Behind Barbed Wire

Margaret Bevege graduated from Kelvin Grove Teachers' College in Brisbane in 1959 and is a qualified primary, secondary and technical teacher. She has taught in Queensland rural and city schools, and in secondary and TAFE colleges in Victoria. Bevege completed an Honours degree at La Trobe University in 1978 with a thesis based on an analysis of Suffragists' arguments when demanding the vote. It won her a La Trobe University Postgraduate Scholarship. She completed her PhD in 1986. Her publications include articles in *Women, Class and History* and *Worth Her Salt*, which she co-edited.

Her interest in internment germinated in her childhood when she was puzzled by a schoolyard argument over whose father had to be locked-up during the war. Years of struggle to gain access to files, forty oral history interviews, and many months of background reading finally produced the answer.

Margaret Bevege now lives in Sydney.

U(Q)P STUDIES IN AUSTRALIAN HISTORY

General Editor: Associate Professor Lyndall Ryan
Women's Studies Unit
Flinders University of South Australia

Also in this series:

Glen St J. Barclay, *A Very Small Insurance Policy: The Politics of Australian Involvement in Vietnam 1954–67*
Tom Cochrane, *Blockade: The Queensland Loans Affair 1920–1924*
Dennis Cryle, *The Press in Colonial Queensland*
Kay Daniels and Mary Murnane, *Australia's Women: A Documentary History*
Ray Evans, *The Red Flag Riots: A Study of Intolerance*
Ray Evans, Kay Saunders and Kathryn Cronin, *Race Relations in Colonial Queensland: A History of Exclusion, Exploitation and Extermination*
Gerhard Fischer, *Enemy Aliens: Internment and the Home Front Experience in Australia 1914–1920*
Ross Fitzgerald and Harold Thornton, *Labor in Queensland: From the 1890s to 1988*
John McNair and Tom Poole (eds), *Russia and the Fifth Continent*
Denis Murphy, Roger Joyce and Margaret Cribb, *The Premiers of Queensland*
Kay Saunders, *War on the Homefront: State Intervention in Queensland 1938-1948*
Stuart Svensen, *The Shearers' War: The Story of the 1891 Shearers' Strike*
Jan Walker, *Jondaryan Station: The Relationship Between Pastoral Capital and Pastoral Labour 1840–1890*

In preparation:

Gail Reekie, *On the Edge: Women's Experiences of Queensland*
Yuriko Nagata, *Japanese Internment in Australia during World War II*
Bill Thorpe, *Colonial Queensland 1840–1900*
Douglas Hassall, *Australia and Nazism*
William Douglass, *From Italy to Ingham: Italians in North Queensland*
Wendy Selby, *Motherhood in Labor's Queensland 1915–1957*
Stuart Svensen, *1890 Maritime Strike*

Behind
Barbed Wire

Internment in Australia during World War II

MARGARET BEVEGE

University of Queensland Press

First published 1993 by University of Queensland Press
Box 42, St Lucia, Queensland 4067 Australia

© Margaret Bevege 1993

Typeset by University of Queensland Press
Printed in Australia by McPherson's Printing Group, Victoria

Distributed in the USA and Canada by
International Specialized Book Services, Inc.,
5804 N.E. Hassalo Street, Portland, Oregon 97213-3640

Cataloguing in Publication Data
National Library of Australia

Bevege, Margaret.
  Behind barbed wire : internment in Australia during World War II.

  Bibliography.
  Includes index.

  1. World War, 1939-1945 — Prisoners and prisons, Australian. 2.
  World War, 1939-1945 — Concentration camps — Australia. I. Title.
  (Series: UQP studies in Australian history).

940.531794

ISBN 0 7022 2492 8

To my personal heroes

The men of the Australian and American forces who fought the Battle of the Coral Sea and in particular:

- the construction workers of the United States Employment Companies, who built the aerodromes around Townsville, Woodstock and Charters Towers;
- the aircrew of the United States Air Force and the Royal Australian Air Force who flew from those aerodromes; and
- the sailors and airmen of the United States Navy and the Royal Australian Navy who fought the enemy to a standstill.

As I lay in my cot on the veranda with the tropical breeze blowing through my mosquito net, I was not aware then as I am now, that but for these men my life might well have taken a very nasty turn for the worse. That I have subsequently enjoyed fifty years of security and freedom is largely due to the efforts and sacrifices that these men made in the first half of 1942.

CONTENTS

ILLUSTRATIONS

ACKNOWLEDGMENTS

I wish to thank the staff of the Australian Archives, in particular Jenny Stokes of Canberra, Sue McKemmish of Melbourne and Mara Seton of Adelaide. The staff of the Australian War Memorial, the National Library, the State Archives of Queensland, and New South Wales were most helpful. The John Oxley Library very efficiently provided key resources. For access to Arthur Calwell's Papers I thank Elizabeth Calwell and for permission to use the material in the Calwell Papers I am indebted to Mary Elizabeth Calwell. Alfred C. Clarke discussed his work on behalf of the Society of Friends and gave me access to its material. I was honoured to talk to and be shown precious souvenirs by Hans Lindau, Olive Hirschfeld, Ethel Punshon, Ben Chodziesner, and Hugo Wolfson. My greatest support came from Dr John Barrett who helped to mould my personal curiosity into a readable form.

For assistance with the original illustrations I am grateful to Dennis Matthews, media teacher at what was then South Melbourne Technical School. Material from the Australian War Memorial is always effective and is acknowledged. Every attempt was made to satisfy the requirements of copyright. Particular thanks to Terry Quinn of the *Courier-Mail* and Sue Bates of the John Fairfax Group. It was a thrill to be in touch with Oswald Bonutto and Noel W. Laimdey who gave me their photographs to use. I also thank Ernest J. Kirby, the executor of the estate of the late Dr Emery Barcs for permission to use his photograph.

Members of the La Trobe University postgraduate history seminars gave warm encouragement, and I appreciated the support of Dr Kay Saunders, Nicola Evans and Paul Rendle in the publication stage. My work benefited from the valuable comments of Dr D.M. Horner, Dr John R. Robertson and Professor W. G. McMinn.

To my husband, Neil, and daughters, Sharon and Fiona, and

to my parents, Tom and Ellie McDowell, I owe the confidence
to proceed that comes from a loving and supportive environment.

The cover is from "Internment Camp: Orange, NSW 'Desola-
tion' " 1941, a woodcut by Ludwig Hirschfeld Mack. My thanks
to his grandson Chris Bell for permission to use it and to the
staff of the Art Gallery of New South Wales for showing me their
copy.

ABBREVIATIONS

ACAC	Aliens Classification and Advisory Committee
AHQ	Army Headquarters
AIF	Australian Imperial Force
ALP	Australian Labor Party
AJWS	Australian Jewish Welfare Society
AMF	Australian Military Forces
ARO	Aliens Registration Officer
AWCM	Advisory War Council Minute
CGS	Chief of the General Staff
CIB	Commonwealth Investigation Branch
CPA	Communist Party of Australia
CPD	Commonwealth Parliamentary Debates
DCGS	Deputy Chief of the General Staff
DDS	Deputy Director, Security Service
DGS	Director General, Security Service
DMI	Directory of Military Intelligence
DMO & I	Director Military Operations and Intelligence
FBI	Federal Bureau of Investigation (USA)
GOC	General Officer Commanding
IO	Intelligence Officer
L of C	Line of Communications
NBS	Naturalised British Subject
NEI	Netherlands East Indies
OV	Official Visitor
POW	Prisoner of War
PWI	Prisoner of War and Internees
RAAF	Royal Australian Air Force
RMC	Royal Military College
R of O	Reserve of Officers
SS	Security Service
UAP	United Australia Party
WCM	War Cabinet Minute

Note on Money and Measurement

There were 12 pence (d.) in 1 shilling (s.) and 20 shillings in 1 pound (£). When decimal currency was adopted in Australia in 1966, two dollars were equivalent to one pound. Subsequent inflation has reduced the buying power of the dollar.

In linear measurement, 1 metre equals 1.094 yards equals 3 feet 3 $1/4$ inches and 1 kilometre equals 0.6214 miles.

In weight, 1 kilogram equals 2 lbs. ozs. 3 $1/4$ and 1 ton equals 2,240 lbs. and 1 tonne equals 2,200 lbs.

In area, 1 hectare equals 2 acres, 1 rood, 35 poles.

The older terms have been kept as modern equivalents would break up the text without increasing understanding.

INTRODUCTION

It is over fifty years since the terrible threat of invasion unsettled Australians. Yet some of the events relating to this period are still sensitive. The fact that thousands of local residents were interned in a direct response to this threat is not generally known and the picture of that time will not be complete until this aspect is added. The post-war migration boom and today's multi-cultural ethos have blurred the dominant British influence in Australia, but in the period leading up to World War II links to Britain were so strong that being an Australian equated to being a British citizen. The minority non-English migrants were not regarded as capable of being British and therefore not true Australians. Their commitment to the country that gave them economic viability and opportunities for their children might be conceded but it did not make them "one of us". This perception was at the heart of the arguments over internment policy in 1942-43 when huge internment camps imprisoned thousands of naturalised and long-term residents as well as thousands of enemy aliens. Now that two new generations have matured it is time to reflect on why so many had to be put behind barbed wire in World War II.

Since internment involves the detention of people without trial, it is the antithesis of the basic principle of *habeus corpus*. It severely curtails civil liberties and in a democratic society like Australia it is rarely invoked except in times of grave crisis such as war time. The aims of this book are to identify the people who had to decide policy and to know the factors they considered, to discover how policy was implemented and by whom, and to trace the experiences of those interned. The focus is on illuminating the role of internment in the evolution of Australia during six years of war, for internment involved a continuous interplay between the basic structure of society — its laws and values — and the demands of achieving victory.

When nations go to war, external and internal security assume a very high priority. The national leaders' major objectives are to protect the physical integrity of their nation, to minimise injury to its people and property and, above all, to ensure the nation's survival as an entity. To achieve these aims, the armed forces are enlarged, essential war industries developed and the workforce expanded and, if necessary redeployed. As events in Europe in the late thirties became increasingly ominous, Australia's leaders began to prepare for the roles the country would be expected to play as a member of the British Empire and as a nation with responsibility for its own defence. In a war with Germany its role would not be dissimilar to the one it played in World War I. Most Australians thought it necessary to provide a second Australian Imperial Force (AIF) to fight as part of Britain's resources. The militia would also have to be increased and possibly even some forms of compulsory military and industrial service introduced. The raising of a large volunteer army was less controversial than was the proposal to use it primarily for overseas service, some of the doubts arising from concern about possible Japanese aggression in the Pacific. To satisfy this concern, Britain had established a large naval base in Singapore and this bastion was to be Australia's security against any opportunistic move by Japan.[1]

Internally the nation had to be secured against saboteurs and subversives. Members of the Nazi Party and the Communist Party were perceived as real threats, but membership was small and could be dealt with by the Commonwealth Investigation Branch (CIB) of the Attorney-General's Department, Military Intelligence, and the police Special Branches. Not so with the tens of thousands of newly-arrived migrants.[2] As migration does not always lead to permanent residence or naturalisation, it was necessary to assess aliens, particularly those with enemy nationality. Refugees could claim to be pro-ally but if they had relatives in enemy hands they might be blackmailed. In a war with Germany and Italy, many long-term residents would become enemy aliens. Naturalised people could not be expected to forget their homeland. To treat long-term residents in the same way as new-arrivals would cause many problems. Long-term residents were used to British justice. They had their families and friends to back them and worked in jobs or owned businesses. The problems of assessing them would be little different from the problems of investigating suspect Britishers. To be accused of planning sabotage is a serious matter, and to

deny the right of a proper defence would normally be unthink-
able. In war time some basic rights might have to be given up,
but to what degree? In a war against a "police state", a democracy cannot become equally repressive.

Another problem was cost. Were the nation's resources better
spent on the armed forces? The guards needed to run camps
would drain manpower and if internees families had to be put
in camp it would increase the expense and complexity of camp
organisation. The greatest problem however, was psychological. A crucial element in a nation's war effort is morale, and
people or actions that undermined the people's will to fight
must be countered. But were Pacifists who would not fight and
Jehovah's Witnesses, who would not stand for the National
Anthem, or Communists, who did not believe in a capitalists'
war subversive to a degree requiring incarceration? People
would react against such dissenting opinion and possibly create
a threat to law and order, but if the authorities overreacted it
might give the impression that spies and subversives were
everywhere.

Many decisions about the necessity and desirability of internment had to be made, not only in the basic legal and social
system of a democracy, but also in a fluctuating war situation.
D.M.Horner has pointed out that decision-making for external
defence fell into three broad phases.[3] At first the overriding
consideration was to support the British. When Japan entered
the war, the need to secure Australia from direct attack was
crucial and, when that was achieved, managing relations with
America was most important. Similarly the criteria for internal
security would differ in each stage of the war. When the major
thrust was to provide the Second AIF to support the British, it
was crucial to protect military and naval areas, but when invasion threatened, every town and every inhabitant were potential enemy targets. In the final phase, when Australia became
the base for suppling the Americans and the actual threat of
attack was removed, a more pragmatic use of manpower might
better suit Australia's best interests.

In addition to the necessity to stay within a framework that
did not ignore legal process, and also to take account of the
different stages of the war itself, the human element of decision-
making cannot be forgotten. Policy is made by people and
implemented by people. In his introduction to *Crisis of Command*, Horner emphasises the personality of the commander as

central to military problems,[4] and there was a significant military contribution to the enactment of internment in World War II. But the human element is equally central to politics, where politicians compete with each other within parties and in the electorates, and also in the public service, where departmental areas of juristiction are jealously guarded.

In World War II there were four Prime Ministers who all bore grave burdens for war-time decisions, and three had to cary these burdens in the difficult context of having to justify decisions to a delicately balanced parliament. These four men, R.G.Menzies, Arthur Fadden, John Curtin and J.B. Chifley brought their previous experience and personal predilections to bear. Of the ministers for the Army, Brigadier G.A. Street, Senator P.McBride, P.C.Spender and Frank Forde, all had important policy decisions to make; and the Attorney-Generals, W.M.Hughes and Dr H.V.Evatt brought very different backgrounds to the problem of balancing civil liberties and national security needs. Politicians from all parties and at both state and federal levels entered the internment debate but often presented their individual opinions. There were no clear party lines. The Labor Premier of Queensland, W. Forgan-Smith, and the conservative coalition from New South Wales, Alexander Mair and M.F.Bruxner actively campaigned to have the rate of internment increased, opposing the policy of minimum internments supported by the United Australia Party (UAP) leader, R.G. Menzies, and the Labor Leader, John Curtin. Backbenchers have the freedom to be more extreme than government leaders, and both Menzies and Curtin were subjected to severe criticism from members of their own parties.

Military leaders such as Lieutenant-Generals V.A.H. Sturdee and C.G.N. Miles and Major-General J.M.A. Durrant had influential views on internment, and it was part of the role of the heads of Military Intelligence, Brigadier B. Combes and Colonels James A. Chapman and C.G. Roberts, to make decisions about when certain groups and individuals should be interned. The CIB head, H.E. Jones, and his state directors shared this responsibility. The heads of the Security Service, E.E. Longfield-Lloyd, W.J. Mackay and W.B. Simpson oversaw internment and releases as an integral part of their job, but in executing their responsibilities they were influenced by their personal style and their differing military, police and legal training. The views of the Police Commissioners of the eastern states were not identi-

cal and the eminent judges who conducted trials when internees objected to their detention, Judges E.E. Cleland, G.H. Pike,
C.G.W. Davidson, Frederick Jordan and G.S. Reed, all expressed
reservations at some aspect of internment.

In fact, the burden of implementing policy often fell on less
prestigious officials. Military officers of middle rank, detectives
and police sergeants often had the responsibility of assessing
the complaints against individuals, actually making the arrests
and supervising detention centres. The responsibility for running camps was borne to a considerable degree by World War
I veterans such as Lieutenant-Colonel W.T. Tackaberry, who
established Tatura, Lieutenant-Colonel C.S. Thane, of Hay, and
Lieutenant-Colonel E.T. Dean, of Loveday. The Garrison troops
were constantly expanded to cope with local and overseas
internees and later they held numerous prisoners of war
(POWs). To cope, a Directorate of POW and Internees (PWI) was
established under Major J. McCahon. Internment created logis-
tics problems that often had to be dealt with amid a fierce
competition for resources. Administration of policy was shared
between all these groups and, while policy was created by
senior public servants such as F.G. Shedden of the Defence
Department and George Knowles of the Attorney-General's
Department, less senior public servants such as CIB investigation officer W.H. Barnwell, and the secretary of the Aliens
Classification and Advisory Committee (ACAC) Noel W.
Lamidey, actually did the work to ensure that the policy was
enacted. The roles and variety of styles of these middle-level
operators inevitably created some interpretative differences.

Nor were the general public silent on the matter. Many
thousands of ordinary citizens expressed their opinions about
internment through letters and petitions. Pressure groups such
as returned soldiers orchestrated campaigns to have all enemy
aliens interned. Some welfare groups appealed for restraint.
Internment was such an emotional issue that the activities of
the ACAC, which recommended many releases, were censored
from the press and have subsequently remained virtually unknown. Yet the experience of the chairman, Arthur Calwell, in
dealing with the internees and their families, influenced his
performance in that vital post-war ministry, Immigration.

Forty years later, when the research for this work was done,
the tangled web of internment policy and the twists of its
implementation could be traced through the departmental files

of the Prime Minister, the Attorney-General, Defence (later Army), Labour and National Service, Security Service and the Queensland Police and Premier's files. There are problems in dealing with a sensitive subject within living memory and the Australian Archives protects the names of, or details about, internees and files had to be screened before being released to the researcher. With access to files on internees being so restricted, the writer augmented the internees' experiences by seeking personal interviews. A field trip to North Queensland was undertaken in June 1979 with this prime objective.

Oral history has its strengths and weaknesses. Factually, it can only be the recollections of people living many years after the event. However, it has the advantage of adding a personal dimension to names on a list or headings on a summarised report. Interviewees sometimes got facts wrong or out of order, but others were very accurate and their details added to the written records. Some former internees showed that strong feeling could still exist even after so long a time, and its intensity seemed to relate to internees' belief in the "rightness" or otherwise of their detention.

Interviews with non-interned locals, while suffering similar defects, bore some interesting fruit. One man declared that all internees had been fascists because decent people like himself went into the army. It came as a surprise when subsequent research found that the local police had listed him as a high priority for internment, but not for being a fascist. British women were more communicative than their men. They had heard their fathers talking, or were told by their husbands what was going on, and years later they were prepared to repeat it "on the quiet" while their menfolk claimed ignorance, spoke in generalities or told diverting tales. Oral history always takes time but on a sensitive topic the problem is exacerbated. An archival file is quicker, more reliable and often as quotable.

The sensitive nature of the topic did limit the usefulness of official files, because the time archives staff spent on clearance work was budgeted for any one researcher. The problem of using internees' real names was solved in thesis stage by placing an embargo on access and quotation. Now that fifty years have passed it is considered fair to publish real names where these are public knowledge and where internees have had a chance to have their say. Substitute names have been used in only a few cases where internees have not been able to be contacted to put their version. Only one internees asked to have his name withheld. Although this work is primarily concerned with the struggle between individual liberty and community security, these theoretical concepts can only be perceived in concrete terms. What happened in Australia in World War II must be shown through its effects on individual's lives and by the thinking and methods of security and intelligence officers. Before the passing of the *Commonwealth Archives Act* of 1983 all Intelligence material was closed. But official material also involved another form of screening. The views expressed were sometimes a consensus, as with cabinet and committee minutes, and personal inputs difficult to fathom. When letters were from a senior official they were frequently drafted by an assistant. Reports were most useful in ascertaining the opinions of those recommending specific policies or actions. Even these were couched in the polite language of the public service.

Consequently officials' personal views took some teasing out, but a study of the signatories of letters over time helped build up a picture of the interners. They were of diverse opinions and their profession or group did not make their opinions predictable. CIB directors had differing views on Jewish migrants, some lawyers had a greater regard for civil liberties than others, and senior army officers assessed security needs differently. Added to this, the legislation covering internment was open to interpretation. Who could be sure what level of internment guaranteed national security or satisfied public opinion? Subjective judgements were forced on policemen, army officers, lawyers and politicians and it is not surprising that recommendations differed. Most importantly these judgements had to be made under stress:— the stress of going to war, the stress of seeing the mother country isolated and bombarded, and the stress of having one's homeland attacked and threatened with invasion. Actions taken in these circumstances were not "normal"; the most that can be expected is that they were reasonable and backed by a justifiable suspicion. Internments and releases were not static for the interners regularly reassessed security needs and reviewed individual cases, trying to balance contradictory pressures to ensure that while the principle of *habeus corpus* could be suspended, it was not forgotten.

As with most studies, some questions can only be partially answered. The gradual opening of more records may reveal the answers to the questions being asked by those looking for an explanation of why a particular group was detained or why they were kept for so long. The continuing closure of relevant British records means some aspects of the *Dunera* internments may not be known in the internees' lifetimes. The gradual opening of the registers of German internees in Australia provides some indication of how many Jews were interned here — or at least how many specified themselves as Jews. The register of Italians remained closed due to a lack of pressure to analyse their cases, in contrast to the concentration on the Germans and the Australia First internees. This has only changed very recently with the challenge by Dr Bob Woods of the Liberal Party and Mr Con Sciacca of the Labor Party to have the government acknowledge "that grave injustices were done to many Australians of Italian descent who were interned during World War II".[5]

This book aims to give the overall view and to cover both the lesser and the more controversial internments with as much detail as was obtainable. Internment policy should be assessed on its success in restraining fascists and enemy patriots as well as on its inevitable mistakes. Its implementation should be judged on the army's ability to return its prisoners in good health if not in altogether good spirits. Those with the responsibility to order internment did not take their authority lightly. The broader group who could recommend internments showed a few signs of being prone to generalisations and prejudice and occasional over-anxiety.

The thousands of citizens who urged more internments displayed a high level of anxiety, a general prejudice against aliens and scant regard for special cases among enemy aliens. The comparative lack of coverage of internment in World War II contrasts with its Great War equivalent, and probably has a number of causes. The recent opening of official records and the protection of sensitive material are undoubtedly important. In addition it flies in the face of Australia's present multi-cultural ethos and could be regarded as a relic of the former positively pro-British nature of our society. A close study, however, reveals not only its interconnections with pre-war times, its reactions to the progress of the war, but its bridging role between pre-war and post-war migration. The Minister for Immigration, Arthur Calwell, Labor's most ardent advocate of immigration of non-British white people to Australia, was head of the Aliens Classification and Advisory Committee for four years and developed an empathy for many internees and a conviction that such migrants would become good Australians.

In the following nine chapters, the theoretical and practical problems of internment are traced from its pre-war planning to the deportations in 1946. It is not a story with the high drama and appalling mortality in the European concentration camps or the Japanese POW camps. It is the story of how a country with a high regard for individual freedom nevertheless considered the detention of 7,000 local residents (and even more overseas civilians) and their subsequent intermittent release necessary for, or useful to, its national survival.

Chapter One

POLICY

At 9.15 pm on 3 September 1939 the Australian Prime Minister, R.G. Menzies, announced that Australia was at war with Germany. While parliament worked into the night on the measures required to galvanise the nation, small groups of police in each state searched out those people whose names appeared on a predetermined internment list. The police knocked on the door, produced a detention order and required their quarry to accompany them to the local police station. Before the dawn broke on the first day of the war, the few hundred people regarded as likely to act against Australia's interests were behind bars. Paul Hasluck, in his history of Australia in war time, says that "this action was considered by the military authorities to have effectively broken up the hostile organisations for the whole of the war".[1]

Yet other writers consider that Australia lacked effective security at the outbreak of war. Noel W. Lamidey, a senior public servant, wrote in his autobiography that the opening of World War II found Australia unprepared to deal with questions of national security because no national corporate body on security existed.[2] In a study of Australia's spy industry, Richard Hall claims that many German anti-Nazis were interned at the outbreak of war because of the crude approach of intelligence agencies.[3] Jessie Street, leader of the United Associations of Women, who later in the war served on a committee to review internment policy, asserted that after the outbreak of war an hysterical campaign was launched against foreigners, and the government in a "state of war fever" even put some refugees into camps. According to Street, some people in positions of authority lost their heads to such an extent that often all legal protections and procedures were ignored.[4] Thus other writers contradict Hasluck's claim that, as a result of intelligence work before the war, a small number of people who were mainly leaders of hostile organisations were rounded up immediately, and a satisfactory state of internal security was achieved.

Security agencies

It is true that before the war internal security matters were the responsibility of a number of groups. Each of the armed forces had its own intelligence section that took an interest in internal as well as external security. The Commonwealth government had an Investigation Branch (CIB) within the Attorney-General's department, with responsibility for aspects of internal security, and Special Branches existed in some state police forces to watch for subversion and treason. All these agencies kept files on organisations such as the Communist Party (CPA), the Nazi and Fascist Parties and the Yabba Club (the anti-semitic, anti-British precursor of the Australia First Movement) and on the individuals associated with them; individuals such as Dr J.H. Becker, first leader of the Nazi Party in Australia. The CIB grew out of the World War I Special Intelligence Bureau and Army Intelligence and Censorship records became the basis of CIB files. According to its Director, H.E.Jones, the CIB was created to provide the Commonwealth with an instrumentality entirely independent of the States to investigate offences against the federal government.[5] The majority of its officers were former members of the military Intelligence services.

The Security Section of the CIB had the responsibility of protecting the Commonwealth from people who openly advocated seizing power by unconstitutional means or who incited the public to rebellion. Consequently they kept a close watch on the CPA, which in Jones' assessment grew proportionately to the decline in economic conditions until 1931 when the full effect of the world depression was felt in Australia. The CIB's other major interest was aliens. The CIB persuaded the government to introduce an Aliens' Registration Act in 1921, but within a year it virtually became a dead letter because state governments demanded payment for administering it. A later amendment compelled aliens arriving after 1 April 1927 to complete a Personal Particulars form (commonly called Form A 42) which required details of finance, relatives, and guarantors, to safeguard the Commonwealth against the alien becoming a public charge. But once completed, there was no further record of the migrants' or visitors' movements.

The increase of migration from Italy in 1926-7 brought a more political aspect to security. The Consular officials urged, coaxed, and even bullied migrants to form fascist organisations. In opposition, the anti-fascists formed the "Matteotti Club" named after an opponent killed by Mussolini. Security Section successfully penetrated Italian Fascism, and also followed the activities of the "Camorra" Society, a criminal organisation from southern Italy. Friction between Yugoslavs and the Macedonian revolutionary society, the "Comitadjis", had an undoubted potential for violence. Besides keeping an eye out for specifically revolutionary literature, the CIB read all the foreign-language newspapers published in Australia and imported from abroad.

But not all security problems were created by communists or foreigners. In 1931 there was unrest over the growth of Communism and Fascism, with some people believing the government was not aware of the potential danger in a clash. A number of private citizens organised themselves into self- protection units such as the New Guard (NSW), the League of National Safety (Vic), the Citizen League (SA) and the Black Shirts (WA). According to Jones, it was the CIB who took action to force the disbandment of these ill-advised bodies, by cutting off financial supplies, and the withdrawing of certain misguided army officers who were directly associated with them. From 1932 to 1935 the authorities took steps to allay public unease by limiting the amount of communist literature allowed into the country. The CIB then concentrated its attention on Italians and Germans, and in 1936 it prepared a comprehensive report on Fascism and a year later it produced a similar one on Nazism.[6] Copies went to Army and Navy Intelligence.

A CIB officer, W.H. Barnwell was detailed to follow the Count and Countess Felix von Luckner during their Australian tour in June 1938. Von Luckner was a World War I naval hero, and his wife an attractive Swede. The von Luckners were greeted enthusiastically by the German-speaking community and entertained by some prominent Australian citizens, but communists and anti-fascists considered von Luckner to be a Nazi spy. While the Count's yacht Seeteufel remained in Sydney Harbour, Barnwell recorded the activities of its owners and crew.[7] He noted von Luckner's socialising with Arnold von Skerst, editor of the pro-Nazi German-language weekly Die Brucke and his visit to the Japanese ship Kamo Maru to meet the German

businessman Robert Henschel, whose firm supplied bombers
to the German Air Ministry. Henschel told the press in Sydney
that he had received orders for new fighters capable of speeds
up to 360 miles per hour from a country "in the East" and that
he considered Japanese pilots superior to Chinese fliers.[8]

Anti-fascists and communists not yet jolted by Stalin's So-
viet-German Non-aggression Pact, demonstrated against von
Luckner at the Sydney Town Hall, in Adelaide, and also in the
North Queensland sugar town of Innisfail. *Die Brucke*'s local
Innisfail correspondent, L. Muller, reported that the Count's
speech had made a great impression and that the Countess had
been entertained by the CWA and the German women. In the
evening the Count gave a lecture which in spite of a demonstra-
tion by the Communists was well attended. The Communists,
in Muller's opinion, "had made themselves very ridiculous by
their behaviour" and had done "no harm to Germanism".
Muller expressed appreciation for the interest of the German
Consul-General, Dr Asmis, who visited Innisfail in May, and to
Dr Neumann from Sydney, who had come and lectured on the
Reading Association and on the political position in Europe.[9]

Dr Rudolf Karl Asmis was Germany's official representative
in Australia from 1932 and he was constantly watched as the
drift to war continued. Security took particular note of the
individuals who accepted Asmis's invitation to join the *SS
Neckar*, three miles out of Sydney Harbour in international
waters, where it became a polling booth for those who wished
to vote in the plebiscite to endorse Hitler's take-over of Austria
— the Anschluss — completed in April 1938.[10] Those who voted
on the *Neckar* were regarded as self-declared Nazis as the vote
was a public declaration similar to that observed in Austria
where few bothered, or dared, to cast their ballots in the secrecy
of a booth.[11] The *Neckar* list, Barnwell's von Luckner list and
those from Asmis's social functions were cross referenced to
find the people with pro-Nazi leanings.

A few months after the Anschluss the international scene
darkened dramatically. Hitler demanded the incorporation of
the Sudeten districts of Czechoslovakia into Germany. Although the Munich agreement temporarily averted war, one
resident reacted. A technical representative for a German firm,
he flew to Germany on 29 September 1938 in response to a
warning from company headquarters. However, as war did not
break out, the technician came back on 13 December 1938,

accompanied by his wife, only to be interned in Australia for the duration because in September 1939 his passport had one day to clear before Germany invaded Poland.[12] Similarly the Vienna Mozart Boys Choir were about to embark at Fremantle at the end of their Australian tour when they heard the newspaper boys shouting that war had started. They had suddenly become enemy aliens, but their youth and their subsequent employment in the choir of St Patrick's cathedral, Melbourne, protected them from consideration for internment at this stage of the war.[13]

After the 1938 Munich crisis the Australian authorities put even more effort into war planning,[14] including internment policy. Internally the nation had to be secured against possible saboteurs and subversives. Wharves, munitions factories, communications establishments and important public buildings would be fenced and guarded against attack, but as prevention is the best security, any enemy agents should be caught before they acted. As spies, saboteurs and subversives are by definition secretive, all groups in which they might be operating became suspect. The Australian Nazi Party and the Communist Party were perceived as real threats, despite their antipathy for each other. The Nazis were closely associated with the German Consulate and directly in touch with the party in Germany. The Communists followed the policy set by Moscow, where Stalin, in an effort to forestall an immediate confrontation with Hitler, would sign a Non-aggression Pact.

In addition to the politically committed, there was danger from the enthusiastic amateur and the agent's agent. The enthusiastic amateur would probably be a patriot who might see it as a duty to harass the national enemy. Consular officials were most certainly patriots but as diplomats they would be immediately restricted and sent home. An agent's agent would be a person who for some reason would act for the enemy. Such people might be paid, or blackmailed, or even bear some overwhelming grudge against the government and the people. The group most likely to include the enthusiastic amateur or the blackmailed agent's agent were short-term residents particularly those who still had strong ties to relatives living under the enemy's control.

Short-term residents could be holiday visitors, employees of international firms temporarily working in Australia, or immigrants who had only recently arrived but who intended to stay.

Visitors might be willing to make a gesture of defiance or
bravado, but their instinctive response would be to rush home.
Employees of enemy firms would normally be solidly behind
their homeland. Those with technical expertise or knowledge
of Australia's business and shipping organisation, and those
with technical expertise, might be too valuable to the enemy to
be allowed to go home. But their families were probably not
dangerous, so were they to be deported or allowed to remain in
Australia under restrictions? Was the safest and possibly most
humane course to intern the whole family? And what of those
employees who regularly visited their firm's headquarters, but
who had resided in Australia for so many years that they
regarded it as their home? Woolbuyers and shipping executives
who lived permanently in the better suburbs of Sydney, were
worthy of investigation. Fortunately their numbers were not
great, and might be handled by such security agencies as Australia had.

It would be a different story with newly arrived migrants. In
the five years prior to the outbreak of war some 9,000 Germans,
10,000 Italians and 20,000 other continental Europeans had
migrated to Australia.[15] Some sought refuge from Nazi or Fascist rule, some were normal economic migrants seeking jobs or
a better life for their children and some were joining family
members already in Australia. In normal times these migrants
would assimilate and after five years confirm their transfer of
loyalty by seeking naturalisation and becoming British subjects.
However the 39,000 migrants who had landed less than five
years before September 1939 had not fulfilled the residential
qualification, so their intentions were not known.

Security required that these new arrivals be investigated, for
nationals do not normally transfer their loyalty overnight, nor
does migration always lead to permanent residence or naturalisation. It was particularly necessary to assess enemy aliens, for
among genuine migrants the enemy might have planted agents
or kept back relatives or property as a means of coercing others.
The numbers involved a massive increase in investigative and
recording work and no organisation was geared to do it. Refugees could claim an understandable commitment to an allied
victory but they often had close relatives in enemy hands and
might be open to blackmail. Perhaps the answer was the removal of the means of implementing any action. If enemy aliens
were not allowed to travel or have short-wave radios or explo-

sives, they could not carry out enemy instructions. Civil liberties might even be invaded to the extent of telephone tapping
and censoring mail.

The more the problem of what level of internment guaranteed security was considered, the more the complexities
mounted up. In the event of war with Germany and her ally,
Italy, many long-term residents would become enemy aliens
and there would be many naturalised British subjects of enemy
origin who could not be expected to entirely quench a natural
love of their homeland. The numbers were not so daunting in
the case of war with Japan, as Asians were rarely allowed
permanent residence. To view long-term residents in the same
way as short-term ones would raise many problems. Long-term
residents were used to the British system of justice. They had
their homes, families and friends around them and they were
economically integrated into their local community. In many
ways the problems of assessing them would not be very different from those of investigating British subjects who for some
reason might be anti-war. They came under three broad headings — ideological, practical and psychological.

Policy considerations

The basis of the British system of justice decrees that a person
is innocent until proven guilty. From this base flow assumptions
such as the right to know the accusation, the right to defend
oneself and question witnesses. To be accused of sabotage, or
even of planning it, is a serious matter, and to deny the right of
normal defence would in peace time be an outrage. Common
sense dictates that, in war time, the requirements of the war
effort might have to override some of these basic rights, but to
what degree? In a war against a police state, a democracy
cannot allow its security to become too oppressive. The greatest
of the practical problems was cost. Should every non-British
person be investigated or were the nation's resources better
spent in training and equipping the army? Most long-term
residents were established in some form of occupation, so any
detentions would be an economic disadvantage and the guards
needed to run camps would draw manpower from other areas.
Families would either have to be interned, and increase the
expense and complexities of camp organisation, or likely become a welfare burden.

The most difficult problem, however, was psychological. A crucial element in a nation's war effort is morale, a belief in the ability to win and a preparedness to make sacrifices. Here the question of subversion is important. Undermining the people's will to fight is dangerous, and the authorities must counter such people. Pacifists who would not fight might influence others, and Jehovah's Witnesses, whose only king was a heavenly one, would not acknowledge the British monarchy. Communists, who did not believe in a capitalists' war, might persuade their co-workers to "go slow" and cause munitions and manufacturing shortfalls. Were such people dangerous to the degree of needing to be removed from the rest of society? The diverse anti-war groups were small and their philosophies were not likely to attract extra converts in a popular war, but the general public could react aggressively, even violently, against dissenting opinion. A threat to law and order would divert resources better used against the enemy.

Another possible reaction could be resentment expressed in the form of withholding complete support. Parents might discourage sons from volunteering if their neighbours were not eligible because they were not British. Aliens might not engage in subversive activities, but the community could attribute it to them. In desperate times the very presence of such people could become an intolerable irritation. But for the authorities to overreact to complaints against all people who were not British subjects might be counterproductive. Clumsy investigation that implied suspected disloyalty might, in fact, provoke it. Nor was there any guarantee that extreme official action would content the general public. Rather than being reassuring, heightened activity could encourage the belief that spies or subversives were everywhere. Many decisions about the necessity and desirability of internment had to be made, not only in the basic legal and social system of a democracy, but also in a fluctuating war situation where defeats or victories would alter perceptions of threat. Guidelines for internment were finally agreed and printed in the Department of Defence *War Book*. The aim of internment was to prevent an individual from "acting in a manner prejudicial to the public safety, or the defence of the Commonwealth".[18] Although the detention of all enemy aliens was considered the only means of total security, it was decided that internments should be kept to the "narrowest limits consistent with public safety and public sentiment".

An Inter-Departmental Committee coordinated war plans between the federal departments and with state agencies and the Commonwealth *War Book* specified that the Attorney- General's department was to hand over the records of the CIB to the Intelligence Section of the General Staff at Army headquarters (AHQ) during the time when war was considered to be imminent. Arrangements were to be made between the CIB, the police and the army for the control and internment of aliens. If the National Security Act, which would legitimize the internment of British subjects, was not passed before war was declared, there was sufficient authority under the Crimes and Defence Acts to detain suspected persons.[16]

The military and security

The decision to give the military both the responsibility for security and for the files and personnel of the CIB was not unanimous and in many ways was a contradiction of the normal role of the military in a democracy, but the army in fact had good reason to feel it had the most knowledgeable of the security networks. A military reporting system covering every country town and district was established soon after Hitler came to power in Germany. Lieutenant-Colonel C.A.K. Cohen remembered the establishment of this internal security system in terms of the "new Lavarack regime".[17] Major Bertrand Combes[18] became Director of Military Intelligence (DMI) in May 1934 and Lieutenant-General John D. Lavarack, Chief of the General Staff (CGS) in April 1935.[19] Combes and the Intelligence section at AHQ moved to establish an intelligence system within Australia. According to Cohen, although British MI5 was in contact with Major Jones of the CIB, it had little confidence in the CIB as its equivalent in Australia. Cohen recalled that conflict soon developed between the services' Intelligence Section and Jones of the CIB, who was supported by the head of the Attorney-General's department, George Knowles. Cohen felt Jones and Knowles wanted an American style Federal Bureau of Investigation (FBI) for Australia. Cohen's impressionistic recollection of the immediate pre-war months was that there were conferences, checks and counter-checks and that by the outbreak of war nothing had been done to establish an adequate security organisation.

Captain C.D. Coulthard-Clark, of the Australian Intelligence

Corps, confirms that from the time of the 1938 Munich crisis the army had the chief responsibility for national security and other organisations were to hand over their material to military intelligence.[20] In February 1939 the Inter- Departmental committee considered setting up a Defence Security Organisation. This could be done either by creating a new organisation as an adjunct to the Defence Department or by expanding the CIB. The army needed a group to secure defence establishments, so efficiency suggested this group take the enlarged role. The CIB's activities included many mundane activities, such as serving bankruptcy notices and following up departmental queries with no security aspect. The cooperation the army hoped for from the CIB did not eventuate and although some records went to AHQ, the CIB resisted the army having the internal security responsibility. Despite the CIB's separatist attitude, the army had collected a considerable amount of internal security information between 1934 and 1939. In the country areas, former World War I officers kept watch on anti-war activists, communists, unemployed groups, foreigners and anarchists. In Victoria, there were military reporting officers (MROs) operating in all major country towns. Twenty-two new MROs had been sounded out on their willingness to do this work and were recommended on 5 October 1936 while five others were terminated as unsatisfactory. In November, an additional eight were added and in October 1938 seven more, including a "Travelling MRO", whose address was c/- Graziers Association, Collins St, Melbourne. In total, 64 men acted as MROs in Victoria.[21]

These former officers collected leaflets handed out at meetings of the unemployed and reported speeches where violence was advocated to redress grievances. They were concerned that the Anti-War League discouraged recruiting in 1935 when there was a possibility of Britain going to war against Mussolini over Ethiopia, and they were very interested in the communists. In the Newcastle area of New South Wales there were files on 300 residents who were active unionists or subscribers to communist publications, together with about 50 files on Jehovah's Witnesses.[22] Coombes had updated the military Intelligence Diaries and Summaries in 1934 to include an extra section on Internal Security and the army's major interests can be deduced from its Monthly Intelligence Notes.[23]

Six themes appeared regularly activities of Japanese, Italians and Germans, Communists, Peace Movement activists and the development of Australian resources. The new mines at Yampi Sound, new dams and irrigation projects and new hospitals and bridges were noted. International Peace Movements and conferences were reported on and while many participants were credited with a genuine desire for world peace, the movements were suspect because of the involvement of communists. The communists' views on defence were frequently quoted and the army was obviously concerned that if there was a war, Australian communists would not fight, except for a Soviet Australia. If they did enter the army, the communists indicated they would either be urging soldiers to demand their rights and decent allowances or be learning all they could about arms storage facilities to use when the time came to overthrow the true class enemy on both sides. The army was convinced that communists were behind certain strikes and that politically they were desperately trying to become part of a united front with the Australian Labor Party (ALP) which found this "most distasteful". Interest in the activities of foreigners was usually centred on Japanese, German and Italian visitors, particularly military men, and their contacts and reception by residents noted. The Japanese economy, its shipping and its army were of great interest.

A full set of Intelligence Summaries for 1936 have been scrutinised.[24] They were the responsibility of Major James A. Chapman, of the Intelligence Section of the General Staff based in Melbourne. Copies were distributed to AHQ, the CIB and local Intelligence officers. Economic details about Japan are highlighted. Japan was the second largest purchaser of wool, taking twelve million pounds worth. The tonnage and routes of her ships and her resource problems at home were frequently mentioned. By comparison, Germany and Italy get little mention, although this would not necessarily hold for 1937-9. Reports from strike meetings are direct quotes and knowledge of union leaders and their political affiliations suggests a broad coverage of industrial activities including Trades Hall meetings. The pro-fascist organisations of interest were the Australia First Movement, the British Racial Guild and the Italian Fascio. The Victorian Council Against War and Fascism was of interest for its anti-war stand as well as its anti-fascist politics. The army was convinced that involved pacifists and clergymen were influenced by the communists. The formation of the Council of

Civil Liberties was noted and in October the graduates of the university's Japanese language course were named.

Of greatest concern was the Communist Party.[25] Two meetings addressed by J.B. Miles, the leader of the CPA, had attracted "between 3-4,000". The women wore red berets or rosettes, and motions condemning the "reactionary" Lyons, Dunstan and Stevens governments and the banning of the anti-fascist play "Till the Day I Die" were applauded. However, the press had not reported these meetings and the army commentator complained that the "ignorance of the general public in the matter of communist activity was extraordinary, particularly as history showed how an organised minority can force its will on an unorganised majority".

The police and security

The third contender for the job of handling internal security was the police force. The state with the biggest Special Branch was New South Wales. Its Chief Commissioner, W.J. Mackay, expressed his views in the following terms.[26] There were some people who lived in Sydney, who enjoyed a lifestyle well beyond their means. They mixed with military and naval officers at official receptions and their movements were not continuously monitored. Some of these people were women. Along the Sydney foreshore lived many aliens who had jobs on the waterfront. "Women agents" could get documents from ships' masters and pass them to enemy agents in Australia. Mackay favoured establishing an Intelligence Bureau on the lines of MI5 with definite liaison between the police, the army and the navy. He had already established some liaison between his detectives and a military officer and the basis for a comprehensive record of possible enemy subjects and suspected enemy agents in New South Wales. Mackay offered the help of the police Special Squad for making specific inquiries into aliens under the cover of its normal enforcement of state liquor and betting laws.

Mackay's concept of a joint Intelligence Bureau was based on cooperation and mutual access to records. Under the pre-war system, information collected by each branch of internal security was not automatically passed to others and aliens bent on espionage could remain undetected. Mackay felt the matter was particularly pressing because Britain had moved to return Nazi agents to Germany, and the United States had discovered that the employees of a German steamship line had an extensive espionage operation underway. Mackay laid out a nine point plan for the establishment of a Military Intelligence section in each state police headquarters and at Darwin, with Melbourne becoming Commonwealth headquarters. Mackay's plan was supported by his Premier, B.S.B. Stevens, who urged the Prime Minister to consider it carefully. It was at the level of the Inter-Departmental Committee created after the Munich crisis that the decision to pass internal security to the army was made. This committee was very much under the influence of the secretary of Defence, F.G. Shedden.[27] However it was Lt-Col. Jones' Commonwealth Investigation Branch that had done the detailed work on the most dangerous aliens. Membership of the Nazi party was regarded as prima facie grounds for internment, so the Attorney-General, W.M. Hughes, ordered the branch to list party members and Jones instructed his state inspectors to invite all known or suspected party members to interviews.

Nazis and Germans

Inspector D.R.B. Mitchell, of the Sydney CIB, interviewed Alfred Henschel, who was in charge of the Nazi Party at this time. Henschel was asked for a list of party members from the treasurer's records, but he refused on the grounds that the Australian group was an integral part of the party in greater Germany. When Mitchell threatened to search the houses of members or raid a meeting, Henschel referred him to Barnwell, whom the Nazis had guessed was an investigator for the CIB. The authorities were helped, though, when material on party membership was found by the treasurer's landlady under the linoleum of his Sydney flat.[28] After his interview with Mitchell, Henschel wrote to Berlin informing them that the Australian authorities did not know all members, and proposing working through subsidiary organisations, such as the Winter Help charity. That this was effected is doubtful. Henschel's letter was intercepted in Britain and a copy returned to Australian security. Nor did the German cultural and charity groups have an overt political ethos.

In assessing the attitude of German-born Australians in the mid-thirties, the German Consul-General, Dr Rudolf Asmis, concluded that the Germans in Australia had been divided before World War I by distance and religious differences. The

first war had brought "the brutal oppression of everything that
was German", and the few people who continued in German
clubs were "strongly anglicised".[29] By contrast the demogra-
pher Charles A. Price's analysis of German settlers in South
Australia states they were slow to become absorbed into British
society.[30] Before World War I the German community had fifty
day-schools, two branches of the Lutheran Church with 20,000
adherents in South Australia, several cultural and social clubs
and a number of German-language newspapers. During World
War I the schools, clubs and newspapers were closed and even
the German names of towns were changed. One branch, the
Evangelical Lutheran Synod of Australia, began to use Austra-
lian-trained pastors and in both branches the number of services conducted in the German language declined. In the 1920s
the German club reopened and later two German-language
newspapers appeared. The German Historical Society successfully re-established most of the old German names and orchestrated a suitable tribute to the German pioneers during the
South Australian centenary of 1936. The German schools never
reopened, but there were Saturday language-schools and Sunday schools where German was used.

Price points out that Dr Johannes Becker, a medical practitio-
ner at Tanunda and a committed Nazi got films showing events
in Germany with portions of speeches by Hitler and other
German leaders. Ernst Starke was the leader of the Adelaide
Nazi branch and was elected president of the German General
Club in 1937. Paul Beckmann, the German consul in South
Australia, took over the Adelaide Nazi branch in 1938 and
succeeded in becoming president of the German club also. The
number of functions to celebrate specifically Nazi occasions
increased and the Winter Help relief fund, which distributed
blankets to the poor in German cities and the women's group
were active. Price claims that through Beckmann's influence the
German consulate in South Australia was "most successful in
its task of penetrating the Australian German community and
in influencing it towards Nazi racial policy".[31]

This is not borne out by Price's own subsequent evidence.
Sections of the Lutheran church were upset by Hitler's efforts
to unite all branches of the Lutheran church in Germany into
one state church, the promotion of Christ as a Nordic hero and
the pagan doctrine of "Blood, Race and Soil". As early as 1935
the *Australian Lutheran*, the newspaper of the Evangelical Lu-

theran Synod, criticised the Racial League of Germans Abroad for one of its racist publications. These Lutherans resented plans to imbue German-Australians with the Nazi spirit and took exception to being classed as German nationals with an implied allegiance to the Reich, and for being treated as material for Nazi propaganda.

Price estimates that in 1938 some 7,000 of the 25,000 people of German origin kept to the German language and culture, that is, over 25 per cent. He estimated that "at least a thousand South Australians succumbed to Nazi influences". Price does not make it clear why he nominated one thousand, as the security services placed party membership in the whole of Australia at only a hundred and seventy.[32] There is no doubt that the German consuls in all parts of the world actively promoted the New Germany and its leader, and that they tried to use the natural sympathies of German descendants to support this promotion.[33] To state that one thousand "succumbed" implies that these people would be influenced to act in Germany's interest even if it was to the detriment of their own native or adopted country. There is no proof that the South Australian Nazi party members had anything like this influence.

Price suggests that the strongest supporters of Germany came from the United Evangelical Lutheran Church in Australia. Yet this branch was unequivocal when it came to a choice of loyalties. Its newspaper, the *Lutheran Herald*, admitted in July 1939 its campaign to promote German culture but protested that this had nothing to do with Nazism from which they considered they held aloof as they were Australian having no other flag than the Union Jack. The paper urged citizens not to resist the National Register and when war broke out the *Lutheran Herald* reminded its readers that their ancestors had come to Australia originally to find religious freedom and urged Lutherans to help Australia preserve her liberty and freedom. Able-bodied readers were exhorted to volunteer for national service and it was suggested to less fit readers that they willingly donate their money and time to the war effort.

Price, in contrast to Asmis, is the external observer very impressed with the survival of the German language, the clubs with a cultural flavour and the few highly publicised Nazis. On the other hand Asmis is the internal observer seeing how far the Australian-Germans had moved from the mainstream in Germany. Asmis' assessment is the more convincing but the line

between interest in a culture and commitment to the political
aims of a foreign power were under continual review and the
fact that Henschel had proposed the use of non-party organisations to promote Nazi aims placed their members under suspicion.

There was a third church which bore Lutheran in its title, the
German Evangelical Lutheran Federated Church of Germany.[34]
It was strongly connected to the German state church and had
only two congregations, Melbourne and Sydney. Among the
Sydney congregation was Dr Asmis and some forty Nazi Party
members and this church deservedly attracted security attention but it primarily served officials and visitors from Germany.
Among its Nazi Party members was A.N. Wolf who is described
as the Leader. Wolf was the party treasurer but may have
succeeded to the leadership as other members returned to
Germany. The immediate pre-war leader was Walter Ladendorff, who had succeeded Becker to the leadership in 1936.

Ladendorff had come to Australia in 1929 and taken out
naturalisation. During a period of severe economic stress he
took to drinking heavily, but after joining the party he worked
so diligently that Asmis recommended him to replace Becker,[35]
who was in disgrace over the mishandling of the Winter Help
relief funds. Asmis and Becker also disagreed about tactics.[36]
Becker had established the Australian Nazi Party and a "Union
of the Friends of Hitler Movement" as political groups that
included naturalised British subjects. Asmis felt this work
among "non-Reich" Germans would undoubtedly lead to interference by the Australian government. Asmis preferred to
cultivate Germanism through broadly-based cultural activities,
and he united the major German clubs into a Bund, called the
"Alliance of Germanism in Australia and New Zealand".

The Alliance co-sponsored Die Brucke, which Asmis insisted
should not overstep the "quite determined conditions" under
which it was allowed to appear. Asmis considered that extreme
material would result not only in official censorship but also in
the Australian reader simply dismissing it as Nazi propaganda.
Asmis worried that Becker's pursuit of outright political activities would mean immediate internment for all Union and party
members in case of war; but he got little change from Becker,
who regarded himself as only accountable to the Foreign Department of the party in Hamburg. When the chance came in
1936, Asmis seems to have outmanouvered Becker, and the

party centre moved to Sydney, where German nationals attached to the big wool-buying, engineering and commercial firms became core members of the party.

Ladendorff had business connections in Singapore and security monitored his journeys there and back. In June 1939 Ladendorff called on Mitchell of Sydney CIB to inform him of an impending trip to Germany. He stressed that he had every intention of returning and that there was no danger of war because his overseas principals would not have refused to pay for his wife if there was any such danger. Barnwell kept up surveillance, and when he reported that Mrs Ladendorff had joined her husband on board ship, this was relayed to Canberra.[37]

Before the Nazi leader left for Germany a "surprise party" was held at the German Club to farewell him, and Detective Constable Norman Spry of the NSW Special Squad got himself an invitation and a seat at the table with Henschel, Dr Neuman and other key party members. The main speaker was the local party leader, Waldeman Weber and also very prominent was Herman Junge the "Master of Ceremonies" who amused the gathering with a comedy monologue in the Bavarian dialect. During the dinner another of Spry's hosts, Eduard Hagedorn, recalled how he had persuaded Admiral von Spree not to bombard the wireless station near Apia, Samoa, early in World War I, because this would have disclosed his position to the British. Hagedorn became a prisoner of war in New Zealand. Later Spry was approached by a member of the club not attached to the Nazi group and reproached for associating with the Nazis. Spry was not sure whether the man was genuinely part of the anti-Nazi faction in the club or a pro-Nazi testing his reaction. About fifty men and "a number of ladies", out of the 280-strong club, were present, and although Spry could not understand German, he noted those who wore the party badge and gave the Nazi salute.[38] Thus the police Special Squad contributed to the drawing up of lists and the compilation of evidence of pro-Nazi sentiment that was being recorded for use in warrants.

Although the Sydney police were the most active, all state police were included in pre-war planning. The Commonwealth would depend on state police forces to arrest persons suspected of being spies, and enforce regulations relating to aliens, including internment. In Chapter III of the Police War Instructions, policemen were warned that persons "of potential enemy nationality", "of hostile association and subversive or evilly-disposed elements" might attempt to obtain defence information, destroy important installations, and lower morale by demonstrations "under the guise of anti-war propaganda".[39] Although the Intelligence organisations of the three armed services were expanding, they were not adequate to keep all suspects under continuous observation and the police were to provide the necessary investigation officers. In the precautionary stage, lists of those considered to need controlling were drawn up. Finally, when war was declared and the legislation passed, the police were to arrest the persons to be interned and hold them in temporary custody for the military.

By mid-1939 all known party members were being constantly watched. When von Skerst travelled to Melbourne in June 1939, Mitchell sent a comprehensive report on him to the Melbourne CIB.[40] Von Skerst was born in Riga, Latvia, of Baltic German stock and became a diplomat for Imperial Russia. He moved in White Russian circles in the twenties and was Foreign Affairs officer for the Chinese Eastern Railway in Manchuria. Migrating to Sydney in 1932 he resigned from the Russian ex-servicemen's association and began cultivating Germans. He established Die Brucke in February 1934 and it claimed a circulation of 3,000. Although it was the official organ of the Alliance or "Bund" created by Asmis, and the German Chamber of Commerce, both of which were regarded as non-political organisations, security felt Die Brucke had become an instrument of Nazi propaganda at von Skerst's direction. Von Skerst changed his wife, religion and nationality on an average of three times each, and was not entirely trusted by either the German or Russian communities.

It was established that von Skerst's income depended on Die Brucke, and he was interned at the outbreak of war. No one could mistake the approving descriptions of anniversaries of the triumphs of the Third Reich. This is Die Brucke's picture of the celebrations of Hitler's advent to power in its issue of 4 February 1939:

> For the celebration of 30th January the big hall of the German Club Concordia was beautifully decorated with Swastika flags and pennants and with evergreen . . . Among those present were: the representative of the Reich, German Consul Dr ASMIS, the representative of German sovereignty Regional Leader of the

N.S.D.A.P., LADENDORFF; the President of the German Alliance in Australia and in New Zealand, Herr O. von DREHNEN; and many others . . . the Acting Local Group Leader of the N.S.D.A.P., W. WEBER, delivered an address. He said Adolf Hitler had led Germany up from weakness and humiliation and given her again equal rights among the nations. He believed in the German people and the German people stood by him . . . After the death of Hindenburg, Hitler became Chief of State. Very important social and other measures are next: marriage loans, racial hygiene, labour law, Winter Relief work, Strength Through Joy, National Socialist Welfare Organisation, Hereditary Farms Law, taxation reform, relief works . . . motor roads . . . arts, big National Festivals, the Olympic Games, the Reich Party Rallies. Thereafter the speaker gave a summary of the Third Reich's successes in foreign policy during the six years of National Socialist government.[41]

The authorities took the view that von Skerst and party members represented a security risk for the whole of the war, a view difficult to disagree with.

Members of the Nazi Party were interned quickly when war was declared, and the files are a testament to the painstaking work of those who had a responsibility for security. Lamidey is wrong to conclude that Australia was unprepared to deal with questions of national security because there was no corporate body called the Department of Security. If war had broken out as a result of the Munich crisis of September 1938, security agencies would have been as unprepared as the rest of the nation, but the CIB, Military Intelligence, and the Special branches of the police used the breathing space to good effect. Whether they caught every party member is unprovable, as party files were deliberately destroyed, but the extensive cross-checks made it unlikely that many slipped through the net.[42]

Non-Nazi internees

Hall, in *The Secret State*, claims that many anti-Nazis were interned so who were these other internees who go beyond Nazi membership? The Secretary for the Army told the Secretary of the Prime Minister's Department on 28 November 1939 that 343 Germans had been arrested and then 66 released.[43] Hall offers only the evidence of the activities of a few gungho military officers lack of trust in politicians and disregard for legal form to support his view[44] and while it is comparatively easy to trace the few prominent Nazis who appear in the investigations prior to the war, become camp leaders, and feature in the newspaper reports of the deportation trials at the end of the war, the evidence on the other internees is not conclusive, but does not favour Hall.

In his study of Fascism and anti-Fascism in Australia, Gian-franco Cresciani sets out the categories of Italians who were assessed as security risks.[45] Those in Category A included people suspected of espionage, former members of the Italian armed forces, and those with Communist, Fascist and Mafia associations. Category B comprised people connected with shipping, port or harbour works, transport or communication systems, factories for war material and public utilities. Category C included all leaders and people of influence in the Italian community, while category D included all Italian males of military age, capable of bearing arms, while O included all ordinary harmless persons. All those listed in Categories A, B and C, and some under D, had detention orders prepared against them, according to Cresciani. A similar categorisation of Germans can be assumed because members of the Fascist Party were interviewed by the CIB at the same time as members of the Nazi Party. Other internees were selected from ex-military men, communist fellow-travellers, criminals, those working in vital industries, ethnic leaders and fit young men. But as the number in these categories far exceeded the number interned, discretion was clearly applied. Being listed was not the same as being arrested. The *War Book* referred to the situation of those in the B category whose employment or place of residence was the cause of concern, and recommended that prohibitions and restrictions be applied.[46] It is unlikely that, with the "narrow" policy of 1939 internments went much beyond category A.

Among newly arrived Germans there were social-democrats and socialists, as well as numerous Jews who fled Germany for their survival. The British had decided in August that there would be no general internment of enemy aliens on the outbreak of war, but some measure of internment exchanges would probably be inevitable.[47] If general internment had to take place because of public opinion, less severe restrictions for refugees should be considered. Only those women who were under suspicion of committing hostile activities would be interned and no children. By 2 September London stated that enemy aliens wishing to leave Britain could apply for exit permits to embark from the larger ports.[48] All aliens would have to register, giving personal details, photograph and address and enemy aliens would be prohibited from travelling over five miles from home without permission. In relation to refugees[49] there was a general desire to avoid treating them as enemies. All Germans and Austrians would be individually assessed by a legal panel in their home district. Friendly aliens would be encouraged to take up work through the employment exchange to ensure they were usefully employed without taking British people's jobs. English householders would not suffer the "unnecessary" difficulty of being deprived of their live-in domestic servants. British women married to foreigners would not have to register but those who had been Germans or Austrians before marriage, would. Overall, the policy would be an assessment through a careful review of individual cases. Thus in accordance with both British and Australian policy, migrants from Germany or Austria were not likely to be interned unless they were actively associated with the Communist Party,[50] or had other factors combining against them.

Age was a factor the military did take into account. When the Minister for Defence requested information about internments, the Military Board explained that the principles observed were to include "enemy aliens of military age", or any others "reasonably suspected" of being likely to act or to "cause disaffection". The Board stressed that the Nazis were the prime target.[51] A man who appears to have been interned on three grounds — nationality, age and disaffection — was Heinrich Flauaus, a fitter by trade who had emigrated in 1929. Flauaus worked as a fencing contractor in western Queensland before getting a tradesman's job with Mt Isa Mines. Flauaus would have also had his three year service with a Pioneer Corps of the German army held against him. Flauaus was released shortly after his internment and returned to his job at Mt Isa Mines, but his workmates refused to go underground with him, so he had to take alternative employment selling ice-cream in Brisbane.[52] Although not trusted by his workmates, Flauaus had no connections with the Nazi Party and his release and that of others may have been the result of the Military Board drawing the attention of commandants to the variety of controls such as prohibiting aliens from moving out of their police districts. A suspect person was "not to be interned unless his being at large" constituted "a potential danger to the public safety or the defence of the Commonwealth".[53]

Another internee released early in 1940, George Edelmann, seems to fit the category of those closely associated with Nazis. Edelmann was arrested on 4 September 1939. He had arrived from Austria in February 1938. He had acquired German citizenship as a result of the Anschluss. A fussy man, very concerned about his diet and health, his ambition was to raise chickens. To save the necessary capital, he took a job with G. Hardt and Company, and placed a deposit on a farm at Quaker's Hill just as war broke out. Hardt and Co. was a declared enemy firm, with Nazi directors, and Edelmann's employment there caused his internment, but his case was investigated by a Review Committee established by the army. The committee comprised senior officers from the Intelligence Branch and the General Staff, and a chairman with the rank of Lieutenant-Colonel. Any recommendations for release were finally approved by the General Officer Commanding (GOC) each area, the same officer who had the Minister's delegated authority to intern. The case against Edelmann was that he was of German nationality, had been in the military reserve in Austria, and had worked for a firm controlled by "a fanatical Nazi". It was reasonable to assume that this director would not have employed anyone who did not subscribe to Nazi principles. However, as there was no record of any Nazi activities on the part of Edelmann, Lt-Col. W. B. Simpson, Chief Legal Officer and Chairman of the GOC's Review Committee, recommended Edelmann's release in February 1940.[54]

The cases of Flauaus and Edelmann provide some clues as to the people on the original list beyond party members. There are also some glimpses of criminals. On 12 February 1940 the *Argus* reported that Alfred Fritz Yackels (alias Joseph Alfred Schmidt) disappeared from the Liverpool internment camp. Yackels was described as being "well known to police".[55] Nor were people necessarily interned even if they had strong associations with German-based organisations. Von Luckner's Brisbane contact was the secretary of the state's German Club and he organised the reception for the Count in Queensland. A British subject by virtue of his father's naturalisation, he joined the German Club in 1934, became vice-president in 1936 and secretary in 1938. A few pro-Nazis successfully gained executive positions in the club but he stayed on as secretary. In early

September 1939 the Club voluntarily suspended its activities
and offered is building in Vulture Street, South Brisbane, to the
Commonwealth government for any purpose but preferably
for the use of the Red Cross. On 15 September 1939, the club's
president and secretary called on R.F.B.Wake, the CIB's inspector in Brisbane, to request that small withdrawals from club
funds be allowed for expenses such as council rates and to
support internees' families. The secretary's home was searched
on 28 September on a warrant issued against supporters of "The
Friends of the Third Reich". In February 1940 the German Club
was searched and the account books, correspondence, Hitler's
photo and the German flag confiscated. The secretary described
the club in Brisbane as having a membership of between 350
and 400 of whom two-thirds spoke German and one-third
English. In the course of his duties the secretary was regularly
in touch with the police in South Brisbane and he was a Justice
of the Peace. He was not a member of the Nazi Party, he was a
long-term naturalised citizen and while a policy of keeping
internments to a minimum prevailed, the Queensland German
Club secretary did not suffer the fate of the newly arrived
Edelmann.[56] There is no evidence that many German anti-Nazis
were interned at the outbreak of war. Some internees appear to
have represented little security risk, and perhaps they were
politically neutral, but they had been investigated individually
for internment and were judged at the time to give cause for
concern. Some, like Flauaus and Edelmann, were soon released.

The reports of the Victorian director of the CIB, Roland S.
Browne, put Hall and Street's criticisms further into doubt.
These reports show that Browne and his colleagues were well
aware of the anti-Nazi feelings of Jewish refugee immigrants.
But Browne went beyond a passive intellectual acceptance of
the Jews' position, he actively defended them. Browne worked
closely with the army and sent in his proposed list for internments to the 3rd Military District HQ well before war began.
When Southern Command took over responsibility for internments in October 1939, Browne explained his recommendations
and gave opinions on aliens, communists and others as requested. A study of six hundred of his reports reveals something of his perspective on the people and issues he dealt with.[57]
Browne believed in migration and often summed up people by
saying they would make excellent citizens. He approved of
family migration in particular. He described Jewish migrants as

anti-Nazis and often added that these people were "highly
thought of in this office". His knowledge of their family and
financial situations suggests conversations beyond mere requests for statutory information. And once he felt he knew a
person, he was unequivocal in his defence of them against
anonymous letter writers or amateur sleuths who found their
activities suspicious. It would be most unlikely that any genuine Jewish migrant would have been interned in Victoria.
Browne was sympathetic to the culturally minded and liberal
thinkers. Such people, despite associations with the German
Club or interest in left-wing politics were not given critical
assessments by Browne. In a report on a member of the Italian
Fascio at Werribee, Browne recommended restrictions for the
man rather than internment. When queried by Southern Command, he justified his opinion on the grounds the local Britishers regarded the naturalised Italian highly and he was not
regarded as dangerous.

This is not to say that Browne hesitated to recommend internment or surveillance or to give adverse reports. Dr Franz
Haslinger, the agent for the "Wanderer" car of Stuttgart, although a man of good address and keen intelligence, was an
enemy subject of military age, deprived of his livelihood, whose
unrestricted presence in the community would be likely to
cause some degree of disaffection and he was recommended for
internment. The subject of report 162 was a Polish Jew, about
whom Browne was prepared to repeat the Sydney branch's
view that the man was "arrogant" and his "behaviour in the
Kings Cross neighbourhood" was known. He was the "type
that gives some understanding of Hitler's attitude towards the
Jews". And although Antonio Agostini, the advertising manager of *Il Giornale Italiano* had not taken out Fascist party membership in Australia, he had "described himself as a Fascist at
heart", and Browne had listed him for internment.[58]

Browne had considerable confidence in his own judgement
and would back it against other agencies or even other state
branches. When a Pole was rejected for naturalisation Browne
protested that he had met the man many times and he knew
nothing against his loyalty and suggested the officer who gave
the adverse report had only a limited knowledge of Polish Jews,
because there were relatively few in his state.[59] Browne quoted
the Society of Friends and Jewish welfare agencies as authorities on refugees and given his clearcut reports, it required some

definite contradictory evidence before the military in Victoria
went against Browne's advice. Not only did Browne have confidence in himself, he had a background that would give the
army confidence in his judgements. Browne was an Intelligence
Officer with the 28th Battalion, First AIF and was wounded in
1916. He began work with the CIB in 1921, was a prescribed
authority for war gratuities from 1923 and in the Militia he was
attached to the 3rd Military District in 1935.[60] The fact that a
Queensland internee, wrote to Browne in February 1940, asking
for release and stating that he had been the only Jewish refugee
in the Queensland camp at Gaythorne and was similarly placed
in the Victorian camp,[61] suggests that very few refugees were
among the original internees.

So newly arrived migrants were not interned merely because
they had just arrived, nor was there an hysterical campaign
against foreigners as soon as war broke out. Migrants from
Germany, Austria, Czechoslovakia and Poland held public
meetings to express their loyalty and gratitude to Australia and
their willingness to enlist an these were reported in the press.[62]
No doubt some individuals did react aggressively but official
policy was not against them. The Prime Minister, R. G. Menzies,
appealed to Australians to refrain from any boycott of friendly
aliens and declared that a display of thoughtfulness and kind-
ness towards enemy aliens would not be incompatible with the
determination to fight for a good cause. It was as important to
preserve justice in Australia as to fight for it internationally.

When a large company belonging to a friendly power found
that its managing-director had been interned they contacted
Menzies. The Leader of the Opposition, John Curtin, claimed
that the Prime Minister ordered the man's release without even
looking at his dossier. Menzies countered that he had requested
that an enquiry be made in case there had been a mistake.
Brigadier G. A. Street, the Minister for Defence, explained that
although the man was released pending the enquiry, he had
been reinterned once his nationality was substantiated.[63] But
the *War Book*'s recommendation that internment be kept to the
"narrowest" limits was not to be flouted. The government
announced that state-based Advisory Committees, presided
over by judges, would be established to hear appeals by aliens
against their internment.[64]

A balancing act

Many considerations contributed to the decision to keep intern-ments to a minimum and the most practical one was money. Concern to keep cost to a minimum was highlighted by the World War I experience. During World War I, some German and Austrian military reservists were interned immediately and in February 1915 they were all taken in. When there was a setback on the war front anti-German feelings increased. Many Ger-mans, thrown out of their employment, had given themselves up for internment voluntarily, and their dependents also had to be housed and fed. All these internees had been added to the public servants from German New Guinea, the crew of the *Emden* and other prisoners-of-war, until 6,739 men, 67 women and 84 children had been interned. It had cost Australia one and one half million pounds for internments in 1914-18.[65] If the new war was to follow the pattern of the old, with the theatres of operations in Europe, the cost had to be weighed against the security risk.

While expense was a fairly straight forward practical consid-eration, the more complex problem was how far authoritarian action in the name of victory would be accepted by the people of a democracy. The relative importance of civil liberties and national security were argued out in parliament in the debate over the National Security Act. Parliamentary members of the Australian Council of Civil Liberties, Frank Brennan and Maurice Blackburn, complained that the Bill was potentially more repressive than its World War I equivalent. Brennan felt it was designed to undermine the authority of representative government and to suspend the power of parliament, but Menzies denied this, claiming that the government also had civil rights firmly in mind. He said, that "whatever may be the extent of the power that may be taken to govern, to direct and to control by regulation, there must be as little interference with individual rights as is consistent with concerted national ef-fort". In Menzies' view the "greatest tragedy that could over-come a country would be for it to fight a successful war in defence of liberty and lose its own liberty in the process". The new powers would be exercised firmly, but "without intoler-ance and with a due respect for the interests of minorities". Maurice Blackburn accepted Menzies' present intentions as "generous and liberal", but his recollections of World War I made him unwilling to rely on the assumption that the government would maintain those liberal intentions for the whole of the war. War changed the opinions of people with the community subjected to great nervous tension. The opposition to the Bill was most vocal against the sections that allowed a ministerial regulation to nullify any previous Act of parliament, a judge to hold "political" trials in secret, and the police to detain suspects for ten days without charge.[66]

But even if basic legal rights were potentially suspendable, it does not follow that legal form was overturned with the outbreak of war. It was not the intention of the government, or of the Military Board, to act repressively. The power to detain naturalised or British subjects did not pass to the military and the Board did not ask for such powers. The "onus of proof", however, was placed on the person concerned to show that he or she was an alien of "a particular class", or was not an alien at all.[67] So one basic legal principle was sacrificed to security: the onus of proof was shifted to the alien, but those claiming to be refugees found that family ties and welfare associations were sufficient evidence for the authorities. At this time, while there was no external threat to public safety, and morale remained high, internments were few and carefully considered. Australia had laid down her internment policy well before war began and despite their overlapping responsibilities the CIB, the military and the police executed it promptly to remove the threat from organisations and individuals who were potential security risks.

Chapter Two

EARLY DAYS

The desire to keep costs down and concern for democratic principles minimised the number of initial internments, and the nature of the war before May 1940 ensured that there was no alteration to this narrow selection policy. Apart from the naval battle of the River Plate, few British servicemen were involved in major engagements before May, and most Australian servicemen were still in training. One third of the 6th Division, Second AIF, went to the United Kingdom, but it did not arrive there until 16 June 1940, after the evacuation of Dunkirk and too late to fight in Europe. It was still "the phoney war".

Australia's defence policy was based on the 1923 Imperial Conference decisions that each dominion would look after its own defence, maintain maritime communications and develop an air force, but the economic depression of the thirties directed priorities away from defence spending.[1] Australia had urged Britain to establish a naval base at Singapore but the Singapore base was still not completed when it was officially opened on 14 February 1938. During the twenties, Colonel H. D. Wynter suggested that the Australian army should be developed to the extent that it could defend the south-east corner of the Australian continent until help arrived, but this was rejected. When the Opposition leader, John Curtin, urged the development of a larger air capacity in 1937, it was considered that Australian industry could not cope with the rapidly changing technology of aeronautical engineering. Thus Singapore was the cornerstone of Australia's defence. When Winston Churchill, the First Lord of the Admiralty, reassured a hesitant Australian government in the early months of the war that any attack by Japan on Singapore would be a "mad enterprise", the 22,000 men who had enlisted in the AIF, and the 11,000 selected for the Royal Australian Air Force, were organised for overseas service.[2]

Registration of aliens

Most Australians believed that the war would be fought "over there", and consequently Australian authorities had no need to intern anyone beyond the few considered to be hostile. The registration of all aliens proceeded in an orderly way. Approximately 50,000 aliens aged sixteen and over were required to complete a registration form at their closest police station. The registration form asked for basic personal information and for details of migration, political allegiance and military service and this information was then processed by the security authorities. Enemy aliens were subjected to restrictions on their movement beyond their police district and had to report to their Aliens Registration Officer (ARO) at the police station every week. Cameras, guns and radio sets capable of overseas transmission had to be handed in. Individual aliens could not anglicise their personal or trade names, and they had to swear not to do anything that might be "prejudicial to the safety of the British Empire".[3] For most enemy aliens these were their only formal hardships and when the war situation improved in 1943 even these restrictions began to be revoked.

The registration procedures highlighted two complications. First, many recently arrived migrants from Germany, and German-held territory, claimed to be refugees and wanted to be classified as friendly aliens; and, secondly, some married women were surprised to find that they had lost their British nationality because they had married a foreigner. To assist the committees classify newly-arrived migrants, Colonel J. Northcott, Director of Military Operations and Intelligence,[4] drew up some guidelines. In Instruction No. 4 he stressed that, although the national interest was paramount, "sympathetic treatment" was to be accorded to enemy aliens who had left their own country on political, racial or religious grounds. Northcott warned that care should be exercised to sift out persons claiming to be friendly, but who were not, although how the committee was to do so was not specified. Former Czechs were not to be classified as enemy aliens as a general rule, but any individual who gave cause for concern was to be restricted. Northcott recommended that each committee should include an intelligence officer and a legal officer and that societies who dealt with refugees should be consulted. Persons judged to be "friendly disposed to the British Empire" and "trusted not to do anything damaging to the national interests" were to be given a certificate "Form Z" which exempted the holders from the restrictions that applied to enemy aliens.[5]

The Jewish Welfare groups had records of the orthodox Jewish migrants they sponsored, and Catholic welfare looked after Catholics. The European Emergency Committee, begun by the Society of Friends (Quakers), helped Lutherans, Old Catholics, members of the Greek Orthodox church and those who were specified as "no religion". The NSW Special Investigation Branch reported that there were 259 refugees on the committee's books, including people with some Jewish ancestry married to Christians, and Christians married to Jewish spouses.[6] Other migrants used the capital J stamped on the passports of non-Aryans by German officials for proof of refugee status, and the Australian immigration form A42 that required migrants to state if they were a Jew was useful to others. In order to screen these thousands of aliens and particularly to assess the enemy aliens, the Intelligence Corps had to be increased. Appropriate men, including some from the Reserve of Officers (R of O) were sought for Intelligence work.[7] In Tasmania, Lieutenant-Colonel C. A. Clowes recommended, among others, Lieutenant E.C. Stephens who had been transfered from the R of O and seconded to HQ as an Intelligence Officer (IO) in August 1938. The latter's legal training had been very valuable to the Security sub-section. Captain E.E. Von Bibra became the IO at Launceston. Men such as these would form part of the assessment and review committees.

Migrants motivated by economic, political or family reasons had to rely on their own credibility, backed by references from friends, family and business acquaintances, for while many German migrants were Jewish refugees, non-Jews were in the traditional stream of seekers of political and religious freedom, family reunions and employment. Germany was a regular source of migration to Australia from as early as 1836 and chain migration followed with significant numbers of Germans settled in South Australia, southern Queensland and the Wimmera district of Victoria.[8] The Lutheran Church also established a number of missions in Australia, especially among the Aborigines, and in New Guinea. There was a break in migration from Germany from 1914 until December 1925, but when it was restored the traditional chain migrants were boosted by the Jewish refugees and other anti-Nazis.

As its contribution to alleviating the world-wide migration pressures caused by Germany's attitude to non-Aryans, Australia agreed to take a quota of 15,000, almost half of whom had arrived by 1940.[9] It was not an easy task for the military committees to screen migrants from Germany, as some political anti-Nazis were communists likely to be sympathetic to the anti-war policy dictated by Soviet Russia[10], but in these early days Jews and political refugees were usually given the benefit of the doubt.

The other group complicating the registration procedure was married women who found they had lost their status of British subject on marrying a foreigner. The laws on nationality at that time were not universal or agreed. A few countries held to the principle that all native-born people kept their original nationality even if they migrated to another country and obtained naturalisation there. Most countries relinquished their claims to nationals who obtained another nationality. Germany and Italy continued the pre-World-War-I practice of giving a woman her husband's nationality. In contrast, American women kept their United States citizenship on marriage, but it did not transfer to spouses. To prevent a woman becoming stateless, Britain, and therefore Australia, adopted the convention that a married woman normally took her husband's nationality, but if this was not possible, she kept her own.[11]

The Australian Nationality Act of 1937 also gave Australian women married to foreigners the opportunity to retain their British privileges while they resided in Australia. Further this act allowed wives to renounce their husband's nationality altogether and to take out British naturalisation for themselves so that they retained British status anywhere in the world. Senator H.S. Foll, the Minister for the Interior, publicised this clause when he found that many married women were "suffering unnecessary hardship" through the registration of aliens procedures.[12] So Australian women married to aliens could retain their Australian privileges, take out complete British citizenship by becoming naturalised, or take their husband's nationality and forgo their claims to either British or Australian resident status. Nevertheless, if they took their husband's nationality, even if it were German, they were virtually exempt from internment.

In the *War Book* it was originally declared that women would not be interned "as a general rule", but when it was necessary they would be "kept in custody". Shortly after war commenced, the Military Board instructed the War Book officer to amend this rule because it was "at variance with British practice", and because gaol was worse than an internment centre. The gentlemanly board felt that there was "no apparent reason why women should be treated more harshly than men". As the original decision was made with the concurrence of AHQ, the *War Book* officer was somewhat peeved at being put in the wrong, but he recommended the alteration.[13] Of the thousands of women of alien birth or acquired nationality in Australia, only seven were regarded as a sufficient security risk to be interned.

Reciprocity

These seven women became the subject of a tug-of-war on an international scale. When the German consul, Dr Asmis, and his staff left Australia, the Consul General for Switzerland, Herr H. Hedinger, undertook the responsibility for German interests. All queries from Berlin concerning Germans and their property in Australia were directed from Berne through London to Hedinger's office in Pitt Street, Sydney. Hedinger contacted the relevant Australian authorities and sent their reply through London to Berne for transmission to Berlin. It became Hedinger's responsibility to protect the interests of the original internees, most of whom were German citizens. The American Embassy in Berlin did the same for British interests and internees in Germany.

The United States urged that the rigorous internments and reprisals of World War I not be repeated[14] and it was proposed that there should be an agreement to prevent these and to guarantee speedy and automatic hearing of appeals by internees. After London had considered the proposal, the Secretary for the Dominions, Anthony Eden, passed the matter on to other governments for their comment.[15] Internees would be treated in accordance with the Prisoner of War Convention (commonly called the Geneva Convention) of 1929. The Germans offered to allow British citizens to leave, if those of military age swore not to bear arms. Britain had already agreed to let women, children and males under 18 and over 60 depart, with only security exceptions, and they were not averse to releasing all internees "having regard to the small number of Germans interned in the

British Empire". However, the Dominions had interned many more than Britain, and Germany wanted to know what would happen to these people. Australia agreed with British policy as far as women, children and non-military age men were concerned, on condition that the Germans reciprocated.

The seven women held in Australia were released in February 1940 having been originally housed in the women's section of Long Bay and transfered on 26 October 1939 to a house on the Hawkesbury River.[16] Also released was Nancy Reichelt, an Australian held in Germany.[17] In March 1940 news came from London that another Australian, Alma Graf, was interned in Charlottesburg Gaol, Berlin.[18] A British woman who saw her there passed on Graf's plea to the Australian government to release a German woman in exchange. Her captors continually told her that she would remain incarcerated for years unless Australia released women internees. Graf was suffering from influenza and becoming morose "on account of the monotony and hopelessness of the dreary prison routine". She ate breakfast before dawn and was sent to bed at 8 pm. Her room was heated and clean, and the food good, but mainly limited to bread and soup. Graf's worst fear was mixing with the other women prisoners who were "convicts".

Telegrams were despatched to the Dominions Office, London, on 27 February and 29 March 1940, affirming Australia's decision to release all women and placing no obstacle in the way of their departure. For some reason it took until 29 May for the British to inform the Germans, who replied through the United States Embassy that they would reciprocate in respect to Australian and New Zealand nationals in Germany. But by the time this decision was relayed to Australia on 4 July 1940 practical difficulties had arisen.[19] Germany had attacked Norway, the Low Countries and France. Demands on shipping for war purposes were great and travel on the high seas dangerous. Thus, while reciprocity became a firmly established principle in internment policy, delays in communication and other factors often frustrated its implementation.

While Australia felt that its behaviour in respect to women was exemplary, there had been an unpleasant incident during the transfer of male internees from Queensland to Victoria. The Quartermaster-General arranged for the movement of 59 internees from Brisbane's Enogerra army camp to Sydney by train as part of the plan to congregate all internees at Tatura, Vic., where a special internment camp had been constructed. The Queensland internees, on reaching Sydney, were to join 94 from New South Wales and sail on *SS Katoomba* for Melbourne, while 27 internees from Western Australia and South Australia came across on the *MV Duntroon*.[20] When first arrested, internees had to spend a few nights in the cells of the local police station, but they were then moved to regular prisons where internment centres were established. The Sydney group, the largest, spent some time in Bathurst Gaol while those in South Australia went from Keswick Barracks to Gladstone Gaol. Western Australian internees went to the Northam Race Course, and Victorians to Dhurringle.[21] Now the time had come for them to go to a permanent Internment Camp.

The Queensland internees were housed in a fenced off section of the Enogerra Military Base referred to as the Gaythorne Internment Camp and on 18 January 1940 Hugo Hilderbrant and Hubert Wunck escaped. They planned to get a boat from Tin Can Bay, a remote fishing spot near Maryborough, and from there to sail to New Guinea. The third member of the escape party, who had the necessary charts, failed to get out, and Wunck was arrested in Urangan, and Hilderbrant at Maryborough.[22] As a result of the escapes, extra precautions were taken. The remaining internees were locked up from 6 pm to 6 am, and roll calls by day and torch checks by night were stepped up. For identification purposes during the transfer trip, the internees' clothes were stamped "P of W". The proposed transfer was not announced until twenty-four hours before being put into effect. More dangerous for its implications for reciprocal treatment, the internees were handcuffed in pairs throughout the journey to Sydney.

The Swiss Consul protested that the treatment in camp after the escapes and on the train "amounted to collective penalties" for the actions of the individuals who escaped, and was in direct contravention of Article 46 of the International Convention.[23] There was no doubt that all the internees, except one who had two artificial legs, and a second who had a broken ankle, were handcuffed for all but three hours of the twenty-six hour journey. The aim was to prevent a concerted rush at the guards as they patrolled down the central aisles of the railway carriages, or during the darkness while going through tunnels.[24] That the internees resented their treatment was clear from their official complaints and their mail, which was always read. One internee felt that the officer from the CIB, whom he possibly remembered from his pre-war interview and consequently identified as his persecutor, was a sadist. Another internee could not understand why civilians should be subjected to treatment that would not be meted out to criminals, and a third internee harboured his grudge and determined to repay Australians in kind when the fortunes of war changed.[25]

The Northern Command officers argued that the drastic restraints were warranted by the "truculent" attitude of the internees and because of the three former escapees who were "considered definitely desperate characters". The precautions at the railway station were necessary because a Brisbane contingent of the Second AIF were also on the train, and there were many people seeing them off, making it dangerous to use firearms to prevent escapes, and their continued use was justified by the long tunnels and broken lights. Major-General H.D. Wynter, backed the Assistant Provost-Marshal, who had experience in the regular army and civil police, and who "was in touch with the temper of the men" and whose responsibility it was to ensure that there were no escapes.[26]

Street replied to Hedinger that the intensified security measures at Gaythorne were not a collective punishment but a precaution against further escape attempts. The internees had been given the option of wearing government-provided marked clothing as an alternative to having their own shirts branded. The presence of the former escapees had heightened tension and anticipation among all the prisoners and made handcuffing necessary, but the handcuffs had been removed for washing and visits to the lavatory. Street indicated he would allow interstate relatives to visit for two hours. Overall, Street supported the guards, but he also confirmed that the policy of the Australian government was not to inflict any unnecessary hardships on internees.[27] After checking that Street's reply was for forwarding to Germany, Hedinger sent it to London.[28]

Most other arrangements in the early days of internment were negotiated with less drama. The Australian post office agreed to carry internees' mail and parcels at the same rate as the Geneva Convention prescribed for prisoners of war. General Wynter told his staff in Brisbane that internees were normally to be treated as prisoners of war with the rank of private. An issue of one pair of ankle boots, dungaree jacket and trousers, two flannel shirts and a white hat was to be made to each

internee. Internees could not be paid for work done around the
camp, but the possibility of their employment was being investigated. Because former itinerant workers and merchant seamen had few savings, they were anxious to have some means
of gaining a small income for, although the most basic needs
were met, the issue of soap, shaving cream and tobacco was
below what they desired, and such items had to be paid for at
the canteens provided. Internees with savings were allowed to
draw a small sum from their accounts each week. Liquor was
banned altogether.[29]

Some internees' families were destitute and, to help them,
the Secretary of the Military Board sought permission for the
payment of a 17s 6d weekly allowance provided by the War
Financial Regulation.[30] Because so many families needed full
accommodation and sustenance in camps in World War I,[31] it
was deemed to be more economical to pay an allowance and
keep the families out of camps. The rate set for internees'
families was the same as the separation allowance for members
of the Australian military forces on war service. In addition to
the 17s 6d a week for wives, 5s 3d was provided for each child
under 14. Some wives tried to join their men in camp and
petitioned Herr Hedinger who pressed Street to have married
quarters at Tatura. This was considered but when the cost was
realised it was abandoned.[32]

The problem of destitute families quickly surfaced with
charitable groups. The Anglican Archbishop of Sydney wrote
to Menzies about the plight of the men of German birth who
had been "dropped from jobs connected with shipping,
whether naturalised or not". The Archbishop was anxious that
if these men remained unemployed a great amount of misery
could result and "the victims" would soon be dependent on the
clergy for help. Menzies wrote to all State Premiers stressing the
undesirability of repeating the World War I experience when
despite appeals to the public to avoid discrimination against
harmless enemy aliens, many had to be interned to save them
from starving. Cleverly, Menzies pointed out that the most
practical and economical way to deal with the problem would
be for the states to continue to use "their machinery for granting
sustenance" to pay unemployed aliens, thus giving the states a
good motive to keep them employed.[33]

Again with the World War I precedents in mind, Official
Visitors drawn from the judiciary of each state's Supreme

Court, were appointed to each camp. Their monthly visits were notified in advance and those wishing to speak to a visitor in private could make an appointment. The Visitor had no influence over releases. His role was to see that the regulations governing the management of camps were being carried out, and he dealt mainly with the camp leaders selected by internees to speak on their behalf. After consulting the camp leader, the Visitor spoke to the camp commandant and dealt with minor matters on the spot. Outstanding matters were then officially reported to headquarters. The Visitor's report went to the relevant army authorities, such as the Quartermaster's branch if the problem was issue of clothing, or the Accounts Branch if the delay in financial transactions was criticised. Matters relating to the area of the camp commandant's area of jurisdiction, such as the physical state of the camp, or camp orders, were referred from headquarters to the commandant for reply. It was policy that an Official Visitor (OV) should be "a gentleman of high position" so that, as in the Great War, foreign powers would be impressed with the Commonwealth's desire to fulfil its obligations to internees.[34]

Another reason is suggested in the comment by Brigadier Street to a request from the *Daily Telegraph* to visit Bathurst gaol to write an article on the treatment of aliens interned there. The military authorities were against press visitors because it would be difficult to discriminate between newspapers and to limit reports to general questions rather than individual cases. Street wrote on the discussion paper that he wanted official visitors appointed in each state "as early as possible".[35] The reasons given for the appointment of Official Visitors in the Official History of Internment are more expansive. There was the World War 1 precedent and the need for civilians to be able to appeal to fellow civilians. Internees were placed in military custody for national security reasons and not as a punishment, and their conditions should be reviewed by civilians who could give assistance with the problems arising from the internees' sudden removal from civilian life. Official Visitors were also appointed to avoid retaliatory action and as a defence against ill-founded complaints. The Official Visitor to Gaythorne was Mr Justice Neal Macrossan, Senior Puisne Judge of the Queensland Supreme Court. In Victoria Mr Gavin Duffy of the Supreme Court visited Tatura, and Sir Fredrick Jordan , Chief Justice of New South Wales visited Liverpool. When camps expanded later in the war, prominent men with legal experience were added to the list including a former Chief Justice of Gibraltar and a judge of the Supreme Court of Malaya.[36]

Appeal system

Once internees were in camp they were given a copy of the rules in their own language, and appeal forms to fill out if they objected to their internment. These objections were heard by a committee or tribunal, who advised the authorities whether they considered the objector had a sufficient case to justify a trial. Although this method of handling objections was designed to streamline hearings, it did not succeed. An internee might object, yet the military claim that because he was a member of the German Labour Front, an organisation closely aligned to the Nazi Party, his internment was correct. The objector would argue that he was at best an a nominal annual subscriber without active participation. With the cross-examination and explanations of the relationship between the Labour Front and the Nazi Party and further arguments as to whether only the active and executive members were significantly devoted to be "likely to act", the hearings were drawn out. They might as well have been trials, for if the committee advised that the objector had a case the whole thing had to be gone over again. Members of the Nazi Party were often refused leave to object outright, and tribunals later combined leave to object and objection hearings.[37]

The Chairmen of Advisory Committees and Appeals Tribunals were, or had been, judges in state courts. The Advisory Committees heard the objections of British subjects and naturalised subjects only. These committees were established in each state on the nomination of the premiers. To support the chairman-judge, two men of high standing in the community were also nominated. The objectors heard by the Advisory Committees were those arrested under Section 26 of the National Security (General) Regulations, while the cases of aliens arrested under Section 20 of the National Security (Aliens Control) Regulations were reviewed by the GOC's committee. Basically all British, naturalised, and alien objectors who protested were reviewed, in secret, according to the criteria for internment set down in the *War Book*.

Advisory Committees were chaired by Justice J.D.Morris

(Tas.), Justice Sir John Northmore (WA), Justice Roslyn
Philp(Qld), Justice Edward Cleland (SA) and Justice Fred Mar-
tin (Vic.). No. 1 Advisory Committee (NSW) was chaired by
Justice Colin G.W.Davidson, supported by W.Monahan, KC,
and W.J.Wilson, and sat intermittently from 26 September 1939
until 7 February 1940 to hear the objections of the naturalised
British subjects of German origin and from 15 July to 23 December 1940 to hear naturalised Italian objectors.[38] To support the
Victorian chairman, the Premier nominated Colonel Rupert
Ryan of Berwick and Mr George Young of Melbourne. Colonel
Ryan was described as "an ex-Imperial Officer" aged about 60
and "a European linguist of some note", and Mr Young was a
partner in a large firm of shipping agents. The Queensland
Premier nominated Hubart J.H.Henchman, the Solicitor-General of Queensland and George W.Watson, Under Secretary in
the Premier's Department. A police magistrate from Brisbane
was omitted as he took up chairmanship of the Defence Department's Committee to investigate aliens recommended for internment.[39] The use of judges and lawyers on Advisory
Committees put a strain on the courts and legal system, especially as some objectors were able to hire senior counsel. Thus
the legal profession was second only to the military in its
involvement in internment procedures. This is an example of
the interaction and "cross-pollenation" between the two groups
over appeals from the correspondence of the Deputy Crown
Solicitor; Lt.-Col. G.L.Mayman, Southern Command's Legal
Officer and Mr Justice Martin of the Supreme Court and Chairman of the Advisory Committee were to meet to discuss appeal
hearing arrangements. The Chief Justice was willing to lend No.
2 High Court and Justice Martin's associate would act as secretary. Mr M.E. Burbank of Counsel was a member of the Army
Legal Corps and an IO who worked on aliens and was "well
acquainted with the dossiers of the appellants", and HQ Southern Command suggested the Attorney-General might nomi-
nate Burbank to appear for the Minister of the Army.[40] But
administrative details and allocating appropriate personnel
were technical decisions and easily achieved, but because the
two groups brought a different perspective to the problem their
overall interaction was not so easy. Lawyers are not accustomed
to the onus of proof being with the accused; on the contrary, the
basic premise of British justice is that the onus of proof rests
with the Crown. The committee men were not insensitive to the

needs of national security, nor did they reject the concept of
secret trials, or baulk at the lack of material witnesses appearing
in court to be cross-examined. They were not comfortable with
this style of tribunal hearing but they knew it was legally
constituted under the National Security Act and was a war-time
phenomenon. Nevertheless, as cases progressed, the funda-
mental differences between the legal men on the committees
and the army prosecution became marked.

In a case where the evidence against an objector lay in his
membership of the Winter Help organisation, a number of
questions arose. The military regarded the Winter Help as a
Nazi-inspired charity, patronised by Hitler and used by the
Nazi propaganda machine to show caring Nazi youths distributing blankets to the poor and underprivileged. The argument
ran that a person who made contributions to such a scheme
must be a Nazi sympathiser and could be a secret member of
the party. Even if he were not, his contribution to an organisation so identified with the Nazi leadership made his sympathies
suspect and warranted his detention. The objector would argue
that he did not deny his contribution to a charity helping the
slum dwellers in his city of origin. Any migrant who had been
successful in Australia would understand the natural desire of
a native son to help his less fortunate kith. The objector would
categorically deny any association with the Nazi Party either in
Germany or Australia, and it was left to the committee to decide
if he was sincere.

The military provided evidence, which the objector could not
see, of agent's reports on the objector's social association with
known members of the party, or of comments made by the
objector, as reported by neighbours. This evidence could not be
cross-examined nor the witnesses produced and in a normal
trial it would be worthless. Mr Justice Cleland, of South Australia, expressed his concern after hearing appeals in late 1940.
These appellants were from a group well beyond the original
internments. He found that his duties were

> particularly distasteful because there is nothing "judicial" about
> them. First of all I understand that the onus of satisfying the
> Committee that any person detained is loyal lies upon the person
> detained and the more general and indefinite the charge against
> him is,the more difficult it is for him to satisfy the Committee.
> Again, on the one hand the Committee had before it the oath of the
> person detained subject to cross-examination and, on the other

hand, the unsworn reports of one or more anonymous individuals (nearly always described as being "a particularly reliable agent") and some of these reports may be possibly malicious, probably honest, and sometimes, no doubt, inspired by patriotic hysteria.[41]

Other matters connected with their committee work also agitated the lawyers. There was a mix up over payments for time and expenses. When Cleland asked for recompense the state government would not back him, but as no arrangements were made to provide a secretary or clerical staff or a meeting place, judges had to arrange for the use of courts and asked their Associates to act as secretaries for the Advisory Committees. Eventually committee members were paid, but amounts were inconsistent and there were lengthy delays.[42]

The military Review Committees, which looked into the cases of aliens, were not hampered by the preoccupation with court procedure that made Advisory Committees nervous. The army's committee was an internal reassessment. As early as 20 September 1939 the solicitor of the Austrian internee, Georg Edelmann, was enquiring about his possible release. Edelmann had written to his former landlady about the unpalatability of camp food, and his wish to complete the purchase of the poultry farm he had saved for; and his landlady's family contacted the solicitor handling the purchase. The solicitor put the facts to the officer-in-charge of the Aliens Squad at police headquarters, Sydney.[43] Before the war actually began, Edelmann had become upset by war rumours and fear of losing his job and agitatedly asked the solicitor for his deposit back, which was the reason he had so much money on him at the time of his arrest. A cautious man, Edelmann had noted the numbers of the bank notes on the inside of his dictionary. When the camp guards noticed the numbers they suspected a code. The solicitor stressed that his firm was not asking for Edelmann's release but was prepared to act for him if the authorities decided that he would be safe enough on the property, which was well away from the harbour. Having acquired "a stake in the country" this "might be considered a satisfactory bond" with the national interest.

The Review Committee decided that, as there was no record of Nazi activities by Edelmann, he could be released on parole and under restrictions, if arrangements were made for him to live on his land. Edelmann agreed to purchase a suitable tent and to depart with this and his bedding and cooking utensils immediately on release. He left Liverpool camp on 7 February 1940, before the remaining internees moved to Tatura.[44] In Edelmann's case the perceptions of security had been modified because the war had not then flared up into a major anxiety for Australia. The combination of facts against Edelmann had not changed, but it was held that his level of security risk did not warrant precautions beyond his living away from the coast and regularly reporting to police. The similar release of Heinrick Flauaus, the German fitter from Mt Isa,[45] confirms that only those who gave some real cause for concern remained interned.[46] Whenever internment ran over into the peripheral categories, corrections were made to return to the policy of keeping internment basically for "prima facie" fascists and those with strong cases against them.

Frictions

Borderline cases were also released for the practical reasons of reciprocity and cost. Reciprocity was highlighted in the treatment of women and the transfer of Queensland internees, but the federal government's problems did not end there. The state government's police forces and judges were being used to implement federal responsibilities and some premiers wanted reimbursement for the use of their resources. State Premiers asked for some recompense for the use of state police forces in making arrests, temporary holding of internees in lock-ups and gaols, and for collecting evidence.[47] The premier of New South Wales, Alexander Mair, was both an outspoken critic of Menzies' narrow internment policy[48] and also anxious to defend his income from federal demands. When his Minister for Health told Mair that an enemy alien from the Bathurst Internment Camp had been placed in the Mental Hospital at Orange on 21 September 1939, Mair complained to Menzies that not only had the patient not been dealt with under the NSW Lunacy Laws but that some mental patients who were internees in World War 1 were still in state institutions . He wanted the situation "regularised".[49]

With the federal government's own ranks there was also friction from the dispute between the Attorney-General's CIB and the Army's Intelligence Branch. The argument centred on the files of accumulated evidence gathered by the CIB on individuals and organisations. While the *War Book* made the control of aliens a military responsibility, the lists for the initial detentions were compiled mainly from the evidence collected by the CIB who still had the responsibility for investigating subversive organisations. George Knowles, secretary of the Attorney-General's Department, insisted that as his department administered the legislation in relation to subversive organisations, the records could not pass elsewhere. Although the army had the legal responsibility to control aliens, and the CIB had files on many aliens, Knowles argued that the Inter-Departmental Committee had, "by a majority only, favoured the transfer" of records to the army, and this recommendation had not received cabinet approval.[50]

The Secretary of the Military Board, C.B.Laffan, complained that the *War Book*'s recommendation that Military Intelligence take over the CIB's records and personnel as soon as war started, had not been adhered to. The Board urged that it was "wrong in principle" to have two authorities concerned with investigation . In the Board's view the proper role of the CIB was to supply its information to the military authorities. In August 1939 the Attorney-General's department was asked to get their inspectors to make arrangements with District Commandants to hand over records on "aliens and others known or suspected to be connected with subversive activities". Part of the problem was that the areas of responsibility overlapped. Subversive organisations had some members who were aliens and others who were British subjects, and subversion could be defined as anything likely to undermine law and order, war production, morale or military efficiency. But the main problem was that each body responsible for security wanted to make the decisions and not to have its judgements subjected to scrutiny by another body. There was a professional rivalry and a definite annoyance in the military that the CIB had flouted the Inter-Departmental Committee's recommendation. Coulthard-Clark wrote that the protests by the Military Board "received no satisfaction". Later the army complained that their reports on individuals were often given less credence than those of the CIB. But while the CIB remained somewhat aloof, the army was working closely with the police, particularly in New South Wales. In 1938 a special squad of 30 police officers had been placed under military control and later army officers took up full time duty directing the Police Commissioner's Military Police Intelligence Section. The group developed a records system on suspect persons,[51] particularly aliens and subversives, which covered more than 12,000 people and firms.[52] The relationship between MI and the NSW police was described by Laffan as having been very good for many years.[53]

The Communist Party was the largest organisation under observation for subversive activities because of their adoption of a pro-Soviet, anti-war line, their tight organisation and their history of participation in the violent overthrow of governments. Intelligence felt there was "a danger in the existence of an active, organised and determined group whose whole sympathy was with a country which was already in alliance with the Allies' enemy and with which the Allies might some day find themselves at war." The Military Board told War Cabinet that the communists had deliberately planted "cells" in army units to stir up trouble, and there had been a case at Ingleburn Base (NSW), where the communists attempted to create discontent over alleged profiteering in canteens. There was also the possibility of sabotage. On 18 January 1940 the *Argus* reported a Sydney CIB investigation into an attempt to wreck the valuable caneite manufacturing machine at CSR's Pyrmont works by placing iron bolts in the gears and between rollers. This attempt was made on 14 December 1939 but not released to the press until mid-January, during the Military Board's submission to War Cabinet on the communists.[54] A communist directive of 9 November 1939 suggested that certain vital areas in each state would become targets if Britain and France declared war on Russia.

The Military Board was supported by the Naval and Air Boards and they wanted the government to declare the Communist Party to be illegal, or failing that, for the military to be given the power to restrict or detain individuals under the National Security (General) Regulations.[55] In effect this would have given the military the right to intern naturalised and British subjects, and regulated the CIB to a minor role in investigating subversives. The army failed to win the day with War Cabinet, but a conference of police and the relevant Commonwealth departments was called for 22 January and chaired by Colonel B. Combes, DMO&I. The service representatives were joined by Lt.-Col.H.E. Jones and Major R.S.Browne of the CIB, and the state police commissioners and a member of the Department of Information. They decided it was not useful to declare the CPA illegal as this would give it too much publicity, but it was desirable to take action against individuals. Methods of obtaining evidence on members needed to be tightened up and made speedier. It was suggested that police be given wider powers of obtaining evidence and that an intense counter-propaganda campaign be undertaken.[56]

After reading the conference report Menzies decided to defer putting it to cabinet because he wanted more details. What was the machinery proposed for uncovering the personnel of Communist and other subversive elements and what would be involved in giving wider powers to the civil police? Menzies instructed Shedden to point out to Combes that the subject matter of the report was of "a highly political nature".[57] Combes explained the conference had put forward general views and looked to cabinet to name the areas where detailed proposals were required. One means suggested for uncovering communists in government and essential industries was to plant agents in the suspect's workplace or social venues but this was subject to local factors and the cost could not be estimated. Combes said the conference members felt there had been a reluctance to launch prosecutions against people for subversive activities because they were required to get the Attorney-General's approval. Energetic action could be achieved if there were some decentralisation of authority to the Police Commissioner and police Commissioned Officer level.[58] But Menzies was more concerned for the infringement of the rights and privileges of innocent persons if approval was "given to principles without regard to the details and methods of implementing them and the provision of safeguards to prevent their abuse".[59]

While the military had not succeeded in its attempt to oust the CIB from its investigation role, the basis was laid for what the Intelligence officer Austin Laughlin described as a feud.[60] The Director of the CIB, Lt-Col. Jones, fought to defend his territory, and his greatest weapon was his long-standing relationship with Britain's security service, MI5. Jones also argued that military officers were not necessarily qualified for the work the CIB was especially trained to do. Neither group wanted to yield precedence to the other and the scene was further complicated when the state police commissioners decided to establish Special Branches in the states that did not have them.[61] The police were used by the military to arrest aliens and the CIB was critical of this, considering itself a better medium to deal with civilians who were not criminals. The Military Board felt the involvement of the CIB would just create extra complications in the execution of warrants.[62]

The draft instructions on arrest procedure recommended that arrests be carried out in daylight but it also urged that they be carried out with despatch.[63] As war broke out after 9.00pm it would have been illegal to have rounded up anyone before the Prime Minister declared war and it could have been dangerous to have waited until the next morning. The bulk of those arrested were Nazi Party members or those regarded as "likely to act" against Australia's interests. They were probably more basic differences behind the CIB's interest in the process of arrest. One document on internment implies that, from shortly after the war started until June 1940, there was a virtual suspension of internment.[64] The army had interned people who were later released and the CIB may have opposed the arrest of these lower-level security risks. At the basis of the friction between the army and the CIB however was the dispute over files and which service would dominate the security field.

Early camps

Meanwhile the internees who had not appealed, or whose objection had been rejected, settled into camp life. In Victoria, internees were guarded by the 17th Garrison Battalion, formed at Broadmeadows on 6 October 1939. Lieutenant-Colonel W.T.Tackaberry was appointed to command the 7 officers and 124 other ranks who were mainly former members of the First AIF. Tackaberry had a vast experience in a military context. Born in 1879, he served in the South African War with the Victorian Mounted Rifles. In World War I he was an officer in the 3rd Light Horse Regiment and the fact that he was chosen to act as Adjutant and Quartermaster when the *Boorara* embarked in May 1917 suggests his organisational abilities. In the Middle East, Tackaberry served with the Desert Mounted Corps and became Town Mayor of Haifa following its capture. After some headquarters training with the 1st Light Horse, Tackaberry again acted as Adjutant to supervise the brigade's embarkation for Australia. After the war Tackaberry stayed on in the army and retired from the Staff Corps of the 3rd Military District in 1936. Now aged sixty, he came out of retirement to take charge of internees in Victoria.[65] The initial members of the 17th Garrison Battalion marched through Melbourne on 18

October 1939 and took charge of the 47 internees from the 14th Militia Battalion.[66] The prisoners occupied the Dhurringle building, a squatter's mansion of eighty rooms built in 1870, the soldiers lived in tents.[67]

They all left Dhurringle for the new camp — a camp of huts this time — at Tatura on 25 January 1940, marching the four miles to the music of an internee band. The detailed instructions for the custody of internees were drawn up before war began, but these carefully worded documents were concerned with preventing escapes, conforming to the Geneva Convention and the correct compilation of the financial and administrative rolls and returns. They took little account of the realities of inmate life. Most internees suffered a traumatic culture-shock, an inevitable result of any sudden change of life style. Civilians do not quickly adjust to living in huts, sleeping in bunks, eating set menus and having a regimented parade and roll call interspersed with long hours of idleness, let alone forced separation from wives and families, and all the other frustrations and humiliations that are inevitably a part of prison life.

The first group did have some advantages over subsequent ones. German was the common language, and some internees were personal friends. Because most had been interviewed before the war, and knew they were shortlisted, they had time to make alternative business and family arrangements. Those working for German firms knew that they and their families would receive allowances. Their morale was fairly high and they confidently believed that Germany would win the war and their incarceration would be short. They began organised physical activities such as table and deck tennis, football, calisthenics, fistball and handball. A library was established and later augmented by the resources of the German Club.[68]

With the move to Tatura, lectures and musical performances were held regularly, an internee showed movies once a fortnight on his own projector, and Dr G. Neumann edited a roneoed camp magazine that painted a picture of friendliness, co-operation and camaraderie. Neumann was a biased reporter, no doubt enjoying the opportunity, albeit enforced, of practising those healthy aspects of the Strength Through Joy program he had enthusiastically espoused on his speaking tours. Also, as a university lecturer, Neumann would have had prestige as an expert on language and literature, and as a prominent member of the party he would have been one of the powerful inner circle. It would not have been such a satisfactory experience for all internees. It is a comment on the internal discipline the Nazis established in the camp that Neumann's camp record broadsheet was not discovered until 1941. In Tatura two exhibitions were organised; one entitled "A Creative People behind the Barbed Wire", and an other called "Our Zeal and Ability", held at Christmas 1940. Hitler's successes in Europe during the middle of 1940 were celebrated enthusiastically, and on 4 September 1940 there was a special party in the A compound to commemorate the fact that "a great part" of the internees had been detained for one year. The traditional harvest festival and other German cultural and religious observances were enacted.

But behind Neumann's facade of camaraderie lay the reality of personal internee stress. The cramped physical conditions forced people together who were not always compatible. Minor irritations were exaggerated, and tender egos placated at other people's expense. Even the Nazis had their own internal rifts. Becker was argumentative, desirous of paying back the "Sydney crowd" who had snubbed him in 1937, and personally affronted when Herman Junge was chosen as camp leader. Von Skerst, always sensitive to his own importance, ruffled many of his fellow Nazis' feathers and resigned from the party.[69]

However these internal squabbles did not undermine the strength of the leadership group. Internal Courts of Honour were elected by the internees and had power to recommend punishments such as solitary confinement and extra work for breaches of camp rules. Although these offences and their punishments were supposed to be reported to the camp authorities there was no guarantee that they were. Men not in total sympathy with the pro-Nazi group kept their opinions to themselves. On top of the oppressive internal discipline, the external restraints and the poor physical conditions,[70] there were worries about how families were faring.

When Yackels, alias Schmidt, the enemy alien with the criminal record, escaped from the Liverpool Camp by hiding under the sanitary wagon to put the bloodhound off the scent,[71] it was to visit his wife who was just discharged from hospital. The police found Yackels by following his wife. Yackels climbed onto the roof, where police caught him and lowered him over the front verandah on a rope. His wife was arrested at the police station later. Strains on relationships were exacerbated for interstate internees by the move to Tatura. Visits were expensive, and two-hours non-contact time once a month, supplemented by two short letters a week, were not much of a family or sex life. Children grew up hardly seeing their fathers, and often desperately lonely wives began to feel that camp life, despite its prison stigma, was a desirable alternative. But that was not possible in these early days, when Australia's policy was firmly for reciprocity on the non-internment of women, children and the elderly. It would have been expensive, and minimum expense was also policy. It also went against the overall policy of only interning the selected few who were "likely to act" and against whom there was some evidence.

In Queensland a number of naturalised men of German origin had not been arrested because evidence against them was lacking. A cafe proprietor was alleged to be a Nazi but Northern Command had no documentary proof, no witnesses to disloyal statements or records an any suspicious activity. Personal details on L.M.Muller, whose article in *Die Brucke* was so admiring of prominent German visitors to Innisfail, were missing and evidence was "insufficient to prepare a case for submission to the Minister". The names were to be resubmitted with the evidence needed to justify the internment of a naturalised person.[72] But the "phoney war" allowed for a breathing space. Major-General Wynter was content to allow these naturalised pro-Germans to develop "a certain amount of carelessness in their organisation", making it easier for the army's agents to get information against them. The additional information would be gathered and a consolidated report containing "the strongest possible case" presented early in the New Year.[73]

On 30 October there were 237 males and 7 females interned of the 50,000 registered aliens.[74] This represented one half of one percent of the aliens registered and two and one half percent of recently arrived Germans. Most,but not all, problems had been anticipated in the *War Book* plans. Friction between the CIB and the army smouldered on, and a few legal men and state officials were uneasy about some aspects of internment. Knowledge of the finer details of the Geneva Convention took a little time to develop, and a few early mistakes were attributable to the newness of the situation. Internees were prisoners of a special kind: they were neither prisoners of war, as captured soldiers are, nor criminals. Army officers tended to liken them to the prisoners they knew — captured soldiers; the police tended to see them more as the prisoners they normally dealt with —

criminals; and to both misconceptions was added the distaste
for treachery that internment implies. Yet the internees congregated at Tatura were not completely unhappy. They were more
homogeneous than any subsequent group. They saw themselves as German patriots, and sang "Deutschland Uber Alles"
and the "Horst Wessel" song with shining eyes and eager
voices. Most considered they were the victims of their physical
location at the outbreak of war, civilian internees whose loyalty
was to Germany. Their position was neither comfortable not
desirable but they could comprehend it and accept it.

Chapter Three

THE "FIFTH COLUMN"

In the middle months of 1940 Britain and her European allies suffered a series of dramatic defeats. In April the Germans successfully invaded Denmark and Norway. In May, Holland, Belgium and Luxembourg came under swift and effective attack. The British Prime Minister, Neville Chamberlain, made way for a new leader, Winston Churchill, who formed a coalition government to cope with the crisis. Sir Nevile Bland, British Ambassador to the Netherlands, returned from The Hague to warn of the new tactics being employed by the Germans, the "Fifth Column".[1] In his report of his experiences in Holland, Bland attributed the decisive victory of the Germans to the effectiveness of this menace. Certainly the Germans had used agents to collect information before the war, and in countries with strategic German-speaking minorities a significant number had associated themselves with the invasion, but it was the parachute landings and the highly-trained troops that won the day for the Germans in the Low Countries. Nevertheless, spies and traitors were fixed in Bland's mind. The sudden loss of Britain's allies on the North Sea coast was credited to the Fifth Column, and Bland considered that, when Hitler gave the word, the same betrayal would occur in England, and that this betrayal would be perpetrated by the Germans and Austrians then living in Britain. Many of these people were refugees from Nazism, and had taken up domestic work to support themselves, but — according to Bland — even the "paltriest kitchen maid"[2] not only could be, but generally was, "a menace to the safety of the country". He recommended that all Germans and Austrians be interned at once.

British internment policy

Britain had provided temporary and permanent homes for 73,000 former residents of Germany and Austria and tribunals

had categorised aliens into security risks: grade A — strong
German patriot who was likely to act or who had skills and
knowledge potentially useful to the enemy, B — anyone who
could not convince the tribunal that they were outright victims
of Nazi oppression, and C — those who were clearly the victims
of Nazi persecution. The British Aliens Tribunals constituted
three local eminent citizens including an experienced lawyer.
In October 1939 some three hundred from category A were
interned and the British government expected that 1,500 at most
would be taken. To accommodate the first internees, two camps,
based on social status, were opened. Those with money could
buy privileges for 4s 6d a day at Paignton while at Seaton camp
the basic requirements were provided. But the original British
policy that had provided for a lower proportion of internments
than even the "narrow" Australian policy, changed with the
Allied losses in Europe. On 12 May 1940 2,000 males of enemy
nationality, including Jews, who were resident in the coastal
counties were arrested "as a precautionary measure". Most of
them were moved into a council housing estate at Huyton near
Liverpool. Another 1,000 men, many of them German merchant
seamen, were held at the Lingfield Race Course. The leader of
the British Union of Fascists, Sir Oswald Mosely, was among
the 60 extreme right-wingers also taken at this time. The police
began to intern Category B risks in the non-coastal counties, and
these 3,000 men swelled Britain's internee holdings to 5,000.

Less than two weeks later the British cabinet was told of the
betrayal of secret communications with the United States by an
American embassy clerk, Tyler Kent, to a German agent, Anna
Wolkoff. A list of members of the Right Club was found among
Kent's papers, and there followed further arrests of right
wingers, the brothers of Lord Haw Haw, Mosely's wife, and
some pacifists and conscientious objectors. As the withdrawal
to Dunkirk began, Category B women and their children began
to be rounded up. Boarding houses on the Isle of Man were
being prepared but many of these 3,600 women had to wait in
prison in the interval.

Peter and Leni Gillman state that General Vernon Kell, the
head of MI5, was replaced and a new body, the Home Defence
(Security) Executive, chaired by Viscount Swinton of Masham
and including the new MI5 chief, Brigadier A. Harker, took over
the control of aliens.[3] The Chief Constables of the counties were
told that they could now intern any Austrian or German man

or woman whose reliability they doubted. Acting on their newly-delegated authority, senior police officers initiated arrests until Britain had over 12,000 internees.

Lord Caldecote, successor to Anthony Eden as Secretary for the Dominions, appealed to Canada for help, but the response was far from enthusiastic, Canada protesting that it had problems with its own enemy aliens, and that fear of the Fifth Column had disturbed its own population. The stories of the Fifth Column activities in Europe had received extensive coverage in the dominions and the losses in Europe and the evacuation of Dunkirk profoundly shocked all British people.

Australia's reaction

In Australia letters to the editor revealed local anxieties. On 22 May 1940 "Vigilante", East Malvern complained that enough was not being done about the menace of the Fifth Column which was organised systematically and skilfully in Australia. "Vigilante" believed that naturalised Germans were the most dangerous, and that there were many wolves in sheep's clothing among the refugees. It was better to intern 100 innocent aliens than risk having one fifth columnist at large. "Precaution", Melbourne, was alarmed at the increase in the naturalisation of Italians, for Italy's leader, Benito Mussolini, showed increasing interest in joining in the war on the German side. "Precaution" considered that a suspension of such naturalisations would create confidence as the danger of the Fifth Column was well-known, and the recent coal strike not reassuring.[4] Official action was to keep in step with this public sentiment.

The naval and police authorities in Sydney were concerned about the vulnerability of the docks[5] from aliens and the army's Intelligence branch was worried about the effects of the "go slow" tactics inspired by the CPA members on the waterfront. These had increased with the outbreak of war between Russia and Finland and consequently the probability of war with the U.S.S.R. The rates of loading raw materials such as butter and sugar and the incorrect storage of wool bales was slowing up the flow of produce to Britain. Aliens could be refused access to wharves under the National Security regulations but many communists were either naturalised or British born.[6] The Naval Board was concerned that among the new naval recruits there were communists and their gravest fear was that of sabotage

and espionage on behalf of Russia.[7] At the conferences on the
situation in January and February, no decisions against the CPA
were taken but the army continued to note the anti-British
Empire, pro-Russian and increasingly anti-conscription tone of
communist speakers at street meetings.[8] On 13 May War Cabinet discussed the dismissal of two communist employees from
the Government Munitions factory. The talk broadened to a
discussion of "acts done with intent to assist the enemy" as
expressed in Regulation 82 and the Attorney-General was
asked to submit "a statement of law" on this later.[9] On the 30
May Combes confirmed that a conference of MI, police and the
CIB would meet in each command to go through all dossiers
and to ascertain leaders for possible internment.[10] Estimated
numbers were to be wired to AHQ and names and dossiers
were to follow.[11]

On 31 May 1940, while Category C male aliens were being
rounded up in Britain, the DMO and I in Australia issued his
13th instruction on Aliens Control,[12] and it represented a major
shift in policy in relation to refugees. Instruction 13 reiterated
that internment was only to be used if other controls were not
adequate, and that there must be a reasonable case against an
individual enemy alien, but the emphasis was changed to give
the benefit of the doubt to the national interest in any borderline
case. In respect to refugees the director pointed out that pressure could be exerted on these people through their relations
and property in Germany. It was desirable that refugees be
given an opportunity of stating their case but the onus was on
them to prove that they had thrown in their lot with Australia
to such an extent that they would not give in to enemy pressures.

The degree of resistance a refugee had to display is impossible to interpret from the wording of the instruction. In one
instance it seems sufficient for him to show that he was "not
likely to be influenced by the possible consequences to relatives", but later it says that he must convince the military that
there was "no prospect of his yielding". But there can be no
mistaking the tone of the new instruction. Refugees were under
suspicion, and those with relatives in German-held territory
were to be reviewed. Details of next-of-kin were recorded on
the Alien Registration Forms and information that had appeared innocuous now took on new meaning. Concern about a
few refugees being Gestapo agents and intimidating genuine

refugees in London in May 1939 was picked up by the Australian press. When W.J. Mackay had included this press item in his submission to establish a joint military police security service before war broke out, his plea had been ignored.[13] But now fear of a Fifth Column and the possibility of refugees being blackmailed[14] fell on receptive ears in New South Wales. On 6 June 1940, hundreds of aliens were arrested in the area under the control of Eastern Command. In Sydney, policemen in groups of three called their listed suspects from their beds, allowed them to dress and took them to metropolitan gaols.[15]

The *Argus* of 6 June 1940 headlined Germany's new offensive into France and later analysed the motives for the round-up of aliens in New South Wales. The raids, according to the newspaper were made by the police working with Military Intelligence and were the result of nine months of meticulous investigation. The round-up indicated that the Federal government had decided to intern "on broader evidence than was hitherto accepted because of the experience of European countries, in which highly organised 'Fifth Columns' existed unknown to the government". The new internees were broadly identified as predominantly Germans living in flats in Sydney's eastern suburbs. Many refugees lived in this area.[16] The eastern suburbs provided superb views of the entry to Sydney Harbour, the most sensitive military target in Australia.

They were in the same plight as the refugees removed from the coastal counties of Britain — they were in the wrong place at the wrong time. Some released internees were re-arrested as the "meticulous research" cited in the *Argus* report probably consisted largely of reassessing people on the new criteria of having close relatives in German hands, combined with living close to Sydney Harbour or overlooking the sea.[17]

Among those reinterned were Heinrich Flauaus, the fitter turned ice-cream seller, and the Austrian, Georg Edelmann. At his trial at the end of the war, Flauaus admitted using a pseudonym when travelling around Australia and writing articles for overseas papers on his travels. He said he pretended to be Swiss to avoid questions about World War I, or about Nazism as he had left Germany in 1929.[18] In the atmosphere of June 1940 such deceptions and activities were seen as typical of Fifth Columnists. Georg Edelmann was reassessed on the same grounds as originally: his employment with G. Hardt and Co. The managing-director of that company, Herbert E. Hardt, had

been the economic advisor to the Nazi Party in Australia and
when he was recalled the doctrinaire Captain Georg Kollat
promptly dismissed all Hardt employees of Jewish extraction.
Party-leader Walter Ladendorff, and persons suspected of being German agents, had been frequent visitors to the firm's
premises, and the company had been declared an enemy firm
in both wars. What damned Edelmann was the Military Police
Intelligence Section's declaration that, under Kollat, no Germans were employed at Hardt and Co. "unless they were true
Nazi sympathisers".[19] Not having engaged in Nazi activities
got him released under the narrow policy, but in June 1940 there
was no benefit of the doubt and association with known Nazis
was sufficient cause.

The increase in internments occurred in all states. In Queensland 41 were taken into Gaythorne. Most of the Brisbane residents in this group were members of the Physical Culture group
associated with the German Club, and others were sugar workers from Innisfail.[20] A late arrival was Ludwig Matthaus Muller
(almost certainly the L. Muller who was the Innisfail correspondent of *Die Bruke*]). He was 58 years old in late May 1940, but
he suffered deep lacerations and cracked ribs when his tractor
turned over on a greasy creek bank.[21] The Queensland Commissioner for Police saw the news item referring to the accident in
the *Courier Mail* and instructed the Innisfail police not to arrest
Muller until his doctor certified he was fit to travel. Conditions
at Gaythorne, according to Neumann's camp record, were not
good. The mess tent was lit by hurricane lamps and with the
latrines next door it was impossible to enjoy meal times. Hot
water was not available and the bunks were lined with "dirty
straw palliasses with three poor blankets". When the new
arrivals increased the numbers, Neumann claims that there
were fights for bread but after a visit from the Swiss Consul
things improved.[22]

The New South Wales internees included former internees
previously released from Bathurst and Liverpool, as well as, in
Neumann's term, "a party of non-Aryans and refugees". They
went from their local police cells to Darlinghurst gaol, then via
"the well known cages in trams" to Long Bay. Hedinger visited
them on 7 June 1940. The prison warders were described as
"viscious (sic) and hateful". It was partly a case of different
expectations — the prison guards treated the internees as criminals, and the internees saw themselves as either upright citizens

of a worthy enemy or twice-victimised refugees. But they were soon to be removed from the control of the New South Wales prison service. So many had been interned that they could not be accommodated at Long Bay.

The first group of 113 internees were moved westwards on 10 June. Another shock lay in store. The army had pressed the Orange Showgrounds into service as an internment centre. The sleeping quarters consisted of a huge, rough built and draughty barn with a dirt floor of clay and broken asphalt. The stalls were divided into bunks and each internee had minimal space for bed and luggage. Recreation and mess quarters were set up under the grandstand. There were fewer seats than internees, and no heating. While Lieutenant Bass, formerly of Liverpool camp, tried to recreate the "happy family" atmosphere of Liverpool, conditions were against him, and it was no comfort to the internees to be reassured that the soldiers were worse off.

In South Australia the internees quartered in a corner of Keswick Barracks. The internees regarded their segregation as "purely formal", with the guards having only revolvers. The record produced by this group contains the only accusation sighted of misconduct by an Australian officer of the guard. According to these South Australian internees one officer "was guilty of robbery" and behaved badly when drunk and was hated by guards and internees alike. Later came more Germans who had lived in Australia for years and some "whose families had settled generations ago". In Western Australia the Fremantle Gaol received Germans from Perth, Kalgoorlie, Wiluna and Norseman, prospectors from the distant areas of the state and farmers from the south. Some of these new internees Neumann specified as Jews. The internees' cells were furnished with straw palliasses and "the famous 'pots' ". The officers and crew of the *Remo* and other Italians came in but were moved to Rottnest Island.

In the Northern Territory the fear of the Fifth Column had grown to such proportions that all Germans in the territory were arrested, including those from Tennant Creek, Mt Brassy and Mt Brady. They were brought to Alice Springs, where, according to Neumann again, they were held in the gaol and forced to do six hours hard labour a day without pay. This was made more unpalatable by the fact that "niggers were housed in the same prison at the same time". In New Guinea the fifteen new internees included traders, gold miners, missionaries and a plantation owner. They travelled steerage on the *Macdui* to Sydney, an indignity usually reserved for natives.

While Australia was hard-pressed to accommodate its new round of internees, probably numbering about five hundred at this time,[23] Britain had both an accommodation and defence problem with its 12,000 internees. The fall of Dunkirk effectively made Britain a fortress and there was a real danger of invasion. Britain wanted to deport its internees, particularly the pro-Nazi sympathisers who would be a source of danger in the event of a parachute attack and for pressing logistic and morale reasons. Britain needed all its manpower for defence, food and war production and its camps for army training centres. British morale had received a great set-back and Churchill, steadying the people's nerve with his stirring, uncompromising speeches, did not want large numbers of internees in the country at all. He even considered St Helena Island and Newfoundland as reception areas. The initial non-committal reply of the Canadians led the British to also ask South Africa and Australia for help.[24]

The South African Prime Minister, Jan Smuts, was "in real difficulties" himself, having interned 2,000 Germans, and suspecting a number of South African nationals as being actively anti-British. Among those interned later was a future leader of South Africa, John Vorster. Smuts also suggested the Falklands, and refused to take any of Britain's internees. Britain's appeal to Australia was cabled on 14 June and Australia gave general agreement within two days. Canada had, by then, consented to take 4,000 internees and 3,000 prisoners-of-war and Australia settled on an overall figure of 6,000.[25] Plans were laid to build an internment centre at Hay and to extend Tatura, for accommodation in Australia was put under further pressure once Italy joined the war on 11 June 1940.

Italians become enemy aliens

Numerically, Italians represented the largest migrant group after those from the British Isles themselves.[26] Early Italian migration included the destitute remnants of the Marquis de Ray's utopian scheme to settle the New Hebrides in 1880, who finally established themselves in the Richmond River District of New South Wales. In 1891 the Queensland government introduced 335 Italian agricultural labourers to help replace the

Melanesian sugar workers who were deported to bring Queensland into line with the other colonies on the White Australia policy prior to federation. Some of these Italian migrants to Queensland pioneered cane farms in the Ingham district and there was constant chain migration to North Queensland, unbroken by World War I because Italy had then sided with Britain against her traditional enemy, Austria. Even earlier, Italians had come to Australia among the men from all nations in search of gold, and an Italian, Raffael Carboni, agitated with Peter Lalor. Miners of Italian origin worked at Broken Hill and other centres. Italians became fishermen at Fremantle (WA), Port Pirie (SA) and on the southern coast of New South Wales; and the Queensland tobacco towns of Texas and Mareeba attracted Italians who wanted to be farmers. Thus Italians were spread throughout the country, although there were concentrations in certain areas and in the cities, where many were restaurant workers, fruit and vegetable sellers and labourers.

In the middle of the twenties the United States government placed a restriction on the immigration of Italians to its shores, and there was a consequent increase in Italian migration to Australia, much of which went to North Queensland, until Mussolini discouraged emigration in the thirties. Suffering the effects of the depression, the Australian government required migrants from Italy to be "called" by an established resident who had to provide for the migrant until he was employed. As a result male migration from Italy dropped further in the later thirties and most newcomers were related to residents. When war with Italy began there were 27,500 persons of Italian origin in Australia of whom 14,000 were naturalised.

Just before Mussolini's declaration of war a boatload of migrants, including some Italians, arrived on the *Remo* and some indignation was expressed in the press. A woman from Geelong West demanded to know who was going to be responsible for their upkeep, and asked whether the Australian government realised that an army would be needed "to keep Italian migrants in order if Italy declared war on Great Britain".[27] But the government was not caught unprepared. Detention orders had long been prepared for the internment of Fascists and others of interest to the authorities.[28] Censorship was used to stop the wrong sort of publicity about security moves.[29] On 20 May 1940 any mention of the despatch of extra police to North

Queensland was banned. This ban was lifted on 7 June but editors were told that to reveal that a squad of special police had been rushed to a specific location in the north for a particular purpose would be indiscreet. On the other hand the censor considered it was desirable that the public should be reassured that the authorities were "taking precautions against eventualities in Queensland by amplifying the police forces". Later the censor urged editors to delete any inflammatory matter from reports from North Queensland and instructed that any speculation on the number of Italians interned was forbidden.

Membership of the Fascist Party did not appear to involve the strength of political commitment shown by the Nazis, and it had a strong social ethos. Fascist groups existed in some areas where sufficient numbers of Italians lived. Each Fascist group, called a fascio, took the name of a "martyr", that is, an Italian who had died in World War I or in the Fascist rise to power. In Victoria, the fascio "Gino Lisa" operated in Melbourne, and there were branches at Werribee and Wonthaggi, but attempts to start branches at Myrtleford, Shepparton and Mildura were unsuccessful. Security placed fascio membership in Melbourne at 100, with 20 in each of the country centres.[30] There were known to be fascios in the capital cities of Sydney, Melbourne, Brisbane, Adelaide and Perth, while smaller branches existed in Babinda, Innisfail and Cairns in Queensland, Port Pirie in South Australia, and Fremantle in Western Australia. A fascio in New Guinea operated among the Italians at Edie Creek.

By far the largest fascio was the "Luigi Platania" in Sydney and its secretary, Dr Icilio Fanelli, was the manager of a shipping company. Fanelli claimed that fascios in overseas countries did not spread fascist propaganda but only reminded members of the loyalty they owed to the motherland, a claim that did not reassure Australian security. Membership was open to naturalised citizens because Italy accepted dual nationality. Some businessmen who traded directly with Italy claimed they joined the fascio to facilitate business arrangements, while some restaurant owners claimed they became members because it brought them customers. Attached to the fascio, or at least operating from the same premises, were sporting and cultural associations and Saturday morning school to teach the Italian language to the young. Italian Clubs, as such, had a much larger membership than the fascios and were broadly based. Their facilities were used for dances, card nights, pool and meetings ranging from the fruit marketeers to the literary Dante Society. Justice G.S. Reed, who studied the interactions of Italians in depth, concluded that the activities of the Italian Clubs would have been "no more harmful" than those of the Scottish community's Caledonian Society if it had not been for Italy's entry into the war.[31]

When Italy did enter the war, those on the original list of fascist sympathisers were arrested during the night as soon as the news came over the radio. An ex-internee journalist went to bed knowing he was short-listed, but convinced that, as the overseas news had stated that the Italian Crown Prince was visiting the front line, war was "not on" that night. The heavy pounding on his door told him of his mistake. He was given time to pack, but not to make arrangements about his books, which he never saw again. By the time he left the building with the plainclothes police, the early buses were running, and the detectives offered him the choice of taking a cab at his own expense or going on the bus. He chose the bus and the men got on, sitting separately so that none of their fellow passengers would realise that one was under arrest.[32]

Also interned in this round up was the Italian aristocrat, Alfonso del Drago, a man aged over sixty, whose social status had made him President of the Italian Returned Soldiers, and of the Dante Society and the senior member of the Sydney fascio.[33] Prince Alfonso attended the Italian Club on special occasions and admitted wearing the full black Fascist uniform to the celebration of the March on Rome[34] every year since he had settled in Potts Points in 1927. The Japanese Consul, who protected Italian interests, approached the Australian government to exchange del Drago, but the Australian authorities did not know the names or importance of Australians being held.[35] The GOC Eastern Command, Lt-General C.G.N. Miles felt that the person exchanged would have to be "sufficiently important to justify the return of a prominent Fascist to Italy".[36] In early December 1940 the US embassy in Rome found that an Australian woman was being held in the Villa Lauri concentration camp in Pollenza, Italy, and by April 1941 six others had been located.[37] Whether or not other arrangements were made for these Australians is unknown to the writer, but del Drago certainly remained in Australia for the entire war.

Besides the Fascists, who were comparatively easy for security to trace because some of Fanelli's receipt books were confiscated intact,[38] there were the strong patriots and probable sympathisers who gave some cause for concern. Security read the Italian-language newspapers, *Vade Mecum, Il Giornale* and *Italo-Australian,*[39] and from these newspapers the authorities extracted the names of the patriotic women who donated their wedding rings to support Mussolini's 1935 Ethiopian campaign, of those in the fasio and those who attended social functions. But arrests of Italians went far beyond the committed Fascists, except perhaps in Victoria where security reckoned there were 140 fascio members. In Victoria a total of 343 men from its 11,530 male aliens were interned giving Victoria the lowest percentage of internees of any state.[40] In New South Wales hundreds of Italians were arrested, placing pressure on Long Bay and even more pressure on the unsuitable Orange Showgrounds. At Gaythorne in Brisbane, the new Italian internees so overcrowded their section of the camp that some had to be redistributed to the German section.[41]

The Italian ship *Romolo* had left Brisbane just before war was declared, and it was chased by *HMAS Manoora*. Rather than have his ship pass into Australian hands, the captain scuttled her. The *Manoora* arrived in time to pick up the survivors. These Italians were first held in Gaythorne. Another Gaythorne internee, Ross Costanzo, was arrested because he was a newly-arrived immigrant who, although he had family to vouch for him, had been a conscript in the Italian army during the Ethiopian war. He described Gaythorne at this time as a turbulent mass of incompatible, unhappy men. He said, "You did not have to choose sides — they were chosen for you. German, Italian, Jew. Every day there was blood! Everyday — blood!"[42]

The situation in relation to fascist sentiment in Queensland, with its concentration of Italians in the sugar areas, is obscure. While security knew of fascios in Cairns, Babinda and Innisfail, and suspected there were also branches in the tobacco areas of Texas, Mareeba and Inglewood, there were none listed in other areas with concentrations of Italians such as Ingham and Ayr. The records of the Queensland Fascist Party were destroyed before the headquarters was raided, but in 1943 Mr Justice Reed made a detailed study of Italians in Australia, and he considered that there "must have been hundreds of members", yet the majority of North Queensland Italians he interviewed protested complete ignorance of Fascist groups in the area.[43] It cannot now be ascertained whether the internees Reed interviewed were deliberately obtuse, or whether Reed overgeneralised from the South Australian situation, especially at Port Pirie, with which he was more familiar. In Port Pirie most Italians came from Molfetta in the Province of Bari. Many were fishermen and naturalised, members of the Fishermen's Co-operative and of the Port Pirie fascio.[44]

One Italian arrested at this time who considered Australia's internment policy towards Italians to be wrong, was Oswald Bonutto. He wrote a spirited defence against his internment in his autobiography, *A Migrant's Story*. In his opinion the Federal government's internment policy caused grief and hardships that were not justified by national security. The policy was "economically and morally wrong" and not beneficial to Australia.[45] Bonutto considered that Italy's conquest of the Ethiopians could reasonably be compared to America's domination of the Red Indians; similarly, if "Australia had been left to the Aborigines, there would be no Melbourne, Sydney or Brisbane". He pointed out that British-born Australians who favoured Italy's actions in Ethiopia were not considered disloyal. It was Bonutto's opinion that the internment of himself and other Italians in June 1940 was a gesture to agitated public opinion. The war was going badly for the Allies at that time, but "instead of blaming the Allied leaders for bungling things" Bonutto considered that all the blame was piled up on fifth column activities. People with non-British names were "either interned or looked upon with suspicion". These people "were made the scapegoats for the Allied defeats".

In the Northern Territory, Giuseppe Zammarchi was taken from his prospecting lease at Tennant Creek.[46] Zammarchi was born in Parma, Italy, in 1901 and emigrated to Australia in 1927. A truck driver, he worked for many years in timber at St Arnaud, Victoria.[47] He was regarded by the Melbourne CIB as a member of the Communist Party and also of the "Victorian Council Against War". In his report of Zammarchi's arrest, the Police Sergeant at Tennant Creek explained that he had been informed that Zammarchi was "an avowed communist" and that he discussed communism with other people. Before migrating, Zammarchi had been a commercial traveller in Western Europe and at the time of his arrest there was a charge pending against him for larceny of a quantity of gelignite. Zammarchi had been in trouble once earlier, when a number of miners became involved in a brawl. Although communistic tendencies

might make Zammarchi a suspected Fifth Columnist, it seems
from the police report that a number of factors worked against
him.

> On the 14th June, 1940, after Italy had entered the war Captain J.D.
> Balfe was sent to Central Australia to investigate the enemy alien
> position, and arrest those that warranted internment. At Tennant
> Creek, Zammarchi's camp was raided and Communistic literature
> was found. At this time feeling amongst the Australian miners
> against Italians on the field was very strong, and it was discovered
> that a Vigilante Committee was in process of formation with the
> intention of running the Italians out of town, Zammarchi being an
> especially marked man. It was decided, owing to Zammarchi's
> Communistic affiliations, his general attitude of truculence, and as
> an aid to his own personal safety, to intern him, and he was taken
> to Adelaide.[48]

Policy in Western Australia

In Western Australia, the senior military officer, Major-General
J.M.A. Durrant, was responsible for the preparation for the
internment of Italians. Major-General Durrant was a permanent army officer with extensive active service in World War 1.
Between the wars he served in senior administrative positions
and when war broke out he took command of the Field Troops
in the 5th Military District. He became the GOC for Western
Command on 13 October 1939.[49] Included in the suggested list
for internments in Western Australia were a number of naturalised citizens and the Army Minister was asked to sign the
detention orders on the understanding that they would not be
executed until war was declared. On 15 April 1940, AHQ asked
all commands to estimate the probable number of internees
who would be taken if Mussolini joined Hitler;[50] Lt-Col. H.D.
Moseley, head of Military Intelligence in Western Australia,
telegraphed that this was impossible.[51] There were 1,900 Italians in the state, living chiefly in Perth, Fremantle and the
gold-mining areas. Moseley considered that the chief danger
lay in the goldfields where the mines and the Kalgoorlie Power
House were dependent on the supply of wood for fuel. The
feeling between the Italians and the dominant wood-suppliers,
the "Slavs", was "always antagonistic", and the Italians on the
goldfields were regarded as "generally anti-British".

Headquarters apparently pressed for further details because,
in May, Durrant wrote to explain the situation and to justify

some names that were on his internment list.[52] It is not unreasonable to assume that these were the naturalised persons, for the Minister, Brigadier G.A. Street, did not sign detention orders for naturalised citizens solely from a list. Durrant explained that the "names were listed in accordance with Aliens Control Instruction No. 6": the men were reported to be members of the Fascist Party. While there was "no absolute proof", the information was considered "fairly reliable", and "on the assumption that it is correct" internment was indicated. Durrant supported Moseley's opinion that the number of probable internments could not be estimated accurately, but that in his view the "only really safe course" in the goldfields area was to intern large numbers and release individuals only after satisfactory subsequent inquiries were made.

When war with Italy was declared, Durrant interned 1,044 Italians in Western Australia, and on 16 August AHQ wanted to know what "local conditions" required the internment of "so large a number". Of the 1,901 Italians and naturalised Italians interned throughout Australia at this time, the huge majority were taken in Western Australia.[53] Durrant gave the reasons for his action,[54] and this provides a detailed explanation of this military commander's interpretation of his responsibilities under the Aliens Control legislation.

In Durrant's estimation the goldfields area was the most dangerous "owing to the feeling that has always existed against foreigners" there and large numbers had to be interned because riots were feared. Durrant's concern was probably based on the 1934 riot in Kalgoorlie following the manslaughter of a local man by an Italian barman. Thus large internments were held to be necessary where there was a threat to law and order. Furthermore, Durrant considered that, in any such riot, mining property might be destroyed, and that this would affect the general war effort and cause a loss of morale. These considerations extended over the whole area that provided the fuel for Kalgoorlie, Boulder, Coolgardie, and the Eastern and Murchison fields. From this area Durrant interned 690 men initially, although 70 were released before Durrant replied to AHQ.

The area Durrant regarded as the next greatest problem was Geraldton. It was a strategic port, and the second largest oil reserves in the west were stored there. There were no military units stationed at Geraldton, and few police, so the oil stocks and the port area could not be guarded, nor could its concentration of Italians be supervised by the police. Durrant interned 65 local tomato growers and 60 fishermen from the Geraldton district. But this had created its own problems. To save the tomato crop, Durrant considered he could release half the farmers "without affecting the interests of national security" by putting them on their parole to stay on their properties and not congregate in Geraldton. Supervision of fishermen was too difficult for release to be contemplated. In the southern areas of Western Australia, only 83 Italians were interned, while 317 were allowed their freedom without any explanation, except that they were mainly farmers and timber workers. In one timber area there had been reports that there would be strikes unless the Italian wood-cutters were interned, but when things settled only a few were taken.

In contrast to their compatriots in the country, few Italian residents of the metropolitan area were interned. Included in those interned from the cities were the 125 taken from the *Remo*, but these were not locals. The reason Durrant allowed the 550 metropolitan Italians to continue to go about their normal occupations was that there were enough police in Perth and Fremantle to watch them. However, the productive capacity bottled up in internment camps was clearly on Durrant's mind, and he assured AHQ that investigations were being carried out "continuously" to release internees to "resume their normal employment and to carry on production". But he was adamant that releases to the goldfields would be minimal, although some of these internees might be released to work on farms in the south.

Durrant's explanation to AHQ shows that he was basically concerned about the damage unsupervised Italians might do, not only on their own initiative but also as victims of anti-Italian feeling. In the gold areas they were likely to be provoked by the Australian miners, and in the wood collection areas by the Slavs, and in the jarrah-cutting areas by their competitive cutters. These antagonisms were based on economic rivalries that long pre-dated the war, which might provide the spark, the excuse leading to a conflagration. This does not seem as evident in the farming areas, but Durrant was not prepared to risk large numbers of Italians unsupervised near key installations. He does not suggest that many were politically active or suspected of being engaged in Fifth Column activities, but Mussolini's attack on France was regarded as a "stab in the back" and, consequently, many Australians credited all Italians with the potential for underhand actions.

Durrant saw it as his responsibility to keep an eye on all Italians, either through the police or, where this was impossible, through internment. In his view this was the only way to achieve security. On the other hand, he was also aware of the value of the Italians' contribution to the economy of Western Australia. Durrant had the responsibility of finding the balance between security and production in the nation's best interests. AHQ felt he had come down too heavily on the side of security, imposing a huge administrative burden and forcing the reopening of the old World War I internment centre at Rottnest Island, and risking the supply of fresh food to Perth.

Differences of opinion

However, Western Command was not alone in being out of step with AHQ over internment. When AHQ asked for the estimated increase in German internees as a result of Instruction 13,[55] Eastern Command indicated that it would have none to send.[56] As the *Argus* report of 6 June, indicating the arrest of "hundreds" in Sydney, was undoubtedly read by Army headquarters staff in Melbourne, Eastern Command was asked why it had none to send. From its answer, the Military Board deduced that there appeared to be a scheme arranged between the Minister of the Army and the State Premier (Alex. Mair), where the State Government was sending up warrants to the GOC (Eastern) Command for executing. The GOC was putting the warrants into effect and people interned on these warrants were being kept in N.S.W. and not being sent to Victoria. So far the State Government had sent up 150 warrants which had been executed and they expected to go up to 500.[57]

This was a flagrant departure from the previous channels of authority. In effect it meant that the right to decide who was to be interned had passed to the State Premier, who disagreed with the Menzies "narrow" policy and who had a reputation for disliking refugees.[58] The conservative coalition partners, Mair and Bruxner, were instituting the internment of persons through the military's delegated authority over enemy aliens. The GOC Eastern Command at this time was Lieutenant-General V.A.H. Sturdee. With a background in engineering, Sturdee had served at Gallipoli and commanded the 4th Pioneer Battalion. He instructed in military engineering and surveying at the RMC, Duntroon and later worked in the War Office and the High Commission in London. From 1933 until 1939 he was the DMO & I, then Director of Staff Duties at AHQ. He raised the 8th Division but suddenly he had to undertake the job of CGS and on him would fall the onerous responsibility of preparing the defence of Australia. In those frightening times, the politicians would rely on him heavily and D.M. Horner has described Sturdee as "the rock on which the army, and indeed the government rested during the weeks of panic in early 1942".[59]

Rock-like in his own loyalty, Sturdee lacked sympathy for enemy aliens and refugees. When asked for his opinion on the desirability of an independent tribunal system to classify aliens, General Sturdee replied that the only really effective way of dealing with enemy aliens was to intern every one and he suggested an immediate start be made by interning all those who had arrived in the previous two years.[60] Nor was the police chief in New South Wales, W.J. Mackay renowned for his empathy with foreigners and his pre-war appeal to his Premier showed not only a general tendency to equal foreigners and criminals but an almost obsession with the treachery of women.[61] The opinions expressed by Jessie Street and Richard Hall, that war hysteria caused many refugees and anti-Nazis to be interned, have some credibility in this period.

The involvement of the State politicians, however, was not the only bone of contention between the Board and Eastern Command. The Board complained that effect should not have been given to such a scheme without first telling the Board, who had the responsibility to decide how and where internees were to be held and to ensure that the relevant Conventions are complied with.[62] They also complained that the policy of concentrating internees away from the coast was not being effected. Defending himself, Lt.-Gen. Sturdee replied that "it was not intended to imply that the internees concerned would never be sent to Victoria".[63] Orange had been selected because the accommodation was "readily available". The site was well away from the coast and secured by a 9-ft fence of wire, outside of which lay loose coiled barbed wire attached to an outer rim of a 6-ft fence also stranded with barbed wire and the internees were guarded by a detachment of the 54th Garrison Battalion. The Chief Engineer, Eastern Command explained that by the "clearing out of certain pens from the main building" bunking accommodation for 638 was installed, and by extending the compound "accommodation could be provided for approximately 1000 internees". The "feeding arrangements" under the main grandstand were considered satisfactory, "but cooking arrangements" needed improvement. Approximately two and-a-half acres were enclosed and the whole of the fence and compound was floodlit from 20-foot poles. Eastern Command received full support from the acting Premier of New South Wales, M.F. Bruxner, who pushed the matter by publicly claiming that dangerous enemy aliens "were left at large", and by writing privately to the federal government urging the internment of women.[64] Bruxner's letter to the federal authorities related to thirteen persons, some of whom were naturalised males, and some women recommended for internment by the NSW Attorney-General, H. Manning, who had examined the police files and felt that these women were too dangerous to be free. The debate over the desirability of giving the military control over naturalised citizens intensified and the suggestion that women be interned was brought again before federal cabinet.[65]

The group branded as Fifth Columnists, and with a commitment to try to alter public opinion, but containing many British subjects was the Communist Party. Faithful Communist Party members in Australia supported the alliance between Stalin and Hitler, instituting strikes and go-slow tactics. Their actions were not generally popular and sometimes the police had to control crowds who wanted to attack communists or to throw them into the river.[66] The military had wanted to be allowed to detain any individuals they considered subversive under the National Security (General) Regulations, but Menzies had been worried about the possible infringement of the rights of innocent people if approval were given for such a sweeping delegation of authority without considering the methods of implementing it.[67] As the war situation worsened, Menzies' concern for safeguards was less popular. What constituted subversion in war time, and to what degree it could be tolerated, were spelt out in the Governor-General's speech on 17 April. The limits to freedom of political thought and action were reached "when men profess an allegiance to a nation other than their own, when they plan to overthrow constitutional government", and "when they direct their activities to the defeat of their own country in a war to which that country is committed".

Colonel Combes' direction to each command to produce, in conjunction with the CIB and state police, a list of communist leaders for possible internment, resulted in a very long list.[68] It was political dynamite. In a nation where freedom of belief and speech are ensured, arrests of this magnitude would create a furore. Actual internments could perhaps be kept to those people against whom there was proof of engaging in activities that aimed at defeating the war effort. While the pros and cons were being debated behind the scenes and in public forums, parliaments and the press, the general public were also having their say. The communists were well aware that their days of freedom could be numbered. The state police forces moved first. When the National Security (Subversive Associations) regulations were gazetted on 15 June they raided CPA headquarters, and a number of officials were arrested.[69]

Why did Australia intern so many men in response to the threat to the British Isles in June 1940? Overwhelmingly of British stock, Australians became overtly pro-British at this time, even though the actual fighting was on the other side of the world. This was completely in keeping with her tradition from World War I, when men flocked to the defence of Britain even though many had no idea who the Archduke of Austria was, or where to find Sarejevo on a map. To most Australians, a generation later, Britain was still "home" psychologically even if not physically. So aggressively pro-British was majority sentiment in mid-1940 that even the citizens of friendly alien countries became nervous at the rising tide of public agitation and the exclusion of anything or any person not British. As an indication of public feeling in June 1940, the following items were reported in two consecutive days.[70] Wild rumours circulated in Sydney, naming "leading citizens of exemplary character" as being interned, refugees were called parasites in one letter to the editor, Poles were hurt at being denied the right to enlist, and Greeks in South Australia decided to wear "conspicuous badges" to distinguish them from Italians. Even some British-born citizens were warned. The Fifth Column was seen as having many facets, and incongruous groups were lumped together. People who have a conscientious objection to bearing arms are not popular in war time, but the consistent fortitude of religious-based groups such as the Quakers (or Society of Friends) in adhering to their beliefs during World War I had won them the respect of the community. Nevertheless even they were warned that they would be exempt from prosecution only if they kept their peace-loving ideals within their own circle and refrained from propaganda. Tolerance of those perceived to be anything less than totally behind the Empire's war effort was wearing thin, and those who were not with us, were increasingly seen as being against us.

Chapter Four

LOYALTY AND LOGISTICS

June 1940 saw a dramatic increase in internments, basically as a response to the losses in Europe and the entry of Italy as an enemy, but in July and August the forces for and against this broader internment policy struggled for supremacy. These forces were various, and many had precedents in World War I, but some were quite new. At the core of it all lay the meaning and essence of nationality. A national is required to be loyal and, in times of war, the fit young men are expected to bear arms. This was a major assumption throughout World War I and World War II. But who is a national? All those born in the country are taken to be nationals and to them are added those who have become naturalised. In peace time the law upholds the equality of both claims to nationality but naturalised persons of enemy origin can be relegated to second-class status in war time. In World War I the status of naturalised citizens was devalued and it was assaulted again in World War II. To further complicate matters in World War II the Nazi government's treatment of its non-Aryan citizens created a class of stateless people. The problem of nationality impinged heavily on internment because it was so interwoven with concepts of loyalty.

World War I precepts

During World War I the original internments were of German and Austro-Hungarian males who were on their countries' military reserves. J.D. Davies has done an extensive study of the Commonwealth government's response to Germans and German descendants in Australia during the 1914-18 period, and he nominates the central problem then as being how to treat different categories of Germans so as to maintain a balance between the adequate military security of the country on the one hand, and considerations of justice, the rights of individuals, administrative practicality and financial cost on the other. Internments went from two thousand in March 1915, to almost three thousand a year later. They peaked in July 1917 with 5411 males detained and fell a little by the end of the war. Because of incomplete records, Davies could not find the precise time of the doubling of internments, but he judges it was sometime in 1916.[1]

The official war historian, Ernest Scott, reported that "when the first long casualty lists from Gallipoli began to arrive the feeling against local Germans became intense". Many Germans were dismissed from their employment, became destitute and gave themselves up for internment. All enemy reservists were taken in Australia in February 1915, after two Turks attacked a train of picnickers outside Broken Hill. In 1916 the camps in the individual states were scaled down and most internees were concentrated at Liverpool. By then, 3,272 Germans who had been resident in Australia before 1914 were interned, along with 393 naturalised British subjects of German origins.[2]

So strong was anti-German feeling in parts of Australia that attacks were made on well-known men of German extraction, some with long records of public service. Herman Homburg, the Attorney-General of South Australia, was forced to resign and a naturalised parliamentarian refrained from standing in the Commonwealth election of 1917. Moves against all naturalised citizens of enemy origins began when W.A. Holman, Labor Premier of New South Wales, suggested removing their privileges.[3] H.V. Evatt, in his biography of Holman, claims that, in a press campaign against people of German origin, Holman was denounced for not moving against the employment of a few former Germans in the public service. In Evatt's opinion, Holman failed to understand that it was the widespread anxiety "of the mothers and wives, the fathers and brothers of the soldiers" that was substantially behind the anti-German agitation and Labor lost an important by-election.[4] Holman quickly learnt the political lesson and became vocally anti-German. W.M. Hughes, the Attorney-General and Prime Minister, disenfranchised Germans on the federal level from April 1917 until six months after the war ended. Hughes felt this move would improve the Yes vote on conscription.[5]

Naturalisation and loyalty

Similar moves against naturalised citizens were made in World War II. Herman Homburg, who had returned to politics, and served a further term as Attorney-General for South Australia from 1927-30, and a term in the Legislative Council from 1933, was again detained.[6] There were also moves to treat naturalised citizens as if they were aliens and these highlighted the complex legal and emotional situation of naturalised people. The German and Italian governments upheld the Delbruck Law of 1913 and gave their natives a permanent citizenship that was not altered by naturalisation elsewhere, so a dual citizenship existed. The problem was further complicated when these rights were passed to children who were under-age when their father became naturalised. The motivations to become naturalised were sometimes as much a matter of commercial expediency, or a necessary prerequisite for owning land, as a definite transfer of loyalty. In many states, licences for fishing-boats depended on naturalisation, and in fishing areas such as Fremantle and especially Port Pirie, Italian fishermen were naturalised while holding office in the local Fascist Party branch. In Queensland, land for farms depended on naturalisation, and some observers felt that migrants took out citizenship for that reason alone. Many Italians made no secret of the fact, but they saw it as the commonsense thing to do, implying no disloyalty to their native nor their adopted land.[7] A great part of the problem was that dual loyalty was not only legally but also emotionally possible. A migrant who took out naturalisation did not expect that there would be a war and, therefore, a conflict of loyalties. But an application for citizenship made in the expectation of continuing cordial relations between the country of origin and the adopted country, is not clear evidence of potential disloyalty. Nor is it logical to assume that migrants who deliberately chose to move half-way around the world, and who found there the economic security they craved, would act to undermine their new country.

The army showed particular mistrust of naturalised persons, and the fact remained that a number of Fascist Party members and the two leaders of the Nazi Party, Dr Becker and Walter Ladendorff, had been naturalised. The military leaders in South Australia were particularly concerned. Brigadier H.C. Bundock, the officer in charge of the SA area, was an expert in artillery and had served as a Commander of Coastal Defences in the thirties.[8] When war broke out he was put in charge of the field troops in Western Australia and also given temporary command of the 5th Military District. In December 1939 he was appointed as the GOC of the 4th Military District. Bundock considered that the power to intern enemy-born citizens should be given to District Commanders. Under the organisational system in operation before the war, the six military districts, together with the militia divisions and independent brigades, reported to and were directed from the Military Board. The Inspector-General, Lieutenant-General E.K. Squires, recommended a major reorganisation with four commands based on Brisbane, Sydney, Melbourne and Perth where senior officers took responsibility for all units in their command.[9] While Darwin kept an independent garrison from October 1939, Tasmania and South Australia came under the control of Southern Command, Melbourne.

As a District commander, Bundock wanted to be able to use his own discretion and intern naturalised people as he was already able to do with enemy aliens. Bundock claimed that the local bank manager regarded most of the "Australian born Germans" of Tanunda, South Australia, as anti-British and in sympathy with Hitler. There was alleged to be a pronounced pro-Nazi feeling throughout the District, and a particular resentment of the withdrawal of fire-arms. The bank manager was also concerned by a drop in bank deposits and little investment in War Savings Certificates. He attributed this "to propaganda by unwitting 5th Columnists" and a lingering suspicion that the government might have been serious about some form of conscription of wealth. Brigadier G.E. Manchester of Tasmania also wanted naturalised citizens stripped of the privileges their British status gave them. He felt they should register in the same way as aliens had to, but he was more concerned that, if the public were not satisfied that action could and would be taken immediately it was thought necessary, civil disturbances could result.[10] This was almost identical to the complaint by the Naval Staff officer at Port Adelaide that there was a popular criticism of the authorities "for their inactivity in not apprehending these people".[11] The public was not aware of the fact that some were already under restriction. These officers complained that while they could detain unnaturalised aliens "if thought expedient", it was extremely difficult to obtain orders against naturalised and "Australian born Germans". They stressed how well off these people were and how many had motor cars. Bundock felt it would only need one more major military success by Hitler in Europe to trigger organised fifth columnist activities such as attacks on the Port Pirie smelters, the Whyalla shipyards and the Islington explosive stores. Bundock wrote that it would be "entirely in keeping with Nazi thoroughness to have hidden machine guns, hand grenades, and light trench mortars ready to produce when required". Bundock considered the law gave "too free a hand to naturalised aliens and their progeny". The District commanders urged AHQ to press the War Cabinet for the necessary legislation and delegated powers.

The GOC Southern Command, Lieutenant-General J.L. Whitham, considered the matter and concluded that some delegation to district commanders would facilitate quick action in an emergency but, to ensure reasonable uniformity of policy, he felt that the Minister's power should only be given to the officers in charge of commands and not to the district commanders.[12] Even in this situation there was some risk of "lack of uniformity, due to the varying personal view points of the officers concerned", but this was minimised because GOC's were advised by a trained, efficient staffs, who knew the local conditions and who could appreciate the repercussions in local public opinion, arising from any proposed action. Basically Whitham did not disagree with Bundock about the principle of military control over naturalised citizens; he differed only over the level at which it should be instituted. But he did not support the de-naturalisation of all enemy aliens. Such action would probably magnify the very problem it was desired to avoid, and would be out of harmony with our whole concept of citizenship in the Commonwealth. Whitham considered the negative effects of any wholesale moves against naturalised citizens. Reputable long-term citizens would feel besmirched and distrusted and their attitude towards Australia could turn hostile. They would lose faith in the British legal system under which they had chosen to live. Furthermore, over the years they had established families and friends who might also respond unfavourably to their relatives' and neighbours' arbitrary detention. Bundock's idea that every naturalised person should be de-naturalised and required to re-apply would have created an administrative and legal nightmare. The government was only prepared to revoke the naturalised status of people who were proven to be disloyal. Evidence of disloyalty was the same as that used for internment, but the evidence had to comply with the terms of the Act. It had to include the source of the information and the dates on which it was obtained. The Director of Military Operations and Intelligence admonished all military area commanders on 1 June 1940 because in certain recent cases the Minister had pointed out that the evidence submitted was insufficient to justify him signing detention orders and he would presumably adopt the same position with incorrectly documented applications for de-naturalisation.[13]

The contrasting attitudes of Whitham and his two district commanders shows the differences between individuals with authority in the internment area. The attitudes of Generals Durrant and Sturdee were uncompromising towards enemy aliens. Bundock and Manchester extend this distrust to include British subjects who originally came from Germany and Italy. Whitham qualified his views and believed that the British system of justice could be understood and appreciated by people from non-British backgrounds and that they could transfer their loyalty. It is always dangerous to speculate, but the comparisons are fascinating. Whitham's comparatively liberal attitude could be due to local factors such as the number of genuine refugees in Melbourne and the influence of the CIB director, Ronald S.Browne. On the other hand, perhaps Whitham's prime concern was to see that only officers at Command level be given such far reaching powers.

Despite Whitham's caution and War Cabinet's decision not to delegate power to detain naturalised people to the military, Bundock remained suspicious of the 60,000 persons of German descent in South Australia. While they were normally loyal and peace-loving, Bundock felt they were being told by pro-German elements that it was their duty to support the Fuhrer and were being enticed by the prospect of getting the rich farms currently owned by Britishers.[14] Intelligence informant No. 214, after two weeks of mixing "with the people in Clubs, Hotels, Bridge parties and Evenings", had found Tanunda people guarded in their conversation, but he had no doubt regarding their sympathies. In his report, No. 214 cited examples of four local men in the area who gave overt signs of pro-German sentiment by actions such as singing "Deutschland Uber Alles", saluting an Australian army vehicle with a "Heil Hitler", and making comments favouring a German victory. However, it is not clear whether No. 214 actually saw and heard these incidents for himself, or whether they were part of the cardparty gossip. Bundock wrote, "Strong bodies of armed and determined men

properly organised and equipped with fast transport and assisted by surprise tactics could cause tremendous destruction
and loss of life before forces could be marshalled to combat
them". Bundock correctly argued that the Australian authorities would be at a disadvantage if such an attack took place,
especially considering that the 4th Garrison Battalion was 77
under establishment, and there was no reserve company or any
organised Home Guard Defence force. On the other hand, there
was no proof that the 60,000 German descendants in his military area, or even a fraction of them, were planning to act as a
mobile, armed raiding party on South Australian facilities.
Because a naturalised person owned a car, it did not mean that
he intended it to become a Fifth-Column armed transport.
Nevertheless, in the heightened tension of June 1940, there was
great pressure put on local authorities to intern more potential
enemies.

As soon as war broke out there were complaints about the
church school at Light's Pass, South Australia. The South Australian State Council of the RSL asked the government to close
it and indeed all German schools in the state. The school denied
it was a "hotbed of Nazi propaganda".[15] The controversy over
the use of German in the Lutheran schools and churches had
precedents in World War I.[16] There was an extended debate in
Victoria over the eleven small schools clustered around Hamil-
ton and Horsham. These schools had an enrolment of 300, were
registered with the Council of Public Education and German
was not spoken during the four hours of standard education
each day. They were controlled by the Luthern Evangelical
Synod in Australia, descendants of a group who had migrated
from Prussia in 1838, eventually settling in Western Victoria as
farmers. A puritanical sect, they considered that the state church
diverged from Luther's teaching. They refused to have anything to do with the celebrations of the Kaiser's jubilee because,
as British citizens, they felt they had no connection with the
affairs of a foreign ruler. When their attitude on this issue
brought condemnation from other German-speaking groups,
they argued that, as they enjoyed the rights and privileges of
British citizenship, they owed it their "full and undivided
patriotism". R.J.W. Selleck claims that the debate on the closure
of the German schools in western Victoria "held up a mirror' in
which Australian attitudes to migrant groups were reflected.
These attitudes are that migrants come to Australia "on the

condition that they absolutely throw in their lot with us" and that "what is good for Australian born boys and girls is good enough for anyone else who comes here". Migrants are expected "to become as English as possible, and as soon as possible". Selleck considers these attitudes are profoundly embedded in the Australian character, and are more conspicuous in wartime.[17]

During the Great War debate over the church schools in Victoria, the government had opposed their closure and its case was most eloquently put by the member for the Western District seat of Lowan, James Menzies,[18] father of the Prime Minister in 1940, Robert Menzies. James Menzies argued that from his 25 years experience with the German settlers he could not express the suspicions, "without discrimination", other members had done. He referred to their pioneering contributions, to the right of access to a religious-based education and to the dead soldiers of the AIF with German names. At the time of his father's defence of the Lutheran schools, Robert Menzies was a twenty-one year old law student. He enjoyed a happy home life in which both his parents imbued him with a sense of fairness.[19] As Prime Minister in World War II he always upheld a limited internment policy and stressed moderation in dealing with enemy aliens, and extreme caution with naturalised citizens. His stand could well have been influenced by his father's defence in World War I of people who the family knew were not a security threat.

Many sections of public opinion were not satisfied with the strictly legal consideration shown to naturalised subjects enunciated by Menzies. Much of this general public unease was based on prejudice and jealousy with agitation in the remoter areas very strong in World War II.[20] The action against large numbers in Sydney in June 1940, and the publicity surrounding it, may have calmed the Sydneysiders, and the availability of police in Perth was a paramount consideration in Durrant's internment policy in Western Australia. City people had the comfort of the proximity of a dominant British population. Isolation, and the existence of non-British neighbours, heightened anxiety in some rural areas. Sightings of "signals", meetings of strangers, and the comings and goings of foreign-born neighbours, were more frequently reported from the country, where people were also very concerned with undefended property, their own and the government's. Railway bridges, power

stations, water-supply pipelines, and the farm equipment of
absent servicemen, are mentioned frequently as potential targets in letters to country members of parliament.

Farmers expressed fears that former migrants coveted their
property. In fact, Australian farmers reciprocated and coveted
the farms built up by hardworking migrants, because the desire
for land in Australia is insatiable, and holdings of good arable
acres are prized above all. Constant expansion is the dream of
farmers and graziers as a buffer against bad times, a chance to
enjoy the economies of large-scale production, and something
to pass on to sons. This rivalry for land, and the envy it provokes
was still at the base of much anti-migrant public opinion. A
similar hostility simmered between Australian city labourers
and migrants over jobs, and the protests against aliens that
came most strongly from the country were echoed from the
working-class suburbs of the cities.

The military and the police had to consider this tension
because it endangered law and order, but there was a limit to
how far their response could include internment. The question
of who should control the internment of naturalised persons
was settled in August 1940 when the Minister stated that he did
not intend to delegate his power over naturalised persons, and
the decision would be reconsidered only if there was an emergency. Evidence supporting requests for the internment of naturalised people had to be "reasonable", and show how it had
been gathered.[21]

Police reaction

The other group with a major input into recommending internments were the police and in contrast to some of the military,
they were not given to making broad generalisations on
grounds of nationality. They showed particular care when dealing with naturalised people, especially the law-abiding ones.
The police were involved in the selection procedure because
they were the reporting officers for aliens. They took down all
the information on aliens in 1939 when registration began, kept
the records and aliens had to report to them every week. In any
selection based on a set of criteria such as "all men of Italian
nationality, who were of military age and who had arrived
between 1938 and 1940", the police took the names from the
registration forms. During the crisis of June 1940 many people

contacted their members of parliament, or the military or the police about individuals in the community whom they thought were disloyal. In the areas outside the metropolitan centres the investigation of complaints was done by the police. The degree to which the police were arbitrary or consistent is relevant to the implementation of internment policy.

A survey of about one hundred such investigation reports shows that the police displayed a fairly uniform caution against precipitous actions.[22] They appear not to have relied on one person's word and they sometimes expressed the opinion that the motives of the complainant were mixed. In one case a naturalised family of German origin in a small town in southern Queensland were reported to be exceedingly pro-German. The police made several enquiries but it was only the accuser who had ever heard the family say anything anti-British. The complainant was born in Durham, England, and had many relatives there. He made his complaint just after a devastating Luftwaffe attack on Durham. The police reported that the man could be described as "prejudiced", and they did not recommend any action. They did however have "a long chat" to an aggressive young man who had painted a swastika on the cow bails of his family's dairy.[23] There are no further entries in his file. Naturalised citizens who were the subject of close police questioning quickly recognised their situation and took a low profile. One couple gave up regular weekday trips to town and confined themselves to a visit of a few hours on Saturday morning, when they quickly did their necessary shopping and restricted their conversation to returning courtesy greetings.[24]

The police did recommend action when there was some evidence to justify the suspicion of disloyalty. For example, one family of brothers painted a large Italian flag and a much smaller Union Jack on the roof of their farm-house. When requested to obliterate the offending flag, they did the job so ineffectively that it remained clearly visible from the road and the air. The brothers were listed together with other suspected Fascist supporters, members of the "Black Hand Gang" and those with criminal records including possession of an illicit still.[25] In another case it was claimed that a man had frequently been seen going off to the neighbouring town centre every Saturday afternoon wearing a black uniform. Although the policeman had not seen this himself, a number of long-term British residents were prepared to swear it was true. Enquiries

among long-term naturalised men of Italian origin revealed
that the man was regarded by his fellow Italians as "a bad man"
who often carried a knife and a shot-gun and was very aggressive towards neighbours. He reportedly beat his wife and the
police discovered that his son had left home because of the
domestic violence. This combination of facts earned the man a
place on an early internment list.

Overall, the police reports tend to give an emphasis to law
and order and to some degree, morality. One man was interned
because ten years before he had stabbed another man in the
hand with a penknife during an argument over work payment.[27] Although his sentence for grievous bodily harm was
served and his naturalisation successfully reapplied for, years
later it was held against him. In the same district there was a
young Italian who had a dispute with some Britishers in 1938
and the argument "finished up in a brawl".[28] The young man
was the son of a naturalised farmer. In the town there was
another young Italian man who had recently arrived with
someone else's wife, causing a violent scene when the irate
husband followed. Both young men had disturbed the peace
and were recommended for internment. The newly arrived
wife-stealer was interned but the fighting son of the farmer was
not. He was already in the army before the blanket internments
in mid-1942 saw his name listed for internment.

The police sergeant from this area reflected on the results of
his pre-war recommendations: There were 240 naturalised Italians in his district and their conduct and that of Italians overall
was "good". However he had listed 23 for internment but when
Italy entered the war only 9 of the unnaturalised men were
taken and none of the naturalised ones. He seemed unaware
that assessments such as "of low moral character", "said to be
a member of the Communist Party" and qualifications such as
"no documentary proof" were guaranteed to be rejected as a
basis for a ministerial warrant.

The same police sergeant took an entirely different view of
46 men, who had been listed by an anonymous writer as "facist
and cumunst all" (sic).[29] The sergeant reported that all but two
were naturalised and many had achieved their migrant dream
of owning a farm. One man had been naturalised in 1913 and
had lived in the district almost from the time it was opened for
selection. There was little likelihood that these men were fascists, for no party branch existed in this district. Nor would their

material success lead them to gravitate towards communism. That they would hold both positions simultaneously was unbelievable. The writer could have been a jealous unsuccessful migrant as the style of writing and spelling on the note suggests, or, as the police sergeant thought, one of the many who had attended a recent "Win the War" rally, where one resolution called for the internment of all enemy aliens, and who had decided to furnish the list "with a view to having the resolution given effect to". The policeman's inquiries suggested that the note be disregarded. Respectable people were protected from outlandish accusations and police judgments were based on local evidence and individual behaviour.

Planning for overseas internees

Australian authorities had no wish to see blatant acts of an anti-British nature go unpunished, but they wanted no unnecessary internments because they were having problems coping with the large number of enemy aliens scooped into camps by the enthusiasm of Eastern Command and Western Command. In addition, the troopship *Dunera*, loaded with about 2,500 internees was approaching Australia. To accommodate these and the 300 internees whom the government of the Straits Settlements had also asked the Australian government to accept, the Military Board proposed to the War Cabinet that £330,000 be allocated to build camps at Hay (NSW), Loveday (SA), and Rushworth (Vic.). The military also requested that £150,000 be reserved for camps for locals or for the 3,000 ex-British internees still to be taken up in the quota Australia had undertaken to receive from the Churchill government. The accommodation of some thousands of overseas internees had suddenly become a major undertaking for Australia's political and military leaders.[30]

There is no doubt Australia desired to fulfil her obligations to internees in keeping with the Geneva Convention; the accommodation and food rations were the same as that provided for the Australian Garrison troops, and where shipments included women and children, extra efforts were made. The Adjutant-General notified the Quarter-Master General, and others who would be involved in this major undertaking, that 2,164 male Germans and 202 male Italians were expected in mid-August, and an even larger mixed group of men, women and children were expected to depart from Britain about the same time.[31] (The large mixed group did not come because of a change of policy in the UK.) From the Straits Settlements, the 145 male and 120 female Germans and 18 male and 14 female Italian internees would include married couples, children and single men and women. The Adjutant-General warned his men that while prisoners of war were of a similar physical standard to Australian troops, internees were arrested irrespective of age and medical condition and that this necessitated modified conditions. Special arrangements would have to be made for women and children, and a suitable ration devised for the Italians who were unused to the foods being supplied at that time. In view of the extreme change of climate extra warm clothing was to be ready when Malayan internees arrived.

On the other hand the government was also conscious of cost. Although Great Britain and the Straits Settlements were willing to contribute to the cost of camps and the maintenance of prisoners, the Military Board's proposed outlay of a half a million pounds was not well received by the Australian War Cabinet.[32] The Minister for the Army was told to review the estimates and check that all proposed expenses were really necessary. The Governor of Singapore and the Dominions Office were informed that Australia would charge the full cost of providing the guards and running the camps. The reply from the Straits Settlements that "reasonable expenditure" would be met was not altogether reassuring, and both expatriating governments were billed while their internees were still on the high seas. Unless the two governments were prepared to accept an averaged per capita expenditure, separate accounts would have to be kept, in addition to providing separate camp groupings for nationality, sex, age and marital status. To further complicate the matter, the British government asked for a further separation. Dangerous enemy aliens were to be kept under "strict custody", but the British wanted Australia to "apply a system of less rigid custodial treatment to genuine refugees from Nazi oppression and those not falling within the potentially dangerous class". The request was somewhat puzzling, given that the Dominions had been asked to take the internees because they were too dangerous to be in Britain. The request for preferential treatment for refugees recognised that these people were actually stateless, and the British authorities were asking for Australia's understanding. But the Australian War

Cabinet at that time was worried about cost, and wanted to know how expensive this further differentiation would be.

The Army proposed the following cost cuts.[33] Cases involving surgery would go to local hospitals and pavilions erected in the grounds if necessary. The Quarter-Master General, Major General E.K. Smart, advised the cabinet and they approved revised estimates. Altogether an expenditure of £278,000 was agreed. Britain was apportioned £127,500,while £150,500 was considered to be Australia's contribution. But the cabinet was upset because someone had authorised spending £16,500 upgrading the Orange Showgrounds camp. The Swiss Consul had been disgusted with the accommodation and threatened to report it to Berlin unless improvements were promptly carried out. While the Consul held his report, the army went to work; however the money had not been released by Treasury and cabinet demanded to know the name of the officer who had authorised the work. The Army Minister refused to comply on two grounds. The report of the Consul would have endangered reciprocity, so that British and Australian prisoners could have suffered, and the money would have been spent anyway, as the Orange camp was to become an Australian militia base as soon as it was vacated by internees.[34] Thus cost and reciprocity again placed parameters on the number of internments. Australia had to keep her own internments within a manageable level if she was going to cope with them and with those about to arrive from overseas.

Overseas internees were not unique to World War II. In the Great War the Liverpool, Bourke and Trial Bay camps became the home of planters and public servants from German New Guinea and Samoa. As with the later internees from the Straits Settlements, there were often family groups and the World War I camp on the Molonglo River was specifically for families. They brought malaria and tropical diseases with them and complained of the dust and cold of outback Australia.[35] However, internees and prisoners of war had not been sent from Britain before, and there was no precedent for the extraordinary group of men who arrived on the *Dunera*.

HMT Dunera

Accounts of the ship's journey cannot help being dramatic.[36] Sections of the ship were overcrowded and some men had to sleep on the tables or under them. Toilets and washing facilities were minimal. Exercise periods were short and the brutality of the British guards comparatively unrestricted. The internees' property was not safe, and was taken from their suitcases in the hold, from their quarters and in body searches. The ship was torpedoed by a German submarine, but not damaged. Two internees died on the journey, one by suicide, and the ship was set alight when an oil lamp spilt.

There were surprises, too, in those deported. Two hundred were survivors of the *Arandora Star*, which was sunk by a U-boat off the coast of Scotland when carrying internees to Canada. Despite barely surviving the shipwreck, these men were arbitrarily reallocated to the *Dunera*. The high death toll of the *Arandora Star* raised questions as to the propriety of deporting prisoners through highly dangerous waters and, when the names of the internees involved became known, serious doubts about the whole policy began to be voiced in Britain and Canada. An interested observer of Britain's internment policy, Francois Lafitte,[37] speedily produced *The Internment of Aliens*, published as a Penguin Special in November 1940. At 6d each, almost 50,000 copies were sold. Lafitte listed some of the eminent scholars caught up in the broad internments at the time of Dunkirk, some of whom were well known anti-Nazi authors. The leader of the Social Democratic Party in Saarland, sculptors and artists whose works were banned by the Nazis, and men who had spent many years in German concentration camps, had been taken into custody.

The public reaction to Lafitte's book added further to the doubts already being expressed within the Home Office and there was also criticism within the Foreign Office.[38] Richard Latham, son of the Chief Justice of the High Court of Australia was a Rhodes Scholar and a Fellow at Oxford. During the Spanish Civil War he drove a supply truck to Republican Barcelona and over Christmas in 1938-9 he visited Berlin to help refugee migration. He urged Australian authorities to drop their demand for landing money, as he considered that among the refugees there was "some splendid human material for Australia". In mid-1940 Latham worked in the Refugee Section of the General Department of the Foreign Office. He criticised internment policy and urged the formation of an advisory committee on refugees. The internment of 27,200 people in Britain almost reached the World War I total of 29,000. Investi-

gators into the deportation of Italians to Canada concluded that
the commanders of internment camps were sent quotas to fill
and, if enough fascio members were not in the camp, the
remainder were selected at random. The Refugee Section concluded that MI5, whose job was to investigate and judge individual cases, had succumbed to the stress of public opinion, and
to "the influence of high authority in the War Office", and
"adopted the rule of thumb that any person of foreign nationality" was presumed to be hostile.[39]

In response to the protests the Home Secretary announced
on 23 July 1940 that category C internees, that is, those who were
refugees, would soon be able to apply for release. The main
reason given for this decision was the need for manpower.
Churchill, who had been an ardent supporter of the broad
policy, reversed his position.[40] In reviewing British internment
the Home Secretary said that mistakes were due partly to haste
and partly "to stupidity and muddle".[41] By the end of the of
August 1940, one thousand internees were freed, but this did
nothing for the 650 who had drowned on their way overseas,
and little for the 7,350 who were in Canada and Australia.

The *Dunera* entered Fremantle on 27 August 1940 and the
Australian authorities got a brief glimpse of a group of men
who claimed that their valuables had been taken, that they had
been denied access to their suitcases for the whole journey, and
that they had rarely shaved. The ship then went directly to Port
Melbourne where the German and Italian seamen and the
survivors of the *Arandora Star* were disembarked.[42] They went
by train to Tatura where the camp commandant was surprised
to discover a man still dressed in the only clothing he had, a kilt
given to him after he had come ashore in Scotland in the first
week of July.[43] The *Dunera* entered Sydney Harbour on 6 September, and the press reported that these internees were "dangerous",[44] but the guards on the train to Hay found them
pleasant, well educated and anti-Nazi. The internees, in return,
were impressed by the guards' humanity.[45]

Hans Hammerstein, a concentration camp survivor, felt that
the fresh fruit, sandwiches and cakes served by the guards on
the train to Hay "were so much the more delicious because of
the manner in which the Australian soldiers distributed them".
Everything was done with a smile, and when an approach was
made, it was done with a "please" or "thank you". At first the
commandant at Hay refused to believe that the British guards

had pocketed internees' goods, had shown a total disregard for
personal papers and possessions and had slashed suitcases
with bayonets to facilitate rifling their contents, but when the
remnants of the battered luggage finally turned up, the Australian officers were "aghast".[46] The officers in charge of the
British guards were entertained in Sydney and in Hay. Lieutenant-Colonel W.P. Scott, the guard commander, was "an impressive kilted figure", who had lost three brothers in "the present
war". The internees were "fed better than any British troops"
he told the press, in contrast to the claims of underfeeding by
the internees.[47] In the Army's weekly report to cabinet on 10
September 1940, the Deputy Chief of the General Staff (DCGS)
pointed out the apparent contradiction between the British
request for differential treatment for internees who were the
victims of Nazi oppression, and the statement of the Intelligence officer from the *Dunera* that all persons sent to Australia
were internment cases. A few internees were recalled to Britain
immediately they arrived in Sydney and they had to be provided with complete sets of new clothing. The DCGS confirmed
that all internees had arrived poorly clad and that the records
relating to them were incomplete.[48]

One thing about the *Dunera* internees soon became evident.
They included hundreds of Jews.[49] Some were practising Orthodox Jews, some were practising Liberal Jews, many were
nominal Jews, a few were Zionists and others were atheists and
socialists — but Jews in terms of Hitler's Nuremberg Laws.
Because of these racial laws many Jews had tried to leave
Germany but most countries restricted their entry. When a
Jewish youth shot the German Embassy's Third Secretary in
Paris, the Nazis took reprisals on the entire German and Austrian Jewish community. On 9-10 November 1938, many shops,
homes and synagogues were destroyed. Because of the amount
of smashed window glass this was referred to as "Kristal
Nacht".[50] Between 20 and 30 thousand Jews were arrested,
(among them Hans Hammerstein) and sent to concentration
camps. Hammerstein and 50 others were released when transit
visas to Britain were arranged. They lived in the Kitchener
Camp with 3,000 others. Many hundreds from the Kitchener
Camp were persuaded to embark on the *Dunera* because their
commandant told them they were going to Canada, and a
release there would leave them on America's doorstep.[51]

Other *Dunera* internees were young men whose families had

urged them to leave Germany. One of them was Werner Pelz. He worked in England on the land but was interned in mid-1940. He heard rumours that the internees would be freed on landing, and this seemed logical to him. He was convinced that no one would dream of sending them halfway around the world just to be put into another camp.[52] The 19-year-old K.G. Loewald was unconcerned about leaving England. Propaganda in the British press against the refugees at the time of Dunkirk prepared him for the possibility of internment. He felt he had nothing to lose and had his bag packed when the official came to collect him.[53] Another young man, Hugo Wolfson, had a permit to enter the USA and was at the Huyton Camp near Liverpool when, with other similar youths, he volunteered to join the *Dunera* because they were told that going overseas would mean more freedom, possibly work and no change to their migration plans.[54] Married men had been told that their families would soon follow and some were given forwarding addresses in Canada. A family man who came through the Kitchener Camp, G.F. Chodziesner, was fortunate that his wife and son Ben escaped to Chile, but on 21 August 1940 he recorded in the diary he kept on toilet paper on the *Dunera* that Jacob Weiss from Vienna, "a comrade of the Kitchener Camp", committed suicide by jumping overboard. Weiss had a mother and brother already in Buenos Aires, but the visa for Argentina that had come through for him just before he was interned had been confiscated at the beginning of the voyage. It had expired on the day of his suicide.[55]

Other internees who were not Jews but Lutheran and Catholic, were also pushed to the brink of despair. Hans Lindau had worked for the Student Christian Movement in Britain and was a member of Toc H and other benevolent clubs. He was devastated by the search he was subjected to when he entered the ship. The roughness with which his person and goods were handled stripped his individuality from him. The soldiers "did not understand" his opposition to Hitler and his basic desire that England and Germany, with their common religious and racial origins, should be allies and friends. For three hours after the search Lindau rested with his head on his rolled up topcoat and agonised with his God. The motion of the boat made him feel seasick but he eventually regained his mental and spiritual equilibrium.[56]

Another internee to draw heavily on his religious strength

was Walter Konig, a Jesuit priest. He had been expelled from the College of St Aloysious in Bad Godesberg by the Nazi authorities in 1939. He taught in Sheffield until he was interned on the Isle of Man. At the Hay camp, Konig recalled five men who had to be removed to a sanatorium, and in his own hut there was a Viennese youth who had seen the Gestapo hurl his parents out of the window of their home. On moonlight nights the lad "ran yelling through the hut". There was also "a highly gifted boy" who "in front of everyone, tried to open the veins of his wrists". Only strong nerves were capable of standing up to the trials through which many *Dunera* men and youths had come. They had been persecuted, they feared they would never be reunited with their families, they were rejected and denigrated by their national government, and there were few welcoming arms in the rest of the world. Finally they had been deported on a "hell ship" to the antipodes where the stars were "upside down" and familiar northern sights and sounds missing. Ludwig Hirschfeld Mack, who had taught mathematics in the famous German Bauhaus Gropius School of Architecture that came under such attack from the Nazis that most of the teachers fled to Britain or America, constructed a relief map of Australia for the Hay camp. Everyone knew that the distance from the camp to the coast held them more firmly prisoners than the strands of barbed wire around their compound and Konig compared the internees to the original convicts of the 1788 penal colony.[57]

Jews interned in Australia

While the *Dunera* internees included many Jews, they were not the only refugees in camp in Australia. Australia herself had gathered up others in the raids following the new guidelines on refugees with relatives in enemy territory, and they were identified by Dr Neuman in his camp record as Jews and "non-Aryans". The trials of internee objectors in 1941 reveal some, but only a guess can be made of the overall number.[58]

In an article on the internment of German-Jewish refugees in Australia, Konrad Kwiet estimates that of the 10,000 local civilians interned "somewhat more than 2,000 would have been of German-Jewish origin".[59] He includes all those who were interned even briefly to arrive at his 10,000 total, but official figures would round out at 8,000. There is no doubt that the second wave of local arrests included German-Jewish refugees. Not only is there the evidence of Neuman, the camp recorder, and of the Swiss Consul, but Kwiet has found the personal papers of 25 Jewish internees who were sent first to Orange and then to the Nazi dominated compound lA at Tatura. The leader of the group, Max Joseph, had been a successful accountant in Berlin until he was sent to a concentration camp after "Kristal Nacht". He migrated to Australia via Holland and England and established himself in a laundry business. According to Kwiet, denunciation caused Joseph's arrest on 10 October 1940. In the Orange camp the group had achieved some segregation but in lA Tatura only their sleeping huts 26 and 27 were their own. The group clung together, stressing their Jewish heritage, celebrating their religious festivals and agitating for release. Joseph was eventually successful and left camp on 12 July 1941.[60] Although the experiences of Joseph's group is a caution against labelling any camp or compound, it does represent the situation of a minority, and a minority significantly smaller than one-fifth. Perhaps Kwiet unconsciously transposed the *Dunera* situation on to local internments. Other overseas internees included a high proportion of Jews, with the internees from Singapore being described as mainly Jews who originally came to the island as refugees.[61]

Queensland records suggest only a few Jews in the earlier groups. The internee registers show that many taken in Queensland were tradesmen living in country towns and some had been in Australia over ten years. Kwiet does not deal with the third wave of local internments — early 1942. At that time all German nationals were removed from the vulnerable northern coast, and this would have included any refugees. But the numbers were small for Jews are traditionally city dwellers. The Sydney experience cannot be transposed to other areas. In 1941, Queensland internee 152 specifies his religion as Jewish and his nationality as German (Refugee). His mother lived in Berlin and this could well have been the reason for his internment. Q191 also states he is a Jew. In the group taken in February 1942 Q202, a pastrycook from Atherton specifies himself as a Jew, as does a former Pole, Q218, and a later internee Q236.[75] But they are a small percentage of the Germans taken in the first half of 1942. Of the approximately 1,200 German internees who were resident in Australia, 240 would have to be Jewish to reach one-fifth and the evidence suggests many fewer. Kwiet's proposition that

2,000 of the 10,000 interned were of German-Jewish background cannot be sustained among the "local" internees, although the proportion of German-Jews among the European
internees held in Australia from all countries, could well be
higher than a fifth because of the large number on the *Dunera*.

To separate refugees from other Germans it was proposed to
introduce a system of independent committees. On 21 June
1940, AHQ notified commanding officers that independent
tribunals might be set up in each military district to classify
aliens. This suggestion was not favoured by any military
leader.[63] Western Command considered that the expense was
not justified. Eastern Command considered that "the only really effective way of dealing with enemy aliens" was to intern
them all before "setting up a tribunal to review the cases of
internees who consider that they can submit proof that they are
traitors to their own country".[64] In Northern Command there
was a feeling that there was already too much opportunity to
appeal in the existing legislation; that command wanted the
right of naturalised citizens and British subjects to appeal to be
abolished and no new tribunals established.

In Southern Command the proposed tribunals were rejected
because the military review committee had frequently allocated
the refugee classification and they considered that the problem
was that their military-assigned "Certificate Z", (indicating
refugee and friendly alien) had not been given legislative status.
Major R.S. Browne had arranged to submit reports on those
who based their claims on the Personal Statement Form A42.
Southern Command was also convinced that the established
military review committee was best able to deal with any
modifications that a changing international situation might
warrant.[65] In classifying aliens, the military review panels had
used files from the CIB and the Special Aliens Branch of the
State police forces, and also Military Intelligence reports. The
military regarded their operational methods and files as secret
and they did not want others to have access to them. They
questioned the dominance of lawyers on the proposed committees because lawyers would look for evidence that would stand
in a normal British Court, but in the tribunals established by the
National Security Regulations the onus of proof was on the
accused. Besides as General Sturdee pointed out, a "really
dangerous enemy alien must necessarily be a man who has
completely cloaked himself with an innocent character".[66] So it

was decided not to proceed with the independent classification committees.

Reaction sets in

The attempts of the New South Wales politicians, Mair and Bruxner, to have internment extended to naturalised and female persons through their police force's access to Eastern Command, created a backlash. Mair sent Menzies a telegram urging the internment of all German aliens on 12 June 1940[67] and Bruxner was reported in the *Sydney Morning Herald* two weeks later as complaining of the Commonwealth's "inactivity" in not interning enemy aliens.[68] Their foray into the public press finally brought condemnation by the Prime Minister,[69] who could see that undermining the confidence of the general public in the effectiveness of the security forces would eventually be detrimental to morale. After Menzies' positive denial that dangerous enemy aliens were still at large, a more balanced press cover of items about enemy aliens developed. Letters in the press and to government leaders pointed out the number of enemy aliens who were actually stateless or had suffered persecution.[70] The announcement of the British government's August White Paper exonerating category C internees gave some critics pause, and rumours of the actual treatment meted out on the *Dunera* began to trouble some consciences.

Added to this mounting concern about the treatment of refugees,[71] was indignation at the number of arrests shown to be trivial. Such abuses were particularly resented by the left of Australian politics. Communist officials of trade unions were harassed and the files of unions were searched, although most members were not communists. Sections of the National Security Regulations were an affront to civil righters.[72] Many of the more active were politically left of centre, and they realised that their chances of free expression rested on overall freedom of expression, but civil rights groups also included many liberal thinkers, pacifists and devotees of legal correctness. Protest peaked when the radical unionists, Horace Ratliff and Max Thomas, were arrested and imprisoned for distributing anti-war literature in December 1940.

A few cases of excessive and stupid zeal threw considerable doubt on security actions. An old couple from Kalgoorlie had their home raided. The house search revealed a newspaper with an item about the internment of their son-in-law, a German-born miner with fifteen years residence in Australia. The parents-in-law were told that if they were only interested in their relative they would have kept only a cutting, and not the whole leftist newspaper.[73] In Sydney, on the Domain, a young woman art student was arrested because she carried a drawing of a head that resembled Mussolini. In court she successfully pleaded that her drawing was modelled on the bust of Beethoven.[74] These trivial arrests certainly went beyond the intent of the legislation, and the criticism of arbitrary arrests and detention of refugees belong to this period — May and June 1940 — when the war first became a reality to many Australians. But there was a reaction to these extremes and, according to Paul Hasluck, a feeling against general internments grew in the later months of 1940.

> [I]nternment of enemy aliens, which had hitherto been exceptional, tended for a time to be general, and individual hardship was imposed on alien refugees who were interned for no other reason than their foreign birth. The injustice of indiscriminate internment, however, roused Australians themselves and, as a result of public protests and appeals, the application of the security powers was made less drastic and at the end of November 1940 enemy aliens were given the right to submit objections to an Aliens Tribunal which could recommend release if it were satisfied that the detention of a person was "neither necessary nor advisable for the public safety, the defence of the Commonwealth or the efficient prosecution of the war", or that the release of the persons "would not be likely to occasion serious unrest in any Australian commnunity".[75]

The decision to give enemy aliens the right to object to their internment was partly the result of representations made to the Prime Minister regarding German missionaries associated with the Roman Catholic Mission at Kimberly, WA. Thirteen Pallotine priests were removed to Broome gaol, triggering a protest by Bishop Raible of Perth. Archbishop Mannix, backed by a public meeting of Catholics and others, appealed to the Prime Minister. Ten were released to return to the mission after an investigation by the Broome stipendiary magistrate ordered by the Minister for the Army, Percy Spender. The remaining three missionaries were paroled to appear before an independent inquiry later. As a consequence, enemy aliens were placed on the same footing as persons interned under Regulation 26, that is, they were to be allowed to appeal against their internment, but this decision specifically excluded internees transferred to

Australia under arrangements made with the Governments of other parts of the Empire.[76]

It would be pleasant to credit Australian altruism and love of justice with being the dominant force behind the second thoughts about internment that prevailed in late 1940. But logistic problems, including lack of accommodation, were probably an equally important consideration. To the end of 1940 the number of local internments in Australia was about half of those in the Great War. As with the Great War, there were assaults on the status of naturalisation but this time they met with no official success. In World War II there was the complicating factor of the Jews whose land of origin rejected them. While Australia was prepared to act to allow any of its own resident Jews, including recently arrived refugees, to appeal through Aliens Tribunals, it hesitated to make decisions about the Jews sent from overseas. The Australian authorities regarded their role as custodial only. While acting as custodian for these thousands of internees and prisoners-of-war from overseas, Australia was at the same time building up her own military forces and mobilising her economy. This placed her organised resources under a great strain and for a time, the standard of care and accommodation for prisoners fell below the level Australia had set herself and promised internationally to provide.

Chapter Five

IMPLEMENTATION DEBATES

In the closing months of 1940 the authorities at Hay struggled to accommodate the Dunera internees who had arrived before the buildings were there to house them, and the internees struggled to accommodate themselves psychologically to being on the opposite side of the world and to adapt physically to an Australian summer in the outback. The army crowded as many as possible into the huts that had been erected, and put up tents for the rest. Although the internees did not complain about the army's efforts in the early days at Hay there can be no doubt that conditions were primitive.[1]

Hay camp and its occupants

The people responsible for reporting on the situation in Internment Camps were the Official Visitors. In New South Wales these were the Chief Justice, Sir Frederick Jordan, and a Supreme Court judge, Mr Justice C.G.W. Davidson. Sir Frederick inspected Hay on 29-30 October 1940 and reported his findings to the Military Board in some detail,[2] although he confined himself essentially to his roles as a commentator on the physical conditions of the camp and its occupants, and as a negotiator between the internees' representatives and the camp commandant. Even so, Jordan found that the internees were preoccupied with matters not related to the camp or their treatment there. In separating the internees' complaints about their journey,[3] from the remainder of his report, Jordan was complying with the National Security (Internment Camp) Regulations which spelt out the rules for the conduct of camps and the role of the Official Visitor.[4] A copy of the Visitor's report went to Eastern Command and the military then put in train their responses and forwarded the report with their responses to the Secretary of the Department of the Army for the information of the Minister.[5]

The internees barely mentioned the accommodation problems, and expressed their appreciation of the camp officers and guards.[6] The camp commandant, Lieutenant-Colonel C.S. Thane took command of the 16th Garrison Battalion in July 1940 and he brought to his job of establishing an internment camp on the dusty western plains, his World War I experience in the 54th Sikhs of the Frontier Force of the Indian Army.[7] The internees were somewhat anxious about the weather as many men were middle aged and they were all unused to the Australian inland climate, with its extremes of temperature, and also about the lack of meaningful activity for the hundreds of student youths in the group.[8] However, they were preoccupied with getting across to the British authorities their protest at being interned at all, and their indignation about their maltreatment on the *Dunera*. The Official Visitor had no jurisdiction over internments, releases, or British troops, but because the complaints were serious, and because the internees utterly refused to have dealings with the Swiss Consul,[9] Sir Frederick undertook to pass on the internees' representations. The internees' spokesmen, H.H. Eppenstein, from Compound 1, Camp 7, and Dr Frankenstein, representing the 250 former Kitchener-camp inmates from Compound 2, and Leonhard Posner, of Hut 33, Compound 1, who represented the Czech-Fund refugees, explained the anomaly of their continuing internment. The Kitchener-camp men had entered Britain on special permits that acknowledged their status as refugees. The Hay camp population was described by its leaders as consisting of up to 90 per cent Jews and "to one hundred per cent of anti-Nazis in every respect".[10]

The Czechs had also entered Britain after "careful scrutiny as to their reliability" and they were maintained by the Czech Fund. They argued that as the British White Paper of 14 July 1940 virtually exonerated all Category C internees, their release was "only a question of time". Being financially independent, they proposed that they live in an Australian town and help the war effort.[11] Other internees asked that releases be effected quickly, as those migrating to Palestine had landing permits due to expire on 31 December 1940. The married men requested that their wives and families be allowed to join them, or, if the situation was to be rectified by the husbands' return to Britain, any crossover be guarded against. Jordan summarised the internees' position.[12] In England the general detention orders of

June 1940 were now realised to have been "unnecessary and unjust", and the White Papers of July and August 1940 had release of many in Britain. The transported internees claimed that they were also "the victims of error" and they asked that someone be appointed by the Commonwealth government to assess their claims. Jordan did not agree. Australia was not in a position to know what precise circumstance led to each British internee's arrest. While they might be on our soil, they were undoubtedly not one of us! However, Jordan conceded that it did seem reasonable to give the internees an opportunity to put their case to the British and he suggested that someone be appointed "to act as a channel of communication with Great Britain".

In relation to the ill-treatment and robbery that the internees alleged against the guards on the *Dunera*, Jordan found their story consistent with two substantive comments by Australian officers at Hay. When the internees had arrived they were "cowed and abject", and the luggage when it finally arrived showed signs of having been broken into by bayonets.[13] While some of the complaints might be exaggerated, and it was necessary to hear the other side, Jordan was of the opinion that there was substance enough to warrant an investigation. He advised the internees' representatives to prepare detailed statements and he knew that the British High Commissioner, Sir Geoffrey Whiskard, was "interesting himself in the matter".

The Military Board passed Jordan's memorandum on to the British authorities, but informed him that there could be no Court of Inquiry as none of the ship's crew were in Australia to give evidence, and turned to answering Jordan's complaints about the physical conditions at Hay, particularly the sleeping quarters.[14] Dust, mosquitoes and flies poured in through a ventilation gap between the top of the wall and the roof. Hay was notorious for its dust storms, and during the war years Australia experienced one of its longest droughts. Jordan wanted some protection against the dust and it was agreed that hessian would be tacked over the ventilation gap to sieve the dust and insects. Mosquito nets on the bunks were ruled out because of the danger of fire.

In each camp there were 36 dormitory huts, each of which held 28 men. The beds are arranged in a double line along the centre of the hut, separated by a partition along the middle. On either side of the partition the bunks are arranged in pairs, one

immediately above the other as in a railway sleeping compart-
ment, and Jordan took a strong dislike to this layout.[15] Bits of
straw filling and dust from the hessian mattresses fell on the
lower sleeper each time the man on the upper bunk moved.
Jordan wanted the dormitories arranged in the same way as
those at Ingleburn Army camp, that is, with single bunks 6 ft
apart along the two long walls of the hut. To back his point, he
quoted Article 10 of the Geneva Convention, which specified
the total area, minimum cubic air space and fittings and bedding material appropriate for internees. He interpreted the
words "as for the depot troops of the detaining power" to mean
that the Hay huts should be laid out in the same way as at
Ingleburn.[16] The army was not impressed. To remove the two-
tiered bunks would mean extra huts to the tune of twelve
thousand pounds, and the army's medical opinion was that
they were not unhealthy. Furthermore, this bunking arrangement "as in vogue at Liverpool during the 1914-18 War"![17]

In other areas the army tried to oblige Jordan. He had noted
that the internees were making hats for themselves from hessian, and sandals from old car tyres. Their few underclothes
were wearing out fast. Although many internees were not poor,
their money was delayed in reaching Australia. A remittance of
over twelve thousand pounds sterling was received early in
November 1940 for credit to individual internees. By the time
the lists were sent to command headquarters, and from there to
camps, three months had elapsed since the arrival of the internees in Australia. [18] Jordan asked that supplies of clothing, hats,
foot wear and toothbrushes be rushed to Hay. He quoted Article
12, which specified that basic necessities be provided, and in
this case the army agreed with him. Basic clothing would be
provided. The problem had arisen because no one had foreseen
that when the men arrived many would have no money and
only the clothes they stood up in. Jordan also commented
unfavourably on the inadequate supply of cooking utensils and
cleaning materials in the kitchens, the smallness of the laundry
and the lack of recreational huts and craft materials for occupational therapy. All these things the army promised to rectify. The
army accepted that the medical, dental and optical services
were inadequate, and they reassured Jordan that there would
be improvements. In the sanitation area they were already
considering replacing the large urine cans, which were sitting
in the open on the earth along one side of the outside of the

latrine, with a trough. Between Jordan's visit to Hay on 29 and
30 October 1940, and the receipt of his report by the secretary
of the Military Board on 6 November, the camp was visited by
E. Sydney Morris, a Quaker and President of the European
Emergency Committee.[19] Morris was in Hay from 1 to 4 November. He found the area unattractive and the surrounding
country "virtually desert".[20] The annual rainfall was eleven
inches and the summer temperature frequently went over 100F
in the shade. After rain the soil became "tenacious mud", but
during most of the year the district was subject to severe dust-
storms. It seemed to Morris that this camp site had been chosen
so that any escapee would have to keep to the Murrumbidgee
River in order to survive.

Morris listened to the internees' stories and thought it "the
most depressing experience" that had ever befallen him. The
internees pressed on him, as they had done on Jordan, their
objection to remaining interned, stressed that the British White
Papers had exonerated the same groups in Britain, and explained their anxieties about families and businesses and visa
expiration. They inquired about the possibility of some internees remaining in Australia, but Morris had to tell them that this
was fairly unlikely as the "Australian Government regarded
itself merely as a trustee for the British". He was concerned
about the depth of the internees' anxiety, some of them being
depressed to a point of hopelessness. Most of the young men
had been sent to England to give them a chance to get training,
and while there was little that could be done about their "mental anguish" for their parents in Europe, Morris considered that
efforts should be made to fit them for life after their internment.
Morris was obviously impressed by the positive attitude of
Captain Carrington, who had formed a Scout Unit and regarded the interned youths as of as high a calibre as any boy
migrants he had placed before the war.[21]

Morris listed a number of items he thought would be well
used; text-books, handicraft materials and Lutheran hymn
books among them. He noted that Lt-Col. Thane was "anxious
to develop the whole camp on a productive basis", and Morris
strongly supported him. If the *Dunera* internees were modern
convicts, then Thane was Arthur Phillip. Thane's plans included market gardening, bread- making to supply the camp,
raising pigs and poultry, tailoring, making mail-bags, and even
constructing a low-level dam across the river to form the basis

of a canal-irrigation system. If internees could be paid pocket money for doing this work, they could buy the basic necessities they badly needed, such as toothbrushes and shaving cream. Morris stressed this aspect of Thane's plan, for Morris was shocked at the destitution he saw. He described the men as having arrived in "ragged" clothes and some men were "forced to clean their teeth by means of a moist finger dipped in sand or grit". Boots were wearing out and some men had to go barefoot. Although Lt-Col. Thane had immediately requisitioned complete outfits for each internee, two months later only 200 outfits had arrived. The delay, as Morris understood it, was largely due to military requirements being greater than suppliers could meet. Some clothing had been sent by the Australian Jewish Welfare Society, but "an enormous amount" was needed.

The internees were well organised and involved in lecture programs and entertainments, and were willing to work inside and outside the camp. The inhibiting factor was the lack of basic equipment. For those who needed special medical care or post-operative specialist treatment a hospital had been established in the old Hay gaol, whose thick walls made it one of the coolest buildings in the district. For less severe cases there was a small sick-ward in each compound staffed by internee doctors. The internee dentists and dental technicians were unable to be of much use because of lack of equipment. "It was rather pitiful," Morris wrote, "to see one of these dentists endeavouring to do what was possible with the aid of a few instruments fashioned out of nails."

The army minister reacts

Morris's report is dated 11 November 1940 and on that same day the Minister for the Army, Percy C. Spender, wrote a letter to General Miles at Eastern Command. Lieutenant-General Charles G.N. Miles was a permanent officer who served in World War I. He was the Director of Military Art at the Royal Military College in the 1920s and its commandant from 1935-9. A member of the Military Board when war began, he was attached to AHQ but took over Eastern Command when Sturdee became CGS. He retired on 19 December 1941.[22] Spender wrote that he had information from "a responsible source, concerning the conditions of the internees at Hay". There can be little doubt that Morris was Spender's source. He repeats Morris' words. The internees were "in ragged clothes", "some are barefoot", many had "neither toothbrushes nor shaving gear" and, in general, the equipment position was "very bad". The Minister did not mince matters. He concluded:

> I take a most serious view of this matter and I require an immediate report showing whether the facts placed before me are substantially true and, if so, advice should be furnished not only in general terms but as to who are the officers responsible and why simple equipment of this description to deal with the situation has not been provided.[23]

General Miles replied that Spender's information was "substantially correct" but action was being taken "to alleviate the position".[24] Greatcoats and sets of clothing had been despatched to Hay but there was "no authority to issue toothbrushes or shaving gear". Educational facilities were being discussed with the YMCA, but money and extra building work would be needed. A policy statement on the employment of internee tradesmen, such as bootmakers, had only just come from AHQ. It was based on the suggestions of Lt-Col. Thane, who was then in Sydney, negotiating with welfare groups, with a two hundred pound grant for each of the three camps to spend. In addition to the army initiatives, the Official Visitor had submitted "a very detailed report" on the inadequacies at Hay but it had only been received on 7 November. General Miles concluded his reply by stating that no officer could "reasonably be held responsible for the conditions at Hay", which were "being rectified as fast as possible".

Spender was not satisfied, and asked for a copy of the Official Visitor's report, and the name of the officer responsible for "the unsatisfactory conditions" at Hay, flatly asserting that the responsible officer should be disciplined.[25] On 16 November, the Military Board contended that Eastern Command was responsible for the conditions at Hay and told General Miles to name the officer and provide a report on the failure "either to provide items or to make the necessary representations".[26] Miles protested, arguing that AHQ held ultimate responsibility, but the Adjutant-General denied this and Spender still wanted an answer to the question "What is being done about the equipment?".[27]

General Miles replied in detail. He had sent Colonel W.B. Simpson, the chief legal officer, to Hay for a five day investigation. Seven hundred sets of clothes were forwarded and 400 were following. Toothbrushes, razors and shaving brushes had now been dispatched. Tools were supplied in part, and the balance was on order. A draft agreement on Thane's land and water project had been negotiated with the state authorities. There were now 72 educational classes being attended by over three hundred internees, but more money was needed for textbooks. Men from the Department of Agriculture were to be appointed as employment officers so outside work could begin. The Catholic church had nominated a chaplain, but other denominations had been unable to supply any. The YMCA was only able to supply some materials but the committee of Public Librarians had agreed to equip each camp with a library. General Miles detailed the considerations that had affected the army's ability to cope with the sudden influx of overseas internees. The highest priority, in Miles' view, had to be provision of food and shelter, and this had been achieved. There had been a lack of definition as to what constituted the "other necessities" required under National Security (Internment Camp) Regulation 12, but in any case, if toothbrushes had been provided to internees on the *Dunera*'s arrival, it would have meant a shortage for the troops of the AIF. Lt-Col. Thane had now been placed in direct contact with supply officers and Miles had instructed them to ensure that there be no delays in meeting requisitions. Lack of funds was holding up the required additions and alterations to camp buildings, but the camp hospital now had an establishment of 110 beds and extra staff. Miles could not resist adding that AHQ generally controlled hospital arrangements, but these were "now likely to be expedited". Miles attached Thane's budget of six hundred pounds for tools, and a request for one and one half thousand pounds for requirements to 30 June 1941. This had the effect of redirecting some of the pressure on to the Minister. Tools and equipment were costly items, difficult to supply and justify when every effort was being put into gearing up industry for war production. Miles still felt that it was unfair to blame any officer in Eastern Command. He had admitted delay in the supply of clothing but he was "not prepared to apportion blame", and he had taken steps to prevent a recurrence.[28]

The Military Board supported Miles, and the Adjutant-General, Major-General V.P.H. Stantke, stressed that the internees had arrived from camps in England and it had been assumed that they had "ordinary personal necessities". Stantke put the blame back where the problem had originated — the hasty round-up and departure from England and the British guards who had looted the internees' possessions.[29] Yet the Minister for the Army was still not moved and members of the War Cabinet were not satisfied with the reply that blame could not be attached to anyone. Unless responsibility could be sheeted home to someone, something was badly wrong with the system![30]

So Miles had to do some more explaining. Eleven days before the Dunera internees had arrived at Hay on 7 September 200 sets of clothing had been ordered, but they were not sent until 14 October because "a junior temporary messenger employed in Ordnance" had "inadvertently filed the original copy in the duplicate requisitions file". When Hay pestered for more outfits it was realised that the original order had not been filled. Hay's second requisition for 800 sets of clothing was reduced to 500, in a mix up between the quartermaster at Eastern Command headquarters and the acting-quartermaster at Hay, but these were sent off on 11 November. The officer at Hay "was found to be unsuitable" as an organiser of supplies and had been transfered while the HQ quartermaster had worked hard since the outbreak of war and had a breakdown in health before being returned to regimental duties.[31] The strains on inexperienced junior staff and untrained senior staff, trying to cope with an unprecedented demand on inadequate resources were showing. The looting of the internees baggage and the camp building contractors' inability to get the labour and supplies to finish the camp in time increased the stress on everyone.

Spender persuaded the War Cabinet on 10 December 1940 to grant large increases in spending on internment camps and recruitment to the Garrison.[32] The Garrison Battalions were to be increased by 9,000 members. This involved a capital expense of £100,000 and other expenditure of £601,500. An additional £135,350 was authorised for capital works on internment camps, and £248,000 on extra maintenance. At the same meeting, the conditions were agreed under which the Apostolic Delegate and other religious representatives should be allowed to operate in visits to internment camps.

While Spender was urging Eastern Command to improve conditions at Hay, AHQ sent Major J. McCahon there to prepare a report for the Director of Personal Services.[33] By early November 1940 there were 2,507 in the three Hay camps and transfers from other commands would bring the group to its full capacity of 3,000. Camp 6 already held 526 Australian-Italian internees, Camp 7 held 955 internees from the United Kingdom, and Camp 8 had 991 German and Austrian internees. There were 35 internees in hospital and 64 were in the compound sick-wards. The senior medical officer at Hay recommended the transfer of 89 UK internees to a more temperate climate. Because of the pressure of numbers, the Orange camp was being re-opened; it could hold 425 men until further permanent camps were authorised and constructed. McCahon stressed that only the new compounds at Orange were to be used. However the garrison troops were still in tents and their conditions were no better than in July 1940 when Lieutenant Bass had told the German internees from Sydney that the guards were "worse off" than they were.[34]

The Official Visitors react

In January 1941 Dr H.O. Lethbridge, MBE, inspected the Hay camps in his capacity as Assistant to the Official Visitors.[35] Lethbridge had been the Government Medical Officer at Narrandera for 30 years and in his experience the weather in the Riverina was healthy provided people dressed correctly. There were periods of extreme heat but they were frequently relieved by a cold front that could cause the temperature to drop dramatically. These cool changes were not harmful in themselves but could bring on diarrhoea if people did not adjust their clothing. Lethbridge strongly supported Thane's plan to plant willows and poplars west of the camps and even suggested the planting of quick growers, such as peppers and wattle, in the compound to minimise the dust. Lethbridge anticipated that as Hay got very cold in winter, further supplies of warm clothing and blankets would be needed.

When Lethbridge met the representatives of Camp 7 he found them willing to speak out.[36] This confidence, so quickly regained in Australia, is to be noted. Jordan had reported the Hay officers' comment on the "cowed and abject appearance" of these internees when they first arrived, but that he himself had found "no trace" remaining of this fear by early November 1940.[37] Now, in January 1941, Lethbridge found them forthright about the unsatisfactory conditions. The urinal pans were still standing in the open and when it rained they overflowed. There

were no water hoses to clean the lavatories which were not
fly-proofed. In the kitchen there were not enough brooms, mops
or tea towels, soda or soap, and some plates were rusty. The
laundry had no proper boiler. Internee doctors lacked sticking
plaster and bandages and optical and dental services were
unobtainable. There was no kit to repair boots and the straw in
the palliasses had been renewed only once since the internees
had been at Hay.

The Official Visitor to the adjoining Camp 6 which housed
Italians interned in Australia, the Hon. Mr Justice Davidson was
angry about conditions there also.[38] In November 1940 he had
visited the camp, and been assured that work to benefit the
internees "would be undertaken immediately". This included
the cementing of the toilet floor and the covering of urine pans,
repairs to the hot showers, a proper wash-house, dust protection, a bread oven and paving around the kitchen. Because he
had been led to believe that everything was available for these
projects, Davidson had passed on the army's assurances to the
camp representative, Prince del Drago, who had now written
to tell him that three months later "nothing whatever" had been
done. Davidson's anger was not lessened by the fact that his
mail from the internees had been marked as passed by the
Censor, an act contrary to the regulations. the Prince's statements were accurate, Davidson considered that either someone
had been deplorably inefficient, or that the military had
breached faith with himself and the internees. Davidson saw
his role as Official Visitor not just to see that the Geneva Convention was observed, "but also to ensure that reasonable
treatment" was being offered to those who were interned. He
threatened the Military Board:

> I can not tolerate for one moment being used as a mere blind to
> enable the public to be deluded with the idea that the proprieties
> are being observed and <u>unless I can ascertain that something is
> being done at once in connection with the matters I have mentioned
> I shall have to resign as a protest.</u>[39]

Further, Davidson stated that he would be writing to the Minister separately. In February, Dr Lethbridge submitted a further
report on Camp 7, where there was "a rather serious epidemic"
of endocarditis, an inflammation of the membrane lining the
cavities of the heart.[40] Sir Frederick Jordan was convinced that
it was related to the "disgraceful" way the internees were
"huddled together in their sleeping quarters owing to the de-

fective layout of the bunks", and particularly to straw and dust falling from the top bunk. Jordan considered that all his and Davidson's representations on the problems with bunks had been met with "an obstinate refusal to listen to reason". To drive home his point he wrote, "I trust that it will not be necessary for a number of deaths to occur before it is realised that the matter is really serious". These vigorous protests by the Official Visitors made an impact.

The Chief Inspector for Army Catering, Major C. Stanton Hicks, and Captain G.G. Hack, of Western Command, visited Hay on 2 March to investigate.[41] They reported that the cementing of the area on which the urine buckets stood was a problem because it had to be sloped so that any runoff drained into the sewage system and incorrect sloping of concrete was a common fault among cement workers in Army Camps. Problems with rusty plates and inadequate soap were straightforward; supplies had been requisitioned but had not come. The supply store was the Drill Hall, and a check of the vegetables there showed that 15 per cent of the potatoes were inedible. The quartermasters in the compounds were untrained and with the Garrison being 200 men short, they had to do other duties as well. To make matters worse, the compounds did not have a stable population: up to 50 men at a time could be absent, appearing before appeal tribunals. Sometimes goods disappeared between the supply store and the compounds, having been traded for drink at local hotels.

In two instances the army's policy of accepting contracts on a price basis had proved a failure. The lower tenderer for the laundry contract had failed to fulfil requirements, and the cheaper meat supply from Deniliquin had to come by roads that were periodically impassable, and some deliveries had been condemned. Freshness of food needed to be a higher priority than fractional price differences, and the inspectors wanted the meat contract to revert to the local butcher, who had continued to supply Kosher meat slaughtered at the Rabbi's instructions because the orthodox Jews who would not eat any other. The two investigators interviewed the two Italians representing Camp 6, Prince del Drago and Captain Qualia of the scuttled *Romolo*. Their camp was now completely occupied by men of Italian origin, so the four negotiators agreed on alternative ration supplies. Veal, rabbit, macaroni, cheese Roman, tomato pulp, olive oil and salami were to replace corned beef, tinned

beef, sausages, tomato sauce, jam and 50 per cent of the oatmeal
and tea supplies.

The inspectors considered that all the essential difficulties at
Hay arose from shortage of staff and delay in carrying out
necessary and authorised works. The Quartermaster had no
staff and there was no Ordnance Officer but on the books stood
"goods to the value of £120,000. The position could reasonably
be described as a company organisation functioning as a Battalion".[42] The sudden increase in internments within Australia
in May and June 1940, and the arrival of the *Dunera* in August,
had created a need for camps well beyond the capacity of the
army contractors to build them, since priority had to be given
to accommodating the thousands of recruits in the AIF and the
AMF.[43]

But the demands on Australia as a reception area for prisoners of one sort or another were not to decrease. The promise to
take 6,000 from Britain still stood, and England continued to
expect it to be taken up. Fighting in the Middle East had brought
the war to Egypt, and one neighbouring base for Australian
troops was Palestine, where there were German-speaking
members of a religious group called the Temple Society, or
Templars, as well as representatives of German firms, both of
whom were considered security risks. There were also thousands of German and central-European Jews in Palestine who
had fled the Nazi advance and entered Palestine illegally. On 9
September 1940 London asked that Australia fulfil its promise.

The War Cabinet agreed to accept an additional 800 civilian
internees from Britain and 1,000 Luftwaffe POWs. Taking into
account the 2,542 *Dunera* internees already in Australia, the War
Cabinet considered they had an obligation to accept 1,658 others, who could be civilian German or Italian internees from the
United Kingdom or Palestine. But the War Cabinet stressed
three points.[44] First, male prisoners were preferred. Secondly,
the capital expense would have to be increased to cover the
accommodation of officers, and Britain should "reimburse"
these expenses. Finally, the acceptance of any aliens for internment in Australia was "subject to their prior internment in the
UK or Palestine and to the distinct understanding that" they
would remain interned in Australia and subsequently be repatriated to the UK or Palestine for release. Australia stuck to these
principles as far as possible. When on 20 November 1940,

Britain wanted Australia to take 3,500 illegal Palestinian immigrants, the cabinet refused.

Cabinet also refused to take the non-interned wives and families of the British internees,45 despite a plea from senior British Ministers that the non performance of their promise to reunite families was a political embarrassment to them. The Australian government could see that the political embarrassment to the British might easily become a double embarrassment to them. When they arrived the UK voluntary family internees might not like the conditions and agitate for release and the families of Australian internees who were finding "their present position difficult" could well ask for the same opportunity to join their men. It seems that 6,000 was considered the limit, and the reports on the accommodation and supply problems at Hay are evidence that the decision was justified.

But even when proof that most of the *Dunera* internees were not enemies became overwhelming, the government stuck to its non-release policy. When the representative of the British Home Office, Major Julian Layton, came to Australia he could offer the British internees some restitution for their property losses, a return trip to England through U-boat infested waters, but not release in Australia.46 While Layton began organising shipping, the *Dunera* internees were transfered from Hay to Tatura and Orange in May 1941, much to their relief.47 Even Konig, who saw a magic and beauty in the glorious colour of the sunsets at Hay, had had enough. He felt he was "no longer equal to the hardships". To another internee, Kurt Fischer, Tatura appeared luxurious. There were "trees, grass and hills" and "the place looked like a holiday resort compared to Hay". The huts "were subdivided into cabins" and each cabin had a separate entrance, a small table, two chairs, two beds and a window. It was "cosy". There were bathrooms with white bath tubs and the food was "good, tasty and plentiful". While Layton continued his work sorting out the internees and trying to arrange passages, questions were asked in parliament about internment policy and practice and about the manpower resources tied up in internment camps.

Questions in parliament

The UAP/Country Party coalition government had not been convincingly successful in the elections in 1940 and held on to power by a thread. There was also a real concern that Australia would soon have to face a powerful enemy in the Pacific area and some internal dissatisfaction about the organisation of the war effort. The Prime Minister, R.G. Menzies, went to London between February and May 1941 to stress Australia's point of view to the Churchill cabinet. He left the shaky coalition government in the hands of Arthur Fadden, the balance of power resting with two independents. The Labor Opposition worked through the Advisory War Council to keep parliamentary friction to a manageable level, but a few individuals within the coalition itself mounted some strong attacks on the government. One came from Archie Cameron, the member for Barker (SA), who went as far as moving a vote of no confidence in the Minister for the Army, Percy Spender, for his handling of internment.

Cameron was furious when the War Cabinet decided in November 1940 to allow enemy aliens interned in Australia the right to appeal to tribunals. Immediately the amendment implementing this decision was gazetted, Cameron moved that it be disallowed. On 2 April 1941, he claimed that the new Statutory Rule 269 was void. Both Spender and the leader of the Opposition, John Curtin, argued against him, but Cameron considered that the Minister for the Army had lost the confidence of the House "because of his handling of the internment, trial and release from internment of certain enemy aliens".[48] Spender persuaded Fadden that such an attack on the Army Minister in war time should be dealt with quickly, so Fadden allowed a full debate.

Cameron began by arguing that while Australian citizens, by birth or naturalisation, "were entitled to all their rights under the law, even in war time", enemy citizens who were in Australia when war broke out should "enjoy no rights whatever". They were "in enemy territory". Cameron claimed that the release of some aliens had "been contrary to the best interests of the country", and he believed that this claim was supported by the police and army officers whose job was to maintain internal security. Statutory Rule 269 placed the Commonwealth "in the hopelessly ridiculous position of appearing before a tribunal to defend its own actions", he declared. Internees were not accused of being criminals, they were merely the citizens of a country at war with Australia who had, in the opinion of those with responsibility for maintaining national security, the capacity to become "a danger to the nation". Enemy aliens "capable of bearing arms or of collecting or transmitting information" were best interned. If such an enemy alien was released he might engage in espionage, and sabotage industry, transport or morale. He might collect and transmit information or interfere with recruiting. It was Cameron's settled opinion that the "proper place" for an enemy alien capable of bearing arms, or of interfering with the war effort, was an internment camp, "unless something very definite" could "be shown to the contrary". To Cameron, nationality was fixed, and a capacity to harm was enough.[49]

Cameron described as "pansy" the government's action in taking the extraordinary situation of refugees into account; it was certainly not the method of the Germans, who had just shot a British officer for putting his head out of a window contrary to camp orders. Cameron claimed that the new regulation did nothing more than elicit information on the political beliefs of the internees before they came to Australia and this new information had "nothing to do" with Australia's security. Cameron argued that tribunals cost too much and that it was a waste of time and effort for army staff to have to prepare evidence and transport internees to hearings. He complained that the police were also put under extra strain in keeping up surveillance on released internees, that there was a lack of uniformity in tribunals procedures and that wealthy internees were favoured because they could hire counsel. To top it all, the government had recently issued a directive that internees were to be heard in the state where they had been arrested, adding even further to costs. The solution, in Cameron's view, was to hear British and non-enemy aliens in the camps and to get "competent authorities" to make a half-yearly report on any changes that might affect the circumstances of enemy aliens.

Despite the opportunity Fadden had given for a debate, not one other member in the chamber would second Cameron's motion and it lapsed. Nevertheless, Spender wanted to reply, both because the charges were serious and because they came from an ex-Minister of one of the armed services. He also wanted an opportunity to put his version for the benefit of the press.[50] He had been charged with being "incompetent or negligent, or perhaps even worse", and although the charges had not been substantiated, they would be published throughout the country, and it would take "a long while to overtake and rebut" them. While the actual attack was on the tribunal system, the political damage would fall on Spender, who resented Cameron using his "dual position" as a member of Army Intelligence and of the House of Representatives. Cameron's sole purpose, in Spender's eyes, "was to indulge his peculiar megalomania in order to get some notoriety out of his action".

No doubt Cameron was playing to the press, but it was an open question whether this was purely personal. As a member of Army Intelligence, how far had he discussed the matter with the army officers and police involved, and how far did his views represent theirs? His words and examples suggested that he was the mouthpiece for at least some officers disgruntled with internees having the use of cars for transport, but how general among army officers was annoyance at having internment decisions questioned, and resentment at being forced to defend their actions? Richard Hall's most trenchant criticism of Army Intelligence's behaviour in World War II was its disregard for the higher level of authority, its lack of "any sense of responsibility" to its "political masters". He points out that in the totality of Austin Laughlin's book, *Boots and All*, they are never referred to. He also claims that Intelligence officers had a sense of being the first line of defence against subversion and the bastion of internal as well as external security. If this attitude was general, and Laughlin is at pains to show how enthusiastically military officers took on their intelligence role, there can be little doubt that they would be irritated by any contravening of their recommendations.[51]

Part of the problem lay with the wording of the act that allowed for a flexible policy, where considerations of the state of the war and "public sentiment" were legitimate factors in internment decisions. In times of national crisis some security officers felt it safer to err on the conservative side, and they judged nationality by birth, and capacity to bear arms, as sufficient reasons for internment. Another part of the problem lay in the original delegation of authority to the army over enemy aliens. Any questioning of the army's handling of enemy aliens by the civil and political authorities was bound to be regarded as impertinent. If the parliament wished to take over the control of enemy aliens it had to introduce new regulations as Spender was doing with Statutory Rule 269. If the government was to become totally disillusioned with the army's handling of internment, it would have to revoke the army's delegated authority. But such a decision in war time, and with the government so tenuously supported, could be very divisive.

The military's political power is an implied but unspoken dimension in the parliamentary debates on internment. There can be no question that in war time the leaders of the armed forces have much more influence than they have in peace time. The people look to them to provide leadership and military victories. The politicians rely on their expert advice. What would be the situation in a case of conflict between the military and the politicians in the heightened atmosphere of war? And how much more leverage would the military have when the political parties were so evenly divided that the desertion of one or two members would change the government? It may be speculation to suggest that Cameron was the spokesman for those sections of military intelligence that wanted the unquestioned right to intern enemy aliens, including refugees, but it is a speculation that would offer yet another explanation of the continued internment of the *Dunera* internees in Australia.

When the Anglican Bishop Venn Pilcher wrote to the Menzies government, suggesting that tribunals be established to classify alien internees, and asking to visit internment camps, Menzies replied that he would be grateful if the bishop would not press his request. Pilcher thought that it was the visit to the camp that would embarrass Menzies, but the problem could have been the whole matter of the continuing internment of refugee aliens from overseas. The Inter-Church Committee prepared a memorandum explaining why the *Dunera* internees could legally be released in Australia, and Cyril Pearl says that the army rebutted the memorandum, contending that there were ample legal grounds for the internment of anyone whose "sovereign or state" was at war with the King.[52] The army minute also stated that an enemy alien had "no rights at all" and concluded that "the position had been made quite clear in Australia by the issuing of internment orders against each internee under the National Security (Aliens Control) Regulations". If the Australian government released the overseas internees, they could be instantly reinterned by the army under its own powers. The government-created tribunals could override the army where it knew the facts about the locally interned enemy aliens, but it would have needed a stronger government to try to assert control if the army was determined to hold the overseas internees about whom there was no local knowledge.

Although Cameron was soundly defeated in April, he returned to attacking the concept of the aliens tribunals on 3 July 1941. In this debate[53] he showed a more overt anti-semitism, there was evidence of government members' dissatisfaction, and the opposition was more restive and inclined to see the issue as an ideological one, where basic civil rights were threatened. Cameron complained that the government was looking after people who had come "to save their own skins" or because "the Nazis wanted to plant them here". This time Cameron was supported by W.J. Hutchinson, the UAP member for Deakin (Vic.), and J.G. Duncan-Hughes, the UAP member for Wakefield (SA). Hutchinson was concerned that aliens suspected of subversive activities, who took "great pains to cover their tracks", would be able to appeal to a court of law where the onus would be on military intelligence officers to prove that the objector was guilty of subversion. Duncan-Hughes, who himself had a military background, was convinced that military trials were more likely to result in "substantive justice" than trials in civil courts, where lawyers required "absolute truth" and complete satisfaction that no injustice could be done. In war time, Duncan-Hughes contended, Australia could "not afford to demand that complete proof be secured", especially when considering alien internees who were "not really members of our own community". Duncan-Hughes recalled the experiences of Holland, France and Yugoslavia early in the war, where fifth column activities showed "how widespread and effective" the Nazi organisation was.

In leading the debate for the Opposition, Frank Forde, the member for Capricornia, rejected the alternative of leaving "the whole matter in the hands of the military authorities". These men were "extremely busy" and consequently internees applications "might be ill-considered". Forde argued that a right extended to naturalised persons should apply to a person who wanted naturalisation but who had not been in the country long enough to apply. Forde described the new system as "a substantial improvement" without which injustice might be done "to loyal members of the community". Eddie Ward, representing East Sydney, spoke of the need for a uniform policy on internments and releases. Ward cited three cases to demonstrate how erratic policy was. An Australian-born returned soldier "was interned without being given the reason" while another man, Philip Hentze, was released very shortly after his internment, without the authority of the appropriate tribunal. From his examination of the NSW police dossier, Ward claimed that Hentze had been employed by the propaganda leader of the Nazi party in Australia, was an associate of three other internees, and was "in a position to obtain information concerning the movements of ships taking Australian wool to England". Ward's third case was a Greek, who had come to Australia at an early age, was well known in the trade unions and had "references from most reputable people". Ward claimed he was not judging any of the cases, only pointing out their inconsistency. Ward's speech also had a more theoretical component. He argued that persons should not be interned "without being given the reason for their internment" and that the government should have "sufficient evidence to support its action". A charge should be laid, for Australian and allied citizens ought not, in Ward's view, be placed in internment without "an open, public trial".

Frank Brennan, a most consistent Labor spokesman against rule by regulation, objected to Cameron's motion on the ground that it infringed civil rights. On these grounds he had originally objected to the 1939 National Security Act and to all the drastic regulations that had subsequently been added to it. Brennan believed that if the principles of democracy were worth dying for, they were "worth maintaining in the face of death itself". Contrary to Cameron's claims that aliens had no rights, Brennan claimed that they had rights the moment they stepped on to British soil. It was part of the British tradition that when men had come to Britain seeking political asylum, they "found sanctuary" there. The principle of democracy, in Brennan's view, required that access to tribunals be given to refugees who obeyed the laws, paid taxes and were entitled to the protection of Australia's laws. Brennan, Forde and Ward were, in effect, challenging any literal interpretation of internment policy that made capacity, and opportunity, and nationality, enough to make a man potentially dangerous. Some in the Labor Party were increasingly worried not only by the application of the internment regulations but also by the Subversive Activities Act. Their continual reference to the broader area of civil rights for all, was in anticipation of a major debate on aspects of the Subversive Activities Act that Labor's most outspoken civil libertarian, Maurice Blackburn, precipitated almost as soon as the aliens tribunal debate was over.

But before that new debate began, Cameron spoke again, pointing out that the government was currently applying harsher laws to alien seamen, and he protested that officials of the Attorney-General's Department were being used to represent the Minister for the Army at tribunal hearings. Spender had insisted that 80 per cent of his representatives were army officers. He acknowledged that alien seamen were subject to a regulation promulgated on 20 June 1941, permitting the arrest and detention of any alien seaman who absented himself from his ship, refused to sail on any ship that offered him a job, or was reported for refusing to perform his regular duties on board. In relation to the methods of appeal, Spender explained the actual practice of the Advisory Committees that dealt with British-born, naturalised and non-enemy aliens, and the Aliens Tribunals that dealt with enemy aliens. All Advisory Committee recommendations came to the Minister, but Spender had found that the dossiers provided by his military advisers sometimes contained "contradictory information". The sources of the information were often not indicated, but assertions could be as different as naming the same man a Nazi and a Communist. Spender had to go through every dossier because he refused "to act as a mere amanuensis" and sign detention orders just because the Intelligence Branch advised him to do so.

With Aliens Tribunals, dossiers and decisions came to the minister only if there was a disagreement between the GOC and the tribunal. Spender conceded that intelligence officers had a difficult task to perform, but he also knew that, in many cases, when the dossiers on which the original detention order had been signed were scrutinised by an Aliens Tribunal, and the objector had a chance to speak for himself, the whole case collapsed. Above all, Spender stressed that the onus of proof, which Cameron kept implying was being devolved on to the interning authority, remained with the objector. In cases where the GOC protested, Spender had sometimes made judgements against the tribunal because when there was any doubt, it "must be resolved in favour of the country". In regard to the particular case of Philip Hentze that Ward had raised, Spender protested that the man was a naturalised citizen and, to his certain knowledge,[54] the man's dossier contained deficient and unreliable information. The whole dossier had gone to a tribunal chairman who decided that there were no grounds for Hentze's internment.

The positions taken by most of those who took part in the debate were predictable, but R.S. Ryan, the UAP member for Flinders (Vic.) made an impressive, reasoned contribution. Colonel Ryan had served on appeals tribunals in the early months of the war and heard about 50 cases. The tribunal had to weigh "the balance of suspicion as to whether an alien is, or is not likely to be a danger". In Ryan's experience the evidence against the interned aliens was often "extremely slight", and 36 were recommended for release. When this went to the Minister, he released some but not others. Ryan was in favour of the new aliens tribunals procedure because if their recommendations were agreed to by the GOCs it meant that the Minister, who was "very much overworked", did not have to sift through large files;[55] on the other hand, contested cases did have a second chance, and through the Minister's "expert advisers" the Army also had a second chance to protest. Ryan's only criticism of the tribunals was the expense involved in transporting the internees down to capital cities under guard; tribunal sittings in the camp would be appropriate and much less expensive. Ryan opposed Cameron's motion to disallow the right of aliens to appeal, and his opinion was supported by the large majority of members.

On that issue of internment the opposition supported the government, but then came the different debate.[56] Maurice Blackburn moved to disallow another new regulation, 42A of Statutory Rule 69 of 1941. The aim of regulation 42A was to prevent people from trying to influence public opinion "in a manner likely to be prejudicial to the defence of the Commonwealth, or the efficient prosecution of the war". It was more punitive than the equivalent British regulation, and it included a clause preventing anyone from being prosecuted without the consent of the Attorney-General. Blackburn was suspicious that this clause would prevent well-known figures being prosecuted, while ordinary people could not "safely discuss any point" of Government war policy. When Spender protested that the courts would use their "common sense", Blackburn replied that he had seen in World War I that in times of crisis "police courts" were "very largely devoid of common sense". He was supported by Arthur Calwell, the new Labor member for Melbourne. Calwell argued that the punishment of six months imprisonment meted out to a Gallipoli veteran (who consequently became a "human derelict") for a drunken outburst, showed that police and stipendiary magistrates could not be relied upon "to deal out even-handed justice in a moment of crisis or public excitement".[57]

Labor men were restive over at least two other cases that influenced their thinking. On 20 June 1941 the ALP member for Wannon, D. McLeod, complained that the police had searched the homes of the executive of the Portland branch of the ALP in April, acting on a tip-off in an anonymous letter accusing the secretary of being a Communist, and McLeod was angry that a "libellous" statement could so easily lead to the embarrassment of a member of a party that had publicly purged all Communists.[58] In a small country town the news of the police raid would spread quickly, and fear of similar treatment might even prevent people from joining the party or taking office in it.

The second case was that of Ratliff and Thomas.[59] Horace Ratliff, an Australian, and Max Thomas, a New Zealander, were charged with preparing and distributing Communist propaganda that was "likely to prejudice the efficient prosecution of the war". When they were arrested in December 1940, the Communist Party of Australia was illegal and the two men were sentenced to six months hard labour. Soon after they were released the military wanted them interned because of their active association with the Communist party and their refusal to desist from further propaganda. On 3 April 1940 the War Cabinet had decided that the "profession of Communism as a political doctrine" would not be enough to warrant internment, and that the Minister for the Army would have to be satisfied that the person had been engaged in subversive or other acts against the national interest, before issuing a detention order. Spender considered extending the grounds for interning communists to include speaking in such a way as to "impede the prosecution of the war", or "undermine the cause for which Australia" was at war but this was not accepted by the Advisory War Council on 18 April. Hasluck states that there is "no record of any objection having been raised to the idea of internment by Ministerial order after release from imprisonment" so when Ratliff and Thomas allegedly continued to spread Communist propaganda after leaving gaol, Spender signed their detention orders and they were interned on 14 June 1941.

About a week later Germany attacked the Soviet Union and

many people felt that this should alter the government's attitude towards the Communist party.[60] Ten days after the entry of the Soviet Union into the war, and one day before the debate on Subversive Activities and regulation 42A, Ratliff and Thomas began a hunger strike to draw attention to their case. Dr H.V. Evatt, a former Supreme Court judge and the newly elected Labor member for Barton, took up their case publicly soon afterwards. With these practical examples of "overkill" in mind, the Labor members took a stand against the government on regulation 42A, despite their granting of supply and their general cooperation with the government. Hasluck claims that this set-back did not have much practical effect on the government's "control over subversive activities", as the original powers given to the police and the military under the National Security Act early in the war remained in force. In Hasluck's view the importance of the debate was that the parliament "had exercised its right and its democratic duty of scrutinising regulations".[61] In relation to internment, these debates are important because they show the thinking of the men who within a few months took office, and into whose hands the policy and practice of internment fell at the time of Australia's greatest security crisis, early 1942.

While this first set of questions on internment centred on civil rights, a second set revolved around the practical consideration of the manpower resources tied up in internment camps. In June 1941 two Labor members asked Spender why internees from Britain and the Malay Straits, who had been cleared and who had specialist skills, could not be paroled to work in industries essential to war production.[62] Labor MPs had been alerted to the presence of the internees by senior Labor parliamentarians in Westminster and, when they visited Tatura, they found "highly reputable members of the Amalgamated Society of Engineers" and other British Labor organisations who had been picked up from the coastal towns when an invasion of the Mother Country seemed imminent. Among the Malay internees there were also well-qualified men who were most anxious to assist with the war effort.

The questioners were impatient that their queries were always met with the response that British internees must be released in England, and the employment of specialist internees was a matter for the Minister for Labour and National Service. When the country urgently needed the skill possessed by some internees, and nothing had been found against them "after six months of investigation", it seemed strange not to release them for work. The questioners realised that it would be "detrimental to the interests of Australian workers if internees of ordinary skills' were released and allowed to take jobs "while Australian people were out of work",[63] but with specialist workers the benefit to the war effort was obvious. Spender replied that while it seemed "harsh" that those internees given "a clean sheet" by Layton could not be released in Australia there were "obvious difficulties in the way of that being done".[64]

These difficulties related to the deeply ingrained resistance to migrants taking jobs when Australians were unemployed, to providing welfare support for ex-internees until they were established, and to the fear of bad publicity to a shaky UAP coalition government if any released internee, especially a German speaker, could be associated with a security leak. Cabinet itself was probably not united on the matter of releasing internees, even specialists; in the minute recording the cabinet's decision to release such people, it was specified that none was to be released without reference to the whole War Cabinet.[65] There is also no doubt that sections of the opposition were against the use of internee labour. At the meeting of the Advisory War Council, even camp-centred work was considered unfair competition to Australian workers; the non-government members did not favour it and asked to be consulted if it was proposed to be introduced in the future.[66]

Australian tribunal results

While the impetus to intern people had been swift, there was much more caution in implementing releases. The procedure of Advisory Committees and Aliens Tribunals was slow, the onus of proof remained with the internee, and the system of checks after the hearings, ensured that the rate of releases of Australia's own internees would be slow. In fact, tribunals established in late 1940 granted fewer than 150 releases after a year of operation.[67] Before the Victorian Tribunal heard any objectors, they had internment policy explained to them by a representative of the Minister for the Army, and they were given a comprehensive account of pre-war Nazi and Fascist organisations.[68] In addition, a senior officer of Military Intelligence, Lt-Col. S.F. Whittington, answered the tribunal's questions on finer points of policy. Colonel Sydney Ferguson Whittington was a militia officer who became a General Staff Officer with Southern Command on joining the Intelligence Corps on 1 November 1939.[69] While the members had no questions about proven Fascists, they did ask for more clarification about those whose cases rested on remote connections, and the policy regarding the internment of enemy aliens professing or alleged to be Communists. The Victorian tribunal was particularly concerned about the internment of refugees whose cases depended on the claim that the enemy would use their relatives to put pressure on them, and they were reluctant to refuse release to a man solely because he had no employment and might be vulnerable to the approaches of enemy agents.

Whittington explained that Communists were interned only if their activities made them potentially dangerous.[70] He assured the tribunal that the military took full account of the rights of citizens and aliens to freedom of speech and ideas, but when a professed Communist combined beliefs with carrying out the party's "active work", he became dangerous. If an enemy alien who was a Communist took part in activities that created "trouble and unrest", he was interned, but if he was not an "agitator", and did not "mix himself up with Union strikes" but "went about his business", he was not regarded as dangerous.

Whittington admitted that some cases might "appear weak", but the tribunal could rely on the opinions of his officers because they were "entirely unbiased". He sympathised with the tribunal having to assess, without the benefit of the normal "legal structure" or "all the information" available to the military, a situation that had taken military intelligence experts "some 15 years or more to appreciate". His strongest argument was that as only about 120 had been taken from an estimated 8,000 Communists and very few Jehovah's Witnesses, the tribunal members should believe that there was a "good reason" in these cases. Lieutenant P.G. Proctor, whose responsibility was to watch the Jehovah's Witnesses sect, considered that their activities were subversive.[71] Their efforts to convert people to pacifism had "an effect on recruiting". Their refusal to recognise the King, by sitting with their hats on during the national anthem, and their defence of their beliefs at public meetings, had created public unrest.

Together with their recommendations, Aliens Tribunal No. 2

sent an explanation of their thinking.[72] They had difficulty in
formulating principles on which to make decisions, for the
regulations gave little help in deciding when the public safety
did not require continued detention. They had to work out their
own rule of thumb. Modern "total war" provided a case for
general internment, as in Great Britain during the latter part of
1918 and, again, in June 1940, but such a policy caused hardship
on individuals, was never practised by the United States, and
nor did the Australian government require it. Internment
seemed necessary at the point when the internee represented a
potential danger, and the tribunal felt that it could release
internees if "there was no reasonable probability or likelihood
of hostile or disloyal activity on the part of an objector". So
Aliens Tribunal No. 2 made its test: were there any reasonable
grounds for doubting the objector's loyalty to this country?
Although each case was different, the tribunal found some
patterns. Reasonable grounds for doubting an objector's loyalty
were membership of the Nazi Party (even if proof was supplied
that the motive for joining had been business reasons), employment in German firms controlled by Nazis, or recent arrival in
Australia with no intention of making it a permanent home.

Ordinary membership of the German Labour Front was not
sufficient for internment, but leadership was. Nor was an un-
willingness to desire a British victory held as crucial. Even a
German who had "thrown in his lot with Australia" would
"hate the thought of his Fatherland being destroyed and his
people suffering". The utmost the Australian could "justly
expect" was that he would "do nothing to stab his adopted
country in the back". This tribunal was unwilling to rely over-
much on camp associations. There was a "natural camaraderie"
among men suffering "a common misfortune". Any "ostenta-
tious dissociation from the Nazi group" would be an obvious
ploy for any internee who wished to strengthen his case for
release. The tribunal was also unwilling to place too much
emphasis on the possibility of persuasion through pressure on
relatives in German hands, or potential unemployment in Australia. They were not convinced that too much emphasis should
be placed on "utterances about the Nazi regime in Germany"
overheard by other people. The tribunal members wrote that
they had "been forced to realise" that "the possibilities of
misunderstanding, distortion, or even sheer invention in such
matters, more especially in times of public excitement or appre-

hension" were great. The tribunal acknowledged the "essentially relative and provisional character" of their judgements on recommending release, for both the military situation and the state of public opinion were variables. They knew that if the country was under immediate threat of actual military operations, public opinion would become "highly apprehensive or inflamed", and a great increase in internment could be "effectively demanded".

The statement that the evidence shown to the tribunal was "meagre" compared with the fullness of army files did not impress. The tribunal had been given their task "by law" and had to make decisions "on the material submitted". They thought it likely that theirs was the first investigation into the circumstances of an objector's detention, and the first chance for new evidence to be shown. In any case, whatever the differences between the army's recommendations and theirs, the ultimate decision lay "with the Minister himself". The Australian Archives has limited research access to the trials of those for whom the tribunals recommended release. The extreme nature of the proof required to warrant a recommendation for release is illustrated by the following cases. It seems that tribunals were very conservative and only the blatant mistakes were approved for release.

Guiseppi Zammarchi, Italian timber-getter turned gold miner, was clearly anti-Fascist. At Zammarchi's trial[73] Mr O.J. Gillard, instructed by the Crown Solicitor, appeared for the Minister for the Army. Mr J.V. Barry, one of the "liberal lawyers" active in the Australian Council of Civil Liberties, appeared for Zammarchi, who had been interned because he was an "avowed Communist", had "communist literature", and had been in arguments around town. After 32 pages of evidence, it transpired that the internee's partner had just won a dispute with a local landowner, that gelignite found in his possession had been taken home from a quarry rather than left for children to find, and that the internee could not remember being in any brawls in Tennant Creek. His "communistic literature" consisted of some anti-Fascist books from the Left Book Club. A timber merchant, a motor dealer and a Justice of the Peace from St Arnaud (Vic.) swore that in nine years of dealing with the internee they had always heard Zammarchi speak against Mussolini. A Melbourne friend declared he was anti-Fascist, having been a member of the Mateotti Club. Zammarchi admitted he

had collected five pounds for the relief of children in Republican Spain for the Victorian Council Against War and Fascism,
and that in 1937 he gave a 2s 6d donation to a Labor Party
member, which entitled him to membership for that year.

The Tribunal recommended Zammarchi's release after assuring him that he had not been interned because of his quarrel
with an influential landowner, or because of his trouble over
the gelignite. They did not want anyone to assume that a desire
for a greater equalisation of wealth, or membership of the
Australian Labor Party, were in any way grounds for internment. Zammarchi had been interned because he was an enemy
alien living in a remote part of Australia, and the Minister for
Defence's only consideration was the security of Australia.
Zammarchi's case vindicated the government's decision to allow internees to explain their position.

Ernst Flegenheimer was another internee who impressed a
tribunal favourably.[74] He was a Jewish refugee whose father
had died of typhus in an overcrowded camp at the foot of the
Pyrenees. His elderly mother, "hungry and freezing", remained
in the camp hut with no windows or furniture. Flegenheimer
stated that he had been "hurt too much" ever to return to
Germany, that he was willing to fight for Australia because if
the British did not win the war he could "buy a rope". He
arrived in Australia in January 1939, having a brother in business in Sydney, and was interned in June 1940. In reply to a
question by the tribunal chairman, he said that he was not taken
in during the September 1939 round-up because of his brother
and the persecution his family had suffered. So although the
military was aware of Flegenheimer's background he was interned on nationality, age and "newly arrived" criteria during
the crisis of June 1940. The army representative did not object
to his release in 1941.

Wilhelm Alexander von Keudell was a Protestant married to
a Jew whom he refused to divorce. His father had been a
Lord-in-Waiting to the Kaiser and his mother an Austrian
countess. Despite his service in World War I, his factory was
resumed by the Nazi government because non-Aryans were
employed there. Von Keudell had tried to have his children
born outside Germany and eventually sent them away while
pretending to remain himself. In a subterfuge reminiscent of the
escape of the Trapp family portrayed in "The Sound of Music",
Keudell left his car parked in the drive, engaged his house-

keeper for a further term and abandoning all claim to the family fortune, headed for the frontier. Hans Dorn on the other hand was a teacher of Occult religion, having lost his Lutheran faith in World War I. He had sheltered a Jewish mother and child for some months in 1935-6, and was arraigned before a special Nazi court in 1937 on the charge of having said that Goering lit the Reichstag fire. The Gestapo forbade Dorn to teach, and he migrated to Australia.

Johannes Eckhardt had lived in Australia since 1912 and had been employed as a wool buyer for many years. Although he admitted an "affection for his birthplace", and regarded the war between his native and adopted land as the "tragedy of his life", he had decided not to become naturalised because in 1916 the naturalised Germans had lost their jobs just as he and other unnaturalised men had done. He admitted making donations to the German Labour Front "to help the poor", and his wife had done some sewing for a group he took to be a church charity group, although the military said the group was a German Women's Club run by Mrs Asmis, the wife of the German consul. He wanted desperately to be released so he could help his wife look after their sick daughter, and to halt the erosion of the family's capital. He said he had signed statements three times, promising not to harm the British Empire, and he knew army personnel who would vouch for him.

Paul J.W. Bauer deserted his ship in 1928 and had worked as an itinerant labourer from Townsville to Port Pirie. He had travelled with a mate at first, but his companion had "fallen off the rattler". Bauer admitted that he had "neglected" to become naturalised. He stated that he had no sympathy for Nazism and "very little" for Communism. He was willing to pick grapes to support himself. While Bauer and the few were recommended for release, the lack of access to the cases of those refused release make it impossible to compare situations. Hasluck's conclusion that the rest were held "for a good reason"[75] should be treated cautiously until a complete analysis can be done.

Oswald Bonutto came before the Queensland tribunal headed by Mr Justice Philp; and E.B. Maher, the leader of the State Opposition, was a witness. Maher had known Bonutto in connection with the tobacco industry and regarded him "as enterprising and industrious", and "a loyal Australian held in high esteem by both Italians and Australians". Bonutto was proud of his ancestry but Maher did not regard this as conflicting with his loyalty to Australia. Bonutto admitted sending money to Italy, but protested that it had gone to his pensionless old mother. He defended Italy's annexation of Ethiopia, seeing it as no different from the imperialistic actions of other European powers. Bonutto was released, but a campaign was waged against Maher's support of him and in six months he was re-arrested. He again came before the tribunal and this time Stan Craves, a vice-president of the Texas (Qld) RSL, insisted that Bonutto had been upset about the prospect of a war between Britain and Italy. Bonutto had written to an Italian-language newspaper urging migrants to disregard any Consul who advised an anti-British attitude. The judge took into account the enmity Bonutto had incurred in the Texas area and recommended his release on condition he sever his business connections there and go to live in another part of Australia. The "good reason" Bonutto was still interned in November 1941 was because he refused to sell his hotel and farm in Texas at the low forced-sale price.[76]

Seven reports to the GOC Southern Command from Aliens Tribunals No. 4 exist and show something of this tribunals's thinking.[77] All the objectors recommended for release had made their permanent home in Australia, were willing workers and had no suspect political associations. Two had served in the Axis forces in World War I; one arrived a few days after the outbreak of war; three were alleged to have made suspect remarks; one had remote connections with German Club activities. Once the objectors had explained their positions, the tribunal assessed them as not warranting continued internment. But their cases did not rest on their own evidence. Six had strong ties with Australians who vouched for them; two were married and one engaged to Australians; one had his family established here since 1927; one had a nephew in the AIF and shared a house with a returned soldier; and another had a long-term friendship with an established refugee Jewish family. How important these ties with Australians were in persuading the tribunal is obvious from the prominence they receive in the reports to the GOC.

Lack of an Australian connection or a steady job were common grounds for army protests against tribunal's recommendations for release.[78] One objector "had extensive knowledge of the road system of Queensland", and Northern Command considered it a bad policy to have semi-vagrant enemy nationals in the community because they caused "alarm to the neighbourhood" and had "quarrels thrust upon them". The army also considered that public sentiment was strongly against releases and that the lack of "war enthusiasm" was due to the government "not exercising stricter control over the enemy population". It is not known how long some of the Army protests took to process, but it involved the tribunals in further justifications of their decisions. Delays also occurred when tribunals went into recess. A naturalised internee of German origin was arrested at Millicent (SA) in November 1940. His appeal was not heard until the following March because of "mishaps to members of the tribunal".[79] Nor was his case unique. In August 1940 a Sydney solicitor wrote to Menzies complaining that his client had been interned for four months, and there were still nearly 40 cases before his. The solicitor urged the appointment of additional tribunals to facilitate "the British principle of bringing a man to a speedy trial".[80] On 17 February 1941, there were 82 appeals outstanding, so Percy Spender asked Sir George Knowles to suggest suitable men to form a second Advisory Committee in New South Wales.[81] Releases were also slow. Zammarchi was brought from Tatura to Broadmeadows for his hearing but had to wait there a month. He was heard on 6 and 7 May 1941, but was not released until September.[82] Given the degree of proof required by tribunals, and the long delay in effecting releases, there is serious doubt about Hasluck's assertion that all the 2,231 local internees who were still locked up in November 1941 were there for a "good reason". It could equally well be argued that the 145 released were a most conservative adjustment to the general internments in the middle of 1940.[83] Even the automatic rejection of appeals where membership of the Fascist party was involved had begun to be questioned.

The New South Wales Advisory Committee chaired by Mr Justice Davidson heard a number of cases of naturalised citizens of Italian origin and he was told to keep three principles in mind: the onus of proof rested with the objector, party membership provided prime facie grounds and, where evidence was "unreliable or unconvincing" or failed to remove the suspicion arising from membership, no release was to be recommended. While many failed to convince the tribunal, Davidson questioned whether this class of internee actually constituted "a menace in the real sense". On the whole, these men were fruiterers and others who had "a very humble station in life". Many had wives and small children dependent on them. They were industrious and law abiding and, although they made a success of their small businesses, few "exhibited much mental acumen". Many had joined the Fascio several years before the contingency of a war between the British Empire and Italy arose. They had not gone to meetings or paid their subscriptions for years, but in their efforts "to exculpate themselves" they gave unbelievable evidence, claiming that they never knew the party was in any way political, and insisting that they regarded it "solely as a social and cultural society", thus ensuring the rejection of their appeals. In Davidson's opinion some of these men, if required to report regularly, would be "no real risk" and the public could be spared the expense of both the man's internment and the maintenance of his family.[84]

Reaction to events overseas

However, while releases in 1941 were few, so too were new internments before the entry of Japan into the war in December. It had been projected "that 2,085 additional Italians were likely to be interned in the event of the AIF becoming engaged in active operations against the Italians", but very few had been detained.[85] The original estimate had been based on the possibility that the contest would result in heavy Australian casualties, but with the first shock of the fighting over and with comparatively small casualty figures, there was a calm public attitude towards Italians in Australia. This fall in demand for accommodation for local Italian internees led to the cancellation of a proposed camp for 1,000 in Queensland. The military's decisions on internment were strongly influenced by battle victories and losses and the anticipated public reaction to casualties.

After their dramatic success in North Africa, portions of the AIF went into Greece and Crete but this campaign led to the loss of 6,000 Australians, many of them taken prisoner. In June, however, the 7th Division went into Syria against the Vichy French. Soon after the entry of Russia into the war, in June 1941, the Iranian oilfields had to be secured and the Australian-manned HMS Manimbla and HMAS Yarra were involved in an action that captured Axis merchantmen. These internees together with civilian internees, many of whom had been em-

ployees of the Anglo-Persian Oil Company, were later brought
to Australia. The first group arrived in August 1941 on the
Queen Elizabeth and the second group came on the *Rangitiki* on
19 November.[86]

The need to replace the casualties and prisoners in the fighting divisions, the pressure to increase munitions production
and the increasingly dangerous situation in the Pacific led the
Prime Minister to broadcast a national appeal for an "unlimited
war effort" on 17 June 1941. He said:

> We have in fact reached a point where your alleged rights and mine
> don't matter . . . The only way we can lose either permanently is by
> losing this war. The only way in which we can win this war is being
> prepared to put into pawn every right that we have until victory is
> attained. If every man is to go on working where he likes . . . if we
> are to live as usual and largely leave the war to others, we cannot
> deserve to win and the perfect equipping of our men overseas must
> be left largely to others.[87]

Lists of reserved occupations were to be overhauled, civil
production reviewed, and the labour of men and women directed. For much of 1941 the AIF fought in North Africa and
part of the 9th Division dug in to defend Tobruk. The 8th
Division went to reinforce Malaya and Singapore and the Japanese occupied Indo-China. Menzies was unseated as Prime
Minister on 29 August. His successor, Arthur Fadden, lost the
support of two Independents and the UAP/Country Party
government was replaced by Labor on 7 October 1941. But
while the war was real enough to the men in the armed forces,
some of the civilian population showed such little awareness of
the seriousness of Australia's situation, that General Blamey, on
a short visit in November, said they reminded him of "a lot of
gazelles in a dell on the edge of a jungle".[88] Their two great
allies, Britain and America had agreed on a strategy of beating
Germany first even if Japan entered the war.[89] Although Canberra had been warned of this as early as February 1941, "its
full import does not seem to have seeped through the govern-
mental structure until 1942".[90] On 7 December 1941 Japan
attacked Pearl Harbour and an all-out war in the Pacific began.
The plans to intern all Japanese in Australia were immediately
put into action.

Chapter Six

THE JAPANESE

Australians had a deep seated fear of Asiatics,[1] and Japan's involvement with the Axis powers and her incursions deep into China during the early part of the war agitated this fear. The Australian government asked both Britain and the United States for assurances of extra military support in the event of further Japanese expansion. In the event of war, it was decided that all Japanese within Australia would be interned.[2]

Policy considerations

This decision was based on four propositions.[3] There was no Japanese equivalent to the Fascist organisations which gave "a guide" to an individual's sentiments, nor were the Japanese absorbed in Australian life as many Germans and Italians were. Japanese sentiment was held to be strongly nationalistic and this could lead to sabotage attempts, and finally, male Japanese could become the "object of demonstrations". The few Japanese women in Australia were not held to be dangerous but they were "likely to suffer hardships" and might best be interned with their men or allowed to depart with the diplomatic staff. Every person born in Japan, or holding Japanese citizenship, or of Japanese descent, was listed.[4] There were over one thousand, including Formosans who bore a similar relationship to Japan as the Austrians did to Germany: they were citizens by conquest. Most long-term Japanese residents lived in the northern areas of Australia and worked in the fishing and pearling industries based on Broome, Darwin and Thursday Island. In other areas they tended to be farmers, market gardeners and operators of laundries. Most short-term residents who were Japanese nationals were members of the consular staff or employees of Japanese firms. Because so many Japanese worked off boats, and because the military were convinced there was a well-organised spying operation among the Japanese in the north,[5] the authorities predicted that some would escape by sea and not have to be catered for in Australia.[6]

Although children were not mentioned, they obviously had to stay with one partner or the other when all males over 16 and all women were to be taken in. The only exceptions were Japanese with diplomatic or consular privileges. The legation archives were to "be regarded as inviolable", and consular premises were not to be searched, "as this would set an undesirable precedent for the treatment of British" diplomatic staff and offices overseas.[7] The Minister for External Affairs, Dr H.V. Evatt, was annoyed when he found that the quarters of the Japanese representative in Melbourne had been "bugged".[8] A desire for favourable reciprocal treatment was also the probable motive for cabinet's decision that Japanese women were only to be interned until they could be "transfered out of the country", and an exchange of internees negotiated.[9] Australia only wanted to hold the men who might be useful to the enemy. On the other hand, to assist the Free French in New Caledonia, and the British colonial administration in the Gilbert and Ellice Islands, the Solomons and the New Hebrides, the War Cabinet agreed to accept their Japanese internees.[10]

Oganisation and implementation

In Northern Command individual warrants were prepared for the Japanese living in Brisbane, but for other areas of the state and for Thursday Island blanket warrants, based on the serial numbers of all the Japanese registered, were organised and paired with search warrants.[11] Military Intelligence were to make the arrests in Brisbane but elsewhere the police were responsible. Once the GOC had signed the warrants, men and transports were to assemble at Victoria Barracks and then be allocated to the round-up parties. The warrants to be executed by the police went to the Police Commissioner. Those responsible for collecting the Japanese were reminded to arrange for the disconnection of phones belonging to internees, to have a truck handy for transporting gear, to procure utensils such as bowls and chopsticks, and to make proper arrangements for searching females.

A detailed operation order for the internment of Japanese on Thursday Island was issued before Pearl Harbour was attacked.[12] The town street plan was divided into four collection areas, and homes and boarding houses where Japanese resided were marked. Immediately the news of war with Japan was telegraphed, the 49th Battalion Details at Links Barracks were to turn out "in battle order" and the police sergeant telephoned. While one party prepared the concentration area - a triangular block between Millman and Hargrave Streets and the sea — the other parties were to guard places such as the Post Office and to proceed to collect the Japanese. The commandant of the internment compound was to be the 2 I/C of the 49th Battalion, and his next ranking officer the commander of the VDC. The commandant was required to prepare standing orders to cover medical examinations, separation of contagious cases, preparation of rolls and issue of numbers, body searches and collection and receipting of articles not allowed in camp. He had to establish routines for ordering supplies and rations, sick parades, camp inspections, censorship of mails, sanitation services, guard rosters, paymaster services and the hearing of internees complaints. Instructions to internees warning them not to disobey or be disrespectful to guards, not to keep more than 10 shillings, not to attempt to escape or go closer than three yards from the boundaries, had to be issued in Japanese. Overall the commandant had to see to the "general well-being of all internees".

A fence was to be built and guard posts set up to cover the boundaries. Ammunition, coils of barbed wire and pickets were stored in preparation. The guards were to come from 49th Battalion and the Torres Straits Infantry alternately, until the VDC was able to assume control. The compound was to be rationed by the 49th's quartermaster and an Intelligence Officer from Northern Command was to be responsible for interpreters, supervision of camp suppliers and visitors, liaison with police and the collection of internees' documents.

When the collection of Japanese began, those service personnel on leave in the town area were to be ordered back to their units. A mobile army patrol was to keep "vigilant watch to ensure against any pillaging or destruction of public or private property", especially of Japanese shops. At the jetty, the navy would land Japanese from the luggers in the harbour. About 340 Japanese were thought to be in the Thursday Island area, but 200 of these were out to sea on their luggers during the fishing season. They were to be collected as soon as they returned to the harbour. The details of the preparations for the internment of this group, the largest community of local Japanese, show how the authorities implemented their policies. There were few possibilities overlooked, either from a security point of view or from the correct legal and International Convention standpoint.

All went well with the round up on Thursday Island on 8 December 1942 and 110 internees were settled into the compound. In the mainland centres of Mackay, Maryborough and Townsville, 29 other Japanese were arrested and arrangements made for their transport to Brisbane by train.[13] Internees from New Guinea were sent from Rabaul and Kieta on the *MV Malaita* and those from Papua joined the ship at Samarai late in January 1942.[14] With the advent of war in New Guinea the *SS Marella* brought the last internees from Port Moresby and Thursday Island to the mainland.[15]

Many of the Japanese internees were poor indentured labourers, and the lists of personal effects show a few lugger captains and merchants with yen, pearls, rings and watches among the many others who only had one razor.[16] The indentured labourers included young men from Wakayama, Japan, who followed the tradition, going back to the 1890s, of diving for Australian-based pearlers.[17] About 400 of these men were interned, and today they recall their four years of sitting out the war in Hay with a philosophic gratitude for the fate that sent them a less demanding role than their brothers who went into the Japanese Imperial Army. Men like these did not contest their internment, and their behaviour in the Thursday Island compound was described as "exemplary".[18] A similar comment was made by the Japanese internees' guards at Camp 14, Loveday. They were subservient and model prisoners because their "fanatical desire to maintain "face" made them easy to handle in their eagerness to obey all orders and instructions to the letter".[19] They rarely complained to the Official Visitor and worked on the farming projects at Loveday and Hay. Their behaviour contrasted sharply to that of Japanese POWs who on the night of 4/5 August 1944 rioted and broke out of their compound at Cowra.[20] Five hundred were pinned down in the broadway between the compounds, and the escapees had to be rounded up around the countryside. As a result 321 Japanese soldiers and 4 Australian guards were killed and 108 Japanese and 4 Australians wounded. When the Japanese at Loveday found out about the Cowra uprising they assured the camp

authorities they were not going to follow suit.[21] They were
labourers, not Samuri, and they were not required to follow the
soldiers' code.

At the Japanese family camp at Tatura a school was established and Ethel Punshon, who had learnt Japanese as a hobby,
was sent to teach the children there.[22] She described the camp
as being on the slope of a hill, with Major F.W.C. Scurry in
charge. There was only one little gaol and she could only recall
one internee ever being put in "to calm down". Punshon's main
responsibilities besides the school were to help supervise the
women's sewing factory (which turned old clothes), take roll
calls and make regular inspections of cooking areas and dormitories. The greatest problem was to prevent the internees running heaters in their wooden huts at night. The duty hours were
long and if a warden had to accompany the nurse to take a
pregnant internee to hospital at night the warden would not get
any sleep until the following night. Children were being born
at what Major Scurry regarded as an alarming rate and Punshon
remembered the Major "laying down the law to the compound
leader" that there were to be no more babies, but to no effect.
While the large majority of Japanese were content in camp, it
was not acceptable to a minority who were long-term residents
or Australian-born. Punshon remembered one incident when
the compound leader expected everyone to bow in the direction
of the Emperor in Japan but a girl, who was the daughter of a
mixed marriage, refused. When the compound leader pushed
her head down she slapped his face, but was reprimanded by
the officer in charge because it undermined the compound
leader's authority to be hit by a girl.

Japanese objectors

Many Japanese lodged objections to their internment, but there
was debate over whether these should be heard. Nationality
alone was the criterion for internment and theoretically, it could
not be challenged except on the grounds of incorrectly designated nationality. It was also the practice of the United States
and Canada to intern all their Japanese.[23] The War Cabinet
seriously considered not allowing any Japanese to appeal but
"such open discrimination" might "react to the disadvantage
of British subjects in Japan" and be "politically embarrassing
after the war".[24] It was hoped that in cross-examinations during

appeals some useful intelligence information might be elicited. After discussing the matter at its meeting on 27 January 1942, War Cabinet agreed that District Commandants refer any release recommendations to the Minister who would reject them all except if the internee was of use to the Defence authorities, or where age, long residence in Australia and family considerations convinced Military Intelligence that the internee represented "no security risk".[25] In addition, the censorship covering all aspects of appeals was tightened. The camp authorities allowed all local internees to appeal, but most withdrew their objection when it was explained to them that they were not obliged to appeal.

The few persevering objectors were heard in February and May 1942, and the appeals followed the pattern set in the earlier hearings of Germans and Italians. A comprehensive report on Japanese associations and activities in NSW was prepared by W.H. Barnwell on behalf of the CIB and at the request of the office of the Deputy Crown Solicitor and the Army Legal Branch.[26] The report was designed so Judge Pike and members of the Aliens Tribunal could acquire a knowledge of Japanese activities before appeals were heard. As in his earlier reports, Barnwell covered the Consular activities, the cultural, social and commercial clubs and the individuals associated with them. He pointed out that before the war there had been friendly contact between the Japanese and German consulates and between the Japanese press agency and some members of the Australia First Movement, particularly the Walsh family.[27] Relations between the Japanese and Italians were less cordial, and the opportunity to cultivate Italians, when Italian interests passed to the care of the Japanese Consulate after June 1940, was not taken up. The published list of the Japanese Society included the "better class people", the white-collar employees of the Japanese trading and woolbuying firms, but not the laundrymen or domestic workers. The Nippon Club was incorporated in 1939 by a prominent woolbuyer with the Mitsui Company to cater for the social needs of the Japanese community in Sydney and to keep the young men "out of trouble". The lease was drawn up in the name of Denzo Kuringu, a laundryman of Chatswood.[28] Meetings of the Athletics Club, the Japanese Chamber of Commerce and the Japanese Wool Importers' Association were held in the Nippon Club in Bond Street. The *Domei* News Agency was established in May 1939 to send news

from Australian newspapers and to make Japan independent
of Reuters. Barnwell pointed out that most of the businessmen
working for Japanese firms left Australia with their families on
the *Kasima Maru* on 15 August 1941.

An association not directly connected with the consulate was
the Japan-Australia Society, formed in 1929 to promote cultural
relations between Japan and Australia, and having a distinguished membership of Australians and Japanese engaged in
trade and commerce.[29] While Barnwell considered this group
to be non-political and devoted to trade and cultural activities,
he felt it was established as part of Japanese policy to forge links
in countries where they traded. At a different social level, the
Japanese Laundrymen's Club, controlled by Kuringu, catered
for the social, cultural and commercial interests of Sydney
laundrymen and their families, including a number of young
people whose mothers were Australian and fathers Japanese.[30]
Overall, the Japanese in Sydney comprised four main groups
— the consular staff, the employees of the Japanese firms, the
long-term residents and the children of long-term residents. In
Barnwell's words:

> Japanese domiciled in New South Wales were mainly of the mer-
> chant and diplomatic class. Others, comprising laundrymen and
> gardeners, were admitted to Australia prior to the Immigration Act
> of 1902 and consequently were permanent residents. In some cases
> these Japanese had married Europeans, and their children (half
> caste) with features predominantly Japanese, acquired [an] Austra-
> lian outlook and ideals of life.[31]

Barnwell listed 80 Japanese nationals who had left Sydney
on the *Kasima Maru*, and about the same number of residents.
Those who had left belonged to the Japanese firms and those
remaining included the long-term residents and their families.
Despite the differences in the background of the Japanese,
Barnwell concluded that behind all their activities was a total
commitment to Japan, and that, in the interests of Australia's
national security, all members of a race so "fanatically determined to serve their country's cause" must remain under
guard.[32] Some long-term residents contested this view.

Appeals were heard by Aliens Tribunal No. 4. The Chairman,
W.H. Sharwood, and members, J.W.K. Freeman and F.J. Quinland, were assisted by Captain O.J. Gillard, who was instructed
by the Commonwealth Crown Solicitor to appear for the Minister for the Army.[33] Objectors were questioned about their

association with anything Japanese, including cultural and social organisations such as the Kokusai Bunka Shinkakai (KBS), a cultural exchange program; the Nippon Kinkwai, the Japanese Athletic Club; and the Nipponshokuda, the Japanese Club in Bond Street, Sydney. They were asked if they attended the Emperor's birthday party at the consulate, whether they had contributed to the Comforts Fund of the Japanese Army during the Chinese War, and whether they had bought any of the China Incident 50-yen bonds collected from loyal Japanese when relations with China worsened in 1937. Buying bonds was viewed by Australian security in a similar way to the sending of wedding rings by Italians to support the Ethiopian campaign, that is, as proof of extreme pro-nationalist feelings. Another analogy was drawn with the German situation. When a Japanase military information collector, Major Haishida, came to Australia on 13 January 1941 and travelled around the country as a tourist accompanied by the Vice Consul, K. Otabe, the Newcastle Trades Hall protested, describing him as the "Von Luckner of Japan". Security took note of his contacts.[34]

Few objectors could answer the questions of the Tribunal on matters of international affairs or current Japanese politics. Most had left Japan over 50 years before. One local Japanese association they were familiar with was the Laundryman's Club, the *Doshikwai*. It was established in Sydney in the early thirties by the Consul-General, Mr Takewaga, and had originally been formed to settle quarrels between the 40 competing small Japanese laundries. It later developed regular gambling activities, particularly on cards and horses. Some objectors were quite knowlegeable about the local racing scene. Some objectors decided to withdraw their application when the tribunal pressed upon them the safety aspect. The people who knew them might well accept them, but there was so much feeling against Japan that "larrikins" and soldiers from out of town might attack any Japanese person.

A significant number who carried on with their appeal, did so with the express desire to be reunited with their wives whose British, Irish, Chinese or Australian nationality precluded their internment. There are glimpses of very tender relationships. A Japanese man aged 73 told the tribunal that he only wrote nice things in his letters to his 66-year-old wife because there was "no need to worry an old woman". Consequently she jokingly referred to the camp as "your Hotel Tokio", (sic) and when she

gave away his Sunday shoes to someone who badly needed
them, she told her husband that he should go into Hay and buy
another pair. When people were "old enough to be dead", the
old man said, there was no point in writing gloomy letters.[35]
Another internee, when pressed to agree that he would be safer
inside, said that he would in "one way" because there was
"protection", but he had been married for 28 years and had
never been parted from his wife for one day. "She could defend
herself, but I would rather be with her to try to help her in every
way".[36]

A few objections were supported by letters from their family,
and from church, school or business associates. The tribunal
succeeded in persuading even some of these that, with the war
so close and feelings so high, they would better off in camp.
When an old laundryman from Rockhampton remained adamant that every day he had served Australian soldiers, the
tribunal raised the spectre of the newly arrived American army,
hot to revenge its defeats.[37] He lost his appeal on a variation of
the danger theme. Concern for the safety of objectors encom-
passed not only the danger from other residents, but the danger
of being killed in a war zone, so the strategic position of the
Queensland coastal towns ensued that no Japanese living north
of Brisbane would be released. The Rockhampton laundryman
was acknowledged to be honest, industrious and popular with
the local people, and he had a son with the 8th Division in
Malaya, but he was considered to be in danger if an invasion
took place as Rockhampton was likely to be "a centre of active
operations".

A similar conclusion was reached in the case of a cane farmer
from outside Mackay.[38] Although he was 65 and the sole support of a de-facto wife, and "there was no suggestion he was
dishonest, associated with other Japanese or displayed any
anti-British, anti-Australian or subversive sentiments", the
threat of invasion decided the tribunal against release. Another
old man from Maryborough was "of irreproachable character",
had many letters of recommendation, and normally it would
have been "a grave injustice" to keep him interned, but conditions were "anything but normal".[39] In these cases the tribunal
recommended favourable reassessment if the international
situation improved. So with the long-term Japanese residents,
considerations of civil rights, common fairness, impeccable
character, family loyalty and local public acceptance, seldom

overrode the tribunal's concern about the dangerous state of the war and the consequential general agitation.

Only in a very few cases did the tribunal allow an objection. This meant that a full-scale trial was possible, but the Crown representative insisted that, unlike other groups, the Japanese were interned on nationality grounds alone. The case most favoured by the tribunal was a young man who defied his step-father to join the AIF early in the war.[40] Although he had been only three months old when he landed in Australia, he was discharged from the AIF "purely on racial grounds". He spoke only English and volunteered to serve in a labour battalion. The chairman was of the opinion that "he was a half-caste at the worst", and there was no real case against him. Captain Gillard stated that he could be described as "a person having Japanese parentage", but admitted that this objector "possibly had the strongest case for release from internment that one could conceive".

The chairman of Aliens Tribunal No. 4, Mr Sharwood, and Captain Gillard were in disagreement over a number of cases and the matter came to a head in the case of a little old lady from East Prahran, Victoria.[41] The army argued that she should remain interned because she would have to shift 15 miles away from the coast if she were released. The chairman argued that the proper function of his members was to decide whether the release of any person would interfere with "the efficient prosecution of the war and the defence of the Commonwealth", and not to go beyond that. If all the Japanese were to be automatically refused release, why were they given the right to object? Gillard replied that although all the evidence was in the old lady's favour even the "philosophical debate on the policy which should be adopted" expounded by Professor Bailey's earlier tribunal team conceded the need for policy to be elastic and to move with the international situation. Gillard explained that "the international condition has reached such a stage that you have to look at these things in a different light from what you did when dealing with the Germans at the beginning of 1940, particularly from the point of view of the home front". The tribunal would be surprised at the amount of correspondence about "the apparent laxity — that is what the public think it is — shown by the administration to foreigners". Gillard maintained that allowing aliens freedom had a detrimental effect on recruiting. There were a great many complaints from mothers

of soldiers about the number of foreigners moving around the
country, free to carry on their work and make money, while
Australian sons were in camp or abroad. The chairman objected
that this could not apply to the woman from East Prahran, who
could support herself and who could not compete for anyone's
job. But the problem, Gillard insisted, was that the woman's
release to live anywhere in the country would have a "psychological" effect on morale. She could not disguise the fact that
she was Japanese. It would not matter to the individual who
met her that she had been here nearly 50 years and knew very
little about Japan. Gillard claimed that it was the aggregate of
all cases and not the isolated case that went to make up the
psychological reaction. He said:

> It is the number of individuals moving round with whom the
> particular person in the community comes in contact. He says,
> "There is a dago B . . . who should have been in six months ago. I
> know he is a Fascist", and he probably does not know at all; "There
> is Schmidt", who has probably been in the town for 50 years, "a
> German; why is not he interned?" "A woman got off the train here
> last night, going to stay at the local hotel, a Japanese; what a great
> administration we have.
>
> That is the way people talk, and they do not take the isolated case.
> They take the whole collection of individuals they have probably
> met, and then they start, and that is how fifth column activity really
> begins, because you are breaking down amongst your own people
> the faith that they should have in the administration both at home
> and in the Army.

Thus with the criterion for release being that no unrest would
be created in any Australian community at a time when feelings
were highly agitated, especially against any person with orien-
tal features, the chances of release for Japanese were slight.
Lamidey's figures show that 97.83 per cent of all Japanese were
interned, that is 587 in 600, and that 4 were released in 1942 and
a further 10 by August 1943.[42] By December 1944 another 45
were released, but most were still subject to restrictions.

One of the four released in 1942 was Sho Takasuka, who had
come to Australia in 1905, aged 5 years. He and his brother later
grew tomatoes at Fosterville in Victoria, but while his brother
joined the 3rd Light Anti-Aircraft Regiment Abroad, Takasuka
was ineligible for naturalisation "on account of his race" and
having arrived after 1902, so he joined the VDC. The brothers
were regarded "as respectable and energetic members of the

community, and were never known to engage in any political discussions or subversive activities". Takasuka was interned because of the army instruction of 26 May 1941 that made it "mandatory on all Commands to intern all Japanese nationals over 16 years of age". Takasuka appealed, and the Aliens Tribunal No. 4 recommended his release, and the Minister for the Army confirmed the decision on 4 June 1942. While Takasuka's political circumspection, his brother's active service, his community acceptance and Victoria's distance from the fighting zone made a strong case, there is another possible contributing factor in Takasuka's favour. His tomato farm was described as a "plantation" and 20 pickers were employed there at harvest time. Takasuka was obviously a useful primary producer, and the build up of Australian forces and the arrival of American troops made a great demand on food production. Just as Durrant had released a few Italian tomato farmers to return to Geraldton after his extensive internment of Italians in Western Australia in June 1940, so the Victorian military authorities may have assessed Takasuka as more valuable back on the farm. It was made a condition of Takasuka's parole, however, that he not go beyond a radius of ten miles from his farm, and that restriction was still in force in June 1946.[43]

A more typical local case was that of Michael Joseph Tenin. Tenin was an Australian-born subject of Japanese origin who worked in a shop in Broome, WA. He was interned in accordance with the AHQ instruction that all Japanese descendants be taken in. The case against him, as summarised in his dossier, was that he was of the Japanese race because both his parents were Japanese, and that three years earlier he had gone on a tour of Japan and brought back a Japanese wife.[44] The Minister for Lands and Agriculture in WA wrote to Intelligence about Tenin saying that he had been educated at "one of Perth's best colleges" and was "an excellent citizen" and "a good Australian". He asked that Tenin's case be reviewed because he had no doubt whatever of the man's loyalty. Inquiries were made, but Intelligence Report No. 117 from Tatura showed that Tenin had decided to stay interned because he felt "public feeling would be against him". The Intelligence Report described Tenin as having only one leg, being "pro-Ally" and a quiet person who spoke the best English in the compound and an efficient teacher at the camp school. He had formerly been in partner-

ship in a Carnarvon shop, but his wife had died and he hoped
to start afresh after the war in another location.[45]

Tenin's assessment of the situation of people with Japanese
connections was a realistic one, as is shown by the cases of the
son and Australian wife of Denzo Kuringu, the Sydney laundryman, and of the Inagaki family of Melbourne. Kuringu's
son, Douglas, was interned and appealed against his internment. He heard nothing by February 1943, so he wrote to the
Official Visitor, complaining that he should not be in the camp
as if he were an enemy alien and dangerous to the country.[46] He
had been born in Australia and gone to the local high school
and to business college. He had never visited any countries
overseas or "taken any great interest in them". Apart from
English, the only other language he knew something of was
French. He wanted to finish his education and live in Australia
and nowhere else. He protested that he was not an alien but had
been treated like one. But Douglas's pleas were in vain, for he
and his father were transfered to South Australia by June 1943
and were still interned in December 1944. Douglas' mother only
escaped internment by going to live 200 miles from the coast.
The case against the mother appears to rest on her high regard
for her husband and an assessment made by a friend of her son,
under Military Intelligence questioning, that she would follow
any instructions her husband had left her.[47] The informant
would not appear before a tribunal, nevertheless Mrs Kuringu
was ordered to reside at West Wyalong, NSW, report to police
each week and not associate with enemy aliens or naturalised
persons of enemy origin. When an influential person with a title
discovered her plight, he rang W.J. Mackay, then the Director-
General of Security, and asked that she be given more time to
make arrangements for her dry cleaning business. Mackay
flatly refused. The conditions had been imposed "after careful
consideration by Military Officers" and "if anything happened,
someone would have to take the responsibility", and Mackay
had "no desire to be the person at whom criticism would be
levelled".[48] Although Mrs Kuringu wrote regularly from her
hotel room in West Wyalong asking for her restrictions to be
eased, the facts that she and her son were registered in Japan,[49]
and she had her name on a list of donors to the Japanese forces
Comforts Fund, told against her. By August 1944 security decided that in "view of the present war position" Mrs Kuringu
could be allowed back to Sydney. In December 1944 the owner

of her business premises, who had the family as tenants for over 20 years, supported her request for the release of her son. On 11 August 1945 the restriction on the mother associating with enemy aliens or naturalised people of enemy origin, was revoked by W.B. Simpson, who succeeded Mackay as Director-General of Security. In October 1946 Mrs Kuringu received the news that her husband was going to be deported, but either through her representations to Jessie Street or through the "good solicitor" hired by her husband for two hundred pounds, Kuringu was finally released.

While the Kuringu family suffered financially and emotionally, they were eventually reunited but the Inagaki family paid a greater price for the "crime" of a mixed marriage. Rose and Moshi Inagaki were married in 1907. Rose had thereby lost her British status, been required to register as an alien in World War I. Furious when the police demanded her fingerprints and photograph for alien registration in early 1940, Rose Inagaki discovered she could apply for the return of her British nationality under Section 18A of the Nationality Act and immediately did so. Her husband, a teacher of the Japanese language at Melbourne University, was interned. At his objection hearing on 24 February 1942, Inagaki's counsel argued that not only would his client not want to do anything anti-British but his strong-minded pro-British wife would not tolerate any such "activities". Mrs Inagaki had been a school teacher and her financial support allowed her husband to continue the work he loved, teaching Japanese at Melbourne University, where he was never given a tenured position. When Rose appealed to the university for moral support and for the opportunity to take over Inagaki's students, the registrar was evasive and expressed confidence in the security authorities. The tribunal felt Inagaki's interests and sympathies were Japanese and he remained interned for the whole of the war. Inagaki's association with the KBS cultural exchange program and a consequent trip to Japan were regarded as evidence of pro-Japanese loyalty. Rose died in August 1943 and her husband was deported. Their daughter married and remained in Australia.[50]

Throughout agitation to get their restrictions lifted and their families reunited, both wives argued on the grounds of civil rights, "common fairness" and economic viability. The Inagakis had always pooled resources and the Kuringu's family dry-cleaning business built up together over many years. Mrs Kur-

ingu was fortunate that her sister was able to help out, but other
Japanese laundries met with less happy fates. Caring for the
property of internees was a major headache for security, especially at times of major round-ups. The army preferred internees to sign over their establishments to a Britisher to manage.
The laundryman from Fortitude Valley, Brisbane, arranged to
sign over his business, furniture and plant to his mistress.[51] The
woman looking after the property of another laundryman, NJ
17055, sold his old washing machine for around five pounds,
and the shirt and collar machine and the old laundry iron for
scrap. The money was supposed to go to the internee's account
at the camp but the woman admitted she had spent it and could
not repay it. The laundry of internee QJ 16053 at Gordonvale,
Queensland, was taken over by the US army some months after
his internment and by then the clothing had been taken by its
owners and "a little was taken by people to whom money was
owing".[52] The proprietor of the Townsville laundry, wrote to the
local police in March 1942 asking for his personal clothes and
news of his laundry but had no reply by April 1943, so he asked
for an investigation.[53] The American army took over the Townsville laundry and it may have been part of the security screen
surrounding the deployment of US troops that prevented this
information being conveyed to the Japanese laundryman. Censorship was in full operation and strictly enforced on letters in
and out of camp. Yet some hint of Japanese property owners
may have leaked out, for Lt-Col. J. McCahon wrote to all states
holding Japanese, telling them that allegations had been made
by Japanese officials that internees' property had been sold at
auction for low prices. McCahon wanted Allied Land Forces
Headquarters informed "urgently" of any "such incidents".
The matter was important because it related to "negotiations
relative to the disposal of the property of British persons in
Japan and Japanese-controlled territory".[54]

Reciprocity in handling internees was always a consideration in the policy and practice of internment, and the Australian
garrison officers and men were well aware of their responsibilities in this regard. The Loveday group history states that "Camp
Administrators kept in mind the fact that many" Australians
were held as prisoners of war by Axis Powers.[55] It "therefore
became incumbent on all ranks to treat their charges in the
correct manner in an endeavour to prevent reprisals". With the
Japanese there was a heightened anxiety. Unlike the Germans

and Italians, the Japanese had not signed the International Convention for the treatment of prisoners, and with 21,649 Australians in their hands[56] the government was worried about their "normal" treatment let alone if any misconduct should be proven against Australian guards or officials. An argument between the British and Germans over the shackling of prisoners began after the Dieppe raid, when Germans had been temporarily handcuffed, and the Germans consequently began a campaign of shackling British POWs for extended periods. Among those who suffered were Australians and Canadians in the German camps Oflag VIIB and IIIC and Stalag VIIIB. The British wished to pursue the matter by increasing the number of German POWs in Allied hands being similarly treated, but Curtin had "little faith in the value of reprisals" especially where the burden would "fall on helpless captives on both sides". A "competition in cruelty" could be "carried on indefinitely with far more embarrassment to us than to the enemy" and the Japanese-held prisoners were most vulnerable.[57]

It should not be thought that Australia's treatment of the Japanese or other internees was solely motivated by desire of reciprocity. The Official Visitors, the camp commandants and all those responsible had a high regard for the country's honour, legal process and humanitarian behaviour. When some Australians expressed annoyance that Japanese POWs were to be buried in the Lutwyche Cemetery in Brisbane near Allied graves, the Minister for the Army, Frank Forde answered the complaints in terms of both reciprocity and regard for international law. "It is only by the observance of this convention that we may expect reciprocal action from the Japanese", Forde wrote, and in addition, while Australia remained a signatory to the convention "we are bound by its terms".[58] During 1942 there were negotiations with Japan about reciprocal arrangements and the possible exchange of prisoners. Most of this work was done at a high level by the British, and prisoners were to some extent pawns in a bargaining game.

A major shuffling of Japanese prisoners from Australia occurred in August 1942 and was something of a mystery to camp authorities at the time. When the fall of the Netherlands East Indies (NEI) was imminent the Dutch authorities had moved almost 2,000 prisoners, mainly Japanese, to Australia.[59] They were interned in Loveday if they were single men, or at Tatura if they were in family groups. On 30 January 1942 Major A.W.

Lott of Loveday's Compound 14C received 536 Japanese from
the NEI. Surprisingly, given the state of the war, 528 Japanese
internees were entrained for Melbourne on 15 August 1942, on
their way to Japan as part of a repatriation exchange. It seems
contradictory that Australia, with all its own local Japanese
interned, should allow this large group to be returned, particularly as they had knowledge of the near North from which the
Japanese military forces were at that very moment basing their
attacks on Australia. Most of those repatriated were nominated
by name from Japan, and Loveday officers believed that "they
were all connected with the production of rubber in Malaya and
other islands". Many others with similar occupations were also
repatriated from Tatura, but not all those described as "rubber
estate" employees were included.[60] Most of the men connected
with Japanese firms such as Mitsui and the Yokohama Specie
Bank were early repatriates. Women and families with many
children tended to be included for repatriation from Tatura.[61]
Most of the repatriates were described as Buddhist, but if there
is one common factor it is that the next of kin were recorded as
being residents of Japan. Those internees whose next of kin
lived in Indonesia or the islands were not repatriated until after
the war.[62] The early NEI expatriates sailed on the exchange ship
City of Canterbury, which left Melbourne on 18 August 1942[63]
and took the former Japanese consul, Tatsuo Kawai, and the
ashes of the Japanese submariners, whose bodies were recovered from the bottom of Sydney Harbour,[64] to Yorktown in East
Africa to meet the *Kamakura Maru*.

While the consular staff and the servicemen's ashes went in
conformity to international law, the internees would logically
be exchanged for some valuable consideration, but little of
value came to Australia. Whether the economic value of these
Japanese internees to the enemy outweighed the manpower
and related costs in keeping them, is hard to assess, but Australia had tended to keep Germans with "skills likely to be useful
to the enemy". When the Dutch decided that their internees
were to be exchanged they would have had their own interests
in mind. The NEI authorities could well have been pressed by
considerations of treatment of Dutch in both Japanese and
German control. The British were afraid in December 1941 that
under such pressure the NEI authorities would repatriate 400
dangerous Germans from a camp in Sumatra, and arranged for
them to be sent to India.[65] Australia tried very hard to have its

Dr J.H. Becker, first leader of the Nazi Party in Australia, was interned as soon as war began, held until after it ended and forcibly deported in January 1947. Seen here between two detectives after trying to escape by stowing away on a freighter to Panama. (F.J. Halmarick, *Sydney Morning Herald*)

Oswald Bonutto migrated to Australia in 1926 and worked as a labourer, cane cutter, tobacco farmer and hotel keeper until his arrest in June 1940. After a successful appeal he was released only to be reinterned and eventually sent to Loveday. In his autobiography, *A Migrant's Story*, he says internees were the scapegoats for the Allies' early military defeats.

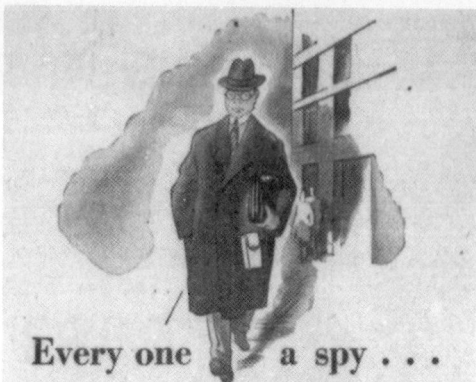

Every one a spy . . .

We saw plenty of them in Australia. They followed many lines of business. One sold silks, another chinaware, one bought wool, another wheat . . . one fished for whales, the other for pearls — they asked lots of questions, they took plenty of photographs. They smiled, bowed, scraped, and though we tolerated them, we hated their obvious insincerity, their filthy tricks of snide business, and we weren't so very impressed with their "Co-prosperity sphere," which sounded to us mighty like a policy of force, annexation, murder and rapine.

How right were our instincts. The Japanese who came to spy out our land, now attempt to return and enslave it.

every one a killer . . .

The record in every conquered country is one of falsity, violence, demoralisation and hateful brutality.

In Formosa, it has driven the aborigines again and again to rebel. Each time the Japs have put them down by massacring them in thousands. In Korea a reign of terror still persists as the Japanese attempt to totally subdue the inhabitants. In Manchuria, it has meant the complete harnessing of all manpower and resources to the Son of Heaven's chariot. In the Marshall and Caroline Islands, it has meant criminal neglect and the degradation of the people. Half the deaths among the natives are caused by tuberculosis; venereal disease is widespread. In Nanking it meant murder, rape, unbridled licence, looting and robbery.

This is Japan's New Order, worked out to include Australia, too. But it won't get here.

Every White Australian, backed by the generous help of our allies, is ready to carry the war right back to Japan.

Every man and woman is at his post —determined, for ever, to halt Japanese aggression and throw back the Jap where he belongs.

We've always despised them—

NOW WE MUST SMASH THEM!

All Japanese were interned immediately after Pearl Harbour. This cartoon is one of a series published in March and April 1942. The language is unequivocal. Every Japanese was vicious and deceitful and bent on enslaving Australians. Unlike European internees, the huge majority of Japanese were held in custody for the duration of the war.

Emery Barcs gazes whimsically from the back cover of the autobiographical account of his war years, *Backyard of Mars*. Expelled from Italy because of his anti-fascist views, he was interned in Australia on 8 December 1941 when his native Hungary entered the war. He was released in February 1942 and called up into the 3rd Employment Company of the CMF in July.

No. 14 Internment Camp, Loveday, held many Japanese. Here two internees use a crosscut saw to cut firewood. In contrast to Japanese prisoners-of-war, internees cooperated with authorities inside camp and on work projects. (AWM Neg no. 64826)

USE THE FINE COMB urged this cartoon. Officials were encouraged not to miss any Fifth Columnists in Australia as the Fifth Column was credited with aiding the Japanese in the battles for Malaya, Singapore and New Guinea. (*Courier-Mail*, 21 March 1942)

Total Internments of persons resident in Australia.

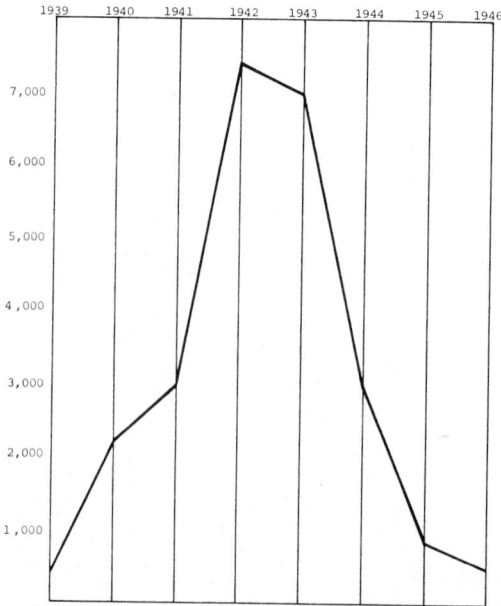

Major-General Durrant was GOC Western Command when Italy entered the war and was GOC Northern Command when the Japanese approached. Here he addresses his staff and unit commanders in Brisbane on 9 January 1942. With the Premier and Police Commissioner he urged mass internments and he and his assistant officer signed warrants for hundreds of residents on the Queensland coast. (*Courier-Mail*, 10 January 1942)

These figures are a compilation from a variety of sources with a basis on Noel Lamidey's *Aliens Control in Australia, 1939-46*. The bulk of internees were scooped up from the coastal areas of Queensland at the height of fear of an invasion. They were released to work in food production or other war related industries when the fighting receded from our shores and political stability was ensured in the 1943 election.

No. 10 Compound, Loveday, near Barmera, South Australia. The huge all male internment group at Loveday held a peak of 5,382 internees in May 1943. Here two internees play on a tennis court between the barbed wire fences and the main hut. (AWM Neg no. 64844)

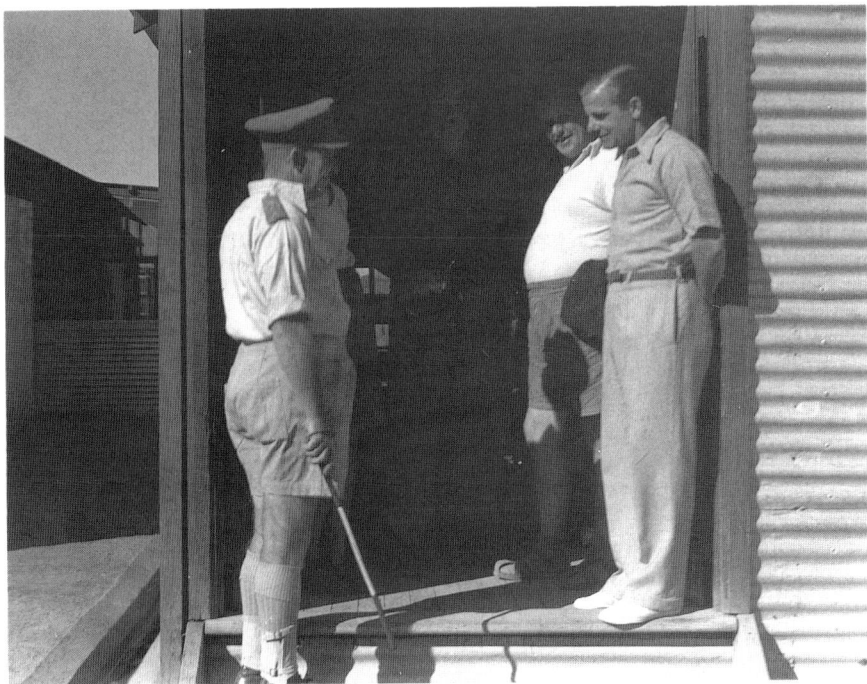

Captain J.F. Winton, Guard officer of No. 10 Compound chats with some internees during his inspection tour. There was regular interaction between the guard officers and the camp leaders. (AWM Neg n. 64878)

Officers of the 25/33rd Garrison Battalion, Loveday POW and Internment Group near Barmera, South Australia in March 1943. Seated from left: Major L. von Bertouch, Major C.E. Hunkin, Lt-Col E.T. Dean DSO,VD (Commanding Officer), Major A. Dick, and Major D.W. Shepherd. (AWM Neg no. 64894)

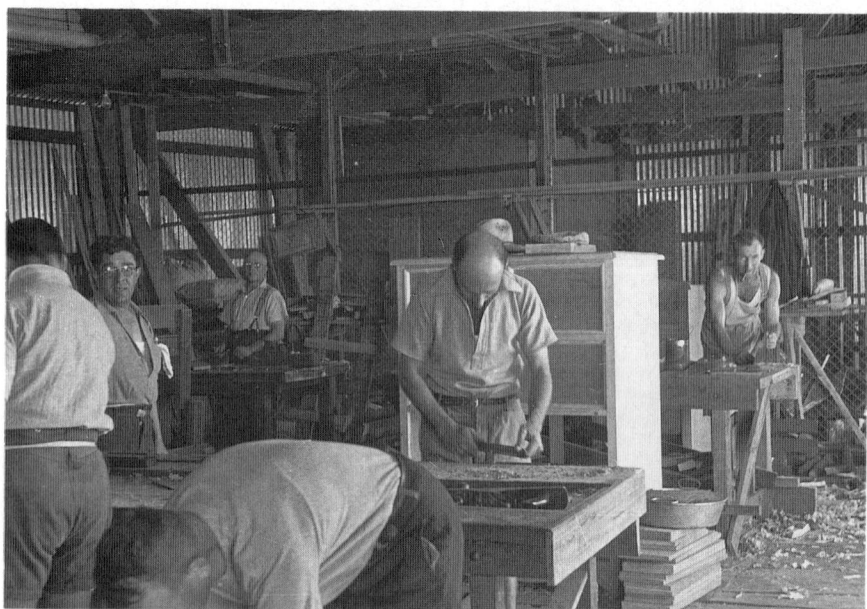

Interior of the workshops at No. 9 Camp, Loveday Internment Group. German internees are making furniture for the various camps of the group. (AWM Neg no. 30198/7)

Women Wardens at No. 3 Internment Camp, Tatura on 15 March 1945. The Tatura Internment Group in Victoria included the family camp. Front left: Wardens L. Moody, Senior Warden L. Murton, J. Watson. Back left: F. Jack, F. McLeod and M. Thompson. (AWM Neg no. 30250/11)

As the danger of invasion passed internees worked on projects to boost the war effort. Here Japanese at Loveday are harvesting pyrethrum daisies — an oil painting by Max Ragless. Pyrethrum was a basic element in insecticides used by the AMF (AWM Neg no. 38870)

The children of overseas internees and their teacher in a class photo at No. 3 CAmp, Tatura 1945. Twenty-four children under ten were among 304 former internees who returned to Europe on 1 December 1947. Many other overseas internees and their children remained in Australia and became citizens. (AWM Neg no. 30245/8)

Noel W. Lamidey, secretary of the Aliens Classification and Advisory Committee, photographed here in his role as Chief Migration Officer in London overseeing Calwell's post-war immigration policy. In 1991, aged 96, Lamidey recalled his own experiences as an impoverished migrant and recounted with amusement the scrapes he got in to in Britain after the war dealing with the backlash of Calwell's enthusiastic style of operating.

officials from Singapore and Timor included in the group sent in return but the Japanese would not agree.[66] Seven other Australian diplomats and 23 civilians were among the 105 Allied people exchanged. When the UK wanted to begin negotiations on a second exchange soon afterwards, Australia understandably resisted, considering the Japanese to have got the best of the first exchange.

Nor was this the end of Australia's problems with the Dutch over their internees on Australian soil. In 1943 Dr Charles Van Der Plas, head of the NEI Commission in Australia, transfered 507 political prisoners from their camp at Tanah Merah, on the Digul River in western New Guinea, to Bowen in North Queensland, on the ship *Both*.[67] Travelling south by rail the prisoners passed a note to fettlers, and the trade unions became interested in the plight of this group committed to Indonesian independence. The Tanah Merah prisoners were placed in the Liverpool camp and in Compound D at Cowra. Rupert Lockwood, in his study of the Indonesians in Australia during the war and immediately afterwards, claims that the Netherlands Indies government had described the Tanah Merah prisoners as enemies of the Allied cause who should be treated as prisoners of war, and the Curtin government had accepted them on this basis.[68] In fact they were political prisoners. Some families had been detained since the republican uprising in 1926. Lockwood charges the Australian government with negligence in accepting this group with the status assigned them by the Dutch, and it might seem surprising that the *Dunera* experience did not alert Australian authorities to the possibility of a false label.

Lockwood berates Curtin for embracing the NEI government-in-exile at all, and for taking 15 months to release the Tanah Merah political prisoners, but Australia in March 1942 was desperate for allies and the circumstances of the arrival of NEI Dutch refugees in Broome, pursued by Japanese Zeros, ensured them of a welcome. Australia had no immediate reason to think the *Both* internees were other than similar to the Japanese internees brought by the *Cremer* in January 1942. Mrs Laura Gapp, of the NSW Civil Rights League, pursued the matter, and Dr Evatt persuaded the cabinet to force the Dutch to take the tuberculosis sufferers into the Princess Juliana Hospital at Turramurra and to free the others from Cowra on 7 December 1943.[69] The NEI government-in-exile had to rely on these Indonesians in their civil service and technical support areas and benefiting from Australian rates of pay and experiencing a freer political system, they became even more determined to achieve independence for Indonesia after the war.[70]

Taken at the same time

Interned at the same time as the Japanese, were a selection of Hungarians, Roumanians and Finns. Australia had considered declaring war on these countries since October 1941, when the United Kingdom was pressed to do so by the Soviet Union.[71] The newly-installed Labor government felt it would damage Russian morale, and be hard to justify publicly not to declare war on the three countries who were fighting against Russia. The date pre-ordained for the declaration was 7 December 1941. Dr Evatt considered the procedure for making a separate declaration by Australia, not wanting to follow the style of Menzies' announcement at the outbreak of war with Germany, that Australia was at war because Britain was.[72] The Labor cabinet considered its internment policy in relation to the nationals of the new enemy countries and the British informed Australia of its policy. In Britain, civilians were to be detained if there was some element of suspicion attached to them on personal grounds", or if "by reason of their knowledge" they were "in a position to damage national interests". In these categories the British expected to take 10 Finns, 10 Roumanians "and about 100 Hungarians". All seamen were to be taken "automatically" and this was expected to net "about 200" Finns and a few others. The persons not interned were to be restricted.[73]

Australia interned 33 Hungarians, 42 Roumanians and 142 Finns.[74] The Hungarians interned in New South Wales elected Dr Emery Barcs to be their spokesman in the Liverpool camp. He calculated that two-thirds of his group had university degrees, and their average age was 32.[75] They spent a lot of time trying to puzzle out why their 30 had been selected from the 300 Hungarian adult males in Sydney, not realising that it was as simple as their being fit, young, intelligent and knowledgable enough "to damage national interests" if they felt so inclined. Barcs was particularly vulnerable. Beside being young and newly arrived, he was a journalist who specialised in international affairs; he was preparing a "Notes on the News" talk for the ABC on the attack on Pearl Harbour when he was arrested.[76] But he had come to the notice of the Military Intelligence Branch, Phillip Street, Sydney because in July 1940 he wrote an article to a Swiss newspaper in German. It contained some well-known facts about Australia and the war. The military intercepted the article in the mail and warned Barcs not to send anything to Europe written in German, "especially about war and defence".[77] Because of his job at the *Telegraph* Barcs was regarded by his fellow countrymen as something of an expert and was often asked what he thought would happen next. When the Hungarian Prime Minister shot himself, and the pro-Axis group gained power, many Hungarians rang Barcs for his opinion on what would happen if they became enemy aliens. He realised his phone was tapped when the telephonist interrupted one of his callers with the demand that he speak up and speak English.[78] No doubt checks on Barcs showed that he had been a war correspondent in Abyssinia, and had interviewed Mussolini's son-in-law, Count Ciano. Barcs was aware that his local Italian fruiterer's brother had been interned, although he had been naturalised for ten years. This "disquieting" information, and a warning from a fellow journalist that "people do strange things when they are frightened" and that the journalist felt Australians were "very frightened", prepared Barcs for his midnight call from the police on 8 December 1941.[79] The fact that Barcs had been expelled from Italy because of his criticism of the Rome-Berlin axis was insufficient to outweigh the combination of other factors. Across the road from the area where the Roumanians, Hungarians and Finns were held was "a small cottage behind barbed wire", holding Japanese internees. The night before, at the police station where Barcs had been taken after his arrest, he had heard the detective tell the policeman on the desk that he had been out arresting Japanese from seven that morning and 250 had been rounded up.

Barcs and his fellow Hungarians spent about six months in captivity, and the Indonesian independence seekers were freed after eighteen months. The Roumanians were released before the rest of those taken in this roundup were moved on to Tatura. Barcs and his friend heard rumours that the Roumanians releases were due to the intervention of the Greek Consul-General, whose wife was Roumanian, or alternatively, to that of expensive lawyers. It was even said that the Roumanians' wives went down "to Victoria Barracks and made a tearful appeal to

the officers of Eastern Command".[80] In fact, Eastern Command
had again moved beyond what higher authority considered
appropriate. Roumanians "against whom no evidence existed"
had been interned. As a result the GOC, Eastern Command had
his authority to intern enemy aliens withdrawn for three
months, and Ministerial approval was to be obtained before
enemy aliens could be interned in New South Wales.[81]

However the major group interned in late 1941, the Japanese,
began a long period in camp. The local Japanese, and the
overseas Japanese not repatriated in late 1942, remained interned in Australia until they departed on the *Yoizuki* or the *Koei
Maru* in 1946. Over 100 Japanese internees never saw their
homes again. They died of malaria, tuberculosis or the diseases
of old age.[82] They were initially buried at Barmera or Tatura,
but were later moved to the Japanese cemetery at Cowra, NSW,
where they lie with their countrymen of more warlike disposi-
tion.[83] Generally, the Japanese were among the most placid of
the internees, and recorded against most of their names are only
the dates of their arrival and departure even after almost five
years of internment. Many were not security risks as such,
although some were of marginal economic value to the enemy.
It was the strength of Australian antipathy to the Japanese race
as a whole that made it necessary in the interests of law and
order, and of morale, to keep them interned for the whole of
their time in Australia or for the duration of the war.

Chapter Seven

THE BIG ROUND UP

In the year 1942 Australian morale was under great strain. While the fighting had remained "over there", Australians at home were remote spectators but the attack on Pearl Harbour and the fall of Singapore, the Philippines, and Java threw the Australian population into the fighting ring. During 1942, Port Moresby, Darwin, Broome, Katherine and Townsville were bombed and midget submarines were discovered in Sydney Harbour.

> So, suddenly, a very old Australian nightmare came to life. Throughout their history Australians had been given to bouts of fear that their remote, underpopulated coastline would tempt a foreign aggressor, probably Oriental, but this terror had been kept at bay by the naval supremacy of the British Empire. After December 1941 that supremacy was no more.[1]

The Australian and New Zealand Chiefs of Staff reported on 26 February 1942 that Australia and New Zealand were in danger of attack.[2] When Singapore fell the "17,000 Australians of the 8th Division were lost to Australia's defence and this shattered any delusion that Australia was safe under the British umbrella. Curtin faced these realities and sought to achieve three things: the safe return of the Second AIF Divisions to Australia; as close a relationship as possible with the United States; and a more stringent gearing of Australia to the war effort.[3]

In the meantime the militia met the challenge in New Guinea, but plans for the defence of Australia revealed that the whole continent could not be defended by the forces available.[4] To secure the area from Brisbane, where a large US base was to be developed, through the industrial heartland of Port Kembla, Sydney, Newcastle and Lithgow, and south to Melbourne, other parts of Australia might have to be abandoned. The commander of the home forces did not recommend the removal of garrisons from places like Townsville or Tasmania for reasons of morale but he insisted that any weakening of the forces in the vital 1,000-mile south-eastern zone by reinforcing "isolated" parts would lead to the defeat of the Australian army and the likelihood of the complete occupation of Australia.

Public reaction

Frank Forde, the Minister for the Army and member for Capricornia, based on Rockhampton, found these arguments disturbing and people in outlying areas clearly felt vulnerable.[5] Many of them wrote to inform the military how unprotected their railway bridges, harbours, power stations and water supplies were. To what degree Australia's nerve was shaken is difficult to assess. According to G.C. Bolton "civilian morale remained on the whole resolute",[6] but Hasluck claims that in the two months leading to the fall of Singapore Australians had come "from complacency or confidence to the threshold of fear for their own survival".[7]

George Johnston wrote in his autobiographical novel *My Brother Jack*, that Port Moresby was undermanned and poorly equipped and a "brooding sense of hopelessness prevailed everywhere". Johnston claims that the picture sent back to the Australian public did not match the reality, but that the dishonesty was "desperately necessary" because the mood at home "was darkened by the realisation that the country's best fighting men were "ten thousand miles away".[8] Lloyd Ross, in his biography of Curtin, describes Canberra in December 1941 as being "in jitters", and he cites one observer as saying that the Australian troops in Brisbane were demoralised, often drunk, and that the whole country was "in the dumps with them".[9] Doubtless all these pictures were partly true, but there is an equally verifiable picture of increased volunteering by women for the services and by men in primary production for the Volunteer Defence Corps which was increased to 80,000 in February and an establishment of 100,000 by the end of 1942.[10] The Army raised a special force to watch for and report any enemy landings between Normanton, Qld and Yampi Sound, WA and many experienced bushmen volunteered.[11] Many thousands of other Australians became active in Civil Defence Organisations and the Red Cross.

The evacuation of the civilian population was included in *War Book* planning and in a few areas, such as New Guinea and

Darwin, women and children were ordered to leave for defence reasons. Within Australia there were perceptible but unofficial moves to the south or inland, but it was officially decided that there would be only "limited evacuation" from areas near possible targets and of young children from congested areas to a safer place in the same city.[12] Some people on the North Queensland coast considered themselves to be in a likely target area and decided to evacuate their families. The evacuation mentality increased when state schools were not allowed to open in February, and the atmosphere of a battle zone increased when rifles, cars and bicycles were impressed, and farmers had their "crawler" tractors taken to help construct aerodromes.[13] Queensland police were directed by their Commissioner, C.J. Carroll, to take statistics from the residents of the coastal towns as a preliminary measure, but this had the effect of unsettling some people.[14]

Disorderly mass movement was dangerous and citizens were told to move only when ordered to "by responsible officials".[15] The VDC were trained to dismantle local machinery, bridges were mined and the volunteers were expected to stay behind and act as a guerilla group in the manner that had been successful in Russia. In the event of a civilian population being trapped behind enemy lines the police were instructed to remain with the people and act as intermediaries between the enemy and the civilians.[16] Hasluck criticises the nation's leaders for their lack of faith in ordinary Australians, their preoccupation with plans to "destroy and withdraw" and their keeping details of the full extent of casualties suffered in the Darwin raids from the public "for fear that the truth might cause panic". He suggests that Canberra appeared "to have been more badly scared than any other part of the continent" and that "undue excitement" was "more evident in political circles" over internment than was shown by the general public. But is Hasluck too severe? Governments are responsible for the safety of the people. If pockets of the population, who could have been saved from enemy hands by quick and pre-planned action, were allowed to be captured, the authorities would have been truly culpable. And, as Hasluck knows, censorship of mail revealed a general and understandable disquiet among the people about the series of military defeats, and the possible disloyalty of aliens.[17]

Many citizens wrote to the Prime Minister and these letters

reveal some of the attitudes of the general public at this time.[18] The writers stressed that they were determined to resist the enemy but there were things that should be done to facilitate success. The problem of aliens was mentioned often.[19] Some writers complained that aliens were taking advantage of the labour shortage created when men were called up for military service. The Deputy Director-General of Manpower in Perth reported that there was "a good deal of irritation in country districts over aliens" who were adopting "an extremely independent manner" and refusing to work "except at exorbitant rates". This "open and unashamed exploitation" of the labour shortage by foreigners caused "deep resentment" among those settlers with sons and brothers in the forces. Curtin replied that it would be necessary for everyone "to readjust" their working conditions in order "to fight desperately to stem the tide of aggression now menacing Australia".[20]

Naturalised subjects of enemy origin were also regarded as a threat because they had built up assets and had the local knowledge that could be useful to the enemy. The Independent member for the South Coast in the NSW parliament, R.N. Beale felt a local German-born man was "hiding under his naturalisation papers" and would harm "our cause" at "the first opportunity". Local Italian fishermen had "been going out to sea in their boats to celebrate" Axis victories, and some young men whose parents were interned were both clever and bitter and "ready to blow up bridges". Basically, "when our sons and daughters" were "risking their lives overseas and on our own shores", and given "the extremely critical position", Australian authorities should not risk leaving foreigners "naturalised or otherwise", at large.[21]

The Shire Council of Mulgrave, Vic., wrote to other Municipal Councils urging them to express their disapproval of enemy aliens having unrestricted liberty. The wholesale and retail fruit and vegetable trade was "almost exclusively controlled by enemy or naturalised aliens" who were benefiting from the call up of Australians, not only by getting higher prices, but by being able to extend "their productive holdings". Mulgrave Council described the situation where some Australians were fighting and dying, where other Australians were being forced off their properties and where Australian housewives had "to pour unwarranted profits into the pockets of freedom-given aliens", as nothing short of "sinister".[22] After noting "the informed views", the Secretary of the Prime Minister's Department sometimes had the letter copied and sent to the Minister and Department of the Army and to the Director of Security Services. Sometimes the writers dealt with particular local situations, but many letters were couched in general terms of principle. The justification for interning all enemy aliens given by the 3,000 petitioners from Ballina, NSW, was fairly typical: a feeling of greater security would exist; loyal women, children and the aged deserved protection; and allowing enemy aliens their freedom gave them the opportunity to endanger life and property and to assist any invaders. The Ballina petitioners felt that there was no certainty that enemy aliens did not have concealed stores of arms and ammunition, so their internment would be for the greater security of Australia. Finally the petitioners pointed out that, with the strength of feeling against enemy aliens rising, they would be safer interned.[23] Hasluck's assessment that politicians got more excited about internment than the general public is doubtful in the light of the enormous correspondence from the public on internment. They wrote in their hundreds and signed petitions in their thousands. The call for greater internment was not combined with a lack of faith in an eventual victory. It was similar to the British reaction to Dunkirk in June 1940, combining a desire to be part of a cohesive, homogeneous group when facing the enemy with a clear-the-decks mentality before battle. The fight was perceived as being between the Anglo-Saxon and Celtic Australians and the Japanese, and potential sympathisers with Japan were best out of the way. The exact degrees to which this "tribal" urge surfaced in the politicians, public, police and the military is speculative, but the urge itself was sufficiently widespread to make community sentiment the basis of internment in the first half of 1942.

On this broad base of concern certain politicians, military leaders and police commissioners were more active in their agitation for something to be done than others. In particular Alexander Mair, who by 1942 was leader of the Opposition in New South Wales, continued to speak against federal policy. On 11 February the newspapers reported that a Japanese controlled radio had broadcast material not made public in Australia, and Mair blamed this on aliens being allowed to remain at large.[24] The theory was that a spy network existed, with a secret radio capable of sending messages to off-shore submarines, thus jeopardising troopships. Mair was also totally opposed to the government's proposal to allow friendly aliens to enlist. The government had made men from Greece, Poland, Czechoslovakia, Holland, the United States and China eligible to join the AIF, and created schemes to use enemy aliens and refugee internees in a civilian corps to work on defence construction. Mair considered the inclusion of non-Britishers in the war effort constituted a grave security risk, and he was supported by the RSL.

The RSL had been active in the campaign to have aliens interned during the crisis of June 1940, but in 1942 it entered into a more aggressive campaign, proportional to the greater depth of the crisis. The 25th Annual Federal Congress considered earlier government response "unsatisfactory" and couched resolution 210 in stronger terms.[25] Because of "widespread public unrest and feeling of insecurity" the congress wanted immediate and more drastic action on internment together with the re- internment of released internees and no more releases. In Queensland, where there was a large concentration of enemy aliens in northern coastal areas and a relatively close proximity to New Guinea, the League's branches strongly supported a call for the internment of all enemy aliens.[26] Queensland's political and military leaders agreed. A conference attended by the Premier, W. Forgan-Smith, the GOC Northern Command, Major-General J.M.A. Durrant, the State Minister for Civil Defence, and Commonwealth and State officers, held in Brisbane on 27 January 1942, recommended that the 13,000 persons of enemy origin in North Queensland all be interned as a matter of urgency.[27] Early in February Arthur Fadden was on a tour of the north, and the North Queensland branch of the RSL asked him, as Leader of the Federal Opposition and as a member of the Advisory War Council, to intern all enemy aliens. On Thursday, 12 February, he replied that "results would be apparent in the near future".[28]

Official response

On the next night and into Saturday morning, what was described as "the most intense round up in Australia since the war began" took place on the coastal areas of Queensland; 2,000 aliens were questioned and "appropriate action was taken by the authorities". The drive extended as far south as the New South Wales border. *The Sydney Morning Herald* reported:

> It is hoped that [this roundup] will help to clear up the spy radio service which has been giving information to Japan. The police forces in the north have been strengthened lately by the promotion of men with an intimate knowledge of the north and the drafting of special men to assist in a possible drive against suspected fifth columnists. The situation in the north has been causing the State authorities much concern, particularly in areas where Italians predominate. Strong pressure has been brought to bear by returned soldiers, who have insisted that appropriate action be taken.

At the same time the Army Minister, Frank Forde, signed an order placing a curfew on all enemy aliens in Queensland, forbidding them to be out of their homes between 8 pm and 5 am. This "drastic action" by Forde was motivated, according to the newspaper, by "the high percentage of alien residents" who often congregated "in colonies", and because Queensland appeared to be in immediate danger of attack.

Although this round-up was described by the paper as "intense" and the largest since the war began, it is probable that the actual number interned was around 200, including 163 listed on a Master Warrant issued at the time.[29] The explanation of the difference between the dramatic tone of the newspaper report and the actual number taken, probably lies in the fact that newspapers were becoming propaganda agents used to boost morale by highlighting positive action and minimising losses.[30] The newspaper did not say to what degree "appropriate action" had been taken. Readers could have gained the impression that 1,000 had been interned. Certainly the number questioned was large, and it was obvious that everyone of enemy origin was under suspicion and that further losses would precipitate further arrests.

The RSL, encouraged by the government's action, stepped up its campaign to get all enemy aliens interned and to give the military control over naturalised persons. The league urged other groups to express their views. Allied organisations such as the Diggers' Association presented a petition with well over 1,000 signatures. Petitions also came from towns in southern Queensland and northern New South Wales, and some trade unions sent telegrams urging more direct action against aliens. The Shire Council of Moree, NSW, urged other local authorities to call for total internment. Other pressure groups included the

Orange Lodge of Leichhardt, NSW (which particularly wanted
Catholic priests interned), the Anti-Enemy Alien Association of
Punchbowl, NSW, War Patriotic Committees, and branches of
the Australian Natives' Association and the Royal Society of St
George.[31]

On 15 February 1942 Singapore surrendered and the next day
the *Sydney Morning Herald* said that more internments in the
north were expected. These would "take out of circulation
'firebrands' among the cane cutters". The cutters were described as a travelling population, largely Italian and thousands
strong.[32] According to the newspaper, "the settled Italian community" had taken the raids quietly, but they were worried that
the newly imposed curfew might be extended to them, and at
the loss of cane cutters who would be needed in June. On 25
February another 93 persons were named on a Master Warrant.[33] Although the trauma to the individuals should not be
understated, the newspaper was misleading its readers about
the number and nature of these internees. Actually the men
taken at this time included some naturalised Germans who had
previously come to the attention of the security services and
those who had failed to register for service under the government's Aliens Service regulations.

The government had introduced the regulations early in
February, giving alien men a fortnight to register for service
with Labour Battalions. The regulations were designed to stop
aliens getting the higher paid jobs that Australians had left for
military service, and to ensure that alien residents made their
contribution to the war effort. Aliens who were eligible but had
not registered were the main target in the second set of raids in
February.[34] On 21 February the *Sydney Morning Herald* contained a report by Major Cameron, that the remarks of the
Minister for Munitions, that broomsticks would have to be used
for training because of the lack of rifles, had not been broadcast
in Australia but appeared in a Japanese radio text a few hours
later, was placed next to the item reporting the hunt for Fifth
Columnists in Queensland. It was claimed that hundreds of
enemy aliens or "naturalised foreigners" suspected of Axis
sympathies were being sought by police.[35] To the general reader
these two consecutive items indicated that the government felt
that spies were sending information to the enemy and that these
spies were to be found among the naturalised Italians and
Germans in Queensland. In reality, as the news from the war

front worsened, the difference between a spy, a Fifth Columnist and a person who was not prepared to work for the war effort began to disappear. And news from the front did get worse.

On 28 February the cruiser *Perth* was sunk in the Sunda Strait with 682 men either drowned or taken prisoner.[36] Refugees poured into Australia from the Netherlands East Indies, and on 3 March, Japanese Zeros strafed Broome, killing 30 people, mainly refugees in the flying boats on Roebuck Bay.[37] If the resources of Java were added to those already captured in Malaya, and if New Guinea were to become an enemy base, a direct assault on the northern portion of the Australian continent was a distinct possibility. The request of the Queensland political and military leaders that the 13,000 persons of enemy origin in the state be interned, whether naturalised or not, had not been agreed to by authorities at the federal level, but on 5 March the *Argus* reported that some hundreds of naturalised and enemy aliens, particularly Italians and Germans, were rounded up in various parts of Queensland by state police "in co-operation with military authorities". Many of these internees had been listed earlier as people suspected of not being completely loyal to the British Empire. They were considered loyal enough to Australia when the war front was remote, but it was felt that their loyalty was basically to the plot of earth they cultivated and not to the democratic process, the government elected by that process, or the British crown. If an invasion came, these successful migrants might be prepared to exchange governments if they could keep their land.[38]

Tension mounted further when the Japanese captured Rabaul and landed at Lae and Salamaua in New Guinea on 8 March 1942. In response, Curtin's government again revised the schedule of reserved occupations, limiting exemptions for men of military age to those doing essential work in food and industrial production and those providing services directly related to the war effort. On 6 March two additional classes of men were called up, and compulsory service was also introduced for the Civil Construction Corps. Cabinet decided to send Dr Evatt to Washington to impress President Roosevelt with the need for more equipment and troops in the Pacific area, and to take part in strategic planning. Evatt was to argue that Australia was in danger of being lost as the best base from which the thrust against the Japanese could be launched. He also went to London, where he persuaded Churchill to send a squadron of Spitfires and their crews to supplement the meagre Australian aerial reserves.[39]

Just as the nation was steeling itself for a terrible struggle with an enemy that seemed to be sweeping everything before it, a most dramatic act of disloyalty was revealed. On the night of 9/10 March, four Western Australians were arrested for planning to receive the Japanese when they landed. One of the group had once written to the Australia First Movement in Sydney asking for information, so sixteen members of the movement there were arrested.[40] The Sydney branch of the Security Service flashed the message to all states. It seemed that 20 people of British descent had been prepared to act as traitors. F.A. Cooper, acting Premier of Queensland, responded to the news of the Australia First arrests by asking that "all naturalised British subjects suspected of subversive activites" in Queensland be arrested.[41] He believed there had been some activity by Australia First in Queensland. There was no evidence of any connection between naturalised Queensland residents and the Australia First movement, and in later, calmer times, it would be shown that there was no connection between the men from Australia First arrested in Sydney, and the four conspirators in Perth, but in the hectic month of March 1942 circumstances gave security a specially high priority.

On 12 March the allied forces on Java surrendered, and a further 2,000 Australian troops were captured. Evatt, the cabinet minister with the highest reputation for protecting civil liberties and legal process, had already left Australia and, on the day after the fall of Java, a further 102 persons were named on Master Warrants in Brisbane. It is fascinating to speculate whether Evatt knew of the Australia First arrests or of the Master Warrants issued at this time. Power to detain any person for ten days without Ministerial approval existed in the original National Security regulations. All the Master Warrants and the Australia First detentions were signed by Forde or his delegated military commander. J.A. Beasley, acting as Attorney-General in Evatt's absence, "twice denied knowledge of the whole affair in Parliament". Whether Evatt would have acted differently is speculation also, for as Craig Munro in his recent biography of P.R. Stephensen points out, "all the various intelligence services, civilian and military" had recommended action be taken against the Australia First Movement.[42]

On 17 March 1942, General Douglas MacArthur arrived in

Australia to a hero's welcome at Spencer Street station, Melbourne. For the next few weeks Curtin and Forde were fully occupied re-organising the military structure with MacArthur as Supreme Commander of the South West Pacific Area, and General Lavarack as head of the Australian forces until Blamey returned. This concrete evidence of a fighting alliance with the United States, together with the relief provided by the arrival of the giant ships, the *Queen Mary* and the *Aquitania*, bearing home the first contingent of the 7th Division, AIF, temporarily heartened both the leaders and the people of Australia.[43] On 23 March the *Sydney Morning Herald* reported that Arthur Fadden found the people of North Queensland showing a spirit comparable with that of Londoners at the start of the Battle of Britain. Under way were Curtin's three strategies: the return of the Australian divisions, the alliance with the United States, and the intensification of Australia's own war effort.

Australia First debate

Throughout these threatening months the total number of people interned had doubled.[44] Frank Forde and John Curtin used this fact as evidence of the government's determination to protect the security of Australia in the debate that followed Forde's dramatic announcement in parliament, on 26 March 1942, that 20 people connected with the Australia First Movement had been arrested and interned, and that documents had been seized, showing that some people had intended to make contact with the Japanese army as soon as it landed, setting out plans for sabotage, and for assassinating prominent people. The morning after this astonishing revelation the *Canberra Times* reported that Curtin had declined to "indicate what punishment, if any," would be inflicted on the people who had committed these "treasonable practices". He did say that the military authorities "might contemplate further action", but reminded reporters that those who had been interned could appeal against their internment.[45]

The Opposition Leader expressed his shock at such a casual response.[46] Fadden demanded that the Australia First internees be put on trial for treason, then quickly moved to a general attack on aliens.[47] In his view public opinion was stirred up because of the number of aliens in Australia whose allegiance was "openly questioned". Since the outbreak of war the han-

dling of the alien question had been "characterised by the usual
British consideration for the individual", but this could no
longer be tolerated "in view of the success which" had "unfortunately attended the Japanese drive southwards". Fadden
linked the disclosures about the Australia First arrests with the
position of aliens in Australia very simply. "The necessity to
control our alien population becomes greater when we learn
that it has been found necessary to arrest and intern twenty of
our own people", he declared.

Fadden's call to intern all enemy aliens was challenged by
Frank Brennan, who pointed out that the internment camps
were full, and by G.W. Martens, the Labor member for Herbert
in North Queensland, who reminded Fadden that 600 people
had recently been taken from two North Queensland districts.[48]
Fadden said that where there was an aggregation of enemy
aliens in coastal areas, there was danger that they "would be an
army to help the Japanese if they landed".[49] He proposed that
enemy aliens should be considered "in parallel with" the Australia First Movement. In his opinion the men should be interned, the women investigated and restricted, those
naturalised within the previous five years should be reported
on, and any suspicious person interned.

Maurice Blackburn considered that Fadden had gone "far-
ther than he really intended to go" and stressed that refugee
Jews were even more afraid of enemy conquests than Australians.[50] Blackburn believed that the Labor government, its
predecessor and the Australian people as a whole, were "ani-
mated by a liberal spirit" and did not assume a man "guilty of
conspiracy merely because of his race or associations". The
member for Moreton, Josiah Francis paid tribute to the authorities who had caught the perpetrators of "one of the most
striking examples of fifth column activity ever revealed in
Australian history". He urged that the personnel of the Investigation Branch, which "in most instances" had done "extraor-
dinarily good work", be increased to keep watch for more fifth
columnists. Francis said that at a Grand Fascist Council meeting
in Mussolini's presence in San Remo, Italy, a speaker had
claimed that Italians in Oceania had been "migrated to the
south seas to prepare the way for Japan, as Japan is the natural
country to drive everything British out of the Pacific".[51]

Curtin replied that two considerations had to be given attention at the same time — the safety of the Commonwealth and

the preservation of the essential principles of British justice and fair dealing.[52] Because of the statement made at the Fascist Grand Council, the government "must watch very closely the conduct of Italians in Australia", but investigations by "Military Intelligence, home security officers, and officials of both Commonwealth and State departments' showed "the irreproachable conduct in this crisis of great numbers of persons" who could technically be described as enemy aliens. Curtin reminded parliament that the persons of whom Forde had spoken were not enemy aliens, but British, and they were being dealt with because Intelligence did have some evidence of their subversive activities. Curtin spelt out the role of the government as he saw it. The government's first obligation was not to judge the evidence or to decide if people were guilty or not, but "to take the elementary precaution of removing them from any possibility of carrying on their activities, until such time as the evidence was examined". The evidence in relation to the 20 people mentioned by Forde was being examined by the Solicitor-General, and there would be "no political interference with the ordinary processes of law". In response to the Opposition's call to intern more enemy aliens, Curtin pointed out that the number interned had doubled in the last four months, indicating that the government did "not need any spur from the Opposition" to know its duty. Curtin concluded that "surely" no member wanted mass internment, and that selective internment necessitated investigation by properly appointed officers, and this was what was happening. The Chief Commissioner of Police in New South Wales, W.J. Mackay, had been appointed Director of the Security department, and while army officers worked under his direction, it was this civilian, "accustomed to the detection of crime and to the preservation of law and order", who was in charge.

Arthur Calwell, the recently elected Labor member for Melbourne, had an antipathy for W.J. Mackay. In Calwell's opinion Mackay was "fascist-minded" and similar to the French police chief, Fouche, "who, during the French Revolution and later, served every government to his own advantage".[53] Nor was Mackay the army's choice. The first director of the Security Service was E.E. Longfield-Lloyd, appointed on 5 March 1941. Other surveillance authorities were not willing to share their resources with the new Security Service. The army was not willing to give it direct access to censorship facilities nor was the Investigation Branch willing to hand over the MI5 cipher code. On 4 July W.M. Hughes asked cabinet for an investigation of the organisation of the Security Service and Percy Spender sought to have Military Intelligence looked at also. The suggested investigator, Lt-Col. J.C. Mawhood of the British army and MI5 was so unacceptable to the Australian Army that cabinet asked A.M. Duncan, the Chief Commissioner of Police for Victoria, formerly of the Special Branch of Scotland Yard, to investigate the Security Service only. Duncan reported to Evatt on 7 January 1942 and Mackay was Duncan's suggestion. The army wanted Brigadier B. Combes who had headed Military Intelligence before the war. Curtin stood by Duncan's advice and told Calwell he could argue until he was "black in the face", but the appointment of Mackay was fixed.[54] Curtin assured the House that the Australia First Movement had been under observation for some time by both the present and previous governments, that a prima facie case had been established by Military Intelligence against those arrested, and that civil authorities would be formulating charges for their trial. The debate was continued by two ideological adversaries: W.M. Hughes, who predictably emphasised the need for tighter security and less "blithering about the Bill of Rights and *habeas corpus* and things of that kind"; and Frank Brennan, who deplored the baiting of aliens, many of whom were "acknowledged to be exemplary citizens".

At a less ideological level, G.W. Martens, who represented the Herbert electorate from which the majority of recently interned men had come, expressed reservations based on personal knowledge. There were men in internment for whom Martens had "a great regard", one being "a very good friend" who had contributed to war loans. Martens would continue to hold such men "in esteem" until it had "been proven" that they had "done wrong". Martens stated that he had been criticised by people in his own electorate for interceding with the Minister on behalf of internees, but his enquiries were basically to ask that certain cases be investigated. Martens had received resolutions passed at many public meetings requesting him to support the wholesale internment of enemy aliens, naturalised or not, but what he knew of many Italians in North Queensland led him "to the opinion that the wholesale internment of aliens, and even of so-called enemy aliens", was "not a proper procedure".[55]

H.L. Anthony, the Country Party member for Richmond, based his support for tighter security measures on his conversations with women who had left the Townsville, Cairns and Innisfail districts for his northern rivers electorate in New South Wales. These people from North Queensland showed "disquiet" about "the colonies of aliens established within easy distance of a landing place". Anthony had no faith in naturalisation as a guarantee of loyalty; he invoked the poem by Sir Walter Scott beginning, "Breathes there the man, with soul so dead, Who never to himself hath said, This is my own, my native land?" Anthony conceded that wholesale internment was "unreasonable and unnecessary", but he felt the government should disperse the congregation of people who might reasonably be suspected of being willing to give the enemy aid. Anthony was supported by John McEwen, the Country Party member for Indi, who said that while in peace-time he would "fight for the personal freedom and security of the individual", in time of peril he had "no hesitation in placing the security of the community above that of the individual".[56] The debate eventually ran out of time and most members were satisfied that Curtin was acting properly. A debate that had been triggered by the public announcement of the arrest of sixteen members of the Australia First Movement in Sydney and four conspirators in Perth, had much more to say about the attitude of Australians to people of Italian origin living on the North Queensland coast. It was not disclosed in the debate that, at the War Cabinet meeting held on 22 March 1942, there had been an extensive discussion on whether there should be total internments in North Queensland, and that the Advisory War Council had also debated the matter.

Coastal Queensland

In the War Cabinet debate the Minister for the Army explained that, as policy stood, people were interned "who were engaged in subversive activities" or in regard to whom there were grounds for suspicion, and the balance of aliens were called up to serve in Labour Units.[57] However, because of the danger of possible invasion, Forde had asked the Director of Military Intelligence for his recommendations "in regard to enemy aliens in the vulnerable area in the north-eastern coastal regions of Australia". It had been suggested to Forde that all naturalised

British subjects of enemy origin should be removed from their homes and compelled to live at least 100 miles from the coast. The men in this group were "of the farmer type" and were alleged to have "nothing less than 3 months supply of food in their homes, which might be used for enemy purposes". Northern Command held the view that everyone of enemy origin — men, women and children, naturalised and unnaturalised — should be removed despite dislocations, accommodation problems and other difficulties.[58] Roughly 7,500 adult males and 15,000 women and children would be involved.

The Chief Commissioner of Police for Queensland, C.J. Carroll, made representations through the Director General of Security in support of the total evacuation of aliens. Carroll put his case "vehemently and passionately", brushing aside any doubts.[59] It did not matter that some naturalised North Queenslanders had sons in the army. From his long years of study of the alien problem, Carroll felt "that everyone of them should come out and come out immediately", and "every naturalised British subject of enemy origin should be given time to get out". In his covering letter Mackay wrote that if removal was ordered, Carroll had intimated that "the Queensland Police would be in a position to give it immediate effect".

In the cabinet debate, the army disagreed with Carroll's view.[60] The difficulties of moving over 22,000 people and providing them with accommodation elsewhere, were too great. Lt-Col. C.G. Roberts, Director of Military Intelligence, pointed out that Italy was the weakest member of the Axis and that the United Kingdom authorities were engaged in a propaganda campaign trying to promote "sympathy between the Italian people and the British Empire". For this reason "and on humanitarian grounds", Roberts felt that Italian women and children should not be "deprived of the protection of their menfolk" and left in an area that might be over-run by the Japanese. Another major consideration was the panic that might develop among other Australians.[61] The vulnerable area could be placed under martial law "when invasion is immediately imminent". This would allow the GOC to "take drastic action against any section of the people hindering operations, including, if necessary, the execution of participants". For the present time, small detachments of a Security Battalion would act as a deterrent to aliens and restore the confidence of North Queensland residents.

The Minister's recommendations to War Cabinet were closer to those of Military Intelligence than to those of Northern Command and Inspector Carroll. While Cabinet agreed that so many people could not be shifted, it decided that as many of the 7,500 adult males as possible were to be caught up immediately for civilian auxiliary service or for military labour units; extra steps were to be taken to remove as many Germans, male or female, as possible; and all strategic areas such as aerodromes and ports, particularly where American supplies were being unloaded, were to be cleared of all alien elements. "Alien elements" in this context included Jehovah's Witnesses. Forde also recommended that the authorities should "filter through in devious official or unofficial ways" to the remaining alien elements "that the males so caught up" would be held "as guarantees for their good behaviour". He felt that the family sentiment of Italians was strong and would prove "a powerful deterrent against hostile activity". When the military passed over the internment policy file to the newly expanded Security Service in September 1942, the covering letter said that the Aliens Service Regulations removed the need for any intensification of the army's internment policy.[62]

The Advisory War Council also debated the matter having been alarmed by press reports on 8 February 1942 that aliens in Queensland had rifles hidden in the cane fields but when the CIB interviewed the reporter, he would not be specific. The police had collected arms and ammunition from aliens, and the Council decided to wait for a report from Lt-Col. Wake as to whether mass or selective internment was preferable in North Queensland. They also considered the United Kingdom procedure of clearing the vulnerable coastal areas and this would have made the coast from Cooktown to Rockhampton a "protected area", from which aliens were removed.[63] After the War Cabinet meeting had decided on a selective internment policy the explanation of the reasons were passed on to the Advisory War Council. The first two reasons given were the dislocation to economic and social life and the effect on public morale. Mass internment suggested "something approaching a state of panic". The strain on manpower and material in the extra guards and camps needed, and the fact that even the one district that was "critical" enough to warrant mass internment had not been recommended for it by the military, were the other two reasons. Other measures were being used to deal with the alien problem, including a prohibition on aliens having fishing vessels and maps. Internments in Queensland had increased markedly and early in March the Minister's powers over naturalised persons had been delegated to the military authorities in Western Australia and on the 17 April to the Commandant, 1 MD, in order to have any suspect person removed from the vicinity of aerodromes, railway junctions and particularly from ports where American supplies were being unloaded.[64]

Nevertheless, between the cabinet and parliamentary debates in March and the victory in the Battle of the Coral Sea early in May, "Omnibus" warrants were used at least twice more in Queensland. On 3 April, 68 persons were interned, and six days later, 208 were arrested. Many of these internees were detained by order of Brigadier A.M. Forbes.[65] There were plans to extend internment to all commands "in accordance with the policy now in force in Northern Command", and the Deputy Chief of the General Staff, Major-General G.A. Vasey asked each district to indicate what internments would follow if they were given the same powers. The GOC Western Command could already "shape his own internment policy".[66] The Eastern Command area quoted the highest numbers, asking to intern 400 immediately and 2,000 in the event of hostilities on the mainland. Southern Command, through Major-General W. A. Beevor Steele, refused to recommend more than 24 for immediate internment and 200 if hostilities came closer. Steele wrote that every effort was made "to investigate and intern the more suspicious members of the community, whether aliens or otherwise", and while the security position could never be regarded "as being entirely satisfactory" it would be improved when the eligible aliens were "drafted into service". There was "no evidence to show that the number of aliens at liberty in 3 MD" had "an adverse effect on public morale". Major-General A.C. Fewtrell, Base Commandant, Eastern Command had originally recommended 3,000 persons be moved from the area within 100 miles of the New South Wales coast but reduced this to 2,000 from a 50 mile danger area.[67] Without Southern Command's support the proposal foundered. There was a higher level of concern about aliens and people of enemy origin in some states than others.

In the states where anxiety was highest, released internees were reinterned, and others who had not been interned earlier, but who had peripheral associations with fascists, were now interned. The secretary of the Queensland German Club was arrested early in the morning of 21 February 1942. The only additional information against him was a statement by his greengrocer, made nine months earlier, that he had made a pro-Nazi and anti-British remark.[68]

A persistent questioner of internment, G.W. Martens, wrote to Curtin protesting that he had been "astounded to see what was taking place in regard to internments" in North Queensland. The policy of the government was not supposed to be "wholesale internment" but Martens considered that in effect it was. He listed about fifteen residents of the Ingham district whom he could not understand being interned.[69] Some had sons in the AIF and others were young men who had arrived in Australia as babies. A few were members of the VDC. Some had collected and given money for patriotic funds. One had been in Australia since 1907. Naturalised and unnaturalised had been interned "willy-nilly", and their wives and children left to look after the farms. Martens alleged, that "without charge or investigation" these men "were put into carriages with barred windows and taken away for God knows why". He told Curtin that the local police claimed they did not report these men. They said there were some "good Torys (sic)", whom they "would very gladly see taken away", still at large. To a radical Labor man a "Tory" was a right-wing conservative or quasi-fascist. Martens believed the internments to be "nothing short of a criminal thing". He assured Curtin that he would not let the matter rest and concluded that there were people in the north who said all enemy aliens should be interned and "apparently they cut more ice with the Brass Hats and the Military Forces than any other Power".

Martens requested the files of the men on his list from the army.[70] Forde replied that the police had concurred in the internments and the Labor government had "consistently opposed the policy of mass internments" which so many Queenslanders had urged when there was an actual invasion threat.[71] The secretary for the Army recommended that the file not be made available since it dealt with several hundred internees, and would be "of little use", because there were "no particulars furnished in regard to the individual internees". Most of the men were interned on bulk orders on the recommendation of the GOC, Northern Command. Colonel J.D. Rogers reported that the dossiers on the men had been transfered to the Security

Service but in any case it was considered to be undesirable to hand "confidential Army files to Members of Parliament at their request".[72] Martens was then referred to the Attorney-General's Department as it was responsible for the Security Service, and Forde passed the problem over to Dr Evatt.[73]

Who then were the people interned in this period? When war began the most dangerous people were taken immediately — people such as Nazi Party members, suspected saboteurs, members of the enemy's armed forces and criminals. The second group of lists comprised those with access to vital installations and to harbours. These people had been sifted and dealt with by internment or restriction if there was any suspicion attached to them. There were three more lists, loosely labelled C, D and O.[74] The category C lists contained the names of "all leaders and people of influence", category D listed all males of military age, capable of bearing arms, and category O listed the "ordinary harmless people". There were divisions within the category C list; List C-3 contained those judged to have an "anti-British" history and a capacity to influence others. What constituted "anti-British" is unclear. On whatever grounds these people were included as being "anti-British", it had not been convincing enough to persuade Menzies' Army Minister, Percy Spender, or Labor's Attorney-General, Dr Evatt, before his departure overseas, to sign for their internment. During the crisis of June 1940 some category C men were interned but, with Menzies' intervention and the great military victories over the Italian army, internment then ceased. But the lists remained and were reactivated when the "barrier" of Singapore fell. After the enemy aliens who had failed to register were rounded up in February 1942, people from category C and D were collected from the northern coastal districts. The category of "leader" or "person of influence" inevitably involved many naturalised people. They owned land, voted and gave advice to newcomers. They may not have perceived themselves as influential, but the very fact that they knew English and translated for others made them appear influential to observers.

Suggesting names for category C was originally the responsibility of the local police but, as the resources of military intelligence grew, certain men in the northern areas were recruited as military reporting officers.[75] These men were often chosen because their employment made them very knowledgeable about the district and they frequently met the locals in the course of their work. Men such as cane or stock inspectors, fuel agents, carters and businessmen were suitable because their work took them around naturally. They "kept their eyes and ears open" and sometimes actively encouraged the alien-born to discuss politics and the war with them. It became known in some communities that these MRO's would be happy to receive information, and that the informant would have complete protection. In such a situation the opportunity for reports based on malice or self-interest are obvious. In comparison with the Victorian MRO's, there seemed less emphasis on having been a World War I officer and there was a committee approach with a team of MROs and the local police sergeant.

When in February 1942, the Army Minister, Frank Forde, granted the GOC Northern Command the power to intern at his discretion all enemy aliens suspected of "anti-British sentiments", and those having "any degree of influence in the community", he also agreed that detention orders for naturalised people could be held in Northern Command and action could be taken without reference to AHQ in an emergency. Northern Command did not have to make "separate recommendations" for each person, but could merely send "classified lists". This removed the ministerial oversight of orders to intern naturalised or native Australians in Queensland.[76]

A naturalised British subject listed in Category C was Augusto Orlandi.[77] He arrived in Australia to cut cane in the 1925-6 migration boom. After years of work, he and two others from the same area in Italy threw in their lot together to raise the one thousand pounds deposit on a farm. Each man returned to Italy to marry, and later had a family in Australia. They were committed to working together until each family was established. In 1940 their farm was flooded and the son of a neighbour was born in Orlandi's bed because no one was able to get to town. On the night of 4 April 1942, about 9.30 pm, three policemen, one of whom Orlandi recognised, came to his house and told him he had to go. Although Orlandi was concerned for his wife, who had been home only ten days since the birth of his own second son, he packed and went. In the gaol were two other locals of Italian origin with whom he had no common interest. He never considered that the criterion of having "a degree of influence in the community" might have been applied. Almost forty years later his only suggestion as to the reason for his internment was his recollection of a conversation with a well-established businessman in the grounds of a local hotel. The local plan in the event of invasion was to move inland and the businessman asked him his views. Orlandi answered, "But how far do you want to go? Will ten miles be safe? Will twenty miles?" Personally he did not want to leave his farm. Other farmers he knew who came from Northern Italy had survived the Austro-German invasion during the Great War. Orlandi felt it would be better for the family to take its chances and remain on the farm rather than to go rushing off into the bush with a limited food supply.[78]

The files show that Augusto Orlandi was listed as suspicious because a relative in Italy had enquired through the Red Cross about a cousin of Orlandi's in Innisfail who had been interned early in the war. Orlandi had worked for this cousin when he first arrived in Australia, and he insisted that the man was anti-Fascist. He also protested in a conversation with a local policeman that he had resented his treatment by fascist officials on his trip to Italy. The police were not convinced. His cousin must have been under some suspicion to be interned and Orlandi's experiences had not put his two partners off returning and marrying Italians. Although the local police said they had no evidence of anti-British sentiments or activities, they felt that "in common with the greater majority of Italian Nationals residing in the district", Orlandi was "an Italian at heart, and his sentiments, although not openly expressed" were "definitely with his native land".[79] Orlandi was unaware that he was also reported on by Military Intelligence's informant TR39. According to TR39 Orlandi was not "sufficiently open" in his anti-British sentiments for any one to declare against him. TR39 understood that a group including Orlandi had been overheard to say that TR39 "would be fixed up if ever their side came out on top", but TR39 could not "get even first hand knowledge of the exact truth of this statement".

Ex-internees from other sugar districts also have their theories about why they were interned. Some feel there was a boundary, that is, all the farmers up to a certain creek were taken, or those in strategic areas such as near sugar mills or on evacuation routes. Some talk of photographs taken when an Italian warship had visited Cairns some years before. Farmers suspected neighbours hoping to take over abandoned farms, while local returned soldiers and freemasons were most widely suspected by ex-internees of making reports against them. A few cane cutters put their inclusion down to attending a meeting protesting against the introduction of labour conscription. Other internees speak of more personal reasons, such as competition with a local policeman over a particular woman, disputes with authorities over other matters, and personality clashes.[80] Some internees after forty years reflection believe that powerful pressure groups forced the government's hand until it became "politically desirable" to intern a significant number.[81] Senator J.I. Armstrong expressed the view in 1950 that, "We all know how the security service worked in North Queensland. My opinion is that a list of Italian canegrowers was compiled and almost every second man named on it was interned".[82] Australian neighbours and townspeople also have views as to why these internees were taken. A number of Australians accept that their neighbours were taken because they were enemy aliens and there was a war on. The issue of naturalisation is rejected as irrelevant. Many thought it was a good thing in principle, but were surprised at their particular neighbour being taken.[83]

Fred Paterson, the Communist member for the Queensland seat of Bowen, that covered the area including Ingham, Home Hill and Ayr, pushed the point of biased internment at the end of the war. In November 1945 he expressed dissatisfaction with the way police had reported on Italians applying for naturalisation and claimed these reports were later used to determine whether men were interned. Paterson referred to the case of the Ingham bootmaker who had left Italy because he was a bitter opponent of Fascism and yet who was interned when some pro-fascists were not. Another Italian, Tardiani was charged in 1931 with assaulting the Italian consul and stealing his Fascist badge. In his evidence the Consul had sworn that Tardiani was an anti-fascist, but Tardiani was one of the first Italians to be interned. Paterson wanted an inquiry into whether any member of the police force had favoured Fascists in recommendations for naturalisation and internments.[84] Paterson could have been correct in suggesting that conservative Italians were more acceptable to the police than radicals, but when Italy first entered the war the Soviet Union had a pact with Germany and active communists were regarded as subversive, and the difference between an active anti-fascist and a communist were not always understood. In any case any history of violence or a police record was a strong contribution to a case for internment.

Many of the men Martens had enquired about, and others such as Orlandi, were interned "on bulk orders signed by the Minister" and these lists were concurred in and sometimes even supplied by the police. On 14 March 1942, Military Intelligence, Brisbane received a letter from Commissioner Carroll enclosing a list supplied by the Inspector of Police, Townsville, giving the names of naturalised British subjects of enemy origin in his district and recommending some for internment.[85] The Inspector of Police at Townsville had sent this list in response to a request from Carroll. The men marked for internment were those it was considered would assist the enemy "if a favourable opportunity offered".

In the early stages of the war the local police had been far from arbitrary in their recommendations for internment but this changed in 1942. Even policemen were affected by the pressures of a war coming closer and closer to the Australian mainland. On 22 February 1942 the sub-Inspector of Police at Innisfail compiled a list of 24 naturalised British subjects and five others and transmitted it south, urging that those listed be interned. He acknowledged that this list differed from previous lists because it included nineteen who had never had a report made about them. They were living at Daradee, Garradunga and Innisfail and despite the fact that no report existed on them, they were now "under strong suspicion regarding their loyalty". Now that the war had "definitely reached Australia" the policeman considered that these men were "more than likely to be a danger to the prosecution of the war", and were "a definite danger to be at large, particularly in North Queensland". Because of the war position, he recommended their immediate internment.[86] Five naturalised British subjects of Italian origin and one of German origin on the list were marked as having been "kept under particular observation" and having had their premises searched. Nothing incriminating had been found or observed. Two-thirds of those on the list had neither been reported on, nor observed nor searched and the majority were naturalised. When the earlier strict adherence to ministerial oversight was practised it would have needed some evidence before these men would have had detention orders signed against them, but now this policeman was recommending that men be interned on suspicion unsupported by evidence. His superiors and the minister concurred.

As internment escalated, even lower levels of security risk

were scooped up. The war situation was critical as Japanese troopships rounded New Guinea just prior to the Battle of the Coral Sea. Inspector Carroll recommended internment for the remainder of men on the list sent from Townsville, that is, even those not marked as being prepared to help the enemy.[87] At the same time he telegraphed that all men of enemy origin aged between 20 and 60 years and living in the Cairns district, were to be interned. All persons of German nationality were also removed. With the extension of internment into the category D Italian group, and with most Germans and all Japanese taken, a state of total internment was approached. Arrested at Mourilyan when this category D "men of military age" list was implemented, was Bruno Agricola.[88] Bruno had come to Australia as a child and his father was naturalised and a cane farm owner. When Bruno turned 21 he registered for the electoral roll, was accepted and voted. His father died just at the outbreak of war, and in the process of executing the will that left the farm equally to Bruno, his sister and his mother, some question arose about the nationality status of the family. When the mother wrote away about it, the official verdict was that the mother was deemed to be naturalised by virtue of the father's naturalisation certificate. His sister was now married to a naturalised man and was covered by her husband's certificate, but Bruno was not covered. He immediately began proceedings for his own naturalisation but was told that there was a moratorium on naturalising people of enemy origin for the time being. Thus Bruno, who for 20 years had considered himself an Australian, and as a primary producer was in a reserved occupation, became an enemy alien living in a coastal area towards which the Japanese could well be heading.

By the time the Allies confirmed that they had won a strategic victory in the Battle of the Coral Sea, over 3,000 of the 6,968 male aliens registered in Queensland, or 43 per cent,[89] were interned and thousands of others were incorporated into the labour battalions. Jessie Street, Richard Hall and G.W. Martens could find plenty of evidence for their claims of unreasonable and arbitrary internments at this time, but Mr Justice Reed from South Australia was of the opinion that when an invasion "was very much feared, prudence dictated that many men should be interned on what was more or less a remote possibility that they might do some damage or act in a subversive way".[90] It was impossible to know, Reed concluded, if this fear had any basis, as "the internment of large numbers, particularly in Queensland, in any event prevented attempts on a large scale". In Reed's view the precautionary internments during this crisis time was justified even if only on the grounds of removing a potentially cooperative workforce from the enemy. If the Axis forces had landed, and the Italians had an opportunity of joining up with them, the position might have been very serious, in Reed's opinion, for the chief risk about the majority of Italians was that, when "in numbers" and "not likely to have to do any real fighting", they would do as they were told by anyone in authority over them.

Such a justification was precisely the view of those in control of internment in Queensland during the crisis period. The Premier, W. Forgan-Smith, the GOC Northern Command, Major-General J.M.A. Durrant, and the Police Commissioner, Inspector C.J. Carroll, had asked in January 1942 for a policy that would remove those of enemy origin from the north-east coast of their state. This policy was also demanded by a large number of Queensland citizens and was allowed to happen by a Minister for the Army, who saw his role as acting on the advice of those responsible for intelligence and not of judging the evidence. Perceptions of security reached to a level where "non-British" virtually equated "potential enemy labourer" and an unacceptable risk.

Chapter Eight

CAMP LIFE

In January 1943 a total of 16,830 prisoners-of-war and internees were detained in Australia. Of these 9,000 were civilians and the remainder predominantly Italian soldiers captured in North Africa. When Rommel's advance in the western desert in 1941 posed a threat to Egypt, the Australian War Cabinet agreed to take 2,000 of the POWs then held there, raising the offer to 50,000 in May 1941, when the situation became desperate, but shipping difficulties kept the number well below this figure. The first group of Italian POWs were sent to Camps 7 and 8 at Hay, and the *Dunera* internees were moved to Tatura and Loveday to make room for them. To accommodate the army of POWs who were to follow, further camps were planned for Murchison and Myrtleford in Victoria, and Hay and Cowra in New South Wales. These camps cost the British government £666,000 in capital outlay and 7s a day per prisoner. In July 1941 the *Queen Mary* brought Italian POWs to Sydney, via Colombo and Fremantle, and from Sydney they travelled by train to Murchison where they lived under tents for some months.[1]

Almost one thousand locally interned Italians were also moved from Hay to Loveday to clear the camps for the POWs, and they arrived there on 11 and 12 June 1941. They were placed in Camp 9 and became the responsibility of Major A. Dick, six officers and 116 guards from the 4th Garrison Battalion.[2] Many of the *Dunera* internees sent to Loveday were soon returned to the eastern states "as most had volunteered for and been accepted as members of British Pioneer Battalions".[3] Major Layton had embarked the first large group of British internees on the *Largs Bay* in May 1941 and the last large group left in July 1942.[4] By the end of 1943 Layton had arranged for 1,148 to return to the UK. The camp they had occupied, No. 10, remained a German-speaking one with Germans from Tatura, and a mixture of locally interned and overseas internees, including men from the Persian Gulf campaign, being housed there. Camps 9 and 10 were built in the rectangular pattern used for the early camps, but the authorities were convinced that the new octagonal design with four compounds would be more appropriate for the Japanese internees.[5] Thus Camp 14 was built with a large broadway dividing the compounds each of which had a capacity to hold one thousand and a guard establishment four times that of Camp 9.

Compound 14B was first occupied when 50 Japanese from Adelaide River in the Northern Territory came in on 5 January 1942. Germans and Italians went into Compound 14D, and Compound 14C took the NEI Japanese, many of whom were inexplicably repatriated in an exchange in August the same year. By the end of February, 115 Italian internees from Gaythorne had moved into Compound 14A and altogether the Loveday group held almost 4,000 internees.[6] In the first part of 1942 the atmosphere was tense, and the guards were doubled because of fog and the restlessness of some internees buoyed up by the Japanese military successes. On 30 April a tunnel was discovered in Camp 10. The German-speaking internees had dug it from within the compound to under the perimeter wire and its discovery prevented a mass escape. In the excitement a few internees were bayoneted.[7] No one was seriously hurt and the Official Visitor considered that a show of force was necessary to convince some internees that the guards meant business.

Throughout the year of large round ups, locally interned Italians and Germans moved through the staging camps to Loveday. As the numbers grew, two wood-camps, Moorook West and Woolenook, were opened up.[8] Here internees chopped wood for camp use and for sale to the Murray River pumping stations. The Group headquarters were originally in Camp 9 but by June 1942 the Camp Commandant, Lieutenant-Colonel E.T. Dean and the administrative staff moved to a new site between Camps 9 and 10. Dean, like the Tatura and Hay commandants, Tackaberry and Thane, was a World War I veteran.[9] Born in 1884, Dean joined the First AIF in September 1915. He commanded the 1st Australian Field Artillery Brigade. Wounded in June 1917, he rejoined after three months and was promoted to Lieutenant-Colonel soon after. He had to be evacuated with influenza and debility in June 1918 but rejoined from hospital in the crucial month of August. At war's end, he returned to his home on Karinga Station, near Angaston, SA. At the age of 56, this pastoralist had been recalled to take charge of the internment complex near the Murray. Internee numbers continued to increase until in November it was decided to form the 33rd Garrison Battalion, and house it in tents at the western end of Camp 14.[10] Lt-Col. Dean remained Group Commandant, and Lt-Col. R. Soden took charge of the 33rd Battalion and the administration of the four Camp 14 compounds just as almost 500 Italians from Western Command arrived and moved into compounds 14A and 14D.

Fantin's death

The sudden uprooting of Western Australian internees from Harvey was due to the discovery of large numbers of weapons concealed in the camp. Razors, sticks, knives, tomahawks and a clip of bullets were among the collection.[11] A Court of Enquiry was held into the administration of Harvey and it considered the Commandant had neglected to carry out the stipulated security measures.[12] He was removed from command and placed on the Reserve of Officers and the internees were moved first to Parkeston, near Kalgoorlie, and then to Loveday. Their arrival precipitated a politically motivated murder. Political divisions between internees had increased with the injection of the mass round-up internees, and compound 14D in particular was a very mixed camp with almost thirty nationalities detained at various times.[13] It held some of Britain's anti-Nazi internees, some Jews and some Italian anti-Fascists, as well as pro-German loyalists and others. The anti-Fascists began a subscription list to send aid to Russia,[14] and when the news of the group's collection reached 14A the tensions between internees peaked. On 16 November Francesco Fantin, an Anarchist, who had been the subject of earlier attacks, was set upon by Giovanni Casotti, a W.A. internee. Casotti claimed that he pushed Fantin in the course of an argument and he fell and hit his head on the wooden upright supporting the water tap, but some witnesses said Casotti hit Fantin with a wooden stick and kicked him when he was on the ground. Casotti did not admit his involvement until three days after Fantin's death, and pleaded it was an accident. He was charged with murder but such a charge raised potentially embarrassing questions about the competence of the army's administration of camps, and of an internment policy that forced Fascists and anti-Fascists to be put in the same camp.[15]

The charge was reduced to manslaughter and the trial was held in Adelaide on 19 March 1943 before Mr Justice Richards. Casotti was found guilty of manslaughter and sentenced to two years hard labour in a civilian prison. Fantin's death was undoubtedly an embarrassment to the camp administration. It is ignored altogether in the published history of Loveday, which only mentions the arrival of the Western Australian internees on 3 November 1942 and the baking of the first loaves of bread in the group's new bakery on 18 November. But mentioned, without explanation, is the fact that on 6 January 1943 the 33rd Garrison Battalion ceased to function as a separate unit, and "the complete control of all camps" came back to Dean.[16]

Fantin had been interned in November 1940 on the basis of a police report that he was "a very militant Fascist". An informant, a British subject, had stated that Fantin "had openly expressed hatred for the British and England", having allegedly said he would rather employ a Hindu or Afghan "than a bloody Britisher". The Brisbane security officer, Commander J.C. McFarlane was inclined to believe the informant because he had given information on several other people that had proved correct. Fantin's objection was heard in Brisbane on 20 March 1942 and leave to appeal was refused. McFarlane conceded on 8 December that the evidence on Fantin's political opinions was conflicting. Fantin was anti-Fascist but he was also an anarchist. Anarchists were regarded as being as opposed to democracy, as they were to totalitarianism, and if Fantin were to be released McFarlane wanted him restricted to the southern states.[17] While Brigadier Simpson was reviewing his case, Fantin was killed. The Labor government received many protests about Fantin's death and the holding of left-wing internees as an apparently unprotectable minority in camps with Fascists.[18] The solution, segregated camps, was not possible because on 15 May 1943 Loveday held its maximum number of 5,382 internees.[19] Nor were the national loyalists or politically neutral internees satisfied with the camp arrangement; in December 1942 a German national complained to the Swiss Consul that loyal Germans were compelled to share the camp with hostile elements such as "communists, Jews, half-Jews and others" who gave aid to Russia. In the confined space, confrontations could flare up and bystanders easily hurt. A number of North Queensland internees remembered that old scores were settled in camp with unscrupulous real estate agents and unsympathetic money lenders being prime targets.[20]

Pressures

It was almost impossible to find solitude and tranquillity in the crowded camps. All camp life was rough and uncomfortable even for the young and fit, and it was considerably less palatable for the middle-aged. It may be lonely for soldiers joining their first units, but the discipline, training and belief in a common cause usually create bonds of purpose and comradeship, and there are periods of home and recreational leave. Life in an internment camp lacked all these compensations, and individual stress often developed into depression. Doctors interned at Hay wrote in late 1940 that there was a growing danger of mental breakdowns.[21] Internees had, within a few years, "suffered shock after shock, starting with their persecution in and their expulsion from Nazi-Germany, followed by their sudden internment in England, the separation from their families, the unexpected shock of the *Dunera* experience, and culminating in the seclusion behind barbed wires in this remote district". Some had, "from sheer desperation", fallen prey to mental diseases. Others were "on the verge of a mental collapse".

Emery Barcs observed that when his group received news that one of them was to be denied the right to appeal, some "seemed to be heading for a nervous breakdown". They banged the table, screamed and shouted until they discovered they were not the person concerned and then they became rational and lucid again, but the one actually involved was so close to madness that the group felt it likely he would kill himself.[22] In his report on the Tatura camps in April 1941, the representative of the International Red Cross, Dr G. Morel, mentioned that the internees of Section D of Camp 3 wanted regular paid work for it would have "a great medical effect" as "an antidote for nervous depression, mental sickness and sexual perversity". The Loveday OVs received a complaint that there was homosexuality in the camp, but felt there was "very little, if anything," that could be done about it.[23]

The only common bond among internees was the fact of incarceration. Apart from a few hours spent on rostered camp duties, the remainder of the day was broken only by the two roll-calls. There was little space between the huts, and even less within them, for activities. Men spent hours talking, but conversations were often guarded for fear of informers who would convey comments to the internal camp power clique or to the Australian authorities. Charles Willyan, a 64-year-old Australian of Welsh parents, interned in 1942, wrote that he was approached shortly after his arrival at Camp 1A Tatura "by a very cordial Australian internee with a disarming 'comrades in adversity' air, and a line of patter inviting reciprocal confidences".[24] He filled the man's head with such fabrications that camp Intelligence called him in. Later he saw an internee leader demand the removal of a detected spy within an hour, backed by the threat that otherwise "he would be thrown over the fence in pieces". Gus Orlandi told a chatty man standing beside him as they were watching the Italian internees playing a hard game of soccer that it was ridiculous to have "the best workers in the world" spending their energies in camp with the country desperately short of manpower, only to discover later that he was talking to an Intelligence Officer.[25] The Australia First leader, Stephensen, refused to speak to von Skerst at Liverpool for 21 months, even though they sat at the same table, because he suspected the authorities were using Skerst in the hope of obtaining information. Stephensen was confronted by Major Hill at Loveday, the morning after an internees' meeting, with quotes from his own speech.[26] The crashing bores who desperately regaled anyone who would listen with a catechism of their woes were also to be avoided.

Each man suffered his own private hell. Tensions, frustrations and worries had untold hours to build up and personality clashes and petty irritations were inevitable. On rare occasions internees attempted suicide. The first successful suicide among the Italians at Loveday occurred on 1 January 1942. Those who suffered nervous breakdowns were sent to mental institutions.[27] Most internee anxieties centred on concern for their families' economic vulnerability, conjugal fidelity or physical safety. For a long time money could not be transfered to Italy and enquiries about a restoration of financial transactions with Italy were constantly directed to the Swiss Consul and to Australian authorities.[28] Dependent wives and children living in Australia were eligible for sustenance from the beginning of the war. On 29 April 1941 de facto wives, other dependents, female crew members and other enemy aliens whose employment or business disappeared because of National Security regulations, became eligible for sustenance also. The Army Pay office in Brisbane recorded that five and a half thousand pounds were paid to the Queensland government for the period 1 April to 30 June 1942. This went to 523 dependent wives and 877 children of internees.[29]

A strong element in a few breakdowns was the psychological inability to accept prisoner status and its dehumanising treatment, lack of individual consideration and above all, its connotations of criminality. The overwhelming majority of internees had never been in gaol before. The first night they spent in the local cell was a traumatic experience. Most country gaols seldom housed anyone but local drunks. Oswald Bonutto wrote of his experience in the Warwick watch-house with five other men arrested at the same time:

> There were no mattresses, palliasses or beds of any description, only some straw and two filthy blankets each, which undoubtedly had been used by drunks and had not been washed afterwards. They had a foul smell of stale liquor and something worse . . . That particular night the temperature was well below freezing point. We spread the straw on the cement floor as evenly as we could . . . and there we spent our first night in jail like drunks or ordinary felons, punished before we were even charged or convicted. Sleep would not come, so we kept talking and tossing about all night. I could hear the Warwick Town Hall clock striking every hour. The night was an eternity.

When Bonutto complained about the "pigsty" of a cell the police sergeant protested that there was nothing better to hand as "this situation was so unexpected". He was able to find some clean blankets and some more straw for the second night.[30]

In the summer of 1941-2 Emery Barcs found the small police cell at Kingsford Police Station, Sydney no better:

> The whitewashed walls and the cement floor looked clean enough, but a penetrating smell polluted the air. Behind a low brick partition a WC out of order explained the stench. A couple of small bedboards stood propped against the wall. I laid one down, sat on it, lit my pipe, and laughed nervously.
>
> I sat there for perhaps half-an-hour, when the door creaked and a young man . . . entered. He glanced at me apprehensively . . .
>
> He takes me for a pickpocket I thought . . . two middle-aged men

joined us and a policeman threw us a bundle of blankets. We didn't need them, for the animal warmth of five bodies turned the small, airless cell into a suffocating hot-box . . .

Soon the fleas which inhabited the blankets were feasting on our blood and, as there was no chance of sleeping, we talked.[31]

On the journey to camp men were confused and anxious and, once at camp, the regimentation began. All their correspondence was prefixed with their number, and sometimes even their huts were allocated by their number. Camp rules were explained as soon as they arrived, and they and their luggage were searched. The most contentious item removed from internees were razor blades and arguments over whether they should be allowed were conducted through the International Red Cross.[32] After the first meal the camp commandant often spoke to large groups explaining the rules and assuring the intake of correct treatment and requiring the internees' cooperation. When individuals joined established camps they were handed over to the internal camp leader for allocation of huts and introduction to rules and regulations. The commandant's speech was often translated by the camp interpreters and included the standard warning to keep three yards back from the wire or the guards would have no option but to shoot.[33] However, no internee was shot by guards and those who died in camps were mainly Japanese with malaria or the complaints of old age.[34] Barcs found his induction speech at Liverpool most candid: "Captain B. delivered a short and (to us) surprising speech. He pointed out that things might not be up to standard, the food could be better and more plentiful, but we newcomers had arrived unexpectedly and the military authorities had no time to supply additional rations. He asked us to be patient, for in a few days the situation would improve. Then he warned us not to pilfer the new tomatoes from the vegetable garden at the end of the camp, because 'everyone would receive some' ".[35]

Shortly after arrival at camp internees were usually given the form on which they could lodge their objection.[36] Some only appealed when prompted,[37] a few claim they never knew they could[38] and merchant seamen, who were interned because they refused to work ships, did not try to obtain release.[39] Most internees did make some attempt to get released and while hopes of an early release were high, camp life was tolerated impatiently and many refused to join in the activities established to relieve the boredom. But when delay followed delay it became harder to ignore the fact that the weekly letter, the occasional parcel, and elementary camp routine were going to be the whole of one's life for longer than expected. Men coped with this realisation and came to terms with their environment and their fellow internees in a variety of ways. Some men gave loyal and professional service to the camp school, and built it up to a high standard from which university entrance was possible, while others worked consistently on musical activities and entertainments. Two notable camp teachers were Hans Lindau and Father Konig.[40]

Another busy minority were the camp "executives". Each compound had a camp executive group comprising a Camp Leader and a Deputy, a Secretary, Quartermaster, Banker, Librarian, Canteen Supervisor, Works Manager and one Hut Leader from each sleeping hut. They met frequently to administer the compound's affairs. It was this group's "ready co-operation" that made the smooth running of the compound possible.[41] While these were full time jobs, and sought for this reason and for the status they gave,[42] they were available only to a fraction of the inmates. Those internees with special knowledge or skill gave occasional lectures and those with a good command of English tutored the many internees anxious to improve their own. Many men also used the opportunity to improve their literacy in their own language. But while time hung heavily, many men could not settle to serious study. Sports were organised and were a useful temporary outlet. The fact was that many internees really missed steady work. Lt-Col. Dean at Loveday saw the need to satisfy this lack, as crucial to camp harmony and morale.[43] The question of payment was a problem, but even before the one shilling a day rate was agreed to, Dean found enough Italian internees at No. 9 Camp on 16 June 1941 to begin work without payment on projects outside the compound.[44] Payment of a shilling a day was sanctioned a month later.

Some Italians took the view that any work was indirectly giving assistance to the national enemy and refused to take part, but, after the military collapse of Italy in 1943, there was a rush to volunteer for work. The few who still considered it unpatriotic formed a "True Italian Movement", but it folded when the commandant gave instructions that it was to cease operation, although for some months afterwards security was convinced that the group in one hut were actively dissuading Italians from joining the Allied Works Council.[45] The threat that they were alleged to use was that they would tell the Swiss Consul that the volunteer was not a loyal Italian and recommend that he not be allowed back into Italy after the war. The Swiss Consul refused to co-operate, and his representative to Loveday, Mr E. Brack, offered his opinion that internees should work to fit themselves for earning a living outside and that while they did not work on munitions, fortifications or transport, they would not be acting against Italy's national interest.[46] The hard-liners still refused to work, but they were so few that their influence was minimal.

Some naturalised Italians felt it was undignified to work because it meant identification with foreign nationals and because there were so many indigent internees who needed the money desperately. Gus Orlandi did not work for this reason. Like many naturalised citizens with some means he was sent the maximum allowed, five pounds per week, from home. The majority of Italians did labour within the compound on their own vegetable plots; they also worked outside the compound on camp projects, and when the opportunity to join the Allied Works Council arrived, they enlisted. Thane and Dean correctly assessed that the need to work was almost integrated into the personality of the recently-arrived Italians who formed the bulk of the early Hay and Loveday camps, and that farming in particular appealed to them.[47]

The Germans were regarded as too great a security risk to be offered work outside the camp until very late in the war, but even then many Germans felt it was totally unacceptable as a matter of principle.[48] The delay in offering work to Germans meant that destitute internees who might have wanted to stay neutral were forced by economic necessity to accept the German government's *Reichgulde* pocket money which carried the understanding that the recipient would be loyal to Germany and seek repatriation to no other country at the end of the war.[49] As the earliest German internees were those aligned with the Nazi Party and who had established themselves as the internal power clique of Camp 1, Tatura, and Camp 10, Loveday,[50] it took a strong-minded individual to reject the pocket money and the commitment to Hitler's Germany that went with it.[51] For those who found the prospect of social ostracism — or worse — too daunting, the safest thing was to go along with the

established group. Welfare workers who visited a youth referred to them by the Student Christian Movement, found him
delighted to see them on their first visit. He was much more
reserved on their second visit, and refused to see them at all
when they came the third time. The visitors were surprised,[52]
but the youth had to make his own judgement as to whether his
best interests were served by a one-hour visit a month from
people regarded as enemies by his fellow internees, with whom
he had to interact every day.

Camp organisation

The style of camp organisation adopted by the military tended
at times to assist the more extreme political activists to gain
power,[53] but some form of a hierarchical system had to operate.
It was the practice in prisoner-of-war camps to leave internal
organisation and discipline to the ranking officers, and with the
shortage of staff in the Garrison there was practically no alternative for internment camps. Camp leaders, chosen by various
methods ranging from a quick show of hands to a full-scale
election, had more and more administrative work devolved on
them. The choice mainly fell on those who were socially and
intellectually prominent, because they were willing to stand
and because the electorate chose to reproduce the external
social structures with which they were familiar. Men like Prince
del Drago, who was camp leader of the Italians at Hay and
Camp 9, Loveday, and von Graf, a German leader at Loveday,
exemplify the deference to social status. Doctors, such as J.H.
Becker and M. Piscitelli were compound leaders, and lawyers
were also frequently chosen. The articulate Oswald Bonutto
was a compound leader, and the journalist Emery Barcs was the
first spokesman for the Hungarians. Men with good educational background had the advantage of being able to perform
the administrative tasks and were frequently literate in more
than one language, so negotiations with camp authorities could
be carried on directly. This pattern of deference to higher status
men was similar in Canada where the grandson of Kaiser
Wilhelm II was the camp leader at Farnham, Quebec, and the
intellectual, Heinz Arnt, was his deputy.[54]
The compound leaders reported to the orderly room every
day. They met camp commandants when specific problems
arose, and some camps had scheduled meetings. The Official

Visitor, and the representatives of the Protecting Power and the Red Cross dealt directly with camp leaders, as did the welfare officers appointed by the YMCA, the refugee organisations and the Society of Friends. Often camp leaders wrote letters on behalf of internees and they were frequently asked for advice. They wrote references for those seeking work outside. A few naturalised Australians who were Justices of the Peace also assisted by witnessing documents until the authorities decided this was inappropriate and had their commissions withdrawn.[55]

Outward mail for censorship and inward mail and parcels passed through the camp leader's office. At Gaythorne the practice of hut leaders collecting mail and delivering it to the sergeant of the Guard led to a complaint that some internees were being intimidated by having their mail held and read by camp leaders.[56] Although the GOC, Northern Command, considered there was no opportunity for abuse, the system was frowned on by AHQ. Other responsibilities of the camp leader, such as rostering camp duties, allocating huts and negotiating with outside representatives gave the camp leader considerable authority and this was usually backed by Australian authorities. Camp leaders could punish internees who offended against camp rules, failed to perform their duties or who were insolent to the camp leader. In one case, at Harvey Camp, the commandant sanctioned a more severe punishment for an internee who was insolent to the camp leader than to one who insulted a guard.[57] All punishments issued by the camp leader were supposed to be reported to the guard officer but this could not be guaranteed. In exchange for this delegated authority, the camp leader had to run an orderly camp.

While it is obvious that the camp leaders had the opportunity to use political influence and to indulge in personal discrimination, they also had to spend a lot of time on paperwork and in enforcing hygiene rules. Because cleanliness was so important, the cook and the sanitary workers were always paid. All other camp work was not paid and was rostered. Loewald recorded his camp duties:

> The highest salary was 3s 6d a week earned by the greasetrap cleaners and the latrine party members . . . I held a variety of positions, beginning as a night watchman . . . it was our duty to prevent the elderly whom the weakness of their bladders drove out of bed at night from emptying them against the huts, to watch for possible

fires, and to wake first the stokers and kitchen staff, and then at 6.15 the entire camp for the first roll-call. We ran two-man, two-hour shifts beginning at 11 p.m. and obtained small extra rations for them from the kitchen.[58]

This was the more typical experience of the majority of internees for, while camps did have some "quality" dramatic and musical performances and some calming religious influences, camps were basically rough and ready places where good order had to be enforced.

Order was not as hard to maintain in some camps as in others. The Japanese were orderly, even submissive, and in the Tatura family camps internees tried to reproduce suburbia by planting flowers around the front steps, providing a good school and keeping up cultural and religious observances. Many internees were not reunited with their families until later in their internment, and then the threat of being returned to the all-male camps in the outback was a powerful one. One of the strongest complaints from the family camp came when the authorities decided to withdraw hygienic towel pads from the free-supply list and put them in the canteen.[59] This is not to suggest that the family camps were politically neutral or indifferent; they were frequently blatantly patriotic in an effort to maintain the children's affinity with the homeland and culture. They were orderly because they were a more sedate group than some of the single-sex compounds. By contrast many of the men in the Loveday camps were from occupations characterised by hard work and hard living. Seamen, charcoal burners, fishermen and miners were used to settling their arguments with their fists, and mothers of boys in the family camps were fearful when their sons became too old to stay and were transfered to Loveday.[60] The roughness did not develop at the family camp, where Ethel Punshon took the Japanese women and children to picnics at the Waranga Dam. Because they would spread out and were slow to hear her shouts when it was time to pack up, one of the guards made her a tin whistle at the camp workshop, and its piercing summons could not be ignored. The interned Japanese acrobats from Wirth's Circus always provided a professional finale to camp concerts.[61]

The rough and ready atmosphere at Loveday was exacerbated when the Italians went out to pick grapes and illicit stills began to operate, and as the older "Digger" guards were replaced by less responsible younger men who were not averse to smuggling in contraband. Gambling was a more popular recreation among the hard-nosed inmates of Loveday than the callisthenics, libraries and concerts of the earlier camps. Fortunately, Dean's persistence against "political indifference which amounted almost to opposition" resulted in the first 2-acre vegetable plot being expanded into 440 acres of cultivated land. Loveday had an initial advantage because it stood in an area that had been a World War I soldier settlement and was reticulated with underground pipes which were fully maintained. Development was never extensive until the cheap labour of the internees made possible a variety of projects, including growing experimental crops of opium poppies for morphine, pyrethrum for insecticides and the Mexican guayule shrub for the production of rubber. In establishing these projects and the internal workshops which were eventually to produce one hundred thousand pounds worth of produce and forty-one thousand pounds in net accumulated profit, Dean's problems paralleled Thane's in the early days of Hay.[62]

At first supplies of stores and equipment for Loveday were difficult to obtain in sufficient quantities to fulfil initial entitlements and replacements were equally hard to get. Clothing and necessaries for average-sized men eventually became adequate but non-standard sizes were always in short supply. There was great difficulty obtaining bread from local contractors as the camp numbers grew, so two large ovens, each capable of holding 380 loaves, were installed in a field bakery, at which young army bakers were trained.[63] The huts in Camps 9 and 10 were originally built with bunks down the centre but these were unsatisfactory "and were replaced by beds". These wooden beds were made by internees in the workshops and provided to all "Europeans". The huge hot-water systems that serviced the ablution blocks were fired by wood cut by internees.

The Official Visitors to Loveday were K.V.F. Sanderson, KC, and W.V. Ray. Sanderson, in particular, took his role very seriously. He warned that the influx of Western Australians into camp 14D Loveday had caused "turmoil" and predicted bloodshed if the different groups were not segregated.[64] He also scrutinised the physical condition of the camps and listened to individual internees problems. He strongly criticised anything he felt was not up to standard or showed a lack of humanity. The lack of fly-proofing in the kitchen and mess huts in Camp 9 brought a protest. When the Group Engineer replied that the flies could be dealt with by "liberal applications of fly spray and swats", Sanderson retorted that using large quantities of kerosene-based spray near food was wasteful and impractical and "would probably lead to contamination".[65] Sanderson also criticised the camp administration for some things over which they had little control. One internee had gone blind and, in all humanity, it seemed reasonable to release him, but these decisions were for tribunals or the Security Service, which in late 1941 was only a minuscule organisation, newly given the responsibility for internment. Another major complaint was misplacement of internees' property and long delays in transfering their money. The property confiscated from the *Romolo*'s crew in June 1940 had not been accounted for by October 1941, and an internee arrested in Tangool, Qld, on 11 June 1940 had no word of two trunks of clothing and tools taken from him at the police station, despite 15 months having elapsed and Mr Justice Davidson's enquiries in March 1941 when the internee was at Hay. Sanderson gave examples of inordinate delays in transfering money from other camps to Loveday, and he was clearly sympathetic with the internees who had to go without the small comforts provided by the canteen, not because they could not afford them, but because their money had not come through. He often punctuated his list of complaints by individuals with sarcastic comments of his own: if "the administration of internees affairs could be raised to the standard of the average Government Department", it would not be asking much, most internees' complaints would disappear and "it would save the Official Visitor a good deal of exasperation and wasted time".[66]

Loveday officers defended themselves against Sanderson's barbs. They were disappointed that the internees had not confided their problems to the camp staff instead of bottling it up for the Official Visitor.[67] There appears to have been a degree of mistrust between the Italians and the original Camp 9 commander. In May 1942 the Camp 9 internees were so bitter about the extreme and sudden censorship of newspapers that they went on strike and ceased working outside the compound.[68] The Camp Commandant also decided to ban the singing of the Italian National Anthem, and the organiser of a concert which ended with the singing of the "Giovinezza" was put in the cells for 28 days, the maximum allowed under the regulations. Brigadier Bundock, Commandant, SA L of C Area, made some transfers[69] that apparently improved matters. When the OVs made their final report in 1942, they wrote that co-operation between the compound leader and the new commandant, Major Hill, "appeared to be excellent".[70]

Sanderson did acknowledge later that many problems were the result of incompetence in "one or more camps in the eastern States" and that the Loveday administration had been "conscientious and painstaking". Most of the justifiable complaints were due to understaffing, particularly in the Paymaster's branch. Nevertheless, Sanderson never pulled his punches and he warned the military that they could expect much more trouble from the Germans if their affairs were not handled more expeditiously than those of the Italians had been. For a time the Germans in camp 10 remained aloof from the Official Visitor, apparently content to use direct negotiations with the camp authorities and to deal with the Protecting Power and the Red Cross. In assessing the roles of the various authorities, Lt-Col. Dean was of the opinion that at times the Official Visitors and the International Red Cross usurped the prerogative of the Protecting Power," thereby causing duplication of work".[71] He may well have also wished for a less biting Official Visitor.

Conditions at Camp 9 obviously improved. When Sanderson made a subsequent visit on 14 and 15 July 1942, the Internees' Representative had "no question of outstanding urgency or importance" and there were only the individual complaints. By this time the inmates of Camp 10 had decided to accept visits from the Official Visitor, and the pattern of problems was similar. Internees had binoculars and cameras taken from them in February 1942, and they had no receipts for them or definite word of whether they had been impressed or not. A group of 18 Hungarians brought to Australia from Basra on the *Rohua* had their money taken from them on board, and it had not arrived at Loveday, leaving the group destitute as the Hungarian government did not provide their nationals with pocket money. Internees from Suez, Palestine, Egypt, and Iraq were still awaiting the balance of their money. Tobacco supplies to the canteen were irregular. The transfer of two particular men believed to be anti-Fascists from Camp 14D to Camp 10 was brought up, and Sanderson "received the clearest possible warning from the German Leader that these two men were likely to be ill-treated if they were left in Camp 10". Sanderson spoke to Lt-Col. Dean and he arranged for one to return to 14D, but the other chose "to run the risk of staying with the Nazis". Overall, Sanderson was pleased with the situation in Camp 10. Morale was "excellent" and, although the camp held the "most potentially troublesome elements" in the Loveday group, there was "practically no sign of ill-will on the part of the internees, and a minimum of friction between them and the staff". Sanderson considered that it was Lt-Col. Soden's "exercise of tact and good sense" that had achieved this commendable state of affairs.[72] It was probably also the homogeneous grouping of the most pro-German internees.

The guards

The criticism of aspects of camp administration must be balanced against the consistent comments of the critics that the men on the job were cooperative and sincere in doing their best for the internees and also against the situation in the overall Australian community. In February bicycles, guns, binoculars and cameras were impressed from everyone who could not show why they needed them in the national interest. In North Queensland, farmers had their crawler tractors taken, and even homes and schools were commandeered. Tobacco was rationed and supplies were unpredictable everywhere, and petty theft was not unknown among postal and railway staff.[73] Backlogs in paperwork were directly related to understaffing and untrained staff. The Garrison Battalions were consistently undermanned and ex-World War I diggers, Class B medical conscripts and the returned wounded did not easily convert into paymasters or typist-stenographers. In other military units the solution was to use women typists, many of whom flocked into uniform, but they were not considered a practical alternative in internment camps.[74] Two features of Australian internment camps must also be kept in mind when the legitimate criticisms of Official Visitors and others are considered. They are firstly that in their custodial role Australian guards were tolerant but effective, and that secondly complaints were individual. There was no systematic theft by Australians like that committed by the *Dunera* guards; nor was there brutality or starvation as in concentration camps run by the Japanese and Germans.

It could be argued that the nature of the Australian countryside made for effective imprisonment. There were few escapes from camps, and from Loveday no successful ones. The black tracker, Jimmy James, lived in the River Murray district, and he found escapees within hours of their departure. The fact that Australia is an island also made total escape difficult and consequently few tried.[75] Only the Italian POW Lt Edgardo Simoni made consistent "successful" escapes. Thus the Garrison's real achievement lay in keeping up the morale and health of their prisoners confined for so long in a dusty camp of huts and flies. The overall lack of epidemics could be partly credited to the internees themselves, but constant regular supervision by the guards was crucial. Food was also more plentiful in Australia than in the war-torn countries, but what continually impressed internees was the fact that they received the same rations as their guards, and that they were similarly housed. It was the Garrison's adherence to the letter and spirit of the Geneva Convention, this sense of fair play, that maintained the internees' morale; it gave them physical security and freedom from fear of their captors.

It must be credited to the Garrison troops that they were able to achieve this success against the odds. Their needs were accorded a low priority, they had few recreational outlets and they were sometimes punished in the same cell blocks as the prisoners. It was not easy to remain enthusiastic, given the isolation, work stress and low status they suffered. In some ways they were as isolated and as much the victim of war's fortune as the prisoners were. When Margaret Pierce and Alf Clarke, from the Society of Friends, visited the Hay camp in January 1941 they talked to soldiers of all ranks. Pierce and Clark noticed among those of higher rank a resentment that the internees had visitors and well-wishers while "no one seemed to give a thought to the needs of the Garrison". When the two welfare workers enquired, they found that there was no Lord Mayor's Comfort Fund and no canteen except one run by volunteer women a mile away from camp. The recreation hut was "cheerless and ill-equipped". Most of the Garrison then at Hay were middle-aged "diggers" whose families lived in other parts of New South Wales. The leave roster took insufficient account of travelling time, so the men did not get home often.[76]

Many internees specifically testified to the humanity of the Australian guards. Konig wrote that when he and his fellow internees left Hay they took leave of the "tough but good-natured guards and the sergeant-major, a former trooper in India", whom he once saw sitting beside a crying boy trying to cheer him up.[77] Barcs wrote that at no time had the internees in

Liverpool or Tatura reason to feel bitter toward the men whose duty it was to keep them there. When a group of Japanese nickel miners from New Caledonia suddenly arrived at Liverpool camp, they were left outside while the other internees went into lunch. Thinking the Japanese would be forgotten, the first group fed them through the window. "No sooner had they finished our lunch", Barcs wrote, "than they were ordered to queue up for their meal: rice with tomato sauce. Each man received huge helpings. "Did you think we wanted to starve the poor devils?" Lieutenant S. asked."[78] The wardress at Liverpool, Mrs Samphia, was "enthusiastically eulogised" by every woman internee Davidson had ever visited there.[79] In the newspaper reports of the Deportation trials, held at the end of the war, a commentator said that it spoke "volumes" for the Australian guards that after fifty cases only one internee at the inquiry had criticised the camps, and then only the food.[80]

Internees' complaints

Internees' complaints were directed against policy and its effects on them as individuals. Camp life was unacceptable to many because they felt they ought not to have been there at all, and because it endangered the economic security that migrants had worked hard to establish for themselves and their families. Being interned was particularly upsetting to the naturalised and long-term residents, and a survey of the Official Visitor's reports on Loveday in 1942 reveals some amazing situations.[81] There were 17 native-born internees from Queensland who petitioned the Prime Minister, only to have the camp commandant invoke a regulation preventing communications with politicians.[82] A man born in Switzerland was naturalised and had lived in Australia for 32 years. His internment left his family destitute, 670 miles out in the bush and away from their home in Mackay. The Official Visitor felt it was "reasonably probable that he had been wrongly interned", and asked that his case be looked into. Another man was an Australian-born Chinese who had been mistaken for a Japanese but who had not been put in the Japanese compound for fear of violence to him. A "Loyal Free Norwegian" seaman was held under Regulation 14A, which stated that he would not be released until he had rejoined a ship, as he had always been willing to do from the day of his arrest in October 1941. Sanderson considered that British justice had come "to a pretty pass" when a friendly alien could be so treated. A naturalised Australian of German origin, who had been told twice by Intelligence officers in Tatura that his internment was a mistake, received his call up to report for duty with the RAAF, for he was on that force's reserve.

Long-term residents, many of them naturalised, also became agitated about the danger to their livelihood. A fisherman's boats were left in the river at Tuncurry, SA, in the charge of his wife and his son, who was not in the AMF. When the boats were shifted, he wanted his boy to be allowed to continue looking after them because if they were not periodically hauled out, scrubbed and painted, the teredo worms would begin eating the planking. The thirteen fishermen from Port Pirie were worried about their boats for the same reason, and also because their Italian friends were afraid of being interned if they took care of them.[83] The son of a tobacco farmer from Texas, Qld, had continued working the family property and used the tractor for cultivating and pumping water, but was stopped from driving, presumably because he was under age. To prevent the crop failing, the interned farmer asked that his son be given special permission to drive the tractor. Another Queensland internee had been forced to leave a blind wife, and his family were "in a pitiful condition". Another wife needed the number of her husband's naturalisation certificate in order to get her clothing coupons but, although the certificate had been handed over to the army, it could not be found. The owner of a bicycle and gunsmith's shop in Hindley Street, Adelaide, had guns belonging to his customers as well as his stock taken without a receipt. A farmer from Innisfail was trying to get his cane cut, but the only member of his family not interned was his 74-year-old wife. His seven-room home had been let out to a bank manager for 35s per week, but the manager unilaterally reduced the rent to 10s a week.[84]

It might be thought that some internees unduly dwelt on their material possessions, but in most cases these internees represented the pioneering generation of their families. They had deliberately left their homeland to make a secure place for their children in a new land, and any economic progress they had made was hard won. At the base of almost all individual complaints was concern for families, and Sanderson was especially outspoken about cases where family ties were disregarded. One internee was informed by his 12 year-old daughter that her 17 year-old sister had been interned and neither he, nor his interned wife in Tatura, had been able to discover her whereabouts. Sanderson wrote that when "the requirements of security have been met by the internment of children, common decency" required that parents be informed immediately. While the Official Visitors had come to regard "a certain amount of stupidity as inevitable", they could not resign themselves "to conduct callous enough for the Gestapo". In another case a man was visited by his mother-in-law and 3 year-old daughter who had come from Melbourne to Loveday. The interned man was not allowed to take the child in his arms. Sanderson asked that in cases like these the regulations be relaxed for this kind of "iron rigidity, backed by law, but not by common sense", made a "deplorable impression on the camp as a whole".[85]

In one way, local-resident internees had an advantage: they had some authority to complain to. There were groups of overseas internees whose problems the Official Visitor was at a loss to know where to direct. Men interned in Teheran were brought via Bombay and told that their cases would be investigated. One claimed to be a member of the Free Austria Movement, had volunteered for a Labour Unit and been sent to pick fruit at Bendigo, before being separated from the unit and sent to Camp 14D without explanation. Major Layton, the Liaison officer sent to deal with the *Dunera internees*, expressly repudiated any authority to deal with any other internees sent by British authorities to Australia.[86] This dilemma also affected the internees from Malaya, Palestine and the British Pacific Islands. A man interned in Singapore had been deprived of his German nationality for writing an anti-Nazi book, and had been told by an Intelligence Officer in Singapore that if the island had not been a naval base, he would have been freed. His case could not be settled in Singapore, the officer told him, and he would have to go to Australia "where it would take only a short time for him to be free". Sanderson asked that some way be found to deal with the situation where an internee could not appeal in the country of detention because he was not there, or in Australia because he had not been detained here.[87]

Those internees at Loveday who saw themselves as enemy nationals were to some degree, more content. They knew they would probably remain in camp until the end of the war. The Japanese were the most placid but the German-speaking Camp 10 also settled to a well-organised routine and much energy put

into making the place comfortable. Dr Morel considered it a
model camp. They had "built schools, cafes, gardens and studios", sometimes using their own money. Good roads had been
established and a stage, a music pavilion, a large bakery oven,
tennis courts and artists' studios built.[88] When the internees
were notified that they would be transfered to Camp 14 as part
of the rationalisation of camps as Italian internees were released, the Germans were upset. The camp leader, von Graf
wrote to the Protecting Power, the Red Cross and the military
authorities, complaining it was a collective punishment. Bundock assured the Germans the transfer was a necessity and as
the war continued everyone "outside the compound as well as
within" was being compelled "to give up one little comfort after
another".[89]

It is very difficult to assess the personal suffering of individual internees, and even more difficult to make a guess at the
collective misery internment involved. It can only be set in the
communal situation in Australia in 1942 and 1943. Many Australian families were torn apart, men were being killed in the
fighting, and lonely women were doing men's jobs, and distress
was widespread over the whole land. Yet one relevant question
is whether the nation gained any advantage in taking naturalised and long-term residents from their jobs and homes, when
nothing but the hysteria of fear suggested that they would do
anything but go about their business. The extra misery that the
internment of these people added to the collective misery of
Australians in their years of crisis, was the direct result of that
general misery, but in no way lessened it. It threw in the faces
of non-British-born citizens the slur that, in the eyes of their
neighbours, they were the same as Fascists and foreigners. It is
here, and not in any resentment of the rough camp life,that the
long-term scar remains.

In addition to the compounded personal misery, there is the
question of whether the national interest was best served by the
holding of 7,000 "local" internees. The need to raise battalions
of guards, the administrative burden on camp commandants,
security officers, Official Visitors and tribunals, the use of building materials for camps, the transport tied up, the welfare
payments to families, the reduced production of sugar, tobacco
and vegetable farms and the severe under-usage of internee
labour, were part of the increasing deficit of internment. It was
costing the Australian government approximately three

pounds per week to maintain each internee.[90] If it was a reasonable precaution to intern the low risk groups when the threat of invasion was real, was it equally reasonable to release them once the Battles of the Coral Sea and Midway stopped the Japanese advance? It would be the greatest security dilemma Australian authorities faced. At what point did American aid and combined military successes guarantee that a reversal would not occur and precipitate another round of internments? How soon after the shock of the fall of Singapore and the bombing of Darwin would public morale accept the return to their communities of people born in enemy countries? A decision had to be made as to where the balance between the escalating costs and diminishing benefits of internment lay.

Chapter Nine

THE LONG WAY HOME

On 21 June 1942 Dr H.V. Evatt returned from his mission to Washington and London. His first responsibility was to inform the Prime Minister about his visit, but very soon thereafter the problem of the Australia First arrests was brought to his attention. A few Labor MPs had raised the matter intermittently with the new member for Melbourne, Arthur Calwell, being particularly insistent.[1] The more time passed after the Army Minister's original dramatic announcement of 26 March that twenty traitors had been caught, the more embarrassing it was for the government to state that only the four people apprehended in Perth would face the courts. The sixteen men associated with the Australia First Movement in Sydney had, in fact, little case to answer. The Perth four had used the name of the Sydney movement without its knowledge or consent.

The most provoking aspect of the Australia First group for the authorities was the threat they posed to law and order. Their anti-semitic, anti-Imperial and anti-Communist ideas annoyed a variety of people, and the communists in particular attended Australia First meetings to disrupt them. Detective-Sergeant G.R. Richards, the controller of the agent Leonard Thomas, who had encouraged the Perth four to produce incriminating documents, knew about the riotous meetings of Australia First in Sydney. When the name Australia First was used by the Perth conspirators, Richards and the military director of Intelligence in Perth, Lieutenant-Colonel H.D. Moseley, wired Eastern Command and recommended the arrest of the Sydney leaders of Australia First. Subsequent investigation showed the lack of connection between the Perth and Sydney groups, but the government could only suggest that they appeal against their internment to the relevant tribunal.[2]

Mrs Adela Pankhurst Walsh, a co-convenor of the Australia First movement, was arrested shortly after the male leaders and she brought a writ of *habeas corpus* before the Supreme Court of

New South Wales. The Chief Justice, Sir Frederick Jordan, criticised the legislation that made it so hard for a person to clear
her name and allowed for such extensive authority over civilians.[3] While the Australia First cases were being reviewed by
Evatt and the Attorney-General's department, the North
Queensland internments queried by Martens were being scrutinised by W.J. Mackay, the second head of the Security Service.
The collective nature of the Master Warrants was becoming
evident.[4] How would the Attorney-General untie this gargan-
tuan knot? The Solicitor-General, George Knowles, pointed out
the contradiction in the government's not formally charging the
Australia First internees when — as Opposition — they had
been so outspokenly critical of the internment of Ratliff and
Thomas without trial.[5] Parliament rose on 4 June 1942 and did
not sit again until 2 September and during this period Evatt
undoubtedly made himself familiar with the relevant documents. He considered that some recommendations for internment appeared "to be unjustified or frivolous".[6] His instinct
was for open trials but the credibility of Frank Forde, the
Minister for the Army, was at stake. Evatt was to be pursued to
the end of his career by the stain of the continued incarceration
of the Australia First members on his civil libertarian image.[7]
His biographer, Kylie Tennant, places the blame squarely on
Forde's naivete in being ready to believe "anything told to him
by an officer".[8]

Policy change

After reading the Australia First file, Evatt probably reached the
same conclusion as Knowles and the Crown Solicitor, H.F.E.
Whitlam, that nothing in the reports on Stephensen showed
that he had contravened "any regulation made under the National Security Act or of any other Commonwealth law".[9] Hasluck is somewhat critical of Forde for not applying the rule
established by Spender that, before issuing a detention order,
the Minister should be satisfied that the person had actually
been engaged "in activities contrary to the interests of national
security", and not merely a member of a suspect organisation
or a holder of political beliefs. Hasluck does concede that every
war "has its casualties" and that "under the strain of wartime
anxiety, the Curtin Government had not fully appreciated the
nature of the actions taken in its name".[10] It may also be relevant

that the Curtin government held office by the narrowest of
margins and the successive falls of Menzies and Fadden were
fresh in cabinet's mind. To go out on a limb for a minute group
of ideologically confused and woolly talkers, who were anath-
ema to both pro-British and pro-Russian elements in the community, at a time when Japanese submarines had penetrated
Sydney Harbour, was an unacceptable political risk.

Another dilemma Evatt had to deal with was Curtin's public
commitment to W.J. Mackay, the police chief who then headed
security.[11] Mackay continued to function as chief of police in
New South Wales, and preferred to work in Sydney.[12] His
concept of using Police Commissioners as Deputy-Directors of
Security was not acceptable to federal public servants. According to Noel Lamidey, who knew the Attorney-General's Department well, the Solicitor-General considered "that the property
of the Commonwealth, could not be transfered to an instrumentality of a State",[13] but Mackay was convinced he was doing the
best thing for Australia's security, and he was not unaware of
the tensions over sharing information and files. Shortly after
assuming office, Mackay wrote to the Service Chiefs and the
Solicitor General declaring his attitude to Security. It was his
intention to use "competent investigators" from all services and
not just the police. He was grateful to the Army for the help
GOCs and Base Commandants had offered and it was his desire
to keep the experienced officers in the area to advise and assist
him. He was arranging for all records of state branches of
Commonwealth Security to be copied and sent to a central
bureau in Canberra for access by the Attorney-General's Department. All these records would "be available and open to
accredited representatives of the fighting services". Mackay
said he wanted "to eliminate any fear that Commonwealth
rights or practices and Service requirements" would "be jeop-
ardised" by his administration "or by the means of carrying out
that administration through the State Police Forces".[14]

Two days later he wrote to General Blamey to congratulate
him on the achievements of the AIF and to welcome him home.
This letter is less formal. Mackay asked Blamey when he was
in Sydney "to have a chat . . . as an old Policeman". Mackay told
Blamey that there had been dissatisfaction with the Security
Service's efforts to achieve "unanimity of purpose among four
investigation organisations in the Commonwealth". As a result
Mackay had been asked to become Director-General of Security

for the Commonwealth. But he had "met with a bit of trouble" and felt some Departmental heads "did not realise what mutual effort means". Because of Blamey's experience as head of the Victorian Police Force, Mackay felt he would understand that men who had a "long and practical experience in dealing with the underworld, the slygrogger and the other excrescences on society, are the best qualified to form the backbone of the investigation side of Security Service". The police were also the best means of approaching people to gain confidence and information.[15] Mackay was rewarded with a warm reply. Blamey was happy to see the Security Service "put in the hands of those who can really use it", agreeing that the police were the only ones with "the skill, expert knowledge and technical training and experience to handle the matter effectively".[16] But in the Attorney-General's Department considerable agitation was aroused and Sir George Knowles managed to head off the implementation of Mackay's plans.[17] Lamidey regarded Mackay's approach as "bull headed" and the man himself as "an authoritative bureaucrat who could not adapt himself with ease to the wider horizons of the Federal sphere". Mackay could have lost his army support when he ordered the relaxing of controls over the movement of aliens, that had been imposed by the military.[18]

Nevertheless when Dr Evatt called a conference for 5 September 1942, Mackay was listed to attend as Director-General.[19] Shortly afterwards Mackay resigned. Lamidey noted that it did not take long before Evatt and Mackay clashed. Evatt was not "an easy man to work either with or under and in many ways Mackay and Evatt were not dissimilar". Both men "drove themselves hard and both would brook little or no interference or opposition to their ideas and plans".[20] So Curtin's choice was overturned and the Security Service was to be given a third leader. The Security Service, created on 31 March 1941 and originally led by E.E. Longfield-Lloyd, had floundered along searching for direction and a defined sphere of operations. Lamidey described Longfield Lloyd as "a gentleman, a person of charm and social grace" who could not always "command the co-operation of some of his colleagues" and who lacked the ability "to translate the spoken word into clear and concise language". Both he and Mackay "suffered the basic handicap of having no written charter of government policy".[21] Evatt chose Brigadier W.B. Simpson,[22] a senior army legal officer, who had served on Eastern Command's committee reviewing alien internments early in the war. Simpson had been sent to Hay to investigate the claims of brutality by the *Dunera* guards and had subsequently served as Judge Advocate-General of the Australian forces in the Middle East. Evatt also appointed a committee to advise on internment matters, the Aliens Classification and Advisory Committee.

While these shakeups were underway, the protests made by G.W. Martens over the North Queensland arrests were being processed. The army was concerned to keep the identity of military reporting officers and informants secret.[23] The protection of sources is a basic principle of security but the army's protest that, as a result of an MP perusing its files the enemy might get to know the extent and limitations of Intelligence's knowledge of subversive activities, was an implied slur on parliamentarians. Forde decided that Martens' representations and the army's protest were to be referred to Evatt.[24] Thus Evatt read Martens' complaints that active Labor Party members in the Herbert electorate were interned, together with men who had collected sums of money for patriotic purposes; and that a man had travelled to internment camp on a train also carrying his son who had just returned from war service in Libya, Greece and Crete. Martens' interned friend Felix Reitano had lived in the Herbert district for 40 years, was married to a Scot and had four sons, of whom one was in the AIF, one in the militia and one in the VDC, while the fourth worked the farm.[25]

Cases like these, coupled with Evatt's own opinions of the Australia First fiasco and his civil libertarian instincts, led him to lay down a firm principle to guide Calwell's committee and Simpson's Security Service. Internment was to be reserved only for those against whom there were "reasonable grounds for suspicion". The narrow policy originally laid down in the *War Book* was to be reestablished. Evatt announced in parliament on 10 September 1942:

> The aim and sole justification of all restrictions upon individual liberty is to prevent injury to the war effort of the country, not to punish the individual. In short, the objective is preventive rather than punitive. This object is clearly embodied in the existing regulations ...
>
> The second principle is that ... restrictions if imposed should be imposed only to an extent sufficient to prevent the evil, full intern-

ment being reserved for cases where the possibility of injury to the nation is undeniable.[26]

The change of policy was not universally popular. When Martens repeated his questions about people from his electorate who were interned,[27] a North Queensland newspaper, the *Sunday Australian*, considered that the speech was motivated by party political considerations such as had marred "successive Commonwealth administrations" in dealing with the North Queensland alien question. The paper went on to protest that it was "inconceivable that the whole of the officers who were involved in the inquiries which preceded the internments were opposed to the Labor Party", and that "the great bulk of internments made in North Queensland were ordered after the Curtin Government had taken office". Any widespread releases would mean that British-born citizens would again become a minority in the north, and the sense of frustration engendered by the return of the foreign born locals might result in "adverse reactions" in the northern war effort.[28]

Yet such talk from Anglo-Saxon North Queenslanders had lost its power. For one thing, the military situation in September was not as bad as it had been in February. The Japanese were being held in New Guinea and support from the United States was increasing every day. Secondly, manpower in Australia was too valuable to be kept locked up if it could be used productively. The sugar industry was most drastically affected, with production steadily falling despite the efforts of the Queensland Sugar Board in organising labour for internees' farms.[29] Nevertheless, a military situation that was holding, and manpower needs that were pressing, do not wholly explain the drastic turn in internment policy. Although the threat of invasion was suspended, the war was still at its height. Rommel's thrust into Egypt was not halted until the Battle of El Alamein was won on 2 November 1942; nor was it sure the Russians were going to be able to defend Stalingrad. On 1 June 1942 the Japanese managed to get submarines into Sydney Harbour, and their army remained entrenched in New Guinea. Their attack on Milne Bay was repulsed on 26 August, but Kokoda was not recaptured from them until 2 November 1942, while the long campaigns to retake Buna, Gona and Bougainville still lay ahead. Continued internments, especially in reaction to setbacks such as the loss of the hospital ship *Centaur* in May 1943, would not have been out of keeping with the established pat-

tern. As for manpower, it was always a secondary consideration
to security. The change of political leadership to a Labor government was the third factor that brought a return to a narrow
internment policy. The influences of H.V. Evatt,[30] and John
Curtin[31] were significant.

Evatt had toured the United States during the middle
months of 1942, aiming to convince Americans that Australia
was totally committed to the war and offering every support to
U.S. troops, which would have inclined him to arguments for
the most productive use of manpower. But, more significantly,
he was against collective internments, on principle, and he
noted that the United States did not institute them against its
own citizens born in Germany and Italy.[32] Although Evatt was
Attorney-General when internment in Australia was at its peak,
none of the arrests that took place between February and May
1942 were authorised by Evatt, and soon after his return from
America he began to reverse the process. It may even be more
than coincidence, although its significance is indeterminate,
that on 16 September 1942, between Evatt's announcement of a
return to a narrow internment policy and his establishment of
Calwell's committee, one of the strongest Labor supporters of
a mass internment policy, W. Forgan Smith, bowed out as
premier of Queensland.[33]

The internment of the naturalised and lowest risk Italians in
North Queensland and the Australia First roundup represented
the pinnacle of internment. After Evatt's return to Australia,
internments were infrequent and involved individual cases.
Only one other group, as such, was sent to camp, and they
actively campaigned to get in. These were the wives and families of the Lutheran mission workers from New Guinea. In the
face of the Japanese invasion, women and children, including
those from the missions, had been evacuated from New
Guinea.[34] The Lutheran women were billeted with families in
South Australia, and after two years the women determined to
join their menfolk by getting themselves interned by becoming
blatantly and provocatively pro-German. This was another
burden for the Lutheran community to bear, as the women's
behaviour naturally brought a reaction from many of the population already stirred up by reports that Lutheran misssionaries
had led, or at least trained their natives to lead, the Japanese
through the Markham Valley. *Smith's Weekly*, the *Adelaide News*
and *Advertiser*, and the national radio all ran the story.[35] The

Australian public were told of native choirs singing the Horst Wessel song, a Nazi armband factory, strategic aerodromes and high-powered wireless sets. Two German nationals attached to the Finschhafen mission — aircraft pilot Werner Garms and mechanic Paul Rabe — took the first opportunity after the war started to fly the mission plane to Dutch New Guinea, from where they returned, via Japan, to Germany.[36] Of the original twenty-six Germans arrested at the outbreak of war by the New Guinea Volunteer Rifles and taken by the *Macdhui* to Australia, sixteen were attached to the Finschhafen Mission and were members of the Nazi Party *Stuetpunkt* led by the mission plantation manager, Hubert Stuerzenhofecker. In June 1940 more missionaries were interned and most of the remainder went in December 1941.[37] It seems that only three were left and the claims of pro-Japanese sentiment or action by them appear ill-founded.[38] Not to be pro-Japanese however, did not make the German members of the mission staff pro-ally.

The former superintendent of Finschhafen expressed the views of the Lutheran missionaries who were German nationals when he said that they had never denied that their loyalty, allegiance and sympathies were with their government and the leader of their nation. Such an attitude towards a nation and its government, was "expected of every honourable Britisher as a matter of course", but the same attitude in a German was "branded as condemnable and disgraceful",[39] he complained. The wives actions worried their church leaders. The Rev. J.J. Stolz wrote to the Rev. O. Theile that he had it "on good authority" that much of the church's "present troubles" were due to their connections with the New Guinea missions. While Stolz was sympathetic to the women's wish to be reunited with their husbands, he considered that the women's outspokenness "would make it all the harder for any one of the missionaries to return" to New Guinea.[40] The Army felt no one should be interned "for reasons other than those of security" because they could agitate at any time for their release. On humanitarian grounds children under 16 could accompany their parents into camp but wives "should not be permitted to voluntarily accompany their interned husbands", nor should children enter camp if one parent was at liberty. The army secretary stressed that if wives and children were allowed into camp the expense of family accommodation, guard personnel, food, clothing and education would necessarily increase.[41] Mackay agreed with

the army's reluctance to expand family facilities but by the end
of 1942 the wives had prevailed.

These women were the exception and policy was moving to
releases. Australian citizens were scrutinised first, and Evatt
released the Communists, Ratliff and Thomas, on their undertaking not to do anything that might impede the war effort, and
to "work for the victory of the British Commonwealth and her
Allies".[42] Adela Pankhurst Walsh resorted to the suffragette
tactic of hunger striking after her unsuccessful tribunal hearing
and thereby gained her release.[43] Seven of the Australia First
men had been released after their appeal to an Advisory Committee, and a further nine were investigated by senior Security
and Intelligence personnel. Five were released under restrictions.[44] Evatt had reversed policy, but he was too busy to attend
to all cases, and analysis of the bulk of internments passed to
the Department of Security, which had taken over control of
enemy aliens from the army.

Administering the Changed Policy

In the changeover from army to the new Security Service there
was a certain amount of friction before the lines of demarcation
in powers and responsibilities were sorted out. The second
Director of Security, W.J. Mackay, was authorised to absorb the
existing security personnel from the three armed services but
they were to continue to be paid by their own service. The army
notified its people that after three months it would no longer
accept any responsibility for them. Security risked losing 167
experienced men. The 110 in the lower ranks were primarily
concerned about the loss of medical and taxation benefits that
a transfer to civilian status entailed, and the officers would not
contemplate their loss of uniform and military rank. Some
chose to transfer to other duties. Mackay appealed to Evatt,
pointing out that after the war servicemen could be discharged,
whereas if security personnel became Commonwealth public
servants they would have to be found jobs after the war.[45]

As the army had been responsible for the great majority of
internments, Mackay felt that it should remain responsible for
those so interned. The army had all the files on these internees,
and knew the circumstances that had led to their internment,
which was also the information on which release would be
determined. Mackay protested that the army had already re-

ferred to him fifty matters related to army-interned individuals, about whom he had no files, while the responsibility for overseas internees and for seamen interned under Regulation 14A, which he had expected, was being kept by the army. Mackay wanted the army to continue paying its staff during their secondment to security, and he wanted the army to sort out "its" internees while he dealt with the overseas group. The army, however, retained its control over overseas internees on the grounds that Major Julian Layton, the Liaison Officer from the Home Office, had to stay in Melbourne to supervise the embarkation overseas of those returning to Britain, and the clearance of those enlisting in the army.[46] On the other hand, the army refused to continue their involvement with the "locals" they had interned in Australia. Colonel J.D. Rogers, Director of Military Intelligence, explained that it would take months to go through the files and a duplication of paper work was foolish.[47] Rogers stated that files outlining general policy and the files of all British-born and naturalised internees could be transferred to Security from headquarters, and those of alien internees were being transfered to the respective State Deputy-Directors. As a final shot Rogers told Mackay that the army now did not have the staff to deal with internment matters.

There was also a basic difference in attitudes to evidence and internment criteria. Mackay considered that recommendations going to the Minister should contain both the evidence backing the recommendation for internment and material favourable to the person under suspicion.[48] Colonel James A. Chapman, DMI, required that full dossiers should be kept containing "all the available information on a suspect", but the precis of the dossier submitted to the persons responsible for signing the detention order "should contain only the information relied upon in justification of the recommendation for detention", as that alone concerned the GOC or the Minister.[49] Objecting to this unbalanced precis, Mackay approached Forde to have it altered. Forde replied that headquarters had told Commands that "any facts which would put a different complexion on an adverse report should be brought out", and tried to avoid making an issue of it by claiming there would be "very little difference in practice" between Mackay's proposal and the army method.[50]

The army's lack of co-operation forced Security Service (SS) to expand its own resources. When the Security Branch in

Brisbane asked the army for a report on a man from Monto, Qld, Major-General J.M.A. Durrant replied that the few Intelligence officers in Brisbane were "fully occupied in military duties" and that the control and investigation of subversive individuals were included in the responsibilities taken over by the Department of Security from the military on 26 June 1942.[51] The government acted to ensure staff for the expanding work of the Security Service. Commander J.C. McFarlane, the Queensland Deputy-Director requested branches for Townsville and Rock-hampton, and when Townsville was bombed on 25 July the RAAF supported the call for "a good man" from security to be appointed there. The first suggestion had been for a corporal, who was to work from his own house. By August a lieutenant and a typist/clerk were ready to move into a three room office in Flinders Street. On 12 October Townsville was a divisional centre with Lt-Col. R.F.B. Wake in charge of a staff of ten and with a one hundred pound establishment fund for secret agents.[52]

When the Security Service took over the running of tribunals it found that as a number had not met for so long, it was best to abandon them. The most active was the tribunal in South Australia. It travelled up to Loveday to hear "13/14 appeals a day, sitting from 9.30 a.m. to 5.00 p.m. and spending 2 to 3 hours in the evening formulating their reports". The chairman, G.S. Reed, KC, used his own car to drive the members of the tribunal, together with Major Millhouse, the army representative, and Captain Sexton of SS to Loveday. Unfortunately Sir Edward Lucas, one of the tribunal members, was 84 years of age and in poor health. The Adelaide Deputy Director, K.H. Kirkman, recommended that Lucas be replaced. The tribunal used Dr Barris, from the Censor's department, as an interpreter, and two sergeant stenographer/typists. Kirkman felt the basis of payment to the tribunal chairman needed revising, as it had been prescribed when sittings were well spaced, but in this hectic period Reed's tribunal was sitting continuously and Reed was unable to devote "any attention to his own practice".[53]

Much of the pressure on the South Australian tribunal came from interstate internees who had moved through Gaythorne to Loveday, and there were sound financial reasons for having this tribunal operating efficiently. On the last day of 1942 there were 5,228 locals held in internment, of whom 3,967 were aliens, 1,097 naturalised British subjects and 164 native born. Since the outbreak of war 7,103 persons had been interned and 1,875 released by the Commonwealth.[54] There were also hundreds of overseas internees from Britain, Malaya, Palestine and Persia, the Dutch East Indies, the Pacific Islands and New Guinea as well as thousands of prisoners of war, being held in camps in Australia. The strains on the Garrison and on the Directorate of Prisoners of War and Internees were enormous. Costs were running at three pounds per head per week, and on top of the cost of guards and administration, this expense was another good reason for releasing low-risk locals in a less threatening military situation.[55] The Aliens Classification and Advisory Committee, chaired by Arthur Calwell, met soon after Dr Evatt announced the committee's establishment in late September 1942. Members of the committee were Senator Walter Cooper (an exserviceman from World War I), Lt A.R. Cutler, VC (wounded in World War II), W.R. Dovey, KC (a Sydney lawyer), and J.V. Barry, KC (a Melbourne lawyer and office holder in the Council of Civil Liberties). Lt Cutler later became Assistant Deputy Director of Security for New South Wales and subsequently Assistant Commissioner of Repatriation, and his place was taken by Mrs Jessie Street, President of the United Associations of Women. Noel W. Lamidey, a public servant from the Attorney-General's Department, served as secretary to the committee.[56] The committee took evidence in Sydney, Melbourne and Canberra from the military, the Security Service, Professor Bailey and other interested parties. The most assiduous representation was on behalf of refugees.[57] The committee accepted the argument that certain people had been designated as refugees before the war, and had been taken into Australia as such. The committee agreed that it was "unjust and morally indefensible" that refugees should be treated as enemy aliens when the German government disowned them, yet they had a long struggle before a Refugee Class was legalised. The committee made its Interim Report in March 1943, and most of this report deals with the status of refugee aliens.[58] Eventually 6,500 former "enemy aliens" were reclassified under the Aliens Control regulations but remained "enemy aliens" under the Aliens Service Regulations and were subject to assignment to the Civil Alien Corps.[59]

Dissatisfied because of the delays in instituting releases, Calwell appealed to the Prime Minister, but Curtin replied that the government was pursuing a policy of releasing internees to

Manpower or the Allied Works Council wherever it could
"without endangering national security".[60] Almost all Albani-
ans and Finns detained as "a precautionary measure" had
already been released and "a systematic review of all internees
of Italian origin", commencing with Queensland internees located in New South Wales, "many of whom had been detained
by the Military Authorities with the primary object of removing
them from vulnerable areas during a critical period", was under
way. Several hundred internees had been released to work and
some naturalised British subjects had been allowed to return to
their farms "under restriction" or were given employment
south of the Tropic of Capricorn.

The Italians

On 28 October 1943 at its twentieth meeting the committee
considered the general question of Italian internees and the
cases of particular Italian internees.[61] Pressure was being applied to release particular Italian internees by a number of
groups including the "Italia Libra" organisation,[62] a coalition of
Italian anti-Fascists and their Australian supporters. G.W. Martens continued to seek information on internees from his own
area, and Calwell was close to Archbishop Mannix, whose
empathy with Victorian Italians as Roman Catholics was well
known. Leading Melbourne businessman, Gualtiero Vaccari,
also took a special interest in Italian internees.[63] At its twentieth
meeting, Calwell's committee considered several cases submitted by the Director-General, and all were decided but one. Most
Italian internees coming under review were being quickly released and put to the "more profitable employment of growing
foodstuffs for the country" and providing labour for other
essential areas of national work.

In order to speed this process Mr Justice Reed, who had
chaired the tribunal in South Australia since May 1941, was
asked for his views on the "political sentiments of internees of
Italian origin, their attitude towards Australia and the British
Empire, and the risks they represented from a security point of
view", and also what "conception" he thought naturalised
Italians had "of their duty towards the Empire". In the course
of his tribunal and committee work, Reed interviewed over
2,000 and concluded that most internees had "no real political
outlook or opinions at all". He felt that they were only slightly

interested "in the form of government of the country, or the institutions by which that government is carried on". They expressed the attitude that it did not make any difference to them who ruled the country, as they would have to work just the same. Reed felt that Italians had some interest in "the personal aspect, for example the amount of taxation or wages and working conditions", and were "quite satisfied" that they had discharged their obligations to Australia if they could say that they had always paid their taxes and respected the laws, and had never been in trouble with the police. While Reed felt that this lack of "real attachment for the land of their adoption" was "regrettable", and their "disinclination to fight anyone" made them a "deadweight of inertia" that could hinder the war effort, he considered that most of them were prepared to work outside the camp and this would involve virtually no security risk.[64]

Simpson was reviewing the internments from Queensland. By the end of January 1943 some 800 cases were yet to be considered and the progress was "unreasonably slow". Those who had been interned under Omnibus warrants had been detained "as a precautionary measure, and nothing of a subversive nature" was recorded against them. Simpson was prepared to release the men in this category. He had made arrangements for them to be called up under the Aliens Service Regulations. They would then "be employed at soldiers' rates of pay in States other than Queensland".[65] Because of "the serious manpower shortage", Simpson felt it was his responsibility to quickly release those who were not a security risk. Between 11 October and 22 November, 708 persons of Italian origin or descent were released.[66]

So many who had been arrested in bulk under Omnibus warrants were released in bulk. To achieve a high rate of release Simpson required the Queensland security chief, J.A. MacFarlane, to read and summarise 40 personal files or dossiers a day and send the summaries and recommendations to Canberra. Among those released from Cowra was Bruno Agricola who went to work cutting wood in Victoria.[67] Augusto Orlandi returned to his farm for Christmas 1943. His wife had organised a petition signed by the town's doctor, local businessmen and neighbouring farmers. The local police pointed out that the petition only claimed that Orlandi was "an honest and industrious farmer" and there were still hostile feelings against

Italians in the district.[68] But because he was naturalised, a primary producer and the case against him so slight, Orlandi was among the few early releases to be allowed back north of the Tropic of Capricorn. Oswald Bonutto was released to work in Adelaide but was allowed back to grow tobacco at Inglewood in December 1943. When the usual "reliable sources" again protested against Bonutto's return, the reply from the Security Service tolerated no such challenge: those who saw the releases as an "apparent laxity" would, "on mature reflection", see that the released internees were "helping our war effort on the production front".[69]

Georg Edelmann, the Austrian interned in 1939 because of his employment by a company with Nazi directors, then released and reinterned in June 1940, was finally released and employed by the Allied Works Council at Alice Springs.[70] The journalist Emery Barcs was heard in Sydney by Mr Justice Pike and released in February 1942; he became a member of the Third Employment Company working on the wharves in July.[71] In February 1944 Lt-Col. Wake reported that he had met the former secretary of the German Club in Queen Street, Brisbane, and he had told Wake that he bore no ill-will over his internment, that he was employed and "doing his best to wipe out the memory of his internment".[72]

As the war continued into 1944 and members of the ACAC became harder to gather together because of their various commitments,[73] Lamidey, the committee's secretary took a more direct role, and together with Flight-Lieutenant Claude A. Philcox, visited Loveday to review the cases of the remaining sixty Italians.[74] Over half were approved for release but Lamidey expressed concern that some internees were choosing to stay in camp, making a drain on the nation's resources, instead of taking the option to go out to work. He described them as "malingerers" who adopted the role of pro-Fascists to ensure that they remained in camp and were thereby "relieved of the obligation imposed upon former releasees of being drafted out to work in the C.A.C."[75]

Work in the Civil Alien Corps certainly had little to recommend it. On the whole it was labouring work of the roughest kind — wood cutting and charcoal burning, fruit picking, railway fettling and aerodrome maintenance. The camps were in isolated areas such as the Northern Territory and along the Commonwealth railway line on the Nullarbor Plain. In addition, the criterion for release — ability to work — sometimes resulted in political opponents being brought together, with consequent brawls reminiscent of camp life.[76] Discipline was strict, the CAC supervisors often regarding with suspicion the newly released internees with their foreign names and accents. Pay was poor, and letters back to camp were not encouraging. Indeed many internees were as entrapped by the CAC and Manpower as they had been when interned. C.G. Jesson, a member of the Queensland parliament, brought Calwell's attention to the plight of ex-internees from his state[77] and Calwell also knew of other cases where "harsh and overbearing treatment" was meted out to aliens in the corps. Calwell had found the Minister for the Interior, Senator J.S. Collings, who controlled the CAC "utterly impossible to deal with on matters of this sort". Collings was "often very insulting when approached on behalf of unfortunate people" who were being pushed around by the Controller of Aliens in the Civil Construction Corps. Curtin was not as sympathetic as Calwell would have wished.[78] Calwell had a direct and sometimes abrasive manner and had not endeared himself to colleagues by his harsh criticism of them, including Curtin himself, who was a very sensitive man.[79]

A bitter wrangle took place, with Calwell and Vaccari (the Melbourne businessman) on the one side, and manpower authorities on the other, over Queensland ex-internees who were sent to work for Cheetham Salt at Laverton, Vic., after woodcutting at Werrimull. These internees, many of whom were naturalised, had been arrested in March and April 1942 on precautionary grounds and after ten months in camp at Cowra, they volunteered to work outside the camp on the assurance they could return to their homes in Queensland earlier than those who did not volunteer. First they went to Laverton, to harvest salt and then to cut wood for the Victorian State Rivers and Water Supply Commission. By September they had achieved their quota and in October they saw the amended Restriction Orders from the Director-General of Security, stating that all naturalised farmers were to be repatriated to Queensland. Despite this and the fact that others who had not volunteered early were going directly from camp to their home state, this group were re-transfered back to Laverton to shovel salt.[80] The Victorian manpower authorities took the view that the men could not be spared, and that the men's requests to be returned to Queensland could not be reviewed before May 1944 and were subject "to continued good behaviour".Vaccari argued that the Ministerial statement of 19 October 1943 by E.J. Holloway, Minister for Labour and National Service, provided that Queensland farmers should be returned to the industry in which they were experts because of the urgent need to produce food. This was not only a humane act but was "the best economic use of the men to meet the needs of the country". Many sugar farms were being worked by female relatives and the tonnages being harvested had dropped dramatically. Land had to be ploughed immediately in preparation for the planting season in March and April 1944 or there would be no crop at all. Calwell appealed to Evatt. He wrote:

> I am afraid there is still a lot of racial, and with some people religious, prejudices where Italian people are concerned particularly amongst the minor officials in the Allied Works Council and the Department of Labour and National Service. I do not know whether you can personally persuade our colleagues, the Minister for the Interior and the Minister for Labour and National Service that the farms of these ex-internees are even a greater asset to Australia than the vested interests of the Cheetham Salt Company which are being so stoutly defended by the officials in the Departments referred to.
>
> If you could do this, it should be easy to secure the return of men who should never have been interned at all. Residing in Queensland at the time of the threatened Japanese invasion, they became the victims of mass hysteria which resulted in arrests on omnibus warrants on alleged precautionary grounds.[81]

Calwell's fears received further confirmation when he was given a report from the local priest at Burra, SA, about a group of 20 internees who were released from Loveday Camp 14D early in 1943 after about a year of internment. They were Queensland cane farmers who were assigned to work with a contractor on tank construction at Hanson, near Burra, SA. One by one, the priest reported, the men were "breaking down and badly". Several were sent away to lighter work or to hospital, for they were "all middle aged men, worn with work and confinement and then turned suddenly on the heaviest of labour". Orazio Patti, a 40-year-old father of five children, died in the Burra hospital on 14 November 1943 after 17 months internment followed by months of forced labour at Burra.[82]

Calwell's efforts were only partly successful and Vaccari was still pursuing the cases of 28 Queensland ex-internees anxious to return to the sugar and tobacco industries in August 1944.[83] These men worked in Victoria at Glenorchy, Creswick, Macedon and Wondong, but their hearts were in Mareeba, Mourilyan, Gordonvale, Dimbula and Silkwood in Queensland. Bruno Agricola was one of them. At Cowra, Bruno had volunteered to cut wood for the Forest Commission in Victoria, where he worked from December 1942 until August 1944. The CAC divisional officer, in supporting Bruno's application for release, described him as "an excellent worker" and "extremely reliable". Bruno's farm was being run by his sister and the yearly production had dropped from 900 to 450 tons. Bruno had again applied for naturalisation (an earlier application had been suspended), and claimed that he was just "a contented resident of Australia", who felt his "continued retention in the C.A.C. whilst the Sugar Farm of which I am Co-Owner is going back to scrub thereby jeopardising many years of hard work constitutes a grave injustice to me personally and to this Country". The government had decided that the nation's best interests now lay in providing support, particularly food, for the army that Macarthur was leading from island to island pushing north towards Japan and Frank Forde defended the release of experienced sugar industry workers to North Queensland because of "the strongest representations of the Food Production Committee".[84] While most Italians were released from internment camps by the end of 1944, a few were kept until the very end of the war. These few were interviewed in 1946 by Simpson, who had become a Federal court judge, but whose experience made him suited to conduct an inquiry into the desirability of deporting the internees then still in camps. Among the possible deportees was Giovanni Casotti, and Antonio Agostini, both nominated by Lamidey as "malingerers".[85] In 1945, Simpson was adamant that Casotti had been "very lightly dealt with" in receiving only two years for the manslaughter of Fantin, which Simpson considered was a case of "plain, unadulterated murder".[86] Because the names on most trials are screened out, and because decisions can only be inferred from the judge's final questions and comments, it is impossible to know whether Casotti was deported; but certainly Agostini, who killed the Pyjama Girl, was deported.

Agostini had been married to Linda Platt, who died in a domestic argument, and he dumped her body in a culvert outside Albury. The corpse was preserved in a formalin bath for

years awaiting positive identification. Agostini's newspaper
articles became increasingly pro-Mussolini and he was interned
immediately Italy joined in the war. Released early in 1944, he
went to work at Romano's restaurant, Sydney, where Police
Commissioner W.J. Mackay observed his depressed demean-
our. Mackay arranged for Linda's body to be made presentable
and persuaded sixteen people who had known her to view the
body. Almost half of them were positive that it was Agostini's
wife, and the ex-internee confessed when Mackay confronted
him. The judge found him guilty of manslaughter and, after
serving only half of his sentence, Agostini was deported in
1948.[87]

Australia First

In the middle of 1944 came a reassessment of the rights and
wrongs of the Australia First internments. A number of people
with experience in internment were involved. Dr Evatt established a Commission of Inquiry under Mr Justice T.S. Clyne[88]
who had chaired the Victorian Appeals Tribunals in 1940. As-
sisting Justice Clyne was W.R. Dovey, QC, a member of the
ACAC. H.J.H. Henchman, a former member of an appeal tribunal represented the Security Service. The hearings began in
Sydney on 19 June 1944 and ended in Melbourne on 17 May
1945. The evidence showed that Intelligence operations and
decisions were not without fault. Conclusions reached by some
operators showed that they did not understand the subtlety of
political thought and they often recorded cliches and selected
extracts, which once they were entered on the file, were regarded as "prima facie" evidence. Constables quickly learned
"to stiffen up a report on a suspect with careful selections from
correspondence in which the innocuous became the seditious".
The lawyer for Masey, Saller, Bath, Hooper and Watts spoke of
"the blithering ineptitude of certain individual military officers" and Dovey did not contradict him. Of the four officers
involved in deciding which, and how many Australia First
members to arrest, each gave a different version of what had
been decided. Of those not arrested there were at least six men
and a number of women who had equally as deep a commitment to the movement and their non-inclusion was not explained.

Another feature of the Clyne Inquiry was the antagonism of

the court to any evidence of anti-British sentiment. P.R. Stephensen refused to admit that his writings were anti-British but he agreed that if a person did attempt to bring Britain into contempt or disrepute in time of war it would be grounds for considering that person for internment. He also agreed with the proposition that "when the presence of an individual in the community was likely to affect the safety of the community, any doubt, from the point of view of common sense, should be resolved in favour of the community". The ultimate justification for internment was the need for the majority to feel secure. The Australia First internments were made in haste, at the moment of Australia's greatest security threat, but in 1945 Clyne concluded that the army had not been justified in recommending the detention of Bath, Clarence Crowley, Hooper, Masey, Matthews, Salier, Tinker-Giles and Watts. Compensation ranging from three hundred and fifty pounds to seven hundred pounds was suggested. Those who were not exonerated by Clyne continued to protest.[89]

The Germans

With the release of most Italians, the investigation of the Australia First cases and the continuing favourable progress of the war, Calwell's committee considered the possibility of releasing the Germans. The ACAC planned to visit Tatura in November 1944 and then to report to the Attorney-General whether the German internees there could safely be released for work. Calwell was not altogether happy about the plan because the Camp Leaders and the Internal Court of Honour were "avowed Nazis". A few internees from this camp had been granted releases but had been intimidated by the others into not leaving the camp. Further, when 50 of the 400 internees in the camp had indicated their desire not to be repatriated to Germany, they had "been subjected to all sorts of intimidation and persecution by the Nazi clique". Calwell placed the blame for this on the Camp Leader, J.H. Becker, and Calwell wanted an "immediate weeding out" of Becker and the Nazis, who would go to another camp so that the committee could test the true feelings of the remainder.[90] Many Germans however, had a strong national loyalty, and would not consider release to work until the war was over.

By the end of 1945 there were 47 Italians and 564 Germans in

camp who had been resident in Australia or her territories when
the war commenced. There were also hundreds of others sent
from overseas and over a thousand Japanese still in camps. Of
the Australian-interned Germans, 357 were males, 85 females
and 122 children.[91] It was decided that the Germans and the
Italians, would be interviewed by Mr Justice (formerly Brigadier) Simpson, who would recommend for or against their
deportation. Many of the missionaries from New Guinea
wanted to return to the missions and after some agitation from
the American and Australian Lutheran Missionary Societies,[92]
many were allowed to do so. Germans whose homes were in
Germany instinctively wanted to return to Germany, but the
plight of German civilians, the lack of food available there for
their children and the division of Germany made some recon-
sider. Newsreels of the horrors of the Belsen concentration
camp, the starvation of civilians and the numerous displaced
persons camps were shown to the internees before their hearings[93] and parents asked if they understood that their children
would be endangered. Naturalised and Australian-born mothers, unlike other wives, were interviewed separately from their
husbands. Most people who chose to return to Germany did so
because they had only ever regarded Australia as a temporary
posting.[94]

All who asked to stay in Australia, and this included those
who had been long-term residents, were closely questioned
about their political views. A number claimed that while their
country was at war they were obliged to give it their loyalty but
with the land they had known now obliterated, they no longer
owed it loyalty. This was acceptable from those who had kept
their original citizenship, but naturalised people and those who
had party affiliations were not viewed kindly. They had to
argue hard to be allowed to stay.[95] Arnold von Skerst explained
that his first life had been destroyed by World War I and since
then he had been knocking around the world "trying to make
a living here and there" as best he could. Simpson summarised
von Skerst's career as being one of service to half a dozen
governments and because this was so widely known Simpson
could never imagine anyone trusting von Skerst's political
outlook again. No one interested in subversive activities would
use such a chameleon. Simpson decided that the man had no
potential as a spy and that it was neither necessary nor advisable to deport him. His reapplication for naturalisation was

rejected and the Prime Minister, Ben Chifley, barred Skerst from representing Australia in a radio Quiz team. On Christmas Eve 1948 Skerst was found dead with his head in the gas oven of his home in Randwick.[96]

Dr Johannes Heinrich Becker, regarded by the press as Australia's leading Nazi, was recommended for deportation. Together with others being repatriated to Germany, Becker had been released from camp on parole to live at his own expense in September 1946, a year after the war was over but still with little shipping available. He also applied for naturalisation but the protest was voluble. Deportation arrangements were made for 20 January 1947 but the Allied Control Council in Germany postponed the move indefinitely. Finally in November 1947, four hundred deportees were gathered at Rushworth for re-grouping prior to departing on the *Kanimbla* from Port Melbourne to be transfered at Fremantle to the US transport *General Stuart Heintzelman*. Becker fled from Adelaide to Sydney under a false name and stowed away on a tanker bound for the Panama Canal but was caught and flown to Fremantle to join the 397 Germans and Italians, 304 of whom had been internees, being returned to Europe. The *Heintzelman* had deposited in Fremantle hundreds of displaced people from the Baltic states. In Europe Becker faced an American de-Nazification court. Dr Gerhard Neumann, the former Sydney University lecturer and Camp Chronicle editor, was also forcibly deported despite his wife's appeal to the newly-engaged Princess Elizabeth, and to Mr Calwell. Dr Greuber, a Nazi Party member and the leader of the Vienna Boys Choir that had been stranded in Australia at the outbreak of war, was also deported from Australia but found a home in South Africa.[97]

The deportees were a minority of internees. Most internees returned to their homes or made new homes in Australia. Of the British internees several hundred remained in Australia. Lt-Col Layton arranged for G.F. Chodziesner's young son Ben to be transshipped to Australia from Chile where his mother had died. Some of the student members of the 8th Employment Company went on to become top-ranking academics and wear the *Dunera* tag with pride.[98] The internees from the Middle East were a dilemma for the Australian authorities and Mr Justice Hutchins from Tasmania was eventually given the responsibility to look into their situation. A significant proportion of the internees from Palestine were members of the Temple Society or Templars. Their return to Palestine where the civil war, that would result in the establishment of the state of Israel raged, was not possible. But the Templars had assets that made them acceptable migrants. On 23 September 1949 Calwell introduced the Temple Society Trust Fund Bill which created procedures for the disbursement of money received by the Australian government on the liquidation of the irrigated citrus orchards, vineyards and dairy farms that the society members and others had owned in Israel.[99] Well over three million pounds sterling were involved. The 574 men, women and children, who were sent to Australia in 1941 because Palestine had become a strategic war zone, had been interned "as a precautionary measure". They had no desire to be transported to Germany and the Australian government was anxious not to be burdened with their internment indefinitely. Could they not become one with us?

Mr Justice Hutchins was satisfied that 504 were suitable for Australian residence but he felt 70 should be returned to Germany. To keep the society together, 270 Templars who had been evacuated to Cyprus from Israel were approved for migration in April 1948. Calwell stated that the Templars' funds were not to be used to establish an alien colony and that the people should be readily accepted into the Australian community. They had high standards of morality and conduct and their farming skill would earn them respect. Calwell told parliament that the Templars would settle successfully in Australia as new Australians "for their own good and in the interests of this great country".[100] Calwell reiterated these themes in speeches at naturalisation ceremonies, at the harbour-sides when migrant boats arrived and at migrant hostels. His Ministerial statements, his autobiography and his biographies attest to his devotion to immigration and assimilation. Another group assessed by Mr Justice Hutchins were the employees of the Anglo-Persian Oil Company and others who had been in camp in Australia since late 1941 including those from the Straits Settlement. In a conference with Forde and Calwell in Canberra, Hutchins asked for a decision as to whether overseas internees held in Australia would be allowed to settle permanently if they wished.[101] The ministers decided they could if they were judged to be "fit and proper persons to become naturalised". Many were released from Tatura in August 1946, most expressing their intention to live in Victoria. Others found it hard to make a decision. Their English was not good, their qualifications might not be recognised and the situation with their property and assets overseas was unclear. Some had not heard from their family for years and wanted to be reunited above all else. The Commissioner had found that in addition to all these problems many suffered "from diffidence and forms of nervousness due to up to seven years in internment". The government decided that it was reasonable to give these people a year to make up their minds about whether to stay permanently. In the meantime they provided fares to places where internees were offered employment and provided some assistance with transfering money and reuniting families. Once an internee decided to stay, the years in camp would be credited for naturalisation purposes. Mr H. Tempy, who had acted as secretary to Mr Justice Hutchins, was appointed as a Welfare officer to meet internees in Melbourne and to direct them to their accommodation and employment.

The Asians

In contrast to his treatment of the European internees, Calwell rejected any moves to allow any of the Asiatic groups, who had been flung on Australia's shores by the fortunes of war, to settle. Calwell, like most other Australians of the period, was committed to the White Australia policy. There was some petitioning to consider the position of former long-term Australian residents, and a few of them were in fact released. Sho Takasuka's restriction not to go beyond ten miles from his farm was lifted just under a year after Japan had surrendered; he went on to become President of the Huntly Shire outside Bendigo. Denzo Kuringu was finally reunited with his family late in 1946.[102] Some of the "Japanese" interned were Formosans, and they were allowed to return to that island rather than to Japan. Other "Japanese" had been residents of Indonesia and the Pacific Islands, and had no desire to return to Japan where the climate was unattractive to them, but the sentiment against anything Japanese aroused by the arrival back in Australia of the emaciated survivors of the Burma railway and the POW horror camps precluded any inquiry into those internees who did not want to return to Japan. When R.G. Menzies, the leader of the Opposition, protested about the deportation of ex-internees and Japanese POWs in over-crowded conditions on the *Yoiziki*, Calwell made one of the most vitriolic replies ever heard in parliament.[103]

The situation with the Indonesian seamen and the employees of the Dutch government-in-exile was more complicated. The Dutch had offended sections of the Australian community by beginning to deport back to Tanah Merah, the prison camp for political prisoners in Dutch New Guinea, their ex-prisoners whom the Australian authorities had released in 1943. The Dutch were moving to have their republican opponents confined. There was an effective lobby group of exinternees working in Mackay, Qld, and they brought the situation to the attention of leading Labor politicians. The Indonesians wanted the deportations stopped and to be allowed to return to their homeland as free people. In all Dutch establishments in Australia Indonesian pro-republican feeling was high, and when some Indonesians refused duty they were interned. The clerks from Wacol, Brisbane, were interned at Camp Lytton and Gaythorne under Australian guards while marines and sailors from Middle Park and St Kilda in Melbourne were gaoled in Geelong. Lockwood claims that in April 1946 there were 820 Indonesians in prison in Australia. The Dutch and Ambonese guards at Camp Victory, Casino, shot at protesting internees, killing two and wounding others. Residents of Casino demanded that this "concentration camp" be closed, and Calwell sent strongly worded protests to The Hague. He threatened that if the Dutch did not free the Casino prisoners the Australian authorities would take action to remove the guards. The refusal of the Indonesians to man Dutch ships and armed services, and the black ban effected by the Australian Seamen's unions, delayed the return of the Dutch government-in-exile and was a contributing factor in the establishment of the Indonesian republic.[104]

The End — or the Beginning?

With the repatriation of the Indonesians, internment in Australia had come to an end and it was virtually forgotten. The Templars and other Palestinian exinternees, the ex-*Dunera* men, the pre-war refugees and migrants who were interned, all slipped quietly into the Australian community and were submerged in the surge of migrants that followed the Balts from the *Heintzelman*. The dramatic impact of one million new settlers in the post-war period, on top of the censorship of the activities of the ACAC has prevented Australians from perceiving the continuity from internment in World War II to the post-war migration boom. Yet the links were there, and one of the strongest of them was Arthur Calwell.

Calwell, who became Minister for Immigration in 1946 and then initiated and promoted Australia's vigorous immigration policy, had spent much of his energies in the previous four years working in isolation on the problems of the internees. For much of this period he was not popular with Curtin or Caucus. He had alienated himself from the Curtin government over conscription and he widened the rift by aggressive and provocative remarks; only his strong position in the Victorian branch got him the last nomination for a junior ministry in 1943. Calwell's biographer, Colm Kiernan, considered that Calwell's immigration policy "had grown in his mind during his period of isolation from Curtin's government". During the years 1942-45 Calwell's main responsibility was the ACAC, and his contact with internees convinced him that "most of them were excellent citizens" and Kiernan considers that, as a result, Calwell "had few fears about bringing more such people to Australia" after the war.[105] The most striking feature of post-war migration policy was its inclusion of large numbers from continental Europe. Migration from Britain created no controversy, but Calwell saw the benefits of a broader policy. Calwell's pro-European view has been attributed to his Irish and American background, and no doubt this provided fertile soil for the germination of his ideas on immigration. He greatly admired the American view of cosmopolitan citizenship, and he promoted the term "New Australians" and gave additional status to naturalisation ceremonies. But while these influences and activities are well known, the contribution of his experiences with internees is not.

This can partly be attributed to Calwell's own failure to mention anything of the ACAC in his autobiography *Be Just and Fear Not*, and the fact that his promotion of a large white population was argued on defence grounds. This justification was necessary to make immigration acceptable to Labor supporters whose depression experiences had made them suspicious of migrants. Defence was also the justification used by the non-Labor government of 1949 who continued to pursue immigration energetically. Calwell's conviction that Europeans were good migrants and his ACAC experiences just dropped out of sight.

Yet his absorption with the status of enemy aliens who were refugees, and with the concerns of hard-working Italian internees and their families, is convincingly documented in his papers. His impassioned pleas to Curtin and Evatt on behalf of these "unfortunate people" are a testament to what was going on in his mind at the time his ideas on immigration were being formed. One of his first acts as Minister for Immigration was to help the families of Australian Jews obtain entry to Australia.[106] In his ministerial statement on Immigration on 2 August 1945 Calwell promulgated his belief that non-British people had a lot to offer Australia and that within a short time assimilation should occur. Australians, in Calwell's opinion, had been "too prone in the past to ostracise those of alien birth", and Calwell stressed that the children of foreign-born parents had helped defend Australia. Also many young Americans, who in Australia's terms were "enemy aliens", had been drafted into the United States forces that had saved Australia. In Calwell's view, Australia would be well advised to incorporate its migrants fully into its life and society in a similar way.[107] Because of its influence on Calwell, internment in World War II is a crucial link in the transition from a traditional British society before the war to the post-war immigration boom that moved Australia towards a more broadly based society.

CONCLUSION

The outstanding feature of internment policy was its fluidity. It had to be fluid because it moved between two concepts that in wartime were not always compatible — the individual's right in a democratic society not to be detained arbitrarily and the need of the people to feel secure. These two principles were evident when policy was first considered and laid down in the *War Book*, and the decision that internments should be as few as allowed by "public safety and public sentiment" reflected both principles, as well as being sensible in terms of cost. Cost, in capital and manpower, was a constant factor influencing internment policy and its implementation, and it was ignored only when security became of overriding importance. After all, the one and one half million pounds spent on internment in World War I had little proven effect on Australian security or on the eventual victorious outcome.

In terms of security Australian authorities were not unprepared at the outbreak of war, and criticisms of the original internments are largely unfounded. Members of the Nazi Party were dedicated to Hitler's regime, and the expatriot employees of German firms were often completely loyal to their native land and thereby did represent a risk. Other measures taken at the beginning of the war — registration of all aliens and restrictions on enemy aliens- were also sensible. The significant fact is that these original internments, together with the equally justifiable internment of members of the Fascist Party when Italy joined the war, constituted only one-twentieth of total interments. The large majority of internments were made because perceptions of security needs changed and because public sentiment demanded it. Both were closely aligned to the progress of the war. There is no proof that security was actually improved by the internment of newly arrived migrants, European socialists, and former Italian soldiers in June 1940, or of Italian farmers from North Queensland in early 1942. These people were free for a large portion of the war and no act of violence to the war effort is attributable to them. But the military losses at these two critical periods brought the war closer and the authorities were concerned that those who did not identify closely with the British Empire might be prompted to act if the authorities did not show themselves determined to prevent such a possibility. Military losses also unsettled the public, whose anxiety was the major factor contributing to most internments.

There is a special psychological state that binds a nation in war time — a belief that the cause justifies the sacrifice of a generation, a belief that victory is possible and a belief that everyone is working together for that victory. If belief in the cause is missing, as happened in the Vietnam War, victory is unlikely. If people do not believe they can win, as a number of European countries realised in the face of Germany's Blitzkrieg, they will surrender and hope to fight another day. If the people do not believe that everyone is working for a victory, as happened in France, the nation will divide and the willingness to fight disappear. Australians, on the whole, never lacked faith in the cause, although some groups were held to be not as committed to it as was required. Communists were regarded as not being wholeheartedly for the war in the period before the attack on the Soviet Union; and the Jehovah's Witnesses and, to a much lesser extent, pacifists generally were regarded with suspicion, but only considered for actual internment if they actively campaigned to disturb the war effort. Enemy aliens and naturalised people of enemy origin were regularly considered for internment because of the fear of disloyalty or divided loyalty. On two occasions — when France fell and when Singapore fell — these sharp reminders that victory would not be quick, or easy, brought a dramatic increase in internments. These were the times when people came closest to questioning whether victory was inevitable. When people feel threatened they look for evidence of action by the authorities to remedy the situation and if a military reply cannot be forthcoming some scapegoat has to be satisfactorily sacrificed to provide a substitute. It is easier to sacrifice the liberty of further groups of enemy aliens, or to throw doubt on the loyalty of naturalised persons than to remind an unsettled nation that lack of foresight, and the priorities of pre-war spending, actually caused the military setbacks.

Arthur Calwell, in his foreword to Lamidey's *Aliens Control* correctly assessed the situation. "When passions are let loose by war", he wrote, "it happens all too often that foreigners, whether or not of enemy origin, and even locally born persons bearing foreign names, become the object of denunciation and persecution."[1] Calwell regarded it as a matter of pride that "popular hysteria did not reach the intensity" of that in the Great War. There was no significant political or press campaign against aliens during World War II. The lack of a public campaign is attributable to the cool-headedness and commitment to fair play exhibited by the Prime Ministers, R.G. Menzies and John Curtin, who never engaged in alien baiting themselves, and publicly denounced it in others. They were supported by senior ministers such as P.C. Spender and Dr Evatt. But internment was not directly in these men's hands, nor did their attitude make them popular. Menzies' temperate approach did not prevent his being ousted from office, and internees from the lowest levels of risk were taken in Curtin's term of office. The fact is that there is little statistical difference between the figures for both wars. The actual number of people interned did not vary in proportional terms, that is, one thousand for every one million in the population.

The explanation lies in the fact that the actual danger increased. In World War I the theatres of war — with the minor exceptions of New Guinea and the chance raider — were far away. In World War II civilians were killed on Australian soil. Many citizens and officials demanded internments and at peak times of war pressure this demand had to be acceded to. Calwell stressed that from the fall of France onwards "a good deal of avoidable human misery was caused" by internments, but he acknowledged that it was probably "inevitable, for war as the democracies wage it is largely a matter of improvisation, and in urgent situations which demand prompt and effective action there is little time to weigh the niceties of human rights". When a nation is suddenly much more threatened than it had been a week before, the population takes fright. This fear can be whipped up in a campaign to emphasise and exaggerate differences between peoples, but it cannot so easily be cooled by soothing reassurances for it is a real fear, and together with actual military action, the government must institute internal security measures to keep up morale.

The most effective way to counter this fear, and to prevent

nervous agitation setting one group against another, is to show that everyone is working equally hard and making equal sacrifices. This is why the Aliens Service regulations were introduced and, although Evatt's explanation of the return to a narrow internment was couched in terms of individual liberty, the policy was defended in terms of the need for manpower and the useful war work ex-internees were engaged in. Everyone had to be seen to be sharing the burden and actively contributing. The most intriguing speculation in the history of internment is whether Evatt would have been able to carry out his return to a narrow policy if the war situation had not improved. The fact that all press reference to Calwell's committee was censored showed that the government was determined to remove debate on internments and releases from the public arena. It was not until after the Labor Government had firmly established itself in office with the 1943 election that the large-scale releases actually took place.

The censorship of release plans prevented open debate and displays of outraged public sentiment, leaving only actual security needs to be considered. Yet nothing lifted morale and calmed the call for internments like military victories. When the Australian and British divisions swept to victory over the Italians in the Middle East, further internments of Italians in Australia in 1941 became a non-issue. When the Australian and American armies recaptured Japanese strongholds in New Guinea in 1943, the question of further internments never revived. Thus the national pattern of internments and releases reflected the fluctuating progress of the war, but variations between states and between nationalities were more complex. Lamidey suggests that the reasons for the difference between internment statistics in the various states lay in the military situation and in the approaches of commandants. So it was both a question of geography and personality. Another aspect, which Lamidey does not suggest but which helps to explain the differences, is the nature of the alien population in each state. But, firstly, there is the aspect of geography. The more distant the state from army headquarters in Melbourne, the greater the number of internments. It was not just a matter of the more northerly (and therefore closer to the fighting) the state, the greater the number of internments. That element certainly explains the high rates in Queensland, where 43.11 per cent of male aliens were interned, but equally important was the sense of isolation. The next highest rates were in Western Australia (32.66 per cent), and in Tasmania (34.33 per cent).[2]

The personalities of the commandants were also important, and variable. A senior officer's concept of loyalty and his interpretation of his duties affected internment levels. Major-General J.M.A. Durrant saw the Italians as undifferentiated, and in Western Australia they had either to be watched or interned. It is not surprising that he also oversaw the high internment rates in Queensland. Brigadier H.C. Bundock, had he been authorised to detain the foreign born, regardless of naturalisation, would undoubtedly have pressed the South Australian rate of 15.65 per cent much higher. Lieutenant-General V.A.H. Sturdee intimated a desire to see all Germans interned whether they had claims to be refugees or not. The halt brought to Eastern Command's internments after a quick roundup in June 1940 and the acrimonious exchanges they precipitated, between Mair and Menzies, and between Eastern Command and AHQ, slowed the rate of internments in New South Wales. The curtailing of Eastern Command's authority after the unauthorised collection of Roumanians during the second peak of internments, held the New South Wales rate at 11.76 per cent. The consistent refusal of Victorian-based commanders to be rushed into higher rates of internment, commensurate with their larger number of alien residents, was justified by the distance from the war zone. The small size of Victoria allowed for regular surveillance and a consequent belief that restrictions were sufficient.

The low rate of 2.97 per cent could also have been the result of the personal judgement of men such as Lieutenant-General J.L. Whitham, Colonel S.F. Whittington and Major-General W.A.B. Steele that Victorian security only required a minimal number of internments. This personal response may have been influenced by intangible factors such as the psychological security of having Australian headquarters and, for a time, American headquarters in Melbourne. An important factor in this lowest rate was the nature of the Victorian alien population and the understanding of this nature by the military's closest advisor on aliens, Major Roland S. Browne of the CIB and, later, of the Security Service. Over half of the Jews who migrated to Australia went to Melbourne, and Browne had met many of them before the war. He knew their anti-Nazi sentiments and he was confident in his judgements. Other personalities may also have had an influence. Archbishop Mannix and General

Blamey were not unknown to the Italian community in Victoria, and the member for Melbourne, Arthur Calwell, and the member for Kooyong, R.G. Menzies, not only knew the communities that made up Melbourne but were, in their different ways, determined advocates of legality and justice.

Another factor in the disproportionate internments between Queensland and Victoria lies in the nationalities of the alien residents. Queensland and Western Australia had the greatest population of Japanese, of whom all were interned, thus driving their overall percentage higher. The differing rates of internment of each national group would logically vary according to the degree of risk they were held to be, but this was not always the case. The Japanese were interned at 98 per cent, Germans and Italians at 32 and 31 per cent, respectively, and the Roumanians at 24 per cent.[3] In sharp contrast to Germans, Austrians were only interned at 6 per cent, which means that the Australian Government disregarded the Anschluss and did not automatically transfer German citizenship to resident Austrians. Nor did the even treatment of Germans and Italians reflect a similar level of risk assessment. The majority of Italians who were interned from the low-risk category were taken only because they were living on the northeast Queenland coast. The Germans were feared because they were held to be thorough, efficient and ruthless — an opinion not held of Italians. At the time of the big round-ups in 1942, not only German men but also their women and children were taken from the vulnerable areas, while only military-aged men of Italian origin were included. The Japanese were all interned, not only because they were of the same race as the army advancing on Singapore, but also because they were obvious targets of abuse. It may not have been necessary for all Japanese to have been interned, for the laundrymen and vegetable growers could have made a productive contribution to the domestic war effort, but it was advisable that they be not released for their own safety, as well as for law and order and morale. Thus the nationalities resident in the different states affected their internment rates. Had there been a Japanese rather than a Chinese community in Melbourne, the Victorian figure would have reflected this.

The personalities of commandants were a factor, but GOCs were not completely free agents. They were influenced by the restraints of their superiors and they paid attention to the advice of their staff. There is no doubt that the overriding factor was geography. Any commandant would have acted to remove the North Queensland Italians, Germans and Japanese in early 1942. And in so doing, the Queensland Commandant would have had the support of the local citizens. Corresponding with the variety in internment rates there was also a difference in the level of demand for internment by the public, with many more petitions coming from the northern areas. However, considerable caution should be applied before concluding that one group of Australians was more xenophobic than another. Queenslanders were most vulnerable. Some Sydney residents reacted to the midget submarine attack on their harbour with a hasty exit to the Blue Mountains. Melbourne was not tested in the same way.

Among the most interesting comparisons are those with World War I. So many aspects were similar. The parallel between internments and the progress of the war, and the emphasis on nationality, and the doubts about naturalisation, were common. In both wars merchant seamen were judged to be as valuable as servicemen, and military-trained and military-aged men were reviewed most carefully. Anti-migrant feeling and competition for land jobs were intermingled with prejudice and fear; spy scares and unjustified suspicions were evident. However, it is the differences that were more telling. The lessons of World War I had been learnt and noted for consideration in World War II. They were that cost, manpower and reciprocity considerations should keep internments to a minimum, and that a system of reviews and reassessments should always be available through appeals. It was the increase in the level of danger that eventually precipitated internments to a rate roughly equivalent with World War I. When that danger decreased a return to a smaller number of internments was possible and was instituted. This fluctuating policy was correct because it allowed for the unpredictability of war-induced situations and resulted in a lack of much long-term hostility by internees.

The most significant justification for a flexible policy was the unusual situation of the German Jews. Amendments to legislation to take account of this special and unexpected situation prevented the continuation of their unnecessary hardships, but this acknowledgement of the Jewish problem and its translation into internment policy were not easy: security fears, anti-Semitism, and anti-migrant feelings had to be overcome. The prob-

lem of the *Dunera* internees would probably have dragged on
into 1944 if the manpower crisis in 1942 had not occurred. The
holding of overseas internees was common to both wars, but
the difficulty of making decisions about releasing internees sent
by allies was a feature of World War II. The solution was not for
Australia to refuse overseas internees, for Australia remained
dependent on allies who asked for this assistance, and incon-
testably the island continent was an ideal gaol. The solution lay
in having some means of applying the flexibility towards the
locally interned, to those who were not Australian internees,
but with no records or assessments available it fell into the "too
hard" basket.

The benefit of adjusting policy is demonstrated by the virtual
lack of any long-term hostility by most internees. The lengthy
incarceration of those with a political and national commitment
to the enemy was acknowledged by ex-Nazis and fierce patriots
to have been warranted.[4] The majority, who served less than
two years, now consider that they were the victims of difficult
circumstances, and prefer to forget their internment. In a study
of the areas of Queensland where the large scale internments of
Italians took place, W.D. Borrie found that by 1951 ex-internees
had again integrated into their communities and were taking
their traditional interest in local affairs; for instance, they were
well represented on primary school committees. They were not
proportionately represented on shire councils or high school
committees, but this had been the case before the war and has
not improved dramatically today. Borrie suggests that the lack
of bitterness of these ex-internees was the result of the care
taken of their farms by their wives and the Queensland Sugar
Board.[5] The economic security they had sought by migration
was basically undisturbed, and they regarded the low yields of
1942-3 as a temporary setback.

In 1979 most ex-internees interviewed confirmed their belief
that the circumstances of war satisfactorily explained their
internment, although a few showed dissatisfaction with generalised explanations and a curiosity about the circumstances of
their own selection. Ross Costanzo shrugged his shoulders —
he had been a newly-arrived migrant who was a conscript in
Mussolini's army and all such men were interned, so he felt no
personal affront. He airly waved the secateurs he used to cut
the capsicums he sold in the southern markets. Since then life
had been good to him. His wife worked beside him, and his

children and their spouses picked the tomatoes in the next field. Australia was a country that protected the "small man". The ABC broadcast the daily vegetable prices and if he was not satisfied with his agent's checque, the Marketing Board would investigate for him. But in the town, the pre-war naturalised and now retired cane farmer, Gus Orlandi, was not satisfied. His eyes flashed and his fist was clenched as he asked for a justification of his internment. Why was a man who had made farming his life, who had two young Australian-born sons, torn from his wife and thrown into prison? When his son was asked at university what his father had done in the war, he had to reply that he had been put in a concentration camp![6]

Of the minority who still search for explanations the *Dunera* internees are the more persistent questioners. In a review of B. Patkin's *The Dunera Internees*, former British internee Felix Werder concludes that "nobody ever learns anything from history" for in his view the middle classes still worship the same materialistic values that they did before World War II.[7] He does not see evidence in today's society that people are more understanding. Henry Mayer, a former *Dunera* internee and now a professor, suggests that the *Dunera* internments should be a part of a broader history of the period with comparisons made "between types of justice" meted out to his group, the Communists, "the quasi-fascist Australia Firsters", and resident refugees.[8] One could add the long-term resident, naturalised Italian farmers to that list. More importantly, Mayer asks where justice can be found and what it would cost. In wartime, justice cannot be purchased at the expense of real security or of the general public's need to feel secure, but the constant questioning by some who were sacrificed to satisfy that need, correctly reminds the nation that the balance went at times cruelly against certain groups.

Few people were prepared to speak out against unjust internments even when the crises had passed. The majority who remained silent did so partly from a mixture of fear, ignorance, parochialism and anti-semitism, but most people accepted that, because "responsible authorites" thought internees were dangerous, they must indeed be so. Mayer blames local Jewish organisations, Dr Evatt and the Labor government for not acting when they could have been expected to have made "some attempt" to fight injustice. Mayer rightly judges that the lack of a quick response by Labor lies in "the atmosphere of the

1940s", and Paul Hasluck pushes this idea even further in his recent review of a biography of P.R.Stephensen.[9]

Hasluck still regards the detention of the Australia First members as a gross infringement of individual liberty, and that "the tardiness in rectifying it", was "a matter of shame". But he also points out that the background of wartime politics was critical. Curtin's government rested on the continuing support of independents who had dumped Menzies because he was not acting dynamically. Internment was action of a kind. A firm stand against action was not possible. It is to Curtin's credit that he was able in early 1942 to use the manpower argument to have the younger *Dunera* internees released, that he expanded recruitment for national service to include aliens and refugees, and that he allowed tribunals to hear Japanese objectors. In mid-1942 he took the control of aliens and internment from the army and returned it to the civil domain. By September 1942 Evatt was able to turn internment policy around, although the enactment of most releases waited a year longer. Curtin, Evatt and Labor do not deserve to be held as more blameworthy than the conformists who lined up with the established authorities. Conformists comprised the bulk of the population, and a democratic nation that expects a higher standard of regard for civil liberties from its leaders than it imposes on itself, is dodging its own responsibilities.

However, together with the shortened terms most internees served, and the economic success that many ex-internees found in Australia, there is another factor that contributed to the general lack of long-term bitterness. All internees stressed their high regard for the men who guarded them, and their general satisfaction with their food and treatment. Accommodation at Gaythorne was unfavourably commented upon, and primitive conditions marked the establishment phase of the camps in the outback areas, but the southern camps, particularly Tatura, were regarded as very good. When the Victorian Official Visitors asked to be relieved of their duties late in 1945, they expressed the opinion that the conduct of the camps and the treatment of internees reflected "credit on the Army".[10]

Not only had internees "been treated justly", but with "a sympathetic understanding". Mr Justice Gavan Duffy and Mr Justice Norman O'Bryan thought "that some other soldierly virtues" were "as conspicuous in our army as valour on the field", and that it was a pleasure for them to have seen the

complete lack of a "malignant rancour against the helpless".
The behaviour of the Garrison troops should not be discounted
as a factor contributing to the successful reintegration of former
resident internees and in the decision of many overseas internees to become Australian citizens.[11]

So humane treatment and a fluid policy circumvented the
worst aspects of internment, but the forces against a peacetime
regard for civil liberties during war time are too powerful to be
counter balanced, even if the offending group are Australians
and their "crime" is extreme political unpopularity. In trying to
assess the "lesson" of the treatment of Australia First internees,
Bruce Muirden could not answer the question as to how far any
individual can be left free in war time. When a community is
physically threatened, how can the authorities handle dissident
opinion and seeming sympathy with the enemy? Is "panic
action destroying civil liberties excusable?", Muirden asks.[12]
The reality is that it is inevitable. The people, in their fear and
anxiety, demand action and particularly the removal of those
considered as not being committed to the cause for which the
young and best people are dying. The authorities must move
against perceived threats, and the community can repent later.
A better solution would be that the nation become a more
integrated, mature and tolerant community, and to some extent
Australia set out to achieve this after World War II. First, citizenship and nationality have been welded together, and rights
and obligations have been made to apply equally to every
citizen. When National Service was required in 1950, it was
incumbent on all 18-year-old males, and when a selective system was introduced in 1964, the authorities tried to be obviously even-handed. Naturalisation is now legally equal to
nationality by birth, and all cultural groups are encouraged to
contribute to the national heritage. It was his experiences with
migrant internees in World War II that motivated Arthur Calwell to begin the process of moving Australia towards those
goals.

Appendix A

ADDITIONAL STATISTICAL INFORMATION

Internments of Resident Aliens by Nationality
(from Lamidey, *Aliens Control*, p.52)

Italians	4 727	Swiss	6
Germans	1 115	Egyptians	5
Japanese	587	Others	5
Finns	142	Yugoslavs	4
Austrians	90	British by marriage	4
Albanians	84	U.S.A.	3
Rumanians	42	New Guinea natives	3
Hungarians	33	Belgians	3
Russians	28	French	3
Portuguese	28	Bulgarians	3
Norwegians	15	Latvians	2
Czechoslovakians	11	Javanese	2
Dutch	10	Chinese	2
Poles	8	Thailanders	1
Estonians	7	Lithuanians	1
Greeks	7	Spanish	1
		Total	**6 982**

Total Internments
(from Lamidey, *Aliens Control*, p.22 of Interim Report)

Aliens resident in Australia	5 475
Naturalised British Subjects	1 388
Natural Born	240
Total	**7 103**

The problem with this figure is that it does not match the figure of 6 982 given as the total number of resident aliens interned in the compilation from Lamidey, p.52. The two sets of figures were compiled at different times. The 5 475 figure for Aliens was dated 31 December 1942 and the 6 982 compilation was

prepared on 31 March 1944, which could mean 1 507 additional
aliens were interned between 1 January 1943 and 30 March
1944. This is unlikely at a time when releases were the policy.
(It would also mean that total internments were 8 610.) A more
probable explanation is that Naturalised British Subjects were
subdivided into their original nationality for the 6 982 figure of
31 March 1944. The addition of the aliens and N.B.S. figures
gives 6 863, which approximates 6 982. It is even possible that
some Australian-born children of alien or N.B.S. parents could
have been included under the nationality of their parent's
country of origin.

Local Internments — 31 December 1942

Aliens

	Males	Females	Total
Apprehended	5 310	165	5 475
Released	1 492	16	1 508
Now interned	3 818	149	3 967

Naturalised British Subjects

	Males	Females	Total
Apprehended	1 339	49	1 388
Released	280	11	291
Now interned	1 059	38	1 097

Natural born

	Males	Females	Total
Apprehended	195	45	240
Released	70	6	76
Now interned	125	39	164

Totals

	Males	Females	Total
Apprehended	6 844	259	7 103
Released	1 842	33	1 875
Now interned	5 002	226	5 228

Lamidey, *Aliens Control*, p. 54

Enemy Male Internments as Percentage of Males Registered in Five Enemy Nationalities

	Total	Interned	%
Japanese	600	587	97.83
Germans	3 479	1 115	32.04
Italians	14 904	4 727	31.71
Rumanians	170	42	24.70
Austrians	1 394	90	6.45

Male Aliens Interned as Percentage of Total Alien Males, by States

State	Total	Interned	%
Queensland	6 968	3 004	43.11
Tasmania	201	69	34.33
Western Australia	5 193	1 696	32.66
South Australia	2 132	334	15.65
N.S.W.	13 060	1 536	11.76
Victoria	11 530	343	2.97

Lamidey, *Aliens Control*, p.53

Tribunal results to 14 November 1940
Number of internees at 31 October 1940

	NSW	VIC	QLD	SA	WA	TAS	NG	TOTAL
Enemy aliens	595	167	328	118	951	34	98	2 291
Other aliens	6	1	2	5	—	—	3	20
British subjects	114	9	55	16	17	—	15	226
All classes	718	177	385	139	968	34	116	2 537

Internees whose appeals and leave to appeal have been rejected from outbreak of war to 14 November 1940

Non-enemy aliens	2	—	1	—	—	—	—	3
British subjects	35	3	24	5	16	—	—	83

Leave to appeal granted but hearing pending

Non-enemy aliens	—	—	—	2	—	—	—	2
British subjects	16	—	2	20	1	—	—	39

Applications for leave to appeal pending decision

Non-enemy aliens	—	—	1	—	—	—	—	1
British subjects	68	—	7	7	—	—	—	82

Note: Arrangements for hearing appeals from those interned to New Guinea was being considered.

(AWM 113 1/1/13)

Releases to 31 December 1944

	Sept-Dec 1942	Jan-Aug 1943	Aug-Apr 1943 1944	Apr-Dec 1944	Total
Italian					
Aliens	29	1 078	1 552	148	2 807
NBS	23	294	365	29	711
Aust.-born	1	10	16	—	27
German					
Aliens	8	47	141	154	350
NBS	39	10	47	36	132
Aust.-born	3	5	19	—	27
Japanese	4	10	20	25	59
Finns	59	—	—	—	59
Albanians	84	—	—	—	84
Others	18	89	75	112	294
Total	268	1 543	2 235	504	4 550

Lamidey, *Aliens Control*, p. 54)

Overseas Nationals Interned in Australia

From

United Kingdom	2 542
Netherlands East Indies	1 949
New Caledonia	1 124
Palestine	834
Dutch New Guinea	524
Iran	495
Straits settlements	284
New Zealand	49
New Hebrides	34
Middle East	18
Solomon Islands	8
Total	7 861

AA MP 842, file 115/1/198

In this file the number of local internees is nominated as 7 485.
On these figures 15 346 persons were accommodated in Australian Internment Camps at some time during World War II.

Overseas internees by nationality

From	German	Italian	Japanese	Sundries	Total
United Kingdom	2 342	200	—	—	2 542
Straits Settlement	222	50	—	—	272
Palestine	664	170	—	—	834
Iran	494	—	—	—	494
Middle East	18	—	—	—	18
Singapore (Foreign Legion)	12	—	—	—	12
New Guinea	—	—	—	525	525
New Caledonia	1	5	1 124	9	1 139
New Hebrides	—	34	—	—	34
N.E.I.	—	—	1 949	—	1 949
Solomon Islands	—	—	3	5	8
New Zealand	—	—	50	—	50
Total	3 753	425	3 160	539	7 877

History of the Directorate of PWI, p.19

Local and Overseas Internees held by AMF by years

		Germans	Italians	Japanese	Other	Total
31 December	1939	278				278
	1940	3 245	1 976			5 221
	1941	3 698	1 957	968	36	6 659
	1942	2 661	3 836	4 022	212	10 731
	1943	2 396	852	3 141	120	6 409
	1944	1 851	226	2 800	97	4 974
	1945	1 576	99	2 764	73	4 512
	1946	202	2	—	4	208

History of the Directorate of PWI, p.212

29 September 1940

COMMAND	LOCAL					OVERSEAS					GRAND TOTAL
	Germans male	Germans female	Italians male	Italians female	Total	Germans male	Germans female	Italians male	Italians female	Total	
Northern	35		294		329						329
Eastern	57		458		515	E1,983				E1,983	2,498
Southern											
3MD	561		166		727	E 345 Z 141	Z 81	E200 Z 34	Z11	E 545 Z 267	1,539
4MD	9		15		24						24
Western			856		856						856
Total	662		1,789		2,451	2,469	81	234	11	2,795	5,246

E = Internees from United Kingdom
Z = Internees from Singapore

12 April 1941

COMMAND	LOCAL					OVERSEAS					GRAND TOTAL
	Germans male	Germans female	Italians male	Italians female	Total	Germans male	Germans female	Italians male	Italians female	Total	
Northern	33		56		89						89
Eastern	61		907		968	E1,870				E1,870	2,838
Southern											
3MD	624	1	5		630	E 449 Z 127	Z 95	E200 Z 30	Z19	E 649 Z 271	1,550
4MD	12		17		29						29
Western			600		600						600
Total	730	1	1,585		2,316	2,446	95	230	19	2,790	5,106

E = Internees from United Kingdom
Z = Internees from Singapore

Captain A.R. Heighway
O/C POW Information Bureau

Appendix B

Senior Appointments to Directorate of Prisoners of War and Internees

Colonel J. McCahon, Director, June 1941 — December 1945
Major F.A. Hosking, AAG, July 1941 — October 1945
Major W.L. Davies, AAG, May 1941 — December 1944
Major E.G. Coffin, DAAG (Employment) January 1942 — April 1946
Major W.H.S. Dickinson, DAAG (Internees), May 1941 — June 1943
The history of the Directorate was compiled by Major D.E. Cleverly (Staff Captain, Enemy POW Section May 1941 — April 1945)
(*History of Directorate of PWI*, pp. 472-3.)

Commandants of Internment Camp Groups

Lieutenant Colonel W.T. Tackaberry — TATURA, 1939-1942
Lieutenant Colonel C.S. Thane OBE V.D. — HAY, 1940—1944
Lieutenant Colonel E.T. Dean DSO V.D. — LOVEDAY, 1940-1946

Other Officers Involved in the Administration of Loveday

Lieutenant Colonel R. Soden E.D. (Commanded 33 Grn Bn)
Major A. Dick DSO (1 I/C Internee and POW Administration)
Major C.E. Hunkin E.D. (2 I/C Security, Loveday)
Captain C.R. Jury (Australian Intelligence Corps)

Camp Commandants (Loveday, January 1943)

No.9 camp	Major W.E.L. Hill
No.10 camp	Major A.W. Lott
No.14A camp	Major C.H. Richardson
No.14B camp	Major J.A. McRae
No. 14C camp	Captain B.B. Buttery
No. 14D camp	Captain G.E. Whitehill, MSM
Woolenook camp	Captain T.S. Brown

(*Internment in South Australia*, pp.6-7)

NOTES

Introduction

1   D.M Horner, *High Command: Australia and Allied Strategy*, 1939-1945, George Allen and Unwin, Sydney, 1982, pp.6-8, points out that two key figures in preparing for war, F.G.Shedden, secretary of the Department of Defence, and Major-General J.D.Lavarack, the Chief of the General Staff from 1935, had different opinions. Shedden stressed the role of the British Navy in Imperial defence and Lavarack wanted a significant force to remain in Australia to avoid complete dependence on the navy.

2   Paul Hasluck, *The Government and the People*, *1939-1941*, Australian War Memorial, Canberra, 1952, (hereafter shown as Hasluck, vol. 1,) p. 593.

3   D.M. Horner, *High Command*, p. xix.

4   D.M. Horner, *Crisis of Command: Australian Generalship and the Japanese Threat*, *1941-1943*, Australian National University Press, Canberra, 1978, p. xvi.

5   *Commonwealth Parliamentary Debates*, 30 May 1991, pp. 4321- 9.

Chapter One

1   Hasluck, vol.1, pp. 593-4.

2   Noel W. Lamidey, *Partial Success: My Years as a Public Servant*, N. Lamidey, Sydney, 1970, p.48.

3   Richard Hall, *The Secret State: Australia's Spy Industry*, Cassell Australia, Stanmore, 1978, p.28.

4   (Lady) Jessie Street, *Truth or Repose*, Australasian Book Society, Sydney, 1966, p. 26.

5   "A Brief Review of the Work of the Security Section of the Commonwealth Investigation Branch", by H.E. Jones, dated 31 December 1943, AWM 67, Long — Papers of Official Historian - H.E. Jones 1-6.

6   Report on Italian Organisations, AA ST 2476/10 and AA AP 501/2.

7   Barnwell's reports to CIB, Sydney, dated 6 and 20 June 1938, AA SP 1714/1,item N40752.

8   Ibid., report of Henschel's interview, *Sydney Morning Herald* dated 18 June 1938.In October 1940 an Army officer from Eastern Command interviewed the von Luckner tour manager. He said there had been trouble between the Count and the German Consul in Adelaide and that von Luckner left his yacht on its return trip and flew directly to Sweden.

9   Letter, L. Muller to *Die Brucke*, date partly obscured, but September 1938, AA SP 1714/1, item N43197. This file also contains translations of *Die Brucke* and material on Dr Asmis.

10 G. Kinne, "Nazi Stratagems and their Effects on Germans in Australia up to 1945", *Royal Australian Historical Society Journal*, vol. 66, part 1 (June 1980), p. 3.

11   William L. Shirer, *The Rise and Fall of the Third Reich: A History of Nazi Germany,* Book Club Associates, Great Britain, 1959, p.350.

12   Internees Inquiry by Mr Justice Simpson, AA MP 798/1, file V38702, folder 8. The technician's name was screened by Archives staff but he was No. 327 and interviewed on 1 March 1946.

13   The story of the Vienna Mozart Boys Choir was presented in "The Class of '39' on Channel 0/28 on 13 and 20 February 1983.

14   For general reactions to the Munich crisis, see E.M. Andrews, *Isolation and Appeasement in Australia: Reactions to the European Crises, 1935-1939,* Australian University Press, Canberra, 1970, pp. 141-64.

15   Hasluck, vol.1, p.593.

16   *War Book,* (July 1939), Chapter VI — Intelligence, p. 4, AA MP 288/17, Drakeford Papers re Defence and Civil Aviation, 1939-1957, item no. 1.

17   AWM 67 Long — Papers of Official Historian — N90, pp. 33-40, for Cohen's comments recalled after the end of the war. Cohen was an Infantry Lieutenant in World War I, served in the Reserve and Militia and became the Military Liaison Officer with the Security Service in World War II.

18   Major (later Brigadier) Combes, a Permanent officer, was the Intelligence officer in Sydney and lectured on tactics. He became Director of Military Operations and Intelligence at AHQ on 2 November 1939.

19   Lieutenant-General Lavarack questioned the British Navy's ability to protect both the Atlantic and the Far East. As CGS he fought for a larger budget for the Army and Air Force. Ironically it was his awareness of Australia's lack of preparedness and his justifiable concern during the Munich crisis, together with his criticisms that left a bad impression with senior politicians who chose the Briton, Lieutenant-General E.K. Squires and later, the militia soldier, Major-General Sir Thomas Blamey, above the CGS of the thirties. See A.B.Lodge, "Lieutenant-General Sir John Lavarack: From Chief of the General Staff to Corps Commander' in D.M. Horner (ed.), *The Commanders: Australian Military leadership in the twentieth century,* George Allen and Unwin, Sydney, 1984, pp. 129-23.

20   Captain C.D. Coulthard-Clark, "Australia's War-Time Security Service" in *Defence Force Journal,* no. 16, May/June 1976, pp. 23-7.

21   Letters, Commandant, 3rd District Base to Secretary, Military Board, dated 5 October 1936, 23 November 1936, 7 April, 22 June, 29 June, 18 August 1937, 25 February, 22 April and 26 October 1938. The 1936 letters specify that the procedure was in response to instruction S688 from the Military Board on 10 August 1934, AA MP 729/6, file 29/401/39. Considerable efforts were made by the writer to find examples of MRO reports but without success. However they are quoted from in Monthly Intelligence Summaries and Notes and occasionally from internees' files.

22   For Newcastle files, see description for CA 904, C 130, CA 3563 and C 458 (formerly SP 26/39, 42, 43). These records on organisational material, on unions,and on communists and others are either presumed or confirmed as destroyed.

23   The following summary of army interests is based on the Monthly Intelligence Notes in AA MP 729/6, file 29/401/468.

24   The Monthly Intelligence Summaries of the 3rd Military District for 1936, AA MP 95/3.

25   In addition to this report on communist activities from the Intelligence Summaries, Lavarack sent an analysis of the National Union of Railwaymen's pamphlet "Shall Communism Rule Australia" to the Defence Minister on 6 April 1936. It was further evidence to "previous papers" on communism, that the CPA aimed to establish a Soviet system of government in Australia, AA MP 429/6, file 29/401/3.

26 Letter, Premier of New South Wales to Menzies, 19 May 1939, includes memorandum from W.J. Mackay. The letter went to Shedden and Combes and was part of the cabinet discussions in August on the Organisation of National Security Intelligence, AA CRS A816, item 25/301/10.
27 Sir Frederick Shedden became Secretary to the Department of Defence in November 1937,aged 44. He remained secretary of the major defence department throughout the war, was a confidant of Menzies and Curtin and became secretary of the War Cabinet and the Advisory War Cabinet. For an assessment of Shedden, see D.M. Horner, *High Command*, pp. 20-2.
28 Major E. Hattam, background briefing to Victorian Aliens Tribunal on Nazism in Australia, given 22 January 1941, p. 13, AA MP 529/3, box 2.
29 Letter, Dr Asmis to Foreign Department of Nazi Party, Hamburg, dated 2 May 1934, AA SP 1714/1, item N43197.
30 Charles A. Price, *German Settlers in South Australia*, particularly pp. 38-76.
31 Ibid., p. 44.
32 Ibid., p. 64 for *Australian Lutheran*, pp. 75-6 for Price's estimate; G. Kinne, "Nazi Stratagems", p. 5, for party membership numbers.
33 John McCarthy, "Australia and the German Consul-Generals 1923-39" in *Australian Journal of Politics and History*, vol. 27, no. 3 (1981), pp. 344-53 describes how Asmis "promoted German interests with considerable vigour and not a little acrimony".
34 Inquiries relative to the activities of German Lutheran Churches throughout the State of New South Wales, signed by Detective Constable J. Fraser, MPI, Sydney, dated 10 December 1940, AA SP 1714/1, item N39016. This file also includes a precis of the History of the Lutheran Church in Australia.
35 Confidential letter to Admiral Menche dated 6 March 1937, SP 1714/1, item N39039. It seems that Ladendorff, like Becker, also came to think of himself as "superior to the German Consul". A detective-constable of the Sydney Special Squad reported on 21 July 1939 that he was told this by Ladendorff when they were discussing the Albury (Pyjama Girl) Murder.
36 Asmis to Foreign Department of Nazi Party, Hamburg, 2 May 1934, pp. 3-4, AA SP 1714/1, item N43197.
37 Letter, Mitchell to the Director, CIB, Canberra, dated 9 June 1939, and letter, Barnwell to CIB, Sydney, dated 22 June 1939, AA SP 1714/1, item N39039.
38 Ibid., Report, "Social Evening at German Club", Spry to Inspector Keefe, Special Squad, dated 17 June 1939.
39 Police *War Book* instructions, Chapter III, p. 1, AA MP 729/6, item 15/402/24.
40 Report "Arnold Von Skerst — German' attached to letter, Mitchell to CIB, Melbourne, dated 19 June 1939, AA CRS BB741, file V-11032/5.
41 Translation of *Die Brucke*, dated 4 February 1939, AA SP 1714/1, item 43197.
42 Internee (name screened) interviewed by Simpson on 26 February 1946 claimed that not all members were interned, AA MP 798/1, file 38702, folder 8; Becker claimed he burnt many files, Extract, Tatura Internment Group Weekly Intelligence Report No. 112, AA SP 1714/1, item N39039.
43 AA CRS 1608, item L20/1/1, part I.
44 Hall, *The Secret State*, pp. 27-8 and Austin Laughlin, *Boots and All:The Inside Story of the Secret War*, Colorgravure Publication, Melbourne, 1951,pp. 81-101.
45 Gianfranco Cresciani, *Fascism, Anti-Fascism and Italians in Australia 1922- 1945*, ANU Press, Canberra, 1980, p. 172. According to Cresciani, the Sydney team responsible for screening aliens grew from 150 men in September 1939 to 250 in September 1940 and by November 1939 over 12,000 aliens had been screened in Victoria.
46 *War Book*, Part 1, Chapter XII, (May 1939), p. 6, AA MP 288/27, item no. 1.
47 Copy of cable, from Secretary of State, London, dated 31 August 1939, AA ACT CRS A5954, box 253.

48 Ibid.; copy of cable from Secretary of State, dated 2 September 1939.
49 Ibid., copy of cablegram from Secretary of State for Dominion Affairs, sent 5 September 1939 consisting of text of statement by Secretary of State for Home Departments on policy on Germans and Austrians in Britain.
50 The CIB's agents had found plans by a few communists to obtain business information for espionage purposes, R. Hall, *The Secret State*, p. 26.
51 Minute Paper for Minister of Defence containing Military Board minute on Principles observed in connection with internment, dated 15 September 1939, AA MP 729/6, file 65/401/7.
52 Details on Flauaus are from newspaper cutting "German Internee Says", labelled *Herald*, 27 November 1945, in AA MP 798, file 38702 and register page 51 in AA MP 1103/2, box 38.
53 Military Board Minute, Principles observed, dated 15 September 1939, AA MP 729/6, file 65/401/7.
54 Summary Report, "George Felix Edelmann, Austrian", W.B. Ball to Captain Lonergan, dated 30 November 1942, AA SP 1714/1, item N26622. On 25 September 1939 the Review Committee comprised Lieutenant-Colonel Simpson, Lieutenant-Colonel A.R.M. Gibson and Major W.J.R. Scott, AA MP 729/6, file 29/401/68.
55 *Argus*, 12 February 1940.
56 Translation of letter headed Brisbane Deutscher Turn-Verein, dated 2 July 1938 and other correspondence in AA BP 242/1, item Q31659. For German Club's suspension see *Argus*, 11 September 1939. The club building was only five years old and had cost more than 4,000 pounds.
57 Reports to General Staff Officer (MI) 3rd District Base and Southern Command, relating to investigations made on behalf of the Army, AA MT 269/8.
58 Ibid., item 528 for Werribee farmer, item 90 for Haslinger, item 162 for Polish Jew and item 522 for Agostini.
59 Ibid., item 596.
60 *Who's Who in Australia*, (hereafter shown as *Who's Who*,) 1950 and *Army List*, 1939.
61 Reports to General Staff Officer (MI) 3rd District Base and Southern Command, AA MT 269/8, copy of letter, dated 18 February 1940 attached to item 444.
62 *Argus*, 13 September 1939.
63 *CPD*, vol. 161 (14 September 1939), pp. 550-1 for Menzies, Street and Curtin on the internment, release and reinternment.
64 Correspondence on the establishment of Advisory Committees in September and October 1939 is in AA CRS A472, item W69, part 1.
65 Ernest Scott, *Australia During the War*, Angus and Robertson, Sydney,1936,pp. 105-137.
66 The debate is summarised in Hasluck, vol. 1, pp. 174-6, and D. Watson, *Brian Fitzpatrick*, pp. 103-5.
67 Copy of letter, Secretary to the Military Board to HQ, 1st Military District, Detention of Enemy Aliens, no date but reply to query 3 September 1939, AA MP 729/6, file 65/401/7.

Chapter Two

1 For a detailed account of Australia's defence policy between the wars, see John McCarthy, *Australia and Imperial Defence, 1918-39'*. For a comprehensive account, see Hasluck, vol. 1, Chapter 2, "Between the Two Wars, 1918-38". The resolutions of the Imperial Conference of 1923 are quoted on p. 17.
2 Wynter and Curtin's comments on defence strategy and Churchill's

reassurance are in John Robertson, *Australia at War, 1939-1945*, pp. 6-7, and p. 10. For enlistment numbers, see Hasluck, vol.1, p.199. Hasluck explains Australia's hesitancy in terms of "uncertainty about Japan", the problem if the NEI was cut off from Holland, and the possible moves of the Soviet Union if it became an enemy, pp. 167-9.

3   Noel W. Lamidey, *Aliens Control in Australia, 1939-45*, for numbers registering (p. 5), conditions applying to aliens (pp. 20-6) and *Argus*, 11 September 1939 for oath.

4   Major-General Sir John Northcott held a number of senior appointments during World War II including Chief of the General Staff under General Blamey, and when Blamey went overseas in April and May 1944, Northcott acted as Commander-in-Chief, D.M. Horner, *High Command*, p. 430.

5   Letter, Northcott to all district HQs, on Control of Aliens: Instruction No. 4, date faded but probably 25 September 1939, AA MP 729/6, file 65/401/79.

6   Report on European Emergency Committee, AA SP 26/5. This undated report confirms that some of these 259 people were interned early in the war but released except in special cases.

7   Letter, Clowes to Military Board, dated 3 October 1939, AA MP 729/6, file 19/401/69 and letter, Commandant, 4th District Base to Military Board, dated 4 October 1939, AA MP 729/6, file 19/401/68.

8   For details of patterns of German settlement in Australia, see W. D. Borrie, *Italians and Germans in Australia*, Cheshire, Melbourne, 1954 pp. 157-79.

9   S.M. Bruce, dissatisfied with Australia's stand at the Evian Conference on refugee migration, suggested a quota of 30,000 but the Lyons government halved this, M. Blakeney, *Australia and the Refugees*, p. 52.

10 D. Watson, *Brian Fitzpatrick*, pp. 64-70.

11 Newspaper article by Elizabeth M. Trout, "Nationality and Marriage", and cutting "Wives of Aliens in Australia', AA SP 1714/1, item N18035.

12 Ibid., Statement for the Press, Copy 40/8854, "British Women Marrying Aliens" and *Argus*, 29 September 1939.

13 Minute Paper, Internment of Aliens, Laffan to Secretary of Defence dated 15 September 1939 and underneath, War Book Officer to Secretary, dated 18 September 1939, AA CRS A816, item 54/301/3.

14 Copy of Aide Memoire from Embassy of the United States of America, London, dated 4 October 1939, AA CRS A1608, item L20/1/1, part 1.

15 Ibid., copy of Cable No. 62, Eden to the Prime Ministers of Australia, Canada and New Zealand, dated 26 March 1940. Australia replied in telegrams on 27 February and 29 March 1940, referred to in Cable 151, Caldecote to Prime Minister, dated 4 July 1940.

16 Memorandum from J.T. Fitzgerald to Secretary, Defence Co-ordination, dated 8 August 1940, states women were released "by direction", AA CRS A816, item 54/301/3.

17 *Argus*, 22 May 1940, "War Prisoner Tells Her Story".

18 "Australians' Fate in Germany", Melbourne *Herald*, 8 March 1940, p. 4. Cutting labelled "Melbne Herald 7.3.40" in AA CRS A1608, item L20/1/1, part 1.

19 Letter, Lt-Col. James A. Chapman, DMO & 1, on Repatriation of Aliens, dated 20 September 1940, AA MP 385/4, file 1940-216. The women's internment numbers were 1156 to 1162 and their files in AA MP 1103 Series 2, box 40 indicate five were later reinterned.

20 Letter, Director of S.T.M. and Q. (Quartermaster-General, AHQ), to Northern,Eastern and Southern Command, dated 6 February 1940, AA MP 729/6, file 63/401/49.

21 Defence Minute Paper, Principals observed in connection with internment, dated 15 September 1939, AA MP 729/6, file 65/401/7.

22 *Argus*, 14 February 1940.

23 Letter, H. Hedinger to Hon. G.A. Street, dated 20 February 1940, AA MP 729/6, file 63/401/49. Lieutenant-General Lavarack, GOC Southern Command, warned the Military Board on 1 March 1940 that Hedinger was "alleged to be pro-Nazi".

24 Ibid., Letter, Assistant Provost Marshal (Lt-Col. Hackney) to Colonel in Charge of Administration, Northern Command, dated 27 March 1940.

25 Ibid., Copies of extracts from Northern Command Internees' mail.

26 Ibid., Wynter to Secretary, Military Board, received 5 April 1940, with Colonel Hackney's report attached.

27 Copy of Letter, Street to Hedinger, stamped 23 April 1940, AA MP 729/6, file 63/401/49.

28 Ibid., two letters, Hedinger to Street, first dated 26 April 1940 and second dated 29 April 1940.

29 Administrative decisions early in World War II are summarised from correspondence in AA MP 729/6, files 63/401/3 and 85 and 65/401/7.

30 Copy of letter from Secretary, Military Board, on Dependants of Interned Aliens, dated 7 September 1939, AA MP 729/6, file 65/401/7. The amounts paid in the Great War were 12s 6d per week for a wife and 2s 6d per child.

31 In World War 1 destitution owing to inability to find work because of general and seasonal unemployment and because of employers' and fellow employees' refusal to allow the employment of enemy aliens, was one of the major reasons for internment. A system of voluntary internment was instituted and the government bore the cost of full maintenance.

32 Copy of two letters, Street to Hedinger, undated but first in response to married women's petition, 1 December 1939 and second follow up letter of 9 February 1940, AA MP 729/6, file 63/401/85.

33 Letters, Archbishop of Sydney to Prime Minister, dated 28 September 1939; Menzies to State Premiers, dated 3 November 1939, AA CRS A1608, item A19/1/3.

34 In World War 1 the Official Visitors included Sir Philip Street of the Supreme Court of New South Wales, Sir David Ferguson, Sir Adrian Knox and Mr Justice Harvey. Correspondence on the appointment of Official Visitors in World War 11 is in AA MP 742/1, item 255/9/587.It includes a statement of the procedure to be observed in connection with the OV's duties and inspections, attached to a letter from the Secretary Military Board, to Northern, Eastern and Western Commands, dated 19 July 1940 describing the suitable type for appointment.

35 Defence Minute Paper, Sinclair to Galbraith, dated 14 September 1939 with Street's handwritten comment of same date, AA CRS A5954,box 253.

36 *History of Directorate of Prisoners of War and Internees, 1939-1951*, (hereafter shown as *History of PWI*), p.32, AA CRS A2663, item 780 1-6, held in Australian War Memorial.

37 General comments on trials are drawn from AA MP 529/1, 529/3, 529/5 and 529/6.

38 Copy of letter, H.M.Ramsay to Secretary, Department of the Army, dated 15 December 1939, AA MP 742, file 255/2/814 for Advisory Committee chairmen; Memorandum, George A.Watson (Deputy Crown Solicitor) to Secretary, Attorney-General's Department, dated 6 June 1941, AA CRS A472, item W69, part 1 for committee sittings.

39 Copy of letter, Premier [Victoria] to Prime Minister, dated 6 October 1939, AA CRS A472, item W69, part 1.

40 Ibid., Letter, Deputy Crown Solicitor to H.F.E.Whitlam, Crown Solicitor, Canberra, dated 8 August 1940.

41 Letter, E.E. Cleland to the Minister for the Army, dated 23 December 1940, AA MP 742, file 255/2/814.

42   Ibid. for Cleland's request and subsequent correspondence. In a letter dated 29 November 1945, T.Playford asked that a state public servant be reimbursed for acting as secretary for sittings between October 1939 and March 1941.

43   Letter, F.Heyes and Wilson, to Aliens Squad, Phillip Street, Sydney, dated 20 September 1939, AA SP 1714/1, item N26622.

44   Ibid. Summary of case prepared by Captain R.Powell, Intelligence Branch, dated 18 December 1939; letter Edelmann to Commandant, Internment Camp, Liverpool, dated 24 December 1939, and Release document dated 7 February 1940.

45   Newspaper cutting, "German Internee says", [Melbourne] Herald, 27/11/45, AA MP 798, file 38702.

46   Memorandum, Secretary of the Army to Secretary, Prime Minister's Department, Information re Germans in Australia, dated 28 November 1939. This stated 66 had been released, AA CRS 1608, L20/1/1, part 1.

47   Copy of letter ready for Prime Minister's signature, to State Premiers, included in communication between Defence Co-ordination, and Prime Minister's Department, confirms Commonwealth reimbursements to state police, AA CRS A5954, box 253.

48   In his book, All In! Australia During the Second World War, Nelson, Melbourne, 1983, pp.44-5 , Michael McKernan nominates Mair as leading the campaign for the wholesale internment of aliens in mid-1940.

49   Letter, Mair to Prime Minister, dated 6 November 1939, AA CRS A1608, item B19/1/1.

50   R Hall, The Secret State, p. 29 refers to the dispute, and correspondence by Knowles and Laffan on this matter is in AA CRS 472, item W601. The military Board's position is set out in a Department of Defence Minute Paper "Internment of Aliens", dated 29 September 1939 and Knowles' counter-arguments are explained in an Attorney-General's Department Minute Paper, dated 5 October 1939.

51   On 9 January 1940 Inspector W.J.Keefe of Police HQ, Sydney, produced a progressive report, "Linking up the activities of the Nazi Party throughout Australia". This report included summaries of fifty men about whom there was "some degree of certainty" that they were party members, AA MP 729/6, file 29/401/100. The report also lists twenty-one German organisations in NSW, the consulate staff and the leaders of the Nazi Party groups . Alfred Henschel was described as a Gespapo agent, and "Manager of all Nazis in Australia". The party began in NSW early in 1934 with six Germans and one naturalised former German.

52   C.D.Coulthard-Clark, "Australia's War-Time Security Service", p. 23.

53   Defence Minute Paper, Naval Dockyard Police, Laffan to Secretary, 8 March 1939, AA MP 729/6, file 29/401/42.

54   Argus, 18 January 1940.

55   Hasluck, vol.1, pp. 587-8.

56   Report, Conference to Consider the Activities of the Communist Party, signed by Combes, dated 23 January 1940, AA MP 729/6, file 29/401/128.

57   Ibid., Memorandum, Shedden to Secretary, Department of the Army, dated 2 February 1940.

58   Ibid., copy of report to Secretary, Department of the Army, initialled by Combes, dated 3 February 1940.

59   Hasluck, vol.1, p.588.

60   A Laughlin, Boots and All, p.108.

61   R Hall, The Secret State, p.29.

62   C.B. Laffan on Internment of Aliens, dated 29 September 1939, AA CRS A472,item W242.

63 Draft Instructions by the Minister for Defence re The Internment of Aliens, undated AA CRS A472, item W242.
64 Memorandum, J.T.Fitzgerald to Secretary, Defence Co- ordination, dated 8 August 1940, AA CRS A816,item 54/301/3.
65 Tackaberry's career is summarised from *Who's Who in Australia*, 1926, the *Army List*, AWM 140 Official Historian's Biographical Cards and H.S.Gullet, *Sinai and Palestine*, 1923, p. 711, (vol. VII of C.E.W.Bean [ed.] *Official History of Australia in the War of 1914-1919*.
66 The replacement of militia by Garrison Battalions recruited from the AIF Reserve was a result of a Defence department review which had shown that a large number of troops were "immobilized in protective duties". Defence Minute Paper, Secretary, Military Board, to Secretary, Defence, War Measures Instituted Since the Outbreak of War, AA CRS A816,item 14/301/127.
67 The War Diary of the 17th Garrison Battalion, AWM 52,item 8/7/21.
68 The general material on camp life comes from ex-internee recollections and a range of files including tribunal hearings, the deportation trials in 1946 and Dr Neumann's camp record in AA MP 529/5, box 1.
69 Extract from Tatura Intelligence Report No. 112, AA SP 1714/1, item N39039, for Becker; Objection hearing, 6 June 1941, AA CRS B741, file V-11032/5, for Von Skerst.
70 The huts at Tatura were unlined, with prop-open windows. There was no hot water or sewerage until September 1940. They were no worse off than the Garrison troops but for civilians it was nothing like home.
71 This was not Yackel's first escape from custody. His other ingenious escape was on 14 November 1930 when he prised open the floor of the police van while it was travelling and dropped through onto the road, *Argus*, 24 February 1940.
72 Copy of letter, DMO & I to HQ Brisbane, dated 12 October 1939 with queries on individuals attached, AA MP 729/6, file 60/401/15.
73 Letter, Wynter to Secretary, Military Board, dated 18 December 1939, AA MP 729/6, file 63/401/30.
74 Defence Minute Paper, War Measures Instituted since the Outbreak of War, p.3, AA CRS 816, item 14/301/127.

Chapter Three

1 In discussing British internment policy the book by Peter and Leni Gillman, *'Collar the Lot!': How Britain Interned and Expelled its Wartime Refugees*, Quartet, London, 1980, has been drawn on heavily. The Gillmans were not given full access to all relevant official documents. Home Office files for September 1939-June 1940, which they felt were vital to an accurate account, were withheld because of potentially embarrassing material about individuals and because they were sensitive and their disclosure would be against the public interest. Most of their information came from Foreign Office files. For Bland's report "Fifth Column Menace", see pp. 101-5.
2 Bland believed a German maid had led German parachutists to one of their targets, Christopher Andrew, *Secret Service: The Making of the British Intelligence Community*, Guild Publishing, London, 1985, p. 477.
3 Major-General Sir Vernon Kell was described by Andrew Boyle as "steady, dependable, but far from creative", *The Climate of Treason: Five Who Spied for Russia*, Hutchinson of London, 1979, p. 222. Kell was blamed for not catching "a mythical German spy" who supposedly caused the sinking of a capital ship and blew up a munitions plant. When some MI5 records recovered after an air raid could not be deciphered, Kell was replaced and Swinton's National

Security Executive created a new two-tier intelligence system. According to Boyle MI5 became the lesser partner, and its new head was Sir David Petrie.

4 *Argus*, 22 May 1940.

5 Correspondence re Naval Dockyard Police, AA MP 729/6, file 29/401/42 and Mackay's submission to Stevens, included in his letter to Menzies dated 19 May 1939, AA CRS A816, item 25/301/10.

6 Copy of report, Communist Party, prepared by Intelligence in December 1939, AA MP 729/6, file 29/401/121.

7 Ibid., Memorandum, Secretary of the Navy to Secretary, Defence Co-ordination, undated but reply to Minute, 22 December 1939.

8 Ibid., Letter, Wynter to Military Board, 20 January 1940.

9 WCM 264, copy in AA MP 729/6, file 29/401/170.

10 Copy, Secret Message, Combes to Commands, Conference on Communist Party, dated 30 May 1940, AA MP 729/6, file 29/401/182.

11 Ibid., List from Western Command, dated 6 July 1940 and from Northern Command, received 18 June 1940.

12 Unsigned copy of Instruction 13, DMO & I to all commands, AA ST 2476/20.

13 Mackay's submission, AA CRS A816, item 25/301/10.

14 C. Andrew, *Secret Service*, gives an example of a Nazi informer posing as a Catholic refugee while sending information on genuine refugees to Reinhard Heydrich, head of the S.S. Security Service (p. 434), and of a British-born photographer forced to work for the German Intelligence Bureau (Abwehr) because of threats to a German relative (p. 441)

15 *Argus*, 6 June 1940. The paper reported that it was expected that these internees would soon be transfered to a country gaol. In the same edition there was a report that the Germans had arrested the British author, P.G. Woodhouse, who lived in France.

16 For refugees' acceptance of apartments in Sydney's eastern suburbs, see Emery Barcs, *Backyard of Mars: Memoirs of the "Reffo" Period in Australia*, Wildcat Press, Sydney, 1980, pp. 36-9.

17 In the objection hearings of these people emphasis was placed on their emotional closeness to overseas relatives and the views their residences commanded, AA MP 529/3, box 1. Lieutenant-Colonel S.F. Whittington, (Intelligence) in his briefing to Aliens Tribunal No. 2 in Melbourne on 5 February 1941 explained that if an enemy alien had close relatives in Germany he was regarded "very frequently as a potential danger" because he was "liable to be used by enemy agents under the pressure of threats ... to his people", AA MP 529/3, box 2.

18 Flauaus' trial was on 27 November 1945. The newspaper account of his trial, labelled *Herald*, 27/11/45, is attached to AA MP 798/1, file 38702.

19 Report prepared by M.P.I. Section, Police HQ, Sydney, no date but after his release, AA SP 1714/1, item N26622. Censorship of the Mail to Edelmann at Orange Camp in August 1940 revealed that he had been contacted by solicitors in Java, because all ex-employees of Hardt and Co. were entitled to pocket-money.

20 Translation of Chronicle of German Internment Camps in Australia, AA MP 508, file 255/711/59 and translation of extracts from the "Record of the German Internment Camp in Australia", confiscated 22 February 1941, AA MP 529/5, box 1, item 3.

21 For circumstances of Muller's arrest, see QSA A/11914.

22 Neumann's camp record contains the information given in the following paragraphs, AA MP 508, file 255/711/59 and MP 529/5, box 1, item 3.

23 Deduced by cross-referencing AA MP 508, file 255/711/59 with AA MP 729/6, file 63/401/85. Further arrests of Germans after 6 June and the entry of Italy into the war boosted this to approximately 2,500 by August 1940. Paul Hasluck

put internee numbers at 2,376 at the end of November 1940, *The Government and the People*, vol. 1, p. 593.

24   P & L Gillman, *Collar the Lot!*, p.163 and p. 166.

25   WCM 388. As the war progressed Australia was often asked to increase the number of prisoners it would take. When in May 1941 the Cabinet offered to take more Italian POWs, the Treasury was nervous. The labour, material and guards needed would be a drain when work on munition factories was "lagging very seriously", memorandum, W.E. Dunk for the Treasurer, dated 1 May 1941, AA CRS A 5954,box 675.

26   For the migration and distribution pattern of Italians, see W.D. Borrie, *Italians and Germans in Australia*, pp. 49-96; and N.O.P. Pyke, "An Outline History of Italian Immigration into Australia", in *The Australian Quarterly*, September 1948. As Borrie shows (pp. 56-9), proportionally fewer Italian-born people lived in the capital cities, mainly due "to the over- whelmingly rural character of settlement in Queensland". In Queensland, where one-third of the Italian-born people recorded in 1933 lived, four out of five settled on the land. The clustering of Italians on the fringes of metropolitan areas was related to their occupation of market gardening, while clustering in inner city areas were expansions on nuclei that had been established well before the 1926 increase in Italian immigration. There are also a number of regional studies including Charles Gamba, *A Report on The Italian Fishermen of Fremantle*, Department of Economics, University of Western Australia, 1952, and Rina Huber, *From Pasta to Pavlova: A Comparative Study of Italian Settlers in Sydney and Griffith*, University of Queensland Press, St Lucia, 1977.

27   *Argus*, 8 June 1940.

28   W.H. Barnwell's report on the Fascist Party in Australia, in AA AP 501/2 and AA ST 2476/10; see also G. Cresciani, *Fascism, Anti-Fascism and Italians in Australia, 1922-45*, pp. 172-3.

29   Correspondence from H.W. Dinning (State Publicity Censor) to Professor J.J. Stable, District Censor for Brisbane and Major Wake of the CIB between 7-13 June 1 940 , AA BP 361 /1, item 1-1 1 .

30   Notes on Fascism, undated, p. 5, AA MP 529/5, box 2 for Victoria and Barnwell's report for Sydney.

31   Justice Reed, Report on Internees of Italian Origin, November 1943, Lamidey, *Aliens Control*, Appendix B, p. 80.

32   Personal interview, details withheld by request.

33   Summary of dossier, Principe Don Alfonso del Drago, attached to letter, Miles to Secretary, Military Board, dated 4 September 1940, AA MP 729/6, file 63/401/111.

34   The March on Rome was a major Italian Fascist festival commemorating Mussolini's arrival in Rome just before being offered the Prime Ministership in October 1922.

35   Letter, Secretary, Department of External Affairs to Consul-General of Japan, dated 24 September 1940, asked for the "names of any Australians suggested as suitable for exchange", AA MP 729/6, file 63/401/111. W.R. Hodgson, the External Affairs Department secretary, asked the Consul- General to find out the names from the Italian Embassy in Tokyo. This at first appears to suggest that the Australian authorities were unaware of the names of Australians interned in Italy, but it might be they were stalling to emphasise their bargaining power.

36   Letter, Miles to Military Board, dated 4 September 1940, AA MP 729/6, file 63/401/111; also mentioned by G. Cresciani, *Fascism, Anti-Fascism and Italians in Australia*, p. 173. Del Drago's own file (SP 1714/1, item N29007) includes much of his correspondence as a camp leader at Orange, Hay and Loveday Camp 9.

37 Copy of Foreign Office message, dated 4 December 1940 for Villa Lauri internee; Memorandum from Australia House to Secretary, Prime Minister's Department, dated 30 April 1941 for list of seven Australians in Italy, AA CRS 1608, item L20/1/1, part 1.

38 Fanelli's receipts covered the period 7 December 1939 to 7 May 1940. Del Drago is 376 and Antonio Agostini, husband of the murdered "Pyjama Girl" was 305, Report of Commonwealth Investigation Officer, p. 65, AA AP 501/2.

39 Translations of extracts from Italian newspapers, AA ST 2476/10.

40 Lamidey, *Aliens Control*, p. 53. Victoria interned only 2.97% of male aliens, while Queensland took the highest, at 43.11%.

41 Translation of Camp Chronicle, AA MP 508, file 255/711/59.

42 Personal interview,4 June 1979. Costanzo considers that he was interned because he was newly arrived and a former Italian soldier. It was over six years before his wife was able to join him but now their family have grown up in Australia and they are vegetable growers in the irrigated Burdekin delta.

43 Mr Justice Reed's report, Appendix B, Lamidey's *Aliens Control*, pp. 73-82. Geoffrey Sandford Reed was born in South Australia and was a KC in Adelaide before being elevated to the bench. In 1949 Reed established the Australian Security Intelligence Organisation (ASIO).

44 Report, A brief history of the Fascio of Port Pirie, prepared by Lieutenant C.F. Sexton in November 1941, AA AP 501/2. In a letter dated 3 August 1938, the Adelaide "Reggente" (Regent of the Fascist Party) points out that the 8 September would be ideal for a visit to Port Pirie because it is "the anniversary of the Madonna dei Martri, an anniversary of great importance for the Molfetta folk".

45 Oswald Bonutto, *A Migrant's Story*, H. Pole, Brisbane, 1963, p. 92. Bonutto's number was 7015 p. 94 . Comments on Ethiopia, pp. 97-8 and final quote p. 100.

46 Zammarchi has recorded his own account of his internment in *With Courage in their Cases: The experiences of thirty-five Italian immigrant workers and their families in Australia*, ed. Morag Loh,F.I.L.E.F., Melbourne, 1980, pp.31-3.

47 For an account of his woodcutting days, see Wendy Lowenstein, *Weevils in the Flour: An oral record of the 1930's depression in Australia*, Hyland House, Melbourne, 1978, pp. 156-61.

48 Transcript of Zammarchi's trial which began in Melbourne on 6 May 1941, AA MP 529/3, box 3. Captain Balfe was a General Staff Officer, Grade 3 with the 7th Military District.

49 *Army List* and D.M. Horner, *Crisis of Command*, p. 288.

50 Message, AHQ to all commands, dated 15 April 1940, AA MP 729/6, file 63/401/119.

51 Copy of telegram, H.D. Moseley to Army, Melbourne, 24 April 1940. Moseley later became Security Service's representative in Western Australia.

52 Ibid., Letter, Durrant to Military Board, dated 4 May 1940.

53 Ibid., Internee returns, dated 10 August 1940.

54 Ibid., Report, Durrant to AHQ, dated 29 August 1940.

55 Message, Military Board to all commands, dated 11 June 1940, AA MP 729/6, file 63/401/50.

56 Ibid., handwritten telephone message from Eastern Command to Military Intelligence at AHQ dated 7 June 1940.

57 Ibid., Letter, Sturdee to AHQ, dated 25 June 1940 acknowledges the arrangements for signing warrants.

58 George M. Berger, "Australia and the Refugees", in *The Australian Quarterly*, September and December 1941. Berger concluded that the N.S.W. leaders "who swayed public opinion against the refugees on anti-semitic grounds or

on possible disloyalty of refugees' were the premier, Alexander Mair, and his deputy, Colonel M.F. Bruxner".

59   D.M. Horner, "Lieutenant-General Sir Vernon Sturdee: The Chief of the General Staff as Commander" in D.M. Horner (ed.), *The Commanders*, pp. 145-6, p. 158.

60   Southern Command's views on Independent Tribunals, AA MP 729/6, file 65/401/79.

61   Mackay's letter to Stevens included in letter to Menzies, dated 19 May 1939, AA CRS A816, item 25/301/10.

62   Copy of letter AHQ to Eastern Command, dated 11 June 1940, AA MP 729/6, file 63/401/50.

63   Ibid., letter Internees — Custody of, Sturdee to Secretary, Military Board, dated 25 June 1940.

64   Letter, Bruxner to the Minister for the Army, Internment of Enemy Aliens, dated 30 July 1940, AA MP 729/6, file 63/401/108. His accusation that dangerous enemy aliens were at large is from the *Argus*, 28 June 1940.

65   Manning's letter is in AA MP 729/6, file 63/401/108; the debate over military control over naturalised persons is in AA MP 729/6, file 65/401/82 and a report to war cabinet on the non-internment of women is in AA CRS A816, item 54/301/3. The War Cabinet considered internment camps for prisoners from Great Britain and Malaya at its meeting of 23 July 1940 and "in view of the danger of enemy agents amongst enemy women" a report on the reasons for the non-internment of women was called for. Menzies, as Minister for Defence Coordination, presented the report on 20 August 1940. J.T. Fitzgerald, Secretary of the department of the Army wrote that "as women are not generally so involved in organising activities inimical to the Empire as men of enemy nationality', few were likely to be interned.

66   Report of anti-communist crowd being controlled by mounted police, *Argus*, 12 February 1940.

67   Hasluck, vol. 1, pp. 587-9, for discussions leading to the banning of the Communist Party.

68   Letter, list attached, Western Command to Military Board, dated 6 July 1940; from Northern Command, received 18 June 1940, AA MP 729/6, file 20/401/182.

69   Brian Fitzpatrick, *The Australian Commonwealth: a picture of a community 1901-1955*, Cheshire, Melbourne, 1956, p. 247.

70   *Argus*, 6 and 7 June 1940.

Chapter Four

1   J.D.Davies, "Some Aspects of the Commonwealth Government's Response to the Presence of Germans and German Descendants in Australia, 1914-1918", PhD thesis, Melbourne University, 1982, p. 2 and p. 197.

2   Ernest Scott, *Australia During the War*, Angus and Robertson, Sydney, 1936, p. 111-5.

3   Ibid. Also see Michael McKernan, *The Australian People and the Great War*, Nelson, West Melbourne, 1980, pp. 164-73, for the worst cases from the Royal Commission in May 1918 enquiring into the origins and parentage of Commonwealth public servants. For an example of anti-German feeling in a provincial centre, see M. Douman, "Townsville during World War 1", in Lectures in North Queensland History, published by the History Department of James Cook University of North Queensland, 1974.

4   H.V. Evatt, *William Holman: Australian Labour Leader*, Angus and Robertson, Australia, 1940, pp. 269-70.

5   E. Scott, *Australia During the War*, p. 114 and Michael McKernan's chapter on

"Manufacturing the war: enemy subjects in Australia", in *The Australian People and the Great War*, pp. 150-77. Using the vote cast at Kapunda, "a solidly German town", McKernan considers it difficult to prove that removing the "German" vote altered the result to any extent, but this does not change the fact that Hughes did it because he felt it would help his side.

6 Homburg was interned on 25 November 1940 and after an appeal, released, but not allowed to return home. He lived in Ballarat for much of the war, AA MP 798, file V24713/5.

7 This is the conclusion of Mr Justice Reed who from 1941 to 1943 questioned some 2,000 men of Italian origin, a substantial proportion being naturalised, Lamidey, *Aliens Control*, Appendix B, pp. 79-82.

8 Bundock had been wounded twice in the Great War and earned a D.S.O. In 1942 he took over the South Australian Line of Communications Area, *Army List*, 1939 and *Who's Who*, 1944.

9 D.M. Horner, *Crisis of Command*, p. 7. The movement of officers to effect the reorganisation is set out in Appendix 3, pp. 286-8.

10 Letter, Lt-Gen. J.L. Whitham to Secretary, Military Board, dated 25 July 1940 and Memorandum, Manchester to Southern Command and Bundock to Southern Command, dated 10 June 1940, attached to letter, Whitham to Military Board, dated 15 July 1940, AA MP 729/6, file 65/401/82.

11 Ibid., copy of letter to Director of Naval Intelligence, dated 11 June 1940.

12 Ibid., letter Whitham to Military Board, 15 July 1940.

13 Copy, SM 2002, DMO & I to all Commands, 1 June 1940, AA MP 729/6, file 65/401/82.

14 Commandant, 4th MD to HQ, Southern Command, dated 10 June 1940, AA MP 729/6, file 65/401/82. Bundock reported that General R.L. Leane, Commissioner of Police in S.A. was also "concerned at the amount of subversive activity in S.A.". This file includes No.214's report, dated 22 May 1940.

15 Argus, 13 and 15 September 1939.

16 E. Scott, *Australia During the War*, pp. 154-5.

17 R.J.W. Selleck, "The Trouble with my Looking Glass": a study of the attitude of Australians to Germans during the Great War", *Journal of Australian Studies*, no. 6 (June 1980), pp. 2-25, particularly p. 20.

18 *VPD* (16 August 1916), vol. 143, pp. 824-8 and pp. 920-3 for James Menzies.

19 For an assessment of Menzies' family life, see Sir Percy Joske, *Sir Robert Menzies, 1894-1978: a new informal memoir*, Angus and Robertson, Australia, 1978, pp. 1-8.

20 The number of representations coming from country areas, and now in archival holdings, such as AA CRS A373,item 1272 is significantly greater than those from the cities, and very much greater when the relative populations are considered. Correspondence over land acquisition by aliens is held in AA CRS A1608, item D19/1/2. A letter from the Longreach and Ilfracombe Districts Patriotic Fund Secretary, dated 27 June 1940 protested against the announced government policy that interned Italians would get their property back at the end of the war.

21 SM 3429, DMO & I to Southern Command dated 8 August 1940, AA MP 729/6, file 65/401/82.

22 These cases are from QSA Police Department, A/1191 (1942), A/11914, A/11916, A/11917 and A/11918 and cover the period 30 April-15 August 1940.

23 Report, Police Constable at Peranga to Inspector, Toowoomba, and Police at Oakey to Toowoomba, QSA A11914.

24 Ibid., Stanthorpe Police to Toowoomba, dated 12 August 1940.

25 List of Italians in the Townsville Police District who it is considered should be

interned in the event of hostilities with Italy, Inspector of Police to Commissioner, dated 30 April 1940, QSA A1191, 1942.

26 Police Constable of Stanthorpe to Inspector, Toowoomba dated 16 June 1940 and Constable at Wallangarra to Toowoomba, dated 26 May 1940, QSA A 11914.

27 Reports, Sergeant at Home Hill, to Inspector of Police, Townsville, dated 28 April and 12 November 1940, QSA Police Department A/11918.

28 Ibid., Copy of Report, dated 19 October 1940, p.4.

29 Ibid., handwritten note attached to Sergeant's report of 19 October 1940.

30 WCM 431, 23 July 1940. The agreement to take 6,000 from Britain and 297 from the Straits Settlements is in WCM 388, 3 July 1940.

31 Army Minute Paper "Prisoner of War and Internees' from Adjutant-General to CGS, QMG and others, dated 19 July 1940 in AA MP 729/6, file 63/401/85.

32 WCM 471 contains discussions on finance and the categories from Great Britain. This was discussed again on 10 September 1940 as recorded in WCM 492. Alternative, less expensive hospital accommodation was discussed in WCM 445. WCM 461 indicates that further consideration of the costs of accommodating internees was deferred until the Acting Chief of the General Staff and the Quarter-Master General could be present.

33 Costing on hospital accommodation for internees is detailed in WCM 585.

34 WCM 608 records that the Military Board later asked for £480,000 to build camps, including Hay for overseas internees and Harvey for Australian internees. The UK government was expected to reimburse £330,000. With regard to the Orange camp, no particular official could be held responsible as all action was taken with "the full knowledge of the Minister for the Army and the Military Board". When the Swiss Consul had severely criticised the camp on 8 July, the Minister had responded by asking what "steps" were being taken. So, given the urgency to satisfy their minister and the consul, "essential improvements were effected as a charge against funds provided for general camp accommodation in N.S.W., pending the provision of funds specifically for internment camps".

35 E. Scott, *Australia During the War*, pp. 115-7; M. McKernan, *The Australian People and the Great War*, p. 174; and Gerhard Fischer, "Botany Bay Revisted:the transportation of prisoners- of war and civilian internees for internment in Australia during the first world war, *Journal of the Australian War Memorial*, no. 5, 1984, pp. 36-43.

36 There are a number of accounts of the *Dunera* passage. Monographs included Benzion Patkin, *The Dunera Internees*, Cassell, Australia, 1979, particularly ch. 3, P.& L. Gillman, *Collar the Lot!*, particularly ch. 22 and Cyril Pearl, *The* Dunera *Scandal: Deported by Mistake*, Angus and Robertson, 1983, particularly chs 3-6. The handwritten diary of Ludwig Eichbaum, of Hut 28, Hay, is held by the State Library of Victoria (MS 9538). A comprehensive article is S. Encel, "These Men are Dangerous", *Nation*, September 1965, pp. 11-13.

37 Lafitte was the stepson of the pioneering sexologist Havelock Ellis, and grew up in a politically radical environment. He took part in street battles against the British Union of Fascists. He visited Vienna before the war and helped Jews and socialists to escape to England where he opened his house to refugees. He was a researcher for the International Miners' Federation and a member of the Political and Educational Planning group, a private ginger lobby group. Rejected for active service, he immersed himself in the refugee problem and wrote *Internment of Aliens* for PEP, P.& L. Gillman, *Collar the Lot!*, p. 174.

38 M. Blakeney, *Australia and the Jewish Refugees*, pp. 156-7 and pp. 167-B and C. Andrew, *Secret Service*, p. 480. R.T.E. Latham joined the RAF and was killed over Norway in 1943.

39 P. & L. Gillman, *Collar the Lot!*, pp. 217-8 and C. Andrew, *Secret Service*, p. 480.

40 Andrew states that Churchill's instructions to Swinton were to "find out whether there is a fifth column in this country and if so to eliminate it" (p. 478), but by January 1941 Churchill wrote that "a more rapid and general process of release from internment should be adopted" (p. 480).

41 P.& L. Gillman, *Collar the Lot!*, p. 231.

42 Copy of Report "Internees ex *HMT Dunera* — Movement" signed by Lt W. Young, HQ, 17th Garrison Battalion, 8 September 1940, AA AP 613/4 Miscellaneous Papers, Loveday Camp.

43 Olive Hirschfeld was told this by the commandant during her welfare visits to Tatura.

44 Headline from Sydney *Daily Telegraph,* 7 September 1940, quoted by S. Encel, "These Men are Dangerous", p. 11.

45 For guards, see B. Patkin, *The Dunera Internees,* pp. 66-7 and K.G. Loewald, "A *Dunera* Internee at Hay, 1940-41", *Historical Studies,* vol. 17, no. 69, October 1977, p. 513.

46 The treatment of their luggage rates very highly with internees, and the reason it made such a deep impression was due no doubt to the symbolic value of that one suitcase. It was, for many, their only tangible evidence of their former lives. For Colonel Scott's explanation, see C. Pearl, *The Dunera Scandal,* pp. 54-6.

47 Press reports and photos from *Sydney Morning Herald, Daily Telegraph* and *Sun,* C. Pearl, *The Dunera Scandal,* pp. 60-4, 66- 8; cuttings from *Riverine Grazier,* 13 and 14 September 1940 provided by Hans Lindau. Asher Joseph refers to "the little food we had" in Patkin, p. 51.

48 WCM 507. In a cable from Perth on 28 August 1940 Captain A.R. Heighway reported that there were 2,544 internees on the *Dunera* but only dossiers for 12 Germans, index cards for 1,900 other Germans, no documents for the Germans from the *Arandora Star* and no documents for any of the Italians. WCM 492 records that the nature of the overseas internees was "specially mentioned" and WCM 471 included the UK request for differential treatment.

49 Father Walter Konig estimated that, of the internees at Hay, 90 per cent were "Jews of most varied religious opinions", W. Konig, "Internment in Australia", in *Twentieth Century,* vol. 18, Spring 1963, p. 7. E. Sydney Morris, President of the European Emergency Committee, nominated 1,700 of the 2,000 Hay internees as "Jewish", "Report on Visit to the Internment Camp, Hay, N.S.W.", provided by A.C. Clarke, Melbourne.

50 W. Shirer, *The Rise and Fall of the Third Reich,* pp. 430- 4. The German insurance companies complained of having to pay out on the insurance claims, Goering, Goebbels and Reinhard Heydrich, who had masterminded the "spontaneous demonstrations" solved the problem by confiscating the payout moneys owed to Jews and collectively fining them one billion marks "for their abominable crimes".

51 B. Patkin, *The Dunera Internees,* pp. 27-8. The protests about the British camp commandant's false promises are also recorded in the *Dunera* internees' statements in AA Army 701, file 255/714/64.

52 Werner Pelz, *Distant Strains of Triumph,* Victor Gollancz, London, 1964, p.74.

53 K.G.Loewald, "A Dunera Internee at Hay,1940-41" in *Historical Studies,* vol.17,no 69, October 1977, pp.512-22.

54 Personal interview with Hugo Wolfson,16 May 1979. Professor Wolfson died in 1982.

55 G.F. Chodziesner, "How I Came to Australia", roneoed sheets in the possession of Ben Chodziesner, Melbourne.

56 Personal interview with Hans Lindau, 21 September 1980. Forty years after the event, Hans Lindau recounted his experiences before, during and after the *Dunera* journey and it was the demotion from an individual to an

indistinguishable member of a prison rabble, which his treatment during the
search implied, that made him visibly upset.

57   W. Konig, *Internment in Australia*, pp. 4-16.
58   Archives policy screens names and, as photocopying is time- consuming, only
     the trials of successful objectors were made available to the writer.
59   Konrad Kwiet, "Be patient and reasonable!":The internment of
     German-Jewish refugees in Australia", in Australian Journal of Politics and
     History, vol. 31, no. 1, 1985, pp. 61-77.
60   Ibid., pp. 64-8.
61   Cablegram from the Officer administering the Government, Singapore, dated
     28 August 1940, AA ACT A5954, box 675.
62   German Internee Registers, AA MP 1103/2, box 38.
63   Views of various commands, attached to Army Minute Paper "Independent
     Tribunals", signed by Major C.G. Roberts, 25 July 1940, AA MP 729/6, file
     65/401/79.
64   Ibid., letter Lieutenant-General V.A.H. Sturdee to the Secretary, Military Board,
     dated 27 June 1940.
65   Ibid., letter Lieutenant-General J.L. Whitham to Secretary, Military Board,
     dated 12 July 1940.
66   Ibid., Lieutenant-General Sturdee's letter dated 27 June 1940, p. 2.
67   Mair's telegram and a draft of Menzies' reply (undated) is in AA CRS
     1608,L20/1/1, part 1.
68   Memorandum for Secretary, Department of the Army, dated 28 June 1940, AA
     A5954, box 253.
69   *Argus*, 28 June 1940.
70   The Anglican Bishop Coadjutor of Sydney, Charles Venn Pilcher, whose
     contacts with Jewish refugees predated his arrival in Australia in 1936, and
     whose theological interest centred on the Old Testament, wrote to Menzies
     asking to visit the overseas internees and passed on documents about their
     plight, M. Blakeney, *Australia and the Jewish Refugees*, pp. 200-1 and letter, C.
     Venn Pilcher to Prime Minister, dated 18 October 1940, AA ACT CRS A5954,
     box 674.
71   On 31 July 1940 a deputation of wives and relatives of the Jews in Orange
     badgered the Jewish Welfare Society to ask for an appeal court that refugee
     Germans could use. In endorsing the request the AJWS offered their files for
     such a tribunal's scrutiny, K. Kwiet, "Be patient and reasonable!", p. 65.
72   For a description of the reactions of the Australian Council of Civil Liberties
     during this period, see D. Watson, *Brian Fitzpatrick*, chapter 5.
73   The old man, John Williams Coleman, was sentenced to four months hard
     labour, but on appeal the sentence was reduced to one month. The ACCL raised
     the one hundred pounds for the appeal, and Dr Evatt contributed five pounds
     of this, Watson, pp. 329-30.
74   B. Fitzpatrick, *The Australian Commonwealth*, p. 248.
75   Hasluck, vol. 1, p. 594.
76   WCM 610 and newspaper cuttings, "Secrecy of Missionary Inquiry", labelled
     D.Telegraph 8-11-40 and "Missionaries released", AA ACT A1608, item
     L20/1/1, part 1.

Chapter Five

1   Hans Lindau, in a personal interview, 21 September 1980, said that some men
    slept on straw palliasses on hut floors for a short time. Hugo Wolfson, personal
    interview, 16 May 1979, insisted that "Hay was OK. No, Hay wasn't that bad.
    It was much better than being on that ship!" K.G. Loewald, "A Dunera
    Internee at Hay", p. 514, comments that although 2,000 were accommodated

in a camp designed for 1,000, the internees were used to a lack of comfort and the camp was "comfortable in comparison with the unlamented *Dunera*".

2   Report of Official Visitor, "Internment Camps at Hay", dated 6 November 1940, AA Army 701, file 255/714/37.

3   Memorandum by Sir Frederick Jordan on Representations made to him, dated 6 November 1940, AA Army 701, file 255/714/64.

4   Letter, F. Jordan to Secretary, Military Board, dated 6 November 1940, AA Army 701, file 255/714/37.

5   Ibid., Army Minute Paper, "Official Visitors Reports - Internment Camps — Eastern Command", C.B. Laffan to Secretary, Department of Army, dated 1 February 1941.

6   Letter, "To His Honour Judge Jordan", signed by H.H. Eppenstein and Dr Frankenstein, dated 26 October 1940, AA Army 701, file 255/714/64.

7   AWM Library, Indian Army List, October 1915 and Index to Australian Military Forces: Appointments, Promotions, etc., LHQ Press, Melbourne, vol. 1, Oct.-Dec.1943, p. 732. Thane was placed at the top in the seniority of the 16th Garrison Battalion.

8   Letter, To His Honour Judge Jordan, signed by H.H. Eppenstein and Dr Frankenstein, 26 October 1940, AA Army 701, file 255/714/64.

9   The internees regarded the Swiss Consul as the representative of the Nazi German government, and they did not want their names forwarded to Germany. Hedinger did forward the basic fact of their arrival and the numbers involved to Germany, but was rebuked for not differentiating between true Germans and stateless persons of German origin, AA SP 1714/1, N60318.

10   Letter to Judge Jordan, p. 12, AA Army 701, file 255/714/64. The high percentage of Jews is corroborated in other sources.

11   Ibid., Letter to High (sic) Judge Jordan, signed by Leonhard Posner and another representative of the Czech Refugee Trust Fund, dated 27 October 1940. There were 138 in the group. They were mainly refugees of German and Austrian origin who had found refuge in Czechoslovakia but who had to move on when Germany occupied first the Sudeten area, then the whole country.

12   Ibid., Memorandum by Sir F. Jordan.

13   Ibid., p.7.

14   Copy of Memorandum for Sir Frederick Jordan from Secretary to the Military Board, dated 3 December 1940, and Report of Official Visitor to Internment Camps, same date, AA Army 701, file 255/714/37.

15   Report of Official Visitor, dated 6 November 1940, p. 4, AA Army 701, file 255/714/37. Jordan admitted that although he had formed "a strong opinion that the layout of the dormitories was unsatisfactory", no exception was taken to them "on this score" by the internees. They did, however, regard them "as being overcrowded".

16   Ibid., p. 5.

17   Ibid., Report of Official Visitor to Internment Camps, 3 December 1940 and Army Minute Paper "Official Visitors Reports — Internment Camps — Eastern Command", Laffan to Secretary, Army, dated 1 February 1941.

18   Ibid., Army Minute Paper, p. 12.

19   The Quakers or Society of Friends were pacifists and interested in welfare, including prison reform. In a personal interview (8 July 1979) A.C. Clarke, told the writer that the British MP, Josiah Wedgewood, who was a critic of British internment policy, had a daughter in Sydney, and she alerted the Australian Society of Friends to the nature of the *Dunera* internees. There were a group of Friends on board. Morris describes the religious composition of compounds 7 and 8 as: 1,700 Jews, 90 Roman Catholics and nearly 200 Protestants, most of whom were associated with the Society of Friends. The European Emergency

Committee was a coalition of welfare groups organised to help refugees. It had a number of Quakers as members.

20 E. Sydney Morris, "Report on Visit to the Internment Camp, Hay", dated 11 November 1940, held by writer, and provided by A.C. Clarke.

21 Cyril Pearl's description of a visit by Miss Constance Duncan of VIREC and Bishop Venn Pilcher in *The Dunera Scandal*, p. 111, supports Morris's report. Pilcher described Hay as having no "grass, no shade, no green thing, a wilderness of blowing dust". Lt-Col. Thane asked if they could supply shoes for the men because he had asked for 2,000 pairs and received only 200. Miss Duncan described the adjutants of the two compounds, Captain Carrington and Lieutenant Bass, as being "extremely popular with the internees" and the relationship between the guards and the internees as seemingly "excellent".

22 *Army List* for Miles' career and D.M. Horner, *Crisis of Command*, p. 51 for his retirement.

23 Letter, P.C. Spender to General Miles, dated 11 November 1940, AA Army 701, file 255/714/31.

24 Ibid., Letter, Lt-Gen. C.G.N. Miles to the Minister for the Army, dated 11 November 1940.

25 Ibid., Army Minute Paper, "Internment Camp Hay", to Mr Harding from Secretary, dated 14 November 1940.

26 Ibid., Copy message to Eastern Command, "Internment Camps, Hay — Conditions", dated 16 November 1940.

27 Ibid., Army Minute Paper, Secretary to AG, dated 20 November 1940.

28 Ibid., Miles to Secretary, Military Board, dated 23 November 1940.

29 Ibid., Army Minute Paper, "Internment Camps, Hay - Conditions", Major-General V.P.H. Stantke, to Secretary, Department of the Army, dated 21 November 1940.

30 Ibid., Percy C. Spender to Secretary, dated 28 November 1940.

31 Ibid., Miles to Secretary, Military Board, 30 December 1940, and Stantke to Secretary, Military Board, received at AG Branch, 29 January 1941.

32 WCM 661. Spender also spoke privately with the Vatican representative about prisoners' welfare. See Percy Spender, *Politics and a Man*, Collins, Sydney, 1972, pp. 137-8. The role of the Apostolic Delegate was also discussed and approved in WCM's 630 and 654.

33 Report of Visit by Major McCahon, dated 12 November 1940, AA MP 508, file 255/714/32.

34 Bass's comment on the condition of the Garrison's quarters is in AA MP 508, file 155/711/59 and refers to July 1940.

35 Memorandum by Dr H.O. Lethbridge MBE, dated 31 January 1941, AA MP 508, file 255/714/32.

36 Ibid., Memorandum submitted by Spokesman of No. 7 camp, dated 30 January 1940.

37 Jordan's comment on the internees' increased confidence is in his Memorandum dated 6 November 1940, p. 7, AA Army 701, file 255/714/64.

38 Copy of letter, C. Davidson to the Secretary, Military Board, undated but file headed 255/714/71, AA MP 508, file 255/714/32.

39 Ibid., p. 2. Underlining in original.

40 Ibid., Report, Camp Seven, attached to Jordan's letter to the Military Board, dated 5 March 1941.

41 Ibid., Copy of Report of Chief Inspector Army Catering, not dated. Captain Hack was familiar with the internment camp at Harvey, WA, where Australian Italians were interned.

42 Ibid., p. 3.

43 On 30 June 1941 it was estimated there were 400,000 men in the three fighting services. To the end of August 1941 the total enlistments for the volunteer AIF

were 188,587. There were about 60,000 in the RAAF and 10,000 new enlistments in the Navy. In October there were 113,687 troops on full-time duty in Australia — 61,396 in the militia, 11,050 in garrison battalions, and 36,357 in the AIF in Australia. Four divisions of the AIF were overseas. See Hasluck, vol. 1, pp. 396-401.

44   WCM 554 for the three points. WCM 642 for the subsequent refusal.

45   Cablegram, Bruce to Prime Minister, dated 8 January 1941, War Cabinet Agendum No. 12/1941, including Views of the Army, signed by P.C. Spender, dated 7 January 1941, AA ACT CRS A5954, box 675.

46   Julian Layton, a Jew and former stockbroker, was in Vienna helping refugees obtain the correct papers for entry into Britain on the eve of Kristal Nacht when he was warned by Adolf Eichmann "to stay out of the way". He acted as a liaison officer between the War Office and the refugees at the Kitchener Camp in Kent in the early days of the war. He sailed to Australia in February 1941 and remained for four years working on the internees' problems. See P. & L. Gillman, *Collar the Lot!*, pp. 255-6. Approximately eighty thousand pounds was paid to ex-*Dunera* internees.

47   W. Konig, "Internment in Australia", pp. 16-17; B. Patkin, *The Dunera Internees*, p. 105 (for Fischer). See also Loewald, p. 521. He went to Orange for "a dose of fresh air". He was reimbursed the full value of the items stolen from his suitcase.

48   *CPD*, vol. 166 (2 April 1941), pp. 504-5 and for Cameron's speech pp. 553-7.

49   At one stage of his speech Cameron said, "Certain Jewish refugees also have been interned, and a lot of "hot air" is being talked about them. I have heard talk of "friendly aliens". I do not know what a friendly alien is. I know that when my country is engaged in a life and death struggle with Germany and Italy any man of German or Italian birth is an enemy alien. If he is friendly to this country then he must be a traitor to his own, and I do not think it is our part to encourage treason". (Ibid., p. 554). Cameron also said, "Enemy nationals owe it as a duty to their country to put us to the greatest possible inconvenience to do everything to injure us ..." (Ibid., p. 555).

50   Ibid., p. 557-60.

51   R. Hall, *The Secret State*, p. 27, and A. Laughlin, *Boots and All*, pp. 81-2. There was little sympathy for internees waiting to appeal. An internee who had waited three months to be heard, protested at having to wait a further two months. He was told there was "no question of a 'trial' ", as he was interned as "a precautionary measure". That a few internees must suffer "inconvenience and hardship" even if they later prove to be "not so dangerous" was "preferable to a display of leniency which conceivably might gravely hamper the national effort", letter, J.F. Fitzgerald to Tebbutt and Sons, undated but reply to request of 16 August 1940, AA CRS A 472, item W69.

52   Cyril Pearl, *The Dunera Scandal*, pp. 128-31. P.A. McBride, Minister for the Army, wrote to the Prime Minister on 13 September 1940 after a deputation on refugees. Those who felt "badly dealt with must bear with such inconvenience for the common good" and "the security of the nation must take precedence over the rights of individuals". McBride urged Menzies to reply "to all similar representations" in these terms, AA CRS A1608, item N19/1/1, part 1.

53   *CPD*, vol. 167 (3 July 1941), pp. 868-80.

54   Hentze was married to Spender's wife's sister, *CPD*, (18 June 1941), vol. 167, p. 105.

55   From the description of AA MP 529, Series 2, it appears that dossiers included police reports, correspondence from censorship and other related authorities, personal details (Form G) and registration as an alien (Form A1), lists of confiscated exhibits and the statements of witnesses.

56   For the debate to disallow regulation 42A of the Subversive Activities Act, see

CPD, vol. 167, (3 July 1941), pp. 880-93. For Hasluck's summary, see *The Government and the People*, vol. 2, p. 373.

57   *CPD*, vol. 167 (3 July 1941), p. 887-8.

58   *CPD*, vol. 167 (20 June 1941), pp. 270-1.

59   Hasluck, vol. 1, Appendix 7, The Case of Ratliff and Thomas, pp. 609-12.

60   Ibid., Appendix 3, The Banning of the Communist Party, particularly pp. 590-1. Bruce Muirden, *The Puzzled Patriots: The Story of the Australia First Movement*, Melbourne University Press, Melbourne, 1968, p. 103, wrote that when Germany attacked Russia "the justification" for the men's internment "virtually disappeared".

61   Hasluck, vol. 1, p. 373.

62   Questions by Holloway and Drakeford, *CPD*, vol. 167 (20 June 1941), pp. 257-9.

63   The registered unemployed at the end of 1940 numbered 70,583 compared with 112,704 at the outbreak of war. Most of the unemployed were unskilled. See Hasluck, vol. 1, p. 388.

64   *CPD*, vol. 167 (20 June 1941), p. 269.

65   WCM 663. As early as 1939 when the move to congregate all internees in Victoria was being considered Shedden noted "that until the present unemployment" was reduced, it might "not be politic to find paid employment for aliens" but to "reduce unrest and assist in the maintenance of discipline, work should be provided as soon as possible", Prisoners of War — Employment, teleprinter message dated 21 September 1939, AA ACT A5954, box 253.

66   AWCM 340.

67   When the new policy became effective there were 2,376 locals interned, and twelve months later it had only fallen to 2,231, Hasluck, vol. 1, p. 594.

68   Briefing by Major E. Hattam given on 22 January 1941, AA MP 529/3, box 2.

69   *Army List*.

70   Lt-Col. Whittington's briefing given on 5 February 1941, particularly, pp. 7-13, AA MP 529/3, box 2.

71   Ibid., Lt Procter's briefing, p. 18.

72   Copy of Preliminary General Observations, signed by C.K. Book, K.H. Bailey and H. Walker, dated 13 March 1941, AA MP 529/5, box 2.

73   The transcript of Zammarchi's trial is in AA MP 529/3, box 3 and his own version is in M. Loh (ed.), *With Courage in Their Cases*, p. 31-3.

74   Flegenheimer was heard by Judge Clyne, Dr T.C. Brennan, and E.R. Stafford, assisted by D.I. Menzies for the Army Minister. The transcripts of his case, and of the others recommended for release — von Keudell, Dorn, Eckhardt and Bauer — are in AA MP 529/3, box 1.

75   Hasluck, vol. 1, p. 594.

76   AA BP 242/1, Q 8375 and O. Bonutto, *A Migrant's Story*, pp.96-104.

77   Reports to GOC, Southern and Eastern Commands, AA MP 729/6, file Aliens Tribunal No. 4.

78   Letters, from Secretary, Department of the Army, to Hon. T.C. Brennan KC, Chairman No. 3 Aliens Tribunal, SM 9883, 9951 and 10870, AA MP 529/5, box 1, item 3.

79   The man from Millicent applied for a writ of *habeas corpus* "on the grounds of unreasonable delay in being heard", but the judge ruled that delay could not turn "a lawful detention into an unlawful one", B. Muirden, *Puzzled Patriots*, p. 120.

80   Letter, H. Tebbutt of Tebbutt & Sons (Solicitors), to Hon. R.G. Menzies, dated 16 August 1940, AA CRS A472, item W69, part 1.

81   Ibid., Spender to Knowles, date faded but probably 17/18 February 1941. Spender's suggestion that Mr Justice Long Innes's Aliens Tribunal might become an advisory Committee was taken up, and it began work on 14 April

1941 and a third and fourth Aliens Tribunal was constituted in Victoria, letter, J.T. Fitzgerald to Deputy Commonwealth Crown Solicitor, dated 28 April 1941, AA MP 529/5, box 2.

82 For Zammarchi's release, see M. Loh, *With Courage in Their Cases*, p. 33.

83 I have been further encouraged in my assessment by the research of John Jenkin of the Physics Department of La Trobe University. Asked to do a biography on the Australian scientist, Henry H.L.A. Brose, Jenkin discovered the man had been interned in Germany in the Great War as a Britisher and was then interned in Australia in the Second War because of his knowledge of Germany and his predeliction for women, including the wives of colleagues. The Advisory Committee that heard his case stated that while no evidence of anti- British activity could be found, Brose was kept interned because he was considered to be an unscrupulous person with plenty of energy and mental capacity who was in need of money and therefore a great potential danger. He was released for Christmas 1943 to work as an agricultural labourer. AA CRS A472/1, W1968.

84 Memorandum to Minister for Defence Co-ordination, signed by Davidson, dated 1 October 1940, AA CRS A472, item W69, part 1.

85 Statement of Position of Internees in Australia, undated, but part of material for War Cabinet meeting on 5 March 1941. At this meeting the cabinet was considering the UK request that 400 dangerous Germans be taken from the NEI, AA ACT CRS A5954, box 675.

86 Letter, D.A. Alexander, to CIB, Sydney, dated 8 August 1946, AA BP 242/1,item Q33792 for internees arrival and Gavin Long, *The Six Years War*, Australian War Memorial, Canberra, 1973, p. 99, for the action in Persian Gulf.

87 Hasluck, vol. 1, p. 363.

88 John Hetherington, *Blamey: Controversial Soldier*, Australian War Memorial, Canberra, 1973, p. 189.

89 Stanley Bruce had sensed as early as November 1939 that Churchill's conception of war strategy was to concentrate British forces to win in Europe "and not dissipate them by trying to deal with the situation in the Far East at the same time". Alfred Stirling went with Bruce to hear Churchill's speech in the debate on Malaya in the Commons on 21 January 1942. Churchill said that while the defeat of Japan would not necessarily entail the defeat of Hitler, the defeat of Hitler would allow allied forces to concentrate on the defeat of Japan, Alfred Stirling, *Lord Bruce: The London Years*, Hawthorn Press, Melbourne, 1974, pp. 142-3, pp. 229-30.

90 John Robertson, *Australia at War*, p. 64.

Chapter Six

1 Before federation, Australia's concern for "the Yellow Peril" centred on China, but the White Australia policy was designed to exclude all Asians. As a concession to Britain, who had an alliance with Japan, "merchants, students and tourists" with Japanese passports were allowed entry. The defeat of Russia by Japan in 1905 alerted Australians to Japan's military capacity and W.M. Hughes protested vigorously over Japan's occupation of the Marshall and Caroline Islands after World War I. For Japan as a consideration in Australian foreign policy, see P.G. Edwards, *Prime Ministers and Diplomats: The Making of Australian Foreign Policy, 1901-1949*, Oxford University Press, Melbourne, 1983, pp. 38, 52-6, 63, 66, 101; and for Japan as a consideration in defence policy, see John McCarthy, *Australia and Imperial Defence*, pp. 7-8, 19-20, 47, 59-63 and 84.

2 WCM 1029, 9 May 1941, and Appendix A "Internment of Japanese", attached to War Cabinet Agendum 45/1942, AA ACT CRS A5954, box 674.

3 Ibid., Appendix A, p. 2.

4   Letter, DMO & I to all Commands, dated 26 May 1941 "Japanese Activities
     -Internment Policy", requested that all dossiers on Japanese be brought up to
     date and included a list of those with diplomatic status, AA BP 242/1, item
     Q39362.

5   On spying see Austin Laughlin, *Boots and All*, pp. 93-9. For an extensive
     analysis of Japanese commercial and espionage penetration into South-East
     Asia, see Eric Robertson, *The Japanese File: Pre-War Japanese Penetration in
     South-East Asia*, Heinemann Asia, Hong Kong, 1979.

6   Report of Conference on Internment Camps, 13 February 1941, signed by
     Colonel T.E. Weavers, Director of Personal Services, AA MP 729/6, file
     63/402/29.

7   Extract from SM 8994, dated 28 July 1941, AA BP 242/1, item Q39362.

8   D.M. Horner, *High Command*, pp. 135 and 483.

9   WCM 1029.

10   WCM 740.

11   Memo "Internment — Japanese", undated, AA BP 242/1, item Q 39362.

12   Ibid., Internment Operation Order, signed by Lieutenant C.I.G. Huxley, dated
     1 December 1941.

13   Ibid., Urgent Telegrams to Commandtel, Brisbane, received 8 December 1941.

14   Copy of letter, S.C. Taylor, Deputy Director of Security (DDS) for NSW to
     Canberra, dated 21 November 1942, AA MP 742/1, item 255/10/12.

15   Ibid., Memorandum for Secretary, Department of the Navy, "Japanese
     Internees", copy to Lt-Col. McCahon, undated but probably early 1942.

16   List of Personal Effects of Repatriated and Deceased Japanese, AA SP 196/1,
     item 5. For example PWJM 16242 had 835 yen, 406 pearls and 2 gold rings
     while 16239, 16248 and 16250 had only one razor each.

17   ABC "Weekend Magazine", TV program 14 October 1979 on pearl divers.

18   Urgent telegram to Milcommand, Brisbane from Fixdef, received 8 December
     1941, AA BP 242/1, Q 39362.

19   *Internment in South Australia*, p. 10.

20   See Charlotte Carr-Gregg, *Japanese Prisoners of War in Revolt: The Outbreaks at
     Featherstone and Cowra during World War II*, University of Queensland Press,
     1978, and Harry Gordon, *Die Like the Carp!*, Cassell Australia, 1978, for
     documentary accounts of the Cowra breakout; and Kenneth Seaforth
     Mackenzie, *Dead Men Rising*, Angus and Robertson, 1951, for a fictionalised
     account based on the author's own experience as a camp guard.

21   Notes from Camp Intelligence Reports — No. 19 — To 7 November 1944, AA
     SP 1714/1, item N38486.

22   Personal interview, 23 November 1979.

23   The Canadians moved their Japanese from Vancouver to the prairies of Alberta
     and the United States moved their Japanese from Hawaii and California to
     camps in Utah. For the American treatment of Japanese see Roger Daniels,
     Concentration Camps, USA: Japanese Americans in World War II, Holt, Rinehart
     and Winston, New York, 1971 and Morton Grodzins, *Americans Betrayed: politics
     and the Japanese evacuation*, University of Chicago Press, Chicago, 1949 and
     George E. Frakes and Curtis B. Solberg (eds), *Minorities in Californian History*,
     Random House, New York, 1971, pp. 88-91, and for Canada, see Forrest E. La
     Violette, *The Canadian Japanese and World War II: A Sociological and Psychological
     Account*, University of Toronto Press, 1948.

24   War Cabinet Agendum 45/1942, p. 2, AA ACT CRS A5954, box 674.

25   Ibid., copy of WCM 1781.

26   Japanese — Report on Associations and Activities, attached to letter, D.A.
     Alexander to CIB, Canberra, dated 15 January 1942, SP 1714/1, item N40344.

27   Ibid., p. 2 and p. 6. Tom Walsh and his wife Adela Pankhurst Walsh visited

Japan just before war broke out as semi-official guests of Japan, and their daughter was employed as a typist for the Japanese Chamber of Commerce.

28 Ibid., p. 6.
29 Ibid., pp. 11-13.
30 Ibid., p. 9.
31 Ibid., p. 1. Some of the people on Barnwell's list of residents (p. 19) had Anglicised their first names to Harry and Sam, and named their children Agnes Elizabeth and Amy Susan.
32 Ibid., p. 20.
33 These cases are in AA MP 529/3, box 5 WOB.
34 The SA *News* of 5 October 1945 claimed that Haishida's efforts to get information were foiled by Australian counter-espionage work. Barnwell's report (p. 18) contains a summary of Haishida's visit and others by Japanese posing as visitors but suspected of being military men. As late as July 1941 a Japanese "sheep buyer" used a trip to an outback station as a cover while trying to find out about the Hay Internment Camp.
35 Name screened, case heard on 14 May 1942, AA MP 529/3, box 5 WOB.
36 Ibid., name screened, case heard on 13 May 1942.
37 Ibid., name screened, case heard on 20 May 1942, p. 4.
38 Ibid., name screened, case heard on 19 May 1942.
39 Ibid., name screened, case heard on 20 May 1942.
40 Ibid., name screened, case heard on 13 May 1942.
41 Ibid., name screened, case heard 12 February 1942. Gillard's quote is on p. 9.
42 N. Lamidey, *Aliens Control*, pp. 53-4.
43 Letter, D.A. Alexander, DDS Melbourne, to Assistant Director, Sydney, dated 20 June 1946, AA SP 26/5.
44 Ibid., Application for Ministerial Detention Order, dated 5 January 1942.
45 Copy of letter, F.H. Wise to Intelligence Section, Perth, dated 14 January 1942, and Copy of Extract from Tatura Internment Group Weekly Intelligence Report No. 117, 24 March-31 March 1945.
46 Letter, Douglas Denzo Kuringu to Dr Lethbridge, dated 20 February 1943, AA SP 1714/1, item N27827.
47 Ibid., copy of signed statement dated 18 February 1942.
48 Ibid., report of phone call signed by W.J. Mackay, dated 13 March 1942.
49 The family concluded that the Japanese consul had forwarded the family's details to Japan when Denzo had asked his help in a dispute with Customs in 1921. As a result Douglas received a call-up notice from the Japanese army and Mrs Kuringu then decided to pay 10s to get naturalised and ensure her British nationality.
50 Ailsa G. Thomson Zainu'ddin, "Rose Inagaki: "Is it a Crime to Marry a Foreigner?" ', in Farley Kelly and Marilyn Lake (eds), *Double Time: Women in Victoria's 150 years*, Penguin Books, 1985, pp. 335-43.
51 Report signed by Lt R.A. Bock, dated 10 December 1941, AA SP 1714/1, item Policy 3.
52 Ibid., Report on disposal of property of Japanese internee Kikuichi Nishniki, attached to Memorandum, A.R. Cutler, Assistant Deputy Director of Security for NSW to Deputy Director of Security (DDS), Sydney, dated 17 July 1943, and Report, District Security Officer, Cairns, to DDS, Brisbane, dated 8 June 1943. Before becoming Assistant DDS for NSW, Lieutenant Cutler V.C. served on the Aliens Classification and Advisory Committee after being wounded in action.
53 Ibid., letter, R. Hayashi to Major W. Cummins, No. 6 camp, Hay, dated 12 April 1943.
54 Ibid., copy of memo "Japanese Internees — Disposal of Property", Lt-Col. J. McCahon to HQ's L of C areas, QLD, NSW, WA.

55 *Internment in South Australia*, p. 10.

56 Lionel Wigmore, *The Japanese Thrust*, Australian War Memorial, Canberra, 1957, pp. 511-642, for the experiences of Australian POWs.

57 Cablegram to the Secretary for Dominion Affairs, No. 456, dated 11 October 1942 and repeated to the Prime Minister of New Zealand, 12 October and signed Curtin. General Blamey urged the government to keep the Southwest Pacific theatre free of the controversy because the Japanese would use it as an excuse "for any sort of inhuman action to our prisoners of war", letter, Blamey to Forde, dated 8 April 1943, AA MP 742/1, item 255/9/219.

58 Letter, Forde to J. Francis MP, dated 18 February 1943, AA MP 742/1, item 255/6/39.

59 In January 1942, the SS *Cremer* brought 1,266 males, 200 females and 322 children and in February the SS *Heemskirk* embarked 100 males, 51 females and 10 children, making a grand total of 1,949. *History of the Directorate of PWI*, p. 18; *Internment in South Australia*, p. 6 records the arrival of the first group and AA MP 1103/1, boxes 6 & 7 contain their Service and Casualty Forms.

60 The Japanese from the NEI numbered 51133 to 51314 were all early repatriates. They were described as employees on estates, clerks, planters, merchants, farmers and peasants. A second group, numbered from 51329 to 51372 and labelled workman or labourer, were also repatriated as were an illustrious group numbered from 50715 to 50723 captured in Batavia. The last group included the General Manager of the Mitsubishi Concern, and the President of Fokindo Nippo, the agent for the Nankoku Company and other company directors and office managers. On the other hand, of a later group, numbered 51462 to 51520, all of whom were fishermen captured in the vicinity of Singapore, not one was repatriated early. The Dutch exchanged the employees of Japanese firms and the rubber workers, but did the British, whose influence with Australia exceeded that of the Dutch, refuse to allow those who knew the waters of the Singapore Straits back into Japanese control?

61 About twenty Japanese women who were nurses or owners of small shops arrived at Tatura from Sumatra on the *Heemskerk* on 14 February and most of these were repatriated in August 1942.

62 Of all the Japanese who came from Indonesia only two appear to have been released in Australia. IJ 50519 Master So was released to the Royal Institute for the Blind "for school", and IJ 57744, who married a Western Australia internee.

63 *History of the Directorate of PWI*, p. 94.

64 Steven L. Carruthers, *Australia Under Siege: Japanese Submarine Raiders 1942*, Solus Books, 1982, p. 156. The midget submarines were given a funeral with full naval honours and it was attended by the senior naval officer, Rear-Admiral Muirhead-Gould, and the Swiss Consul in the hope "that such a civil act would spur the Japanese to similarly honour Australian war dead overseas".

65 *History of Directorate of PWI*, pp. 17-8.

66 Ibid., pp. 94-5.

67 Rupert Lockwood, *Black Armada*, Australian Book Society, 1975, pp. 15-23.

68 Ibid., p. 21.

69 Ibid., pp. 23-6.

70 Ibid., pp. 33-8.

71 The situation with Roumania and Hungary was fairly straightforward, for their extreme right-wing governments were pro-German, but Finland's fight with Russia was seen by many as a legitimate response to the Russian invasion on 30 November 1939. An Allied action to support Finland had been seriously considered. See W. Shirer, *The Rise and Fall of the Third Reich*, pp. 682ff.

72 Paul Hasluck, *The Government and the People, 1942-1945*, Australian War Memorial, Canberra, 1970, pp. 5-6.

73   Cablegram from Secretary of State for Dominion Affairs, dated 5 December
      1941, AA CRS 1608, item L20/1/1, part 2.
74   N. Lamidey, *Aliens Control*, p. 52.
75   Emery Barcs, *Backyard of Mars*, pp. 103, 106-7.
76   The Australian public were not immediately deprived of Barcs's knowledge
      of world affairs, however, for the ABC broadcast his "Notes on the News" just
      as he had finished washing up after his first meal at Liverpool. In ibid., p. 108,
      he wrote:

      We listened, then froze into incredulity. I was on the air, or rather an ABC announcer
      was reading the script I had finished the previous night before my arrest, and which
      my wife must have delivered to the ABC. From across the road we listened to snippets
      of my denunciation of the sneak Japanese attack on Pearl Harbor, to my analysis of
      the situation, and to my hopes that American participation in the war would make
      ultimate victory inevitable,however grim might be the days ahead.
      We just stood there smiling and shaking our heads. "Some day this will be very
      funny," Frank said.

77   Ibid., pp. 65-6.
78   Ibid., pp. 87-90.
79   Ibid., pp. 98-9.
80   Ibid., p. 124.
81   AWCM 715, dated 26 January 1942, in AA CRS A5954, box 675.
82   Of the 134 internees who died at Loveday camp, 108 were Japanese. *Internment
      in South Australia*, p.25.
83   Letter from Office of Australian War Graves to writer, dated 19 November
      1979. One occasion when concern about a possible breakout by internees was
      feared was in the period when the invasion of Japan was imminent, letter
      Captain L.W. Parkes, Camp 14A/B to HQ Loveday Group, dated 21 May 1945
      and letter, E.T. Dean to HQ, SA L of C Area, dated 1 April 1945, AA AP 613/1,
      file 162/1/64.

Chapter Seven

1   G.C. Bolton, "1939-1951", in F.K. Crowley (ed.), *A New History of Australia*,
     Heinemann, Melbourne, 1974, p. 464.
2   P. Hasluck, *The Government and the People, 1942-1945*, (hereafter shown as
     Hasluck, vol. 2), pp. 91-2.
3   The Australian government received warnings of the weakness of Malayan
     defences from (among others) Major-General H. Gordon Bennett and V.G.
     Bowden, the Trade Commissioner at Singapore. Although Curtin reminded
     Britain of its promise to Menzies in April 1941 that there would be a
     reallocation of air resources "to meet the dangers on all fronts", Sir Earl Page,
     Australia's representative to the British War Cabinet found the British baulked
     at applying "the immediate means", D.M. Horner, *High Command*, pp. 144- 7
     and 161.
4   P. Hasluck, vol. 2, pp. 87-9. J. Robertson, *Australia at War*, pp. 101-2 points out
     that the deployment of troops in February/March 1942 left North Queensland
     "lightly defended". D.M. Horner, *Crisis of Command*, p. 40 records that civil
     leaders in Perth were "indignant about the lack of troops in their area".
5   Letters of concern about strategic points being vulnerable to surprise enemy
     attack or sabotage by aliens are contained in AA CRS A1608, particularly item
     N 19/1/1 part 1, item L 20/1/1 part 1, item H 19/1/1, item W 19/1/1 part 1
     and item D 19/1/2.
6   G.C. Bolton, 1939-1951, in F.K. Crowley, *A New History of Australia*, p. 465.
7   Hasluck, vol. 2, p. 4. Hasluck further discusses the people's reactions to the
     military setbacks on pp. 55- 69. In early February 1942 it was reported that

6,000 people had left Cairns and Townsville as a private precautionary measure.

8   George Johnston, *My Brother Jack*, Fontana, 1964, pp. 297-8.
9   Lloyd Ross, *John Curtin: A Biography*, Macmillan, Melbourne, 1977, p. 243 and p. 265. D.M. Horner, in *High Command*, cites some cases of agitation and stress among senior people. Professor W.E.H. Stanner felt Forde "tended to panic during this period" and Sturdee found the tone of a paper by F.R. Sinclair, the Secretary of the Department of the Army, on a possible guerilla army, indicated "complete defeatism; (p. 143). Recalling the months, January to April 1942, when he was putting Australia's case to the British War Cabinet, Page wrote that he went through a "period of acute mental distress", (pp. 159-61).
10 Hasluck, vol. 2, pp. 61-4. A VDC patrol from Ingham went to investigate the reported landing of Japanese paratroops on Hinchinbrook Island, "Q 218123", "Fighting Patrol in the North" in *On Guard with the Volunteer Defence Corps*, Australian War Memorial, Canberra, 1944, pp. 106-7.
11 Captain Amoury Vane, "The Surveillance of Northern Australia: The story of Stanner's Bush Commando, 1942", in *Defence Force Journal*, no. 14, Jan/Feb 1979, pp. 15-30.
12 Hasluck, vol. 2, pp. 66-9.
13 For a picture of North Queensland in 1942, see Ian Moles, *A Majority of One*, University of Queensland Press, St.Lucia, 1979, pp.103-14, and Margaret Bevege, "Some Reflections on Women's Experiences in World War II in North Queensland", in Margaret Bevege,Margaret James and Carmel Shute (eds), *Worth Her Salt; Women at Work in Australia*, Hale and Iremonger, Sydney, 1982, pp.99-110.
14 For criticism of the police survey, see *Home Hill Observer*, 20 March 1942.
15 *Sydney Morning Herald*, 14 and 24 February 1942.
16 Letter, John Curtin to the Premier of Queensland dated 1 May 1942, QSA 6475, no. 187/15. At a conference of Chief Commissioners of Police called by W.J. Mackay in his role as Director of Security on 20/1 March 1942, the police had "desired a direction" as to what policemen were to do in the event of hostilities in their area. Curtin's view was that where any portion of the civilian population remained in the area the police were to remain also. They were not to carry rifles or take part in hostilities but they were to carry pistols openly for crowd control. If the area was overrun the police were to "act as intermediaries between the enemy and the civilian population" and to try to alleviate the civilians' position.
17 Hasluck, vol. 2, pp. 125-33. The Censorship reports for January 1942 reveal criticism of the authorities, "fear of fifth columns, fear of defeat ... and further criticisms of aliens".
18 Letters to Curtin are in AA CRS A1608 and AA CRS A373, items 1272 and 2026.
19 Schedules of Representations requesting the Internment of all enemy aliens, prepared by the Secretary of the Prime Minister's Department, dated 31 March 1942, and Further Schedule of Representations, dated 27 April 1942, AA CRS 373, item 1272.
20 Letter, Secretary, Upper Blackwood Road Board to Hon. J.H. Prowse MP, dated 22 September 1941 and letter, Deputy Director-General of Manpower, Perth to Secretary, Department of Labour and National Service, dated 21 April 1942, and copy of latter, John Curtin to Mr. Prowse, dated 13 December 1941, AA MP 574/1, file 220/2/6.
21 Copy of letter, R.N. Beale to John Curtin, dated 21 March 1942, AA CRS 373, item 1272.
22 Copy of letter, Shire Secretary to Municipal Clerk, "Enemy Aliens", dated 3 February 1942, AA CRS A1608, item W19/1/1, part 1.
23 Petition of Ballina and Northern Rivers district residents, attached to letter

from secretary to H.L. Anthony MP, dated 13 March 1942, AA CRS A373, item 2026.

24 *Argus*, 11 February 1942.
25 Extract from letter from the General Secretary, Federal Executive, R.S.S. and A.I.L.A., dated 16 January 1942, AA CRS 373, item 1272.
26 Ibid., Schedule of Representations contains some 50 communications from Queensland RSL branches, dated from 27 December 1941 to 24 February 1942.
27 Cablegram from Hon. W. Forgan-Smith, sent 27 January 1942, AA CRS A1608, item L20/1/1, part 2.
28 For the reports of the RSL request, Fadden's response and the raid, see *Sydney Morning Herald*, 14 February 1942.
29 N. Lamidey, *Aliens Control*, p. 51; the Master Warrants are in QSA A/1191 1942.
30 The best known case of censorship was the minimal coverage of the bombing of Darwin. Although 243 people were killed and the town and port badly damaged, the government decided to withhold the details from the public.
31 The Moree Municipal Council considered "the present time appropriate for the internment of enemy aliens" and the Diggers' Association wrote that while they were "not unappreciative" of the government's handling of internment in recent weeks, they felt more power should be given to the military authorities, AA CRS A373, item 1272.
32 A reader unfamiliar with the sugar industry could infer that cane cutters roamed around in large groups; in fact they lived in barracks on the property, and a large gang numbered about fifteen. The sugar areas are distributed along a one thousand mile coast line.
33 N. Lamidey, *Aliens Control*, p. 51.
34 Letter, A/D DMI to MLO, Security Service, Canberra, dated 22 September 1942, AA CRS A373, item 1681.
35 *Sydney Morning Herald*, 21 February 1942. The *Sydney Morning Herald* directly endorsed the broader internment policy. In a follow-up story on 24 February, the paper's Innisfail correspondent reported that shouts of "Viva Italia" had come from the internees and the 200 people who gathered at the station to farewell them. This was taken as "an emphatic indication of the wisdom" of the federal government's decision to round up aliens on a large scale in North Queensland.
36 Only 229 men from the *Perth* returned. British troops captured in Malaya and Singapore numbered about 150,000 and they included over 20,000 Australians, 7,777 of whom would die in captivity, L. Wigmore, *The Japanese Thrust*, p 642.
37 R. Lockwood, *The Black Armada*, pp. 41-8.
38 The assessment of these naturalised men was based on police reports made in mid-1940. To be under suspicion virtually only meant the police had reported on the individual. The initiative for the report might have been a neighbour's unsupported claim of a disloyal utterance. In his report on Italians, in N. Lamidey, *Aliens Control*, Appendix B, Mr Justice Reed said of naturalised men that they generally regarded Australia as "a very good place in which to live, and if possible to put together a fortune, but that their duty to the country" did "not extend further than keeping out of trouble with the law".
39 For Evatt's mission to Washington and London, see Kylie Tennant, *Evatt: Politics and Justice*, Angus and Robertson, 1970, pp. 139-46; D.M. Horner, *High Command*, pp. 191-3, and Allan Dalziel, *Evatt — The Enigma*, Lansdowne Press, Melbourne, 1967, pp. 22-4.
40 For a detailed account of the events preceding the Australia First arrests see Bruce Muirden, *The Puzzled Patriots*, particularly chapters 6-9; for an excellent summary of the whole affair, see P. Hasluck, vol. 2, Appendix 5 "The Australia First Movement", pp. 718- 42; and for a study of the movement's leader, see

Craig Munro, *Wild Man of Letters: The Story of P.R. Stephensen*, MUP, Melbourne, 1984.

41 Telegram, Cooper to Prime Minister, dated 11 March 1942, QSA A/6477, bundle 188/25.
42 B. Muirden, *Puzzled Patriots*, p. 149 and Craig Munro, *Wild Man of Letters*, p.215.
43 Watching the masts and then the ships appearing over the horizon, Mary Alice Evatt recorded, "soon everyone in Sydney began to know. People were rushing on motor-bikes with the news ... We all felt wonderful. From then on we felt things were going to be better." Kylie Tennant, *Evatt: Politics and Justice*, p. 138.
44 In a letter to Shedden as Secretary of the Advisory War Council, dated 30 April 1942 Forde stated that at the end of November 1941 there were 2,246 residents interned but by early 1942 there were 4,269, "exclusive of the 1,000 odd Japanese" taken when Japan entered the war. Of the 2,000 increase, 90% were from Queensland, AA CRS A373, item 419.
45 *CPD*, vol. 170 (26 March 1942), p. 462, (27 March 1942), p. 533.
46 Ibid., p. 515, for motion, pp. 516-7 for Fadden's speech.
47 Ibid., p. 516. Fadden said "The time is opportune to link the disclosures made yesterday with the position of aliens in this country."
48 Ibid., pp. 528-30 for Martens' speech.
49 Ibid., p. 517.
50 Ibid., pp. 517-8 for Blackburn's speech.
51 Ibid., pp. 518-9 for Francis' speech.
52 Ibid., pp. 519-21 for Curtin's speech.
53 Ibid., pp.520-1 for the clash over Mackay. Calwell may have held against Mackay his presence at the riot where a miner was killed at Rothbury in 1929, but he was generally acceptable to Labor because he had stood up to the New Guard in the early 1930s.
54 See F. Cain, *The Origins of Political Surveillance*, Angus and Robertson, Australia, 1983, pp.277-8.
55 *CPD*, vol. 170 (27 March 1942), pp. 528-30 for Martens speech.
56 Ibid., pp. 530-3 for Anthony and McEwen.
57 The War Cabinet Agendum no. 181/1942 "Enemy Aliens- North-East Queensland Coast", AA CRS A373, item 1681, p. 1.
58 Northern Command's views are in "Appendix B", Agendum no. 181/1942.
59 Ibid., Representations by Mr C.J. Carroll, forwarded by W.J. Mackay to Forde, "Appendix A". Carroll's views had been previously put to a conference convened by Mackay in Melbourne on 20 March 1942. A summary of this conference is in AA SP 26/3.
60 "Appendix B", Summary of points for and against removal, signed by Lt Col. C.G. Roberts, DMI, dated 22 March 1942, attached to War Cabinet Agendum no. 181/1942, AA CRS A373, item 1681.
61 Ibid., Conclusions by F.M. Forde, p. 2.
62 Ibid., Letter, A/D DMI to MLO, Security Service, Canberra, dated 22 September 1942.
63 AWCM 746, 11 February 1942, and Agendum no. 24/1942, dated 24 March 1942, and Notes on War Cabinet Agendum no. 181/1942, AA ACT CRS A5954, box 253.
64 Ibid., Notes on Supplement No. 1 to Advisory War Council Agendum no. 19/1942, including Report by Minister for the Army dated 30 April 1942.
65 N. Lamidey, *Aliens Control*, p. 51 for statistics. Forbes signed Master Warrant Lists 5, 6, 9, 13, 14, 15, 17, 18, 19, 21 and 26, in QSA A/ll91(1942).
66 Letter, Major-General G.A. Vasey to Secretary, Department of the Army, dated 13 April 1942, AA CRS A373, item 1681. In the Northern Territory martial law gave the senior officer control of all civilians. John Curtin, in response to reports of "anti-ally feeling" among Aborigines in central W.A., recommended

State authorities be asked for information, letter, Curtin to Forde, dated 24 July 1942, AA MP 729/6, file 29/401/626. According to Humphrey McQueen, a mobile army group rounded up all unemployed Aborigines from areas of W.A. in June 1942 and gaoled them as "possible potential enemies". See Humphrey McQueen, *Social Sketches of Australia, 1888-1975*, Penguin Books, Ringwood, 1978, p. 168.

67   Letter, Major-General W.A.Beevor T. Steele, Base Commandant, Southern Command, to Army HQ, dated 1 April 1942, and A.C. Fewtrell to Army HQ, dated 23 March 1942, AA CRS A373, item 1681.

68   AA BP 242/1, item Q31659.

69   Letter, Martens to Curtin, dated 30 April 1942, with list attached, AA CRS A373, item 1357. The names are screened but the descriptions suggest about fifteen.

70   Ibid., Letter Martens to Forde, dated 26 June 1942 and copy of letter, Forde to Martens, dated 2 July 1942.

71   Ibid., Army Minute Paper, "Files Requested by Mr G.W. Martens MP", dated 3 July 1942.

72   Ibid., Letter, Rogers to Secretary, Department of the Army, dated 17 July 1942.

73   Ibid., Army Minute Paper, "Dossiers of Internees requested by Mr Martens MP", Secretary to the Minister, dated 26 July 1942. At the bottom of the minute Forde wrote, "Mr Martens representations together with the points raised in this minute to be referred to the A-G for a decision", dated 31 July 1942.

74   The categories A-O are described by Gianfranco Cresciani in *Fascism, Anti-Fascism and Italians in Australia*, p. 172.

75   The activities of reporting or home security officers were described by the majority of a group of 40 long-term residents of North Queensland interviewed by the writer during a field trip in June 1979.

76   Copy of SM 2700, Internment Policy, Director of Military Intelligence to Command HQ's, received 13 February 1942, AA CRS A373, item 1681.

77   A copy of the detention order, dated 4 March 1942, AA BP 242/1, item Q8389, and List 8, C No. 2, includes Orlandi's name, QSA A1191 1942.

78   Personal interviews, 5 and 8 June 1979.

79   Summary of File No. MI 18/4/1656 as at 11 November 1941 and letter, Sergeant to Inspector of Police, Townsville, dated 11 November 1941, AA BP 242/1, item Q8389. TR39's comments are in Report, IO, Townsville to ISGS, Northern Command, dated 6 October 1941, attached to Summary of File MI 18/4/1656.

80   For the theories from other ex-internees I am indebted to Lyn Henderson, whose honours thesis on the Hinchinbrook Shire involved her in interviews with ex- internees whose opinions have been generalised here.

81   Diane Menghetti, "Their Country, Not Mine" (Second Conference on Italian Culture and Italy Today), p. 206. A second group of ex-internees believed the decision was based on nationality, political involvement and being reported to police as a Fascist or trouble maker while a third group considered arrests were the result of "non-cooperation with the manpower authorities" (p. 205).

82   B. Muirden, *Puzzled Patriots*, p. 95.

83   From a series of personal interviews with 40 people who were resident in the Lower Burdekin, Townsville and the Atherton Tableland in 1942, June 1979.

84   Newspaper cutting, "Paterson Demands N.Q. Police Probe", labelled Old Guardian 2/11/45, AA BP 242/1, item Q33794.

85   Letter, W.J. Mackay to Director of Military Intelligence, dated 15 May 1942, AA CRS A373, item 1357.

86   Letter and list, Sub-Inspector of Police at Innisfail to Brisbane, dated 22 February 1942, QSA A/11914.

87   List to Intelligence Corps, Northern Command, from Ingham Police, dated 28 April 1942 and list from Cairns, dated 1 April 1942, QSA A/11916.

88   Bruno is listed in a Master Warrant, List 26, signed by Brigadier A.M. Forbes on 13 April 1942, by authority delegated to him on 30 January 1942, QSA A/1191, 1942. Bruno's explanation of his case and his appeal to return home are in the Calwell Papers, (MS) MP 1444, box 44 in the National Library in Canberra.
89   N. Lamidey, *Aliens Control*, p.53.
90   Ibid., pp. 77-8.

Chapter Eight

1   Alan Fitzgerald, *The Italian Farming Soldiers: Prisoners of War in Australia, 1941-1947*, Melbourne University Press, Melbourne 1981, pp. 24, 6 — 7. K.G. Loewald, "A Dunera Internee at Hay", p. 521, records that when rumours circulated among the *Dunera* internees that prisoners of war were to be the camp's next inhabitants, they made a bonfire of the "chairs, benches, tables and other items" of comfort they had made.
2   *Internment in South Australia*, p. 5. The 4th Garrison Battalion was redesignated the 25th Garrison Battalion in February 1942.
3   Ibid., p. 6.
4   C. Pearl, *The Dunera Scandal*, pp. 148, 201 and 205.
5   *Internment in South Australia*, pp. 3-4.
6   The Loveday head-count of internees on 1 March 1942 was 962 (in Camp 9), 764 (Camp 10), and Camp 14 held 115 (Compound 14A), 1,000 (14B), 970 (14C), 140 (14D) — a grand total of 3,951.
7   The Official Visitor's Report No. 10, dated 23 May 1942, noted a formal protest lodged by the Camp 10 leader against the bayoneting of men by the soldiers "at the time of the excitement when the tunnelling was disclosed". The Official Visitors considered that the show of force was justified and was only "sufficient to restore order at a time when feeling was running high", AA MP 508/1, file 255/716/111. The discovery of the tunnel is also recorded in *Internment in South Australia*, p. 6.
8   Moorook West was opened by 210 Italian POWs originally from Murchison. An allocation of 138 Japanese internees took up the work on 1 March 1943. By the end of the war more than 56,000 tons of firewood had been supplied to the Murray pumping stations, and 10,000 tons had been cut for army use in the area. *Internment in South Australia*, p. 28.
9   AWM 140, Official Historians Biographical Index Cards, 1914-1918 War.
10   *Internment in South Australia*, p. 6.
11   AWCM 912, dated 16 April 1942, AA CRS A5954, box 674, and AHQ Intelligence Summary No. 170, AWM 123, "Special Collection II", Records of the Defence Committee.
12   Ibid., letter, Forde to Spender, dated 27 May 1942.
13   *Internment in South Australia*, p.14.
14   See Peter Sekuless, *Jessie Street:A Rewarding but Unrewarded Life*, University of Queensland Press, St Lucia, 1978, p.55, for aid to Russia. Jessie Street was Chairman of the Russian Medical Aid and Comforts Committee (RMACC) and travelled the countryside examining fleeces for the "Sheepskins for Russia" campaign. By 1942 there were 28 branches of the RMACC in NSW and support for the Soviet Union in Australia was probably as high as at any time in the two countries' relations.
15   G. Cresiani, *Fascism, Anti-Fascism and Italians in Australia*, pp. 176-9. Newspaper report "Internee on Killing Charge. Quarrel Over Aid For Russia", labelled the "News", 22/12/42 and "Camp friction over aid for Russia", labelled Sunday Telegraph, 24 January 1943, and cutting "Criminal Sittings", labelled

Advertiser 23/12/42, AA CRS A373 item 3744. Fantin complained of attacks by Fascists in a letter, dated 17 August 1942, AA MP 742/1, item 255/12/12.

16 *Internment in South Australia*, p. 6.

17 Deputy Director of Security, Qld, to Director- General, Canberra, dated 8 December 1942, AA CRS A373, item 3744. The problem of categorising non-native English speakers was fraught with the possibility of misunderstanding. Few Australian officials, military or police officers spoke any language other than English, so they had to rely on second-hand information. They often asked long-term naturalised men to give an opinion. These men were believed because they were well-established economically, but financial success and conservatism often go hand in hand and in the first part of the war any type of radical or socialist views were suspect because of the Nazi-Soviet pact. Zammarachi, who was a socialist, was arrested for this reason, but the discrepancy in Fantin's case is much greater. Perhaps it was because there was no equivalent to anarchism in Australian politics but it could equally well be a deliberate act of "dobbing" by the informer, incensed by Fantin's "knocking" the British. Informants could have any number of old scores to settle. Some Italians were denounced by Yugoslavs who had national and job disputes as motives.

18 Letters of protest about the Fantin case and requests for segregation are in AA MP 742/1, item 255/12/12. This includes a strongly worded letter from Bishop C. Venn Pilcher, dated 9 December 1942. Army correspondence on segregation at Loveday includes a complaint by Major Layton about Camp 10 Loveday dated 4 May 1942 and Major-General V.P.H. Stantke's reply of 11 June 1942, AA MP 508, file 255/716/250. Extracts from the Official Visitor's Report No. 16, p. 3 where he predicts trouble in Camp 14D and Stantke's reply of 30 November 1942 are in AA MP 742/1, item 255/11/54.

19 *Internment in South Australia*, p. 7.

20 Intelligence Report No. 183, dated 8 December 1942. This report deals with tension between Fascists and anti-Fascist elements in the compound. Copies of this report and of two letters by Fantin describing his loneliness in camp and how his Fascist enemies tormented him are in AA MP 742/1, item 255/12/12. In her paper "Their Country, Not Mine", Diane Menghetti told the Second Australian Conference on Italian Culture and Italy Today, at Sydney University (6 August 1982), of the ex-internees recollections.

21 Appendix IV, p. 2, attached to letter to His Honour Judge Jordan, dated 26 October 1940, AA Army 701, file 255/714/64.

22 E. Barcs, *Backyard of Mars*, pp. 150-1.

23 Report on the Inspection of the Internment Camps at Tatura, Victoria, signed by Georges Morel dated 24 April 1941, Chapter 2, p. 9, AA MP 385/3, file 156/2/591, and Report No. 17, dated 5 January 1943, p. 2, AA MP 742/1, file 255/12/37.

24 Willyan has written and published his story in *Behind Barbed Wire in Australia: The Amazing Experiences of an Australian Citizen*, C. Willyan, Murchison, 1948. See pp. 20-2 for camp spies. The reasons for Willyan's arrest are difficult to fathom. He had clearly annoyed a local landowner, he implied the local policeman was one of the Victorian Police Force's "mistakes" and that false evidence was given about a conversation and the running of the local Public Building, on which supervising committee he served. In more general terms he claimed Murchison people had "the small-town mentality" and puts Frank Forde's defeat at the 1946 elections down to resentment against Forde's signing of orders to intern hundreds "under powers that were never intended to be used indiscriminately". As a result of his experiences Willyan persuaded his son to desert from the army.

25 Personal interview, 5 June 1979.

26 B. Muirden, *Puzzled Patriots*, p. 127. Stephensen considered some internees would "make up reports to curry favour with the authorities".

27 *Internment in South Australia*, p. 6, for first suicide. On 27 November 1942 Loveday had recorded seven attempted suicide cases. Names are screened but Archives staff deduced that the nationalities represented were two German, one Italian, and four Japanese or Formosans. One swallowed phenol, one bit off his tongue and the others slashed their wrists or otherwise wounded themselves. Of the seven only one (a Japanese) died, and one was evacuated to Japan on 15 August 1942, AA AP 589/1, file 551067. The mental cases from Loveday went to the Enfield Receiving House. On 23 November 1942 the Deputy Director of Security in South Australia reported there were "several internees" in the Government Mental Hospital. Two were from Queensland and their property could not be administered by the SA Public Trustee because it was not in that state, nor by the Queensland Public Curator because the internee was not confined in that state, AA AP 589/1, file 551064.

28 For example, Copy of letter, G. Vaccari to Dr Evatt, dated 24 April 1944, AA MP 742, file 115/1/151.

29 Memorandum, Relief Payments to Dependants of Interned Aliens, from A/District Finance Officer, Qld L of C Area, dated 17 September 1942, AA MP 742/1, item 255/4/37. The NSW Premier resisted using state funds to sustain released internees, and their families. The situation had "arisen out of the Commonwealth's handling of" internment and McKell wanted the Commonwealth to continue to re-coup his state for assistance to released internees, ibid., letter W.J. McKell to Prime Minister, dated 24 November 1941.

30 O. Bonutto, *A Migrant's Story*, p. 93.

31 E. Barcs, *Backyard of Mars*, pp. 99-100.

32 Letter, Dr Morel to Dr Evatt, dated 15 March 1943, AA MP 742/1, item 255/8/15. An I.R.C. cable complained that razorblades "and sometimes tobacco" were not allowed in parcels to Loveday 14A. Morel informed Australian authorities that razor blades should be passed on to internees as they were made available to Australian POWs and internees in Germany. Morel began his work as IRC delegate in February 1941. He died as the war was ending. His reports are scattered throughout internment files and show that he was thorough and was able to establish good relations with internees and camp commandants. For examples of his reports, correspondence with camp leaders, and army responses, see AA MP 385/3, file 156/2/591.

33 Ross Costanzo, Personal interview, 4 June 1979.

34 *Internment in South Australia*, p. 25 says that 134 internees and 1 POW died at Loveday. Of these 108 were Japanese. The Office of Australian War Graves in a letter dated 19 November 1979 states that 145 Japanese, of whom 110 were internees, were buried at the Barmera Garden of Memory. They were later exhumed and interred in the Cowra Japanese War Cemetery, N.S.W. The large majority were aged between 50 and 77 years when they died.

35 E. Barcs, *Background of Mars*, p. 111.

36 Ibid., p. 99. Barcs received his objection form at the police station, but was told to fill it out later.

37 Japanese internee heard by Aliens Tribunal No. 4 on 10 February 1942 said that he/she and friends completed appeals forms because they were "asked by the officials", AA MP 529/3, box 5 WOB.

38 Some Lutheran missionaries from New Guinea denied that they knew of tribunal hearings until after the war, H. Nelson, "Loyalties at Sword-point", p. 206.

39 Merchant seamen who refused to ask for release included six Finns mentioned by Barcs, pp. 120-1, and 17 Chinese noted in Davidson's report on Liverpool

in December 1942, AA MP 742, file 255/10/5, as well as Javanese later in the war, AA CRS 1608, item A20/1/2.

40 W. Konig, "Internment in Australia", p. 21.

41 *Internment in South Australia*, p. 8. The executives are described as "carefully selected" by Camp Commandants but later they are referred to as "appointed" by the commandants. All internee sources refer to elections of their hut and camp leaders and the reference to appointed by the commandant probably meant that the camp executives had the administration's delegated authority and that they could be removed from their positions by him. A bitter contest over the rejection of a camp leader at Camp 10 in the first months of 1943 led to 48 internees getting detention for participating in a protest. They refused to answer "Here, sir" at roll call or answered merely "Here". The matter was resolved by a fresh full scale election and the "moderate" candidate who got the largest vote was appointed. Although the "extremist" gained slightly more votes the commandant, Major Lott, was convinced this was due to the support of the boys who had come from the mixed camp and were under the domination of a Nazi "who was removed from the leadership of his camp at Tatura", AA MP 613/1, file 90/1/139.

42 These positions were very important to the morale of the people who held them. In interviews and written accounts those who held such positions emphasise the fact and in the few camp records sighted by the writer where the positions were terminated the internee involved reacted angrily or went into a decline. The duties of the Compound Leader are set out in Camp Standing Orders for Prisoners of War by Lieut-Colonel E.T. Dean, dated 1 September 1940, AA AP 613/4 Miscellaneous Papers, Loveday Camp.

43 *Internment in South Australia*, p. 14, includes this comment. "The fact that such paid employment was made available very materially assisted in the smooth running, administration and health of the internees themselves ... Men constantly employed were healthier and happier in mind and less inclined to complain of their internment."

44 Ibid., p. 5.

45 Report "True Italian Movement: Note", signed Captain C.R. Jury, OC Section Aust. Intelligence Corps, dated 6 October 1943, AA AP 538/1, file 21163.

46 Ibid., Report on "True Italian Movement", July 1943.

47 The occupational groupings of aliens during World War II (drawn most probably from the Aliens Registration forms) is Appendix "C" in N. Lamidey's *Aliens Control*. The statistics have been organised by nationalities and districts. There is a predominance among Italians of work related to growing and selling food. In New South Wales in the metropolitan area fruiterers and market gardeners were most common, while in the country districts tobacco, banana, vegetable and fruit growers clearly outnumbered the few industrial employees at Wollongong and mine workers at Broken Hill. In Queensland, sugar, tobacco and maize farmers predominate. One ex-internee remembered that they were warned that their plots were getting dangerously close to the wire and that on notification of release, internees often "willed" their plots to their friends.

48 Copy of Extract from Weekly Intelligence Report No. 72 Tatura, dated 21 May 1944, AA SP 1714/1, item N60318.

49 The *Reichgulde* rate was three pounds per quarter. The Japanese government also made pocket money available to its indigent internees.

50 Letter, Camp Commandant to HQ Loveday Group, dated 16 March 1943, AA AP 613/1, file 90/1/139.

51 Zammarchi saw one German who did refuse to be intimidated, at Tatura when the June 1940 Italian intake had arrived. There was trouble among the hundreds of Germans. The Germans fascists and anti- fascists brawled, and

sometimes the fascists themselves argued. "There was a sect among the Germans, Jehovah's Witness "who would 'never have anything to do with the fascists,and one of them, one small chap, he didn't stint, he insulted them ... On Hitler's birthday the fascists had a big turn out and they put out a table with some money they said Hitler sent to them and anyone who went there they were given a few shillings. This Jehovah's Witness, he pass there and they call him over and he went and spit on the money. "They are Hitler's money, they are blood money". He had guts.',M. Loh (ed.), *With Courage in their Cases*, pp. 31-2.

52   Olive Hirschfeld, personal interview, 25 September 1979.

53   G. Cresciani, *Fascists, Anti-Fascists and Italians in Australia*, p. 175, argues that the tolerance shown by the Australian authorities and the "considerable degree of personal freedom enjoyed by internees soon brought about a revival of political activities within the camps' and that Fascist camp leaders were elected and encouraged "manifestations of sympathy for Fascism and Nazism among Italians in camp".

54   S. Encel, "These Men are Dangerous", p. 11.

55   Letter, Director-General of Security to Deputy Director, Adelaide, dated 8 October 1942, AA AP 308/1, file SS 1057.

56   Letter, Major-General R.E. Jackson to Secretary, Military Board, received 20 February 1941, and Army Minute Paper, "Internees Mail: Gaythorne Camp", Colonel James A. Chapman, dated 27 March 1941, AA MP 742/1, file 255/714/241.

57   In his report of 6 March 1941 the Official Visitor to Harvey, Mr Justice A.A. Wolff, showed that one internee received 28 days solitary confinement for refusing to obey an order, for insolence and abusive language to internee F— while another internee got only 14 days "for refusing to obey an order, insolence to Camp Commandant with abusive and obscene language", AA Army 701, file 255/717/18.

58   K.G. Loewald, "A Dunera Internee at Hay", p. 515. E. Barcs, *Backyard of Mars*, p. 114, was invited to join the sanitation unit on the enticement of the pay. For Barcs' account of Tatura, see pp. 129-45.

59   On complaint from family camp, see Morel's report on Tatura in AA MP 385/3, file 156/2/591.

60   When boys reached 16 years of age they were transfered from their families at Tatura and sent to Loveday. This was a decision of the family internees themselves, taken with a view to protecting the adolescent girls. However, the fears of the youths" mothers had some basis in fact. A fair, good-looking member of the Vienna Boys Choir was sent to Loveday and was "never the same again". His fellow choristers are of the opinion that he was probably abused by the Foreign Legionnaires interned in the same compound, as they said in interviews for "Class of '39", Channel O TV program, 20 February 1983.

61   Ethel Punshon, Personal Interview, 23 November 1979.

62   Outline of Loveday Employment Projects, reprinted from *The Advertiser*, 4 December 1945, in *Internment in South Australia*, pp. 26-8. On the early days at Hay, see AA Army 701, file 255/714/31 and AA MP 508, file 255/714/32. In 1942, Thane was annoyed at the delay in the purchase of a Ayrshire bull to service the Hay dairy herd. Why an expert from the Department of Agriculture was needed when he had the advice of "numerous men" in the Garrison, who had spent a lifetime in dairying, Thane could not understand, letter C.S. Thane to NSW L of C Area, dated 7 September 1942, AA SP 196/1, item 9.

63   *Internment in South Australia*, p. 11.

64   Official Visitors Report No. 16, p. 3 reproduced in AA MP 742/1, item 255/11/54. In his reply to Sanderson on 30 November 1942, Major-General Stantke explained that the transfer from Parkeston was made to release some

200 guards and to avoid the use of building materials, both needed in Western Australia. Not to have effected these "vital economies" just "because of prospective difficulties" would "make a valuable contribution to the cause of our enemies" (pp. 2-3).

65 Copy of Report No. 4, dated 24 October 1941, AA AP 613/4.

66 Copy of Official Visitor's Report No. 3 (Extracts), dated 30 September 1941, AA AP 613/4, Unnumbered file, Report No. 3.

67 Ibid., reply to Report No. 3, p. 3, signed E.T. Dean.

68 Adjutant-General to HQ, SA L of C Area, SM 9732, AA AP 613/1, file 90/1/70.

69 Commandant, SA L of C Area, to Major-General Stantke, LHQ, Melbourne, date missing but file headed 90/1/117, AA AP 613/1, file 90/1/117.

70 Report No. 17, p. 3, AA MP 742/1, file 255/12/37. Major W.E.L. Hill was a popular commandant. When he was transfered from 14D, the leader of the Italian Section of the camp, asked the OV to apply "to the proper sources" to have the move stopped. Hill "knew each case personally" and his participation "in all spheres of Sport, Concerts, and individual cases' had given "a definite lift" to morale, letter to W. Ray, dated 13 October 1942, AA Army 701, item 255/716/221.

71 *Internment in South Australia*, p. 15.

72 Report No. 12, dated 29 July 1942, AA MP 508/1, file 255/716/111.

73 On these points, see Margaret Bevege, "Women's Experiences in North Queensland during World Nar II" in *Second Women and Labour Conference Papers*, vol. 2, 1980, pp. 604-5 and Nance Kingston, "My experiences in the AWAS during World War II", in *Worth Her Salt*, edited by Margaret Bevege, Margaret James and Carmel Shute, Hale and Iremonger, Sydney, 1982, pp. 118-19.

74 In *Dead Men Rising*, p. 38, Seaforth Mackenzie describes how a half-blind Garrison guard was promoted to corporal and transfered to Group HQ within a week because the Adjutant discovered he could type. Good typists were "as rare as joy in the unconsidered garrison units". A woman stenographer was employed for a tribunal hearing in New South Wales in August 1940 but the committee and counsel found her presence embarrassing where "obscene statements concerning the Empire, His Majesty the King and other British institutions' might be heard and she had to be replaced by a male, Memorandum to Secretary, Attorney-General's Department, dated 21 August 1940, AA CRS A472, item W69.

75 For Loveday escapes and Jimmy James, see *Internment in South Australia*, pp. 12-3. *The Argus*, 8 May 1942, reported that Wolfgang Kuchl and Paul Lechner were discovered 15 miles from camp, near the radio station 5RM between Berri and Renmark, by Jimmy James who had followed their trail of discarded orange peels. They were asleep under a tree on the Murray Flats and gave no trouble when apprehended.

76 Margaret Pierce and Alfred C. Clarke, Report on a Visit to Hay Internment Camps, roneoed sheets, in the possession of A.C. Clarke, Melbourne. In the early days of Loveday, troops on leave had to walk four miles to Barmera and they asked for "a two horse dray" to use for leave and bathing transport, AA MP 385/3, file 156/2/591.

77 W. Konig, "Internment in Australia", p. 16.

78 E. Barcs, *Backyard of Mars*, pp. 130-1, 155-6.

79 Report, dated 11 December 1942, by the Honourable Mr Justice Davidson, last page, AA 742/1, file 255/10/5.

80 Newspaper article "Belsen Horror Wiped By Tatura Internees", labelled *Truth*, 17 November 1945 in AA MP 798, file 38702.

81 For the Queensland internees and all subsequent complaints of wrongful detention or problems with internees property or families, see AA MP 508/1,

file 255/716/111. This file contains Reports nos 8-12 by K.F. Sanderson and W. Vernon Ray, Official Visitors to Loveday. They cover the period May-July 1942.

82   The army's responses to the report of 23 May 1942 is in AA AP 613/1, file 90/1/70. Here the army agrees that petitions by Australian-born citizens from Queensland may be forwarded "through official channels", but they should be addressed to the Minister for the Army "if the subject relates to internment", p. 6.

83   The situation of the Port Pirie fishermen had given Forde some concern. Although many had joined the local Fascio, they were also naturalised. They claimed they joined the Fascio to facilitate getting their wives out from Italy. They needed to be naturalised to obtain a fishing permit. Forde suggested that as many had wives and young families to support they be given employment on the East-West Railway line, but the army felt all fascists should be interned and Forde signed the orders on 26 February 1942, Army Minute Paper, Orders for Internment, signed by Sinclair, dated 26 February 1942, AA A373, item 1075.

84   Report No. 12, dated 29 July 1942, p. 3, AA MP 508/1, file 255/716/111. By the end of October 1942 the OVs felt they could not continue dealing with problems relating to the administration of internees' property. The authorities would have to get lawyers and accountants in or farms, hotels, houses, boats, and machinery would be wasted assets, Report No. 15, dated 28 October 1942 and army reply, AA Army 701, file 255/716/221.

85   Report No. 11, dated 23 June 1942, p. 2, AA MP 508/1, file 255/716/111.

86   Ibid., p. 7.

87   In July 1944 the government appointed Mr Justice Hutchins to chair the Overseas Internees Investigation Board to look into the position of internees in this situation. His findings are discussed in Chapter Nine.

88   Letter, Morel to General (sic) H.C. Bundock, dated 20 January 1944, AA AP 613/1, file 90/1/238.

89   Ibid., Commandant,SA L of C Area to Camp Leader, dated 20 January 1944.

90   N. Lamidey, Aliens' Control, p. 54.

Chapter 9

1   Arthur Calwell and others asked questions or brought attention to the Australia First internments on 30 April, 20 and 27 May, 2, 3/4 June, 2 and 9 September 1942 and 28 January and 5 March 1943. See CPD, vol. 170, p. 702; vol. 171, pp. 1395-7, 1565, 1827-8, 2147- 8; vol. 172, pp. 43-60, 98; vol. 173, p. 155, and vol. 174, p. 1302. Dr Evatt dealt with the Australia First internments in a speech on National Security on 10 September 1942, ibid., vol. 172, pp. 152-7.

2   Bruce Muirden, The Puzzled Patriots, pp.77-87.

3   For criticism of the legislation by Jordan and Davidson, see Muirden, pp. 124-5 and for legislators' reaction see CPD (19 May 1942), vol. 171, p. 1336.

4   Letter, Mackay to Director of Military Intelligence, dated 15 May 1942, AA CRS A373, item 1357, and letter, Mackay to Forde, dated 20 May 1942, item 419.

5   Paul Hasluck's summary of the events surrounding the Australia First arrests and his analysis of the issues involved is in Appendix 5 of The Government and the People, vol.2, pp. 718-42. Knowles' minute is on pp. 732-3. Knowles also pointed out that there were 167 Australians in camp and the release of Australia First members without appearing before an Advisory Committee would create "an awkward precedent".

6   Letter, Mackay to Deputy Director of Security, Sydney, dated 25 August 1942 refers to the Attorney- General's minute dated 22 August 1942, AA SP 1714/1, item Policy 3.

7　Allan Dalziel, *Evatt — The Enigma*, Lansdowne Press, Melbourne, 1967, pp. 24-7. Dalziel concludes that Evatt's "welter of activity" in putting Australia's case in Washington and London made him "unable to deal with the rapid sequence of events that was taking place on the Australian scene under National Emergency powers" and that Evatt "was never happy with the whole business" which Dalziel believed "would not have happened had [Evatt] not been overseas on his vital mission".

8　Kylie Tennant, *Evatt — Politics and Justice*, p. 147.

9　asluck, vol. 2, pp. 731-2.

10　Ibid., pp. 735-6 and p. 742.

11　Noel Lamidey, who was attached to the Security Section, described Mackay as an "earthy" man who "by dint of hardwork, drive and efficiency and an aggressive personality" had come from a constable in Glasgow to the highest rank in New South Wales, *Partial Success*, p.50.

12　Mackay's preference for Sydney is clear in his appeal to Evatt for support over files and staff on 1 August 1942, AA CRS A373, item 1336.

13　Ibid., p. 51.

14　Letter, Mackay to Lieutenant-General V.A.H. Sturdee, (copies to other Chiefs and Knowles), dated 28 March 1942, Blamey Papers, AWM 3 DRL 6643, item 54.7.

15　Ibid., letter, Mackay to General Sir Thomas Blamey, dated 30 March 1942.

16　Ibid., letter, Commander-in-Chief to Mackay, dated 31 March 1942.

17　Frank Cain, *The Origins of Political Surveillance*, p. 289.

18　N. Lamidey, *Partial Success*, p.51.

19　Security Conference, Canberra, "Anticipated Attendance", 5 September [1942], AA ACT CRS A472, item W69, part 2.

20　N. Lamidey, *Partial Success*, p.51.

21　Ibid., pp. 48-9.

22　F. Cain also mentions that Simpson was "a school and university associate of Dr Evatt", *The Origins of Political Surveillance*, p.291. Simpson took office on 23 September 1942.

23　Army Minute Paper, "Dossiers of Internees Requested by Mr Martens, M.P.", Sinclair to the Minister, dated 26 July 1942, AA CRS A373, item 1357.

24　Ibid., Forde's handwritten footnote is dated 31 July 1942.

25　Ibid., list attached to Martens' letter to Curtin, 30 April 1942.

26　*CPD*, vol. 172 (10 September 1942), pp. 152- 7.

27　*CPD*, vol. 172 (10 September 1942), pp. 193-4, (24 September 1942), p. 860.

28　The *Sunday Australian's* reaction in its edition of 4 October 1942 immediately after a summary of Martens' speech.

29　The production of sugar in 1941 was 696,815 tons, in 1942 it was 605,296 tons, and in 1943 it slid to 486,354 tons. Some of this must be attributed to a shortage of fertiliser, particularly super-phosphate, but the removal of farmers and sugar workers in the planting time of March to May 1942 was a key factor. See Mr Justice Mansfield, Royal Commission on the Sugar Industry, 1942- 1943, vol. I, and statistics available from the Cane Growers Council, Brisbane.

30　Not only did Evatt establish the ACAC, Calwell states that Evatt "showed great personal concern" over aliens control and was always willing to improve legislation and review restrictions. See Foreword to Lamidey, *Aliens Control*. Recalling this period in 1955 Evatt said that there was a struggle" with Military Intelligence when it was deprived "of the terrific power" of internment of civilians. He had found 7,000 people interned in 1942 and thousands of them "should not have been interned", K. Tennant, *Evatt — Politics and Justice*, p. 333.

31　Curtin's calmer approach to the Australia First affair and his refusal to bait aliens indicate his attitude and B. Muirden states that Evatt said in 1956 that

Curtin took the initiative to move the jurisdiction over internment away from Military Intelligence and to pass it to a civil organisation, *Puzzled Patriots*, p.130.

32   Canada had interned only 928 Europeans by 4 December 1942, Calwell Papers, NLA (MS) MP 1444, box 41, and in the United States, German and Italian resident males were drafted into the army.

33   W. Forgan-Smith's departure was officially made on the grounds of ill-health but he continued as a Minister without portfolio in the Cooper government for a time and actively campaigned for Curtin's conscription policy in November 1942. He became Chairman of the Central Sugar Cane Prices Board in December 1942. In his article "William Forgan-Smith: Dictator or Democrat?", Brian Carroll mentions the strains between Forgan-Smith and his federal Labor colleagues over the uniform taxation legislation and comments that Forgan-Smith was not "particularly friendly" with Curtin or other federal leaders. He regarded them as "all too far to the left for his liking", D J. Murphy and R.B. Joyce (eds), *Queensland Political Portraits, 1859-1952*, Uni of Queensland Press, St.Lucia, 1978, p. 423.

34   H.N. Nelson, "Loyalties at Sword-point: The Lutheran Missionaries in Wartime New Guinea, 1939-45", *Australian Journal of Politics and History*, vol. 24, no. 2 (August 1978), p. 204. A case of a German wife's determination to be interned is recorded in the "Synopsis of events effecting (sic) National Security" collected by the Military Police Intelligence Section, Sydney. In the week ending 4 April 1942 a wife, describing herself as a "Good German", called at the Section and demanded to be interned. Her husband was already in camp. In the week ending 14 April, the synopsis records that Mrs B——, "has now been interned", AA SP 26/3.

35   Official reports and newspaper clippings on Lutheran Missionaries are in AA AP 538/1, file SA 20502. It is clear from AA SP 1714/1, item N39016 that every Lutheran church and mission in Australia was investigated as a result of an instruction from Major C.J. Roberts of Military Intelligence on 21 October 1940.

36   H.N. Nelson, "Loyalties at Sword-point", p. 204.

37   Ibid., pp. 201-3.

38   Ibid., pp. 208-10.

39   Ibid., p. 205.

40   A report on the families departure for Tatura, Extract from Security Service Report, fortnight ending 18 December 1942, and Stolz's letter, dated 17 March 1944, Post and Telegraph Censorship Bulletin No. 75, AA SP 1714/1, item N39016. Following a decision by the Department of External Affairs that former New Guinea residents might return some missionaries were released and cleared to return, letter, R.S. Browne, Assistant DGS to DDS, Melbourne, dated 9 September 1946, AA AP 538/1, SA 20502.

41   Copy of Memorandum, "Internment for other than Security Reasons", F.R. Sinclair to Director General of Security, dated 17 August 1942, attached to Mackay's letter to Deputy Director of Security, Sydney, dated 18 August 1942, AA SP 1714/1, item Policy 3.

42   Ratliff and Thomas were released on 21 October 1941 shortly after Labor's assumption to power, Hasluck, vol. 1, pp. 611-2.

43   B. Muirden, *Puzzled Patriots*, p.128.

44   Hasluck, vol. 2, p. 734 and p. 739.

45   Letter, Mackay to Evatt, "Army personnel engaged in Security Service", dated 30 July 1942, AA CRS A373, item 1336.

46   Ibid., Memorandum, Sinclair to Director-General of Security, No. 94118.

47   Ibid., copy of letter, J.D. Rogers to Director-General of Security, "Restrictions and Internments — Transfer of Files", dated 18 July 1942. For further details of Mackay's problems in establishing the Security Service in the various states

see F. Cain, *The Origins of Political Surveillance*, pp. 288-92. According to Cain when Mackay lost his job to Simpson, he took files and staff with him causing Simpson similar problems to those Mackay had experienced with the army. The ACAC also had trouble getting unrestricted access to Simpson's Security Service files later.

48   Letter, Mackay to Forde, dated 20 May 1942, AA CRS A373, item 419.
49   Ibid., copy of letter, Chapman to I.S.G.S., Eastern Command, dated 4 September 1941. There is a clear case of a selective use of words in Bonutto's file. (AA BP 242/1, item Q8375.) In a dossier dated 10 April, 1940 the submitting officer stated that Stanthorpe police reported on 25 September 1939 that Bonutto's hotel in Gordonvale was "a rendezvous for foreigners". In their submission on Bonutto's request to buy a block of flats in August 1946, the Commonwealth Investigation Branch followed the exact wording of the original report that stated that the hotel was "a rendezvous for foreign and British alike".
50   Ibid., letter, Forde to Mackay, dated 10 July 1942.
51   Letter, Durrant to Deputy Director of Security, Brisbane, dated 2 July 1942, AA CRS A373, item 1715.
52   Ibid., McFarlane to Director General, Canberra, dated 10 July 1942 and subsequent correspondence.
53   Memorandum, Kirkman to Director General of Security, dated 17 August 1942, AA CRS A373, item 1336. Kirkman described Reed as "a man of standing in this State" who was an Acting Supreme Court Judge for some months. Reed had "all the responsibility of arranging and dealing with the reports of the Tribunal".
54   N. Lamidey, *Aliens Control*, p. 22 of Interim Report, March 1943. Of the 5,228 remaining interned on 31 December 1942, men numbered 5,002 and women 226. Further information on release rates is included in Appendix 1.
55   The cost of holding Australia's 5,228 locals was therefore almost sixteen thousand pounds per week. The cost of overseas internees was debited to the United Kingdom but the loss of manpower to the active war effort was a cost to Australia.
56   Many committee members went on to very senior positions. Arthur Calwell, MP, became leader of the Labor Party after Evatt, Lt A.R. Cutler, VC, eventually became Governor of New South Wales, W.R. Dovey, KC, became a judge in the Divorce Court in New South Wales, and J.V. Barry, KC, was made a judge of the Victorian Supreme Court in 1947. Mrs Jessie Street was chosen by John Curtin as a member of Australia's delegation to the foundation conference of the United Nations Organisation. Noel W. Lamidey moved to the Immigration department and went to London as Chief Migration officer.
57   Aliens Classification Committee Itinerary, attached to letter, S.F. Whittington, Deputy Director of Security, Melbourne to DDS, Adelaide, dated 21 December 1942, AA AP 308/1, file SS 1006.
58   Interim Report, second part of N. Lamidey, *Aliens Control;* Summary of Events — 1943 (re Refugee Class), Calwell Papers, NLA (MS) MP 1444 SI, box 41, item 287.
59   N. Lamidey, *Aliens Control*, pp.33-4.
60   Letter, Curtin to Calwell, dated 30 July 1943, (in reply to Calwell's representations), NLA (MS) MP 1444, box 42, item 295.
61   Aliens Classification and Advisory Committee, Record of Proceedings of 20th Meeting, 28 October 1943, NLA (MS) MP 1444, box 41, item 287.
62   G. Cresciani, *Fascism and Anti-Fascism and Italians in Australia*, pp. 204-5.
63   Evatt made Vaccari a Liaison Officer between Commonwealth Departments and the Italian community. Copy of letter, Evatt to Vaccari, dated 26 November

1943 and copy of memorandum, W.R. Hodgson to Secretary, Department of Defence, dated 30 November 1943, AA ACT A5954, box 674.

64   Reed's Report on Italians, November 1943, is Appendix B of Lamidey, *Aliens Control*. G. Cresciani, *Fascism, Anti-Fascism and Italians in Australia*, p. 246, reaches similar conclusions to Reed's. Isolated by religion, language and socio-economic status from Australian political life, most Italians "shunned active participation", but that this was "reminiscent of the political apathy" and alienation they exhibited in Italy.

65   Letter, W.B. Simpson to DDS, Brisbane, dated 20 January 1943, AAA BP 242/1, item Q33742.

66   Internment Position — Persons of Italian Origin, dated 9 December 1943, NLA (MS) MP 1444, box 41, item 287.

67   Copy of sworn statement headed "re Bruno CAC", attached to letter, G. Vaccari to Manpower Directorate, Sydney, dated 25 August 1944, NLA (MS) MP 1444, box 44, item 326.

68   Letter, Sergeant to Police Inspector, Townsville (includes testimonial) dated 19 February 1943, AA BP 242/1, item Q8389.

69   Letter from Security Service, Brisbane, to A/DDS, Brisbane, dated 17 February 1944, signature screened, AA BP 242/1 item Q8375.

70   Letter, DDS, Melbourne, to DDS, NSW, dated 12 October 1943, AA SP 1714/1, item N26622.

71   Barcs describes his tribunal hearing and his employment in the 3rd Employment Company in *Backyard of Mars*, pp.158-218.

72   For Record Purposes, R.F.B. Wake, SS, Brisbane, dated 29 February 1944, AA BP 242/1, Q31659.

73   Barry was involved in Commissions of Inquiry into the bombing of Darwin, the suspension of civil administration in Papua and was a member of the Regulations Advisory Committee. Dovey assisted in the Australia First inquiry. Calwell became the Minister for Information. A.R. Cutler became Assistant DDS for NSW and Jessie Street stood in the 1943 and 1946 federal elections.

74   Letter, Camp Commandant 14C to HQ, Loveday Internment Group, dated 13 December 1944, AA AP 308/1, file SS 1006.

75   Report of Mr Noel W. Lamidey and Ft. Lt. C. Philcox, Interim Report, 11 December 1944, NLA (MS) MP 1444, box 41, item 284.

76   The government received many petitions highlighting the refugees' problems with the Allied War Council, including a lengthy report and appeal from a distinguished group led by C. Venn Pilcher, the Anglican Bishop Coadjutor of Sydney, dated 11 October 1943, AA MP 742, file 115/1/95. For an account of the Allied Works Council, see Hasluck, vol. 1, pp. 595-8.

77   Letter, Jesson to Calwell, dated 30 June 1944, NLA (MS) MP 1444, box 41, item 281.

78   Ibid., letter, Calwell to Curtin, dated 26 July 1944.

79   For Calwell's relationship with Curtin, see Arthur A. Calwell, *Be just and fear not*, Rigby, Adelaide, 1978, pp.53-9.

80   Series of letters dated January 1944, NLA (MS) MP 1444, box 42, item 301.

81   Ibid., letter, Calwell to Evatt, dated 5 January 1944.

82   Ibid., "Ex Queensland Internees in South Australia", dated 18 November 1943.

83   Letter, Vaccari to Calwell, dated 25 August 1944, with lists and sworn statements attached, NLA (MS) MP 1444, box 44, item 326.

84   Statement by the Acting Prime Minister, 29 November 1944, AA ACT CRS A5954, box 74.

85   Report of Lamidey and Philcox p 3, NLA (MS) MP 1444, box 41, item 284.

86   Ibid., Letter, W.B. Simpson to Calwell, dated 15 June 1945.

87   Alan Sharpe, *Australian Crimes*, Ure Smith, Sydney, 1979, pp. 107-14.

88   The following account of the Clyne Inquiry is from B. Muirden, *Puzzled Patriots*, pp.140-50.

89   Nancy Krakouer applied for leave to appeal from Tatura on 16 January 1943, AA CRS A373, item 4252 and was represented at the Inquiry by T.H. Hughes, Muirden, p. 142.

90   Letter, Calwell to Minister [of Army], "Review of Internments — Tatura", NLA (MS) MP 1444, box 39, item 262.

91   N. Lamidey, *Aliens Control*, p.54.

92   H.N. Nelson, "Loyalties at Sword Point", p. 215.

93   Calwell recommended this procedure in a letter to J.M. Fraser (Acting Minister for Army), dated 26 May 1945, NLA (MS) MP 1444, box 42, item 298 and questions at Deportation trials indicate such films were shown, e.g. No. 318, AA MP 798/1, file 38702, folder 8.

94   Trial of No. 305 is typical. The wife was allowed to stay and listen, then asked to say if she agreed. Warned of conditions, she still said she wanted to take the children and go with her husband.

95   Herman Junge was a long-term resident who had been interned in World War I, was a member of the Nazi Party in Sydney in the thirties and a camp leader at Tatura. At his trial he stated that he considered the National Socialist government had been "the only government for Germany", although no government was "without fault". He wanted to retain his German nationality which had been "good enough" for 56 years. Nevertheless he had sufficient funds to look after himself and felt that any man could be "a decent member in any other country". He claimed he was personally against war in modern times for the brutality seemed to go "from bad to worse". He wished that nations would "live together in peace". Junge was heard on 23 November 1945.

96   A copy of von Skerst's appeal of 6 June 1941 and newspaper cuttings of his rejection for naturalisation and the Loans Quiz, and his suicide, are in AA CRS B741, V-11032/5. His deportation trial is in AA MP 798/1, file 38702 and he was heard on 19 February 1946.

97   Newspaper accounts of Becker's attempted escape and Neumann's deportation are in AA SP 1714/1, item N41719. Dr Greuber's deportation was mentioned in the TV program, "The Class of '39" on Channel O/28, 13, 20, 27 February 1983.

98   The *Dunera* reunions began in 1972 and receive press coverage. The details of Layton's reuniting of father and son are in a letter from G.F. Chodziesner, dated 4 December 1980.

99   *CPD*, vol. 204 (23 September 1949), pp. 550-3.

100 Ibid., p. 553.

101 Summary of a Conference between the Commissioner and the Minister, dated 28 June 1946, AA BP 242/1, item Q33794. Adverse press reports are also in this file.

102 For Takasuka's later career I am indebted to Dr Richard Broome; Kuringu file is AA SP 1714/1, item N27827. Letters of support for Calwell's actions to deport former Asians are in NLA (MS) MP 1444, box 39, item 259.

103 In the *Yoiziki* debate Calwell was described by Menzies as "a piece of scum" and Calwell retorted that Menzies was "the worst pro-Japanese agent in this country". See *CPD*, vol. 186 (13 March 1946), pp. 206-226 for full debate. The exchange between Calwell and Menzies is on pp. 221-2. In his speech, the Prime Minister, Ben Chifley, claimed that these internees were suffering no more inconvenience than soldiers, and in being given the opportunity to travel home, were better off than stranded war-brides. The Formosan and Korean ex-internees had arrived in Adelaide in "a deplorable condition" early in 1942 and had been maintained for four years on more regular rations than some

Australians. The *Yoiziki* carried 1,005 Formosan and Korean prisoners of war and Formosan civil internees including 209 women and children.

104   Rupert Lockwood, *The Black Armada,* pp. 84-91,135-48.
105   Colm Kiernan, *Calwell: A Personal and Political Biography,* Nelson, West Melbourne, 1978, p. 80, pp. 68-9.
106   A.A. Calwell, *Be just and fear not,* pp.101-3. Problems arose when Jewish sponsors wanted to fill their "scarcely seaworthy" chartered ships with Jews. The Immigration Department insisted half the accommodation be sold to non-Jews, because there were stranded Australians, war brides and others waiting to come out also. Calwell states bluntly that a full boat load of Jews "would have created a great wave of anti-Semitism and would have been electorally disastrous for the Labor Party".
107   *CPD,* vol. 184 (2 August 1945), pp. 4911-7 contains Calwell's full statement His quoted comments are on pp. 4914-5.

Conclusion

1   N. Lamidey, *Aliens Control,* foreword.
2   Appendix A for internment rates by states.
3   Ibid., for internment rates by nationality.
4   For example, Herman Junge at his deportation trial on 23 November 1945 clearly saw himself as a defeated enemy and made no criticism of being interned, AA MP 798/1, file 38702.
5   W.D. Borrie, *Italians and Germans in Australia,* Chapter VII, especially pp. 97-101, 115-23 and 141-51. Economic success remains the aim of most ex-internees and their families. In Cairns the Italian consul, Elvio Meoli, is the largest individual sugar farmer in the district. Meoli came to Innisfail in 1938. He described the population then as 90 per cent Italian and 10 per cent Chinese and says that the "Black Hand ran the place". He was studying law when war broke out, enlisted "but was interned, came out, gave law away" and worked on his father's farm. See Janet Hawley, "The Sugar Millionaires" in *Age,* 14 March 1981.
6   Interviews, June 1979.
7   Felix Werder, "The *Dunera* Internees', *Age,* 8 September 1979.
8   Henry Mayer, "The *Dunera* Affair: An Inside View", *National Times,* 27 January to 5 March 1983.
9   Paul Hasluck, "The Unfulfilled Patriot, Full of Steam", *Age,* 28 July 1984.
10   Letter, Major-General J.S. Whitelaw, GOC Vic. L of C Area, to HQ, AMF, dated 24 November, AA MP 742/1, item 255/9/587.
11   G. Cresciani, from his reading of George Morel's reports to the International Red Cross, concludes that life in Australian internment camps was "not physically burdensome", treatment was "excellent" and relations between internees and guards "cordial", see *Fascism, Anti-Fascism and Italians in Australia,* p. 174.
12   Bruce Muirden, *Puzzled Patriots,* p.181.

BIBLIOGRAPHY

ARCHIVES

Australian Archives Files can usually be traced through the Accession prefix, e.g.

Canberra	CRS	
Melbourne	MP	MT*
Sydney	SP	ST*
Adelaide	AP	
Brisbane	BP	
Perth	PP	

* P are permanent file numbers and T are temporary numbers. Sydney temporary numbers have in one case acquired a permanent accession number during the period of research. ST 1604/1 is now SP 1714/1.

Archives file headings have been used when available, otherwise appropriate titles have been assigned by the writer.

CA5 Attorney-General's Department

CRS 472 Correspondence files "W" Series (War) 1939-1945
   item W69 part 1 Advisory Committee 1939
   item W69 part 2 Advisory Committee — National Security (General)
   Regulations
   item W242 Internment of Aliens- 1939
   item W601 Internment of Aliens — Procedure

CA12 Prime Minister's Department

CRS 1608 Correspondence File. Secret and Confidential Series (Fourth System) War 1939
   item A19/1/1 part 1 Aliens Control Policy 1939-1943
   item A19/1/3 Aliens. Employment of During War
   item A20/1/2 Internment Camps — General 1944-1945
   item D19/1/2 part 1 Acquisition of Land by Aliens 1939-1941
   item H19/1/1 Aliens — Lutheran Church 1935-1940
   item J19/1/1 Alien National Schools in Australia 1939-1942
   item L20/1/1 part 1 Enemy Aliens Internment — Policy 1939-1941
   item L20/1/1 part 2 (inc. Merchant Seamen, Australians Interned Abroad 1941-1943)

item N19/1/1 part 1 Positions of Refugees and Aliens in time of war 1939-1940

item W19/1/1 part 1 Aliens Control. General Representations 1941-1945

CA46 Department of Defence (III), 1942-

CRS A816 Correspondence files, multiple number series Class 301 (Classified) 1935-1957

item 1/301/24 War Emergency Legislation — Pre War Action

item 14/301/127 Early Internments

item 25/301/10 Liaison Arrangements — Intelligence and State Police authorities

item 25/301/180 Intelligence Reports for Minister of Home Security

item 54/301/3 Internment of Aliens — Treatment of Women 1939-1941

CA495 Advisory War Council

CRS A2682 Advisory War Council Minute [Books] 1940-1945

CA660 Security Service, Central Office 1942-1946

CRS A373 ASIO 1 Security Service. Correspondence Files, Single Number Series 1941-1949

item 419 Submissions for Internment and Restriction Orders 1941-1942

item 1075 Internment of Port Pirie Fascists, 1942

item 1255 Alleged Tokyo Broadcasts (1942)

item 1272 Internments and Releases Policy — Representations by Various Organisations 1942

item 1336 Aliens Tribunals: Submission of Reports 1942

item 1357 Dossiers of Internees Requested by Mr Martens, M.P.

item 1680 Refugees from Pacific Area

item 1681 Internment Policy (1942)

item 1714 Internment and Release Policy — Frenchmen in Emergency

item 1715 Establishment of Townsville Office

item 2026 RSL Requests for Internment of All Aliens (petitions)

item 2695 Investigation into the Integrity of Naturalised British subjects 1942

item 3063 Aliens Classification and Advisory Committee. Right to View Files on Interned Aliens

item 3744 Anti-Fascists in Internment Camps 1942-1943

item 4252 Request for Release — Nancy Krakouer 1942-1944

item 7099 Review of Internments 1942-1945

item 7226 Ingham District Office 1943

item 8244 Chronicle of the German Internment Camps in Australia 1941-1943

item 8689 Innisfail and Ingham sub-offices 1944-1945

CA 747 Investiqation Branch — Central Office, Melbourne and Canberra (1919-1946)

CRS A367 Correspondence files, single number series with C Prefix 1916-1953
    C3075 D Supervision of Aliens, Form A-42
        E Aliens- USA Johnson Law
        K RSL on Aliens March 1938
        Complaint over question — Is/is not a Jew
        AD Aliens supervision — suggestions from State branches

CA 1468 War Cabinet Secretary (1939-1946)

CRS A2643 War Cabinet Minutes [Books] 1939-46

Department of Defence III, collected by Sir F.G. Shedden 1911-1952

Shedden Papers (formerly MP 1217)
    AA 5954 box 252, box 253, box 674, box 675

Melbourne
CA5 Attorney General's Department

MT 269/8 Reports to General Staff Officer (Military Intelligence) Southern Command, relating to investigations made on behalf of the Army
    items 1-600 Reports by R.S. Browne

MP 529/3 Transcripts of evidence, 1941-1942
    box 1 Transcripts — Germans recommended for release
    box 2 Briefings by Hattam, Whittington, Proctor
    box 3 Zammarchi's trial. Aliens Tribunal No. 3
    box 4 Transcripts — Italians, Germans
    box 5 Transcripts- Japanese

MP 529/5 Correspondence relating to Aliens Tribunals
    box 1 Extracts from Camp Chronicle
    box 2 Observations for guidance of Aliens Tribunals
    Notes on Fascism
    Preliminary General Observations by Aliens Tribunal No. 2 (Victoria)

MP 529/6 Correspondence with other Tribunals and Alien Advisory Committee 1941-1944
Aliens Tribunal No. 4 (Victoria) — Reports to GOC
Series 6 S.A. Aliens Tribunal, February 1943

MP 798 Commonwealth Investigation case files
    V24713/5 Hermann Homburg
    V26219 Alleged Subversive Organisation
    V39585 Disposal of Dossiers PWI, 1947

MP 798/1 General Correspondence 1931-1962
    38702 Report of Proceedings before His Honor Mr Justice Simpson

CRS B741 Commonwealth Investigation Branch Correspondence files, single number series with "V" prefix, 1924-1962
    file V11032/5 Arnold von Skerst

CA36 Department of the Army

MP 508 Correspondence files, multiple number series 1939-1942
    255/711/59 Camp Chronicle
    255/711/70 Sporting Material for Internment camps
    255/711/108 Camps and Censorship
    255/711/141 Restriction of public access to camps
    255/714/32 Official Visitors on Hay
    255/714/72 Internees to sit for University exam
    255/714/241 Nazi and Fascist organisations in camps
    255/716/23 Official Visitor to No. 9 Camp, Loveday
    255/716/111 Official Visitor to Loveday Group, Report No. 12
    255/716/150 Official Visitors Report No. 7
    255/750/226 Japan and the Geneva Convention

MP 729/6 Secret Correspondence files, multiple number series (class 401)
    1/401/8 War Plans
    1/401/34 National Security (General) Regs: Information and Rumours
    14/401/21 Planning (Victoria) early 1942
    19/401/68 Intelligence Organisation, 4 MD
    19/401/69 Intelligence Corps — Personnel
    19/401/104 War Establishment — Qld Garrison Battalions
    22/401/104 Italian Consuls and Staff
    22/401/119 Italian Consul's Office
    22/401/222 French to be interned in emergency
    29/401/3 Shall Communism Rule Australia
    29/401/34 Local German Views
    29/401/39 Military Reporting Officers
    29/401/42 Naval Dockyard Police
    29/401/47 Junkers representative
    29/401/61 Draft Regs. Local Security Officers
    29/401/66 Customs Officers as MROs
    29/401/67 Japanese Activities
    29/401/68 Adelbert Gruber (Junior)
    29/401/89 Reconnaissance of the Queensland Coast
    29/401/100 Nazi Party throughout Australia (Police Report)
    29/401/121 Communist Activities 1939-1940
    29/401/128 Conference on Activities of CPA (Feb 40)
    29/401/138 Nazi Activities
    29/401/165 Coal Strike
    29/401/170 Communist Activities
    29/401/182 Conference on Communist Party (Aug 40)
    29/401/204 Intelligence Reports and Summaries
    29/401/232 Communist Activities — 6th Division
    29/401/211 Italian Vice Consul at Adelaide
    29/401/468 Monthly Intelligence Notes

29/401/626 Loyalty of Aborigines
55/401/8 Arrest W.A. missionaries
57/401/25 Hermannsburg Mission Station
63/401/3 Custody of Internees
63/401/10 Internees — Women and NBS
63/401/15 NBS of enemy origin — Qld 1939
63/401/16 Internment Aliens 6 MD
63/401/30 Control of Aliens Instructions No. 2
63/401/44 Draft Regs. Maintenance of Discipline among POWs
63/401/49 Hedinger on Transfer from Qld.
63/401/50 Transfer to Orange
63/401/85 Distribution of Internees July 1940
63/401/108 Recommendations for internment Women and NBS
(NSW)
63/401/111 Exchange for Del Drago
63/401/119 Internment of Italians (WA)
65/401/3 Custody of Internees
65/401/7 Principles of Internment Policy
65/401/79 GOC's on Independent Tribunals
65/401/85 Bundock on Pro-Nazi sentiment S.A.
65/401/99 Italians in North Queenslans (Nov 40)
65/401/133 Italians in North Queensland (Aug 41)
66/401/1 Powers of Arrest Auxilary Police Force
15/402/24 Police War Instructions
15/402/34 Sabotage and Fifth Column Precautions
63/402/17 Italians at Hay October 1940
63/402/129 Conference on redistribution of internees in camps

MP 742/1 Correspondence files, multiple number series, 1943-1951
115/1/23 Deportation of Aliens
115/1/37 Post-War Migration
115/1/69 AMF drafted to cut cane
115/1/73 German Club at Belgrave
115/1/95 Australia and the Refugee
115/1/119 Italiaras holding land in N.S.W.
115/1/150 Ex-Servicemen (Qld) on Enemy Aliens
115/1/151 Remittances to Italy
115/1/198 Refugees, Evacuees, Internees, POWs
115/1/249 RSL on Aliens
115/1/292 Internees visiting dying relatives
115/1/294 Indonesians at Lytton
115/1/301 Cables, return of Indonesians
115/1/315 Aliens in forces
115/1/316 Ex-Employment Company men and naturalisation
115/1/382 G. Vaccari's role
115/1/378 Dutch at Casino camp
255/1/126 Locations of Australian POWs
255/1/173 Australian POWs
255/2/282 Merchant Marine Officers and Seamen
255/2/283 Hungarians, Roumanians, Finns

255/2/298 Indonesians appeal to Australian government
255/2/686 Australian Internees Shanghai
255/2/692 Allied prisoners in the Philippines
255/2/811 Formosans at Takua
255/2/814 Payment to Advisory Committees
255/4/37 Relief payments to Internees' dependants
255/4/261 Internees hobbies and handcrafts
255/4/432 Maintenance of deportees
255/4/689 Financial arrangements for deportees
255/7/35 Property of Internees
255/7/87 Internees claims — loss of baggage
255/8/15 Red Cross on Razorblades
255/9/57 Transfers from W.A.,
255/9/219 Handcuffing of internees
255/9/587 Official Visitors on Australian guards
255/10/5 Report on Liverpool Camp
255/10/12 Japanese internees from New Guinea
255/10/166 Monthly return — Internees & POWs
255/11/54 Segregation requests by OV on Loveday
255/11/56 Additional Memorandum — H. Natanson to OV
255/11/69 Internee "A. Mortimer"
255/11/238 E. Simoni
255/12/12 Fantin and interneee political fighting
255/12/37 OV Report No. 17 and Army reply
255/13/426 Overseas Internees (not Japanese or from UK)
255/14/226 Overseas Internees
255/14/228 Overseas Internees
255/14/232 Release of Overseas Internees
255/18/219 Vienna Mozart Boys Choir
255/19/310 Forde's defence of releasing Italian internees
255/19/346 Civilian Internees December 1943
255/19/367 Overseas Internees Investigation 8card
255/31/21 Instructions to employers of POWs
255/714/241 Internee Mail arrangements'
274/1/246 Repatriation of German Internees

MP 1103/1 Records of the Directorate of P.O.W. and Internees
box 5 NEI Japanese internees roll
box 6 NEI Japanese internees roll

MP 1103/2 Prisoners of War Information Bureau Reports on P.O.W./Internee 1939-1945
box 38 Germans interned in Qld.
box 40 German women

CA1843 Command Headquarters, Southern Command, Australian Military Forces

MP 70/2 Security Classified (Secret) Correspondence 1935-1941
file 1939/46A State co-operation — War planning
file 1939/155 Guard to implement Intelligence plans

MP 70/3 Security classified correspondence, 1939-1941
    file 1939/32 Authorized Establishments and Organisation HQ 3rd
    District Command

CA1844 Headquarters, Victorian Lines of Communication Area

MP 70/1 Security classified general correspondence 1940-1945
    36/101/86 Death of Internees Schiessel and Grahl
    48/101/20 Establishment of L of C Areas

MP 385/3 General Correspondence 1919-1946
    32/101/59 Internees escapes
    36/101/327 Dental treatment — internees
    36/104/10 Donation German POWs to Internees families
    53/101/53 Precautions during Blackouts
    53/101/54 Personnel to supervise employment projects
    53/101/65 Escape of 3 Kormoran crew
    53/101/66 PWI — Employment and surplus production
    53/101/84 Visit of Australian Red cross and Y.W.C.A.
    53/102/16 Methods of escape
    53/102/23 Escape of internees
    156/2/591 Dr Morel's Report on Tatura Group
    156/4/2348 Escape of Internees (1946)
    1940-216 Repatriation of Aliens
    1940-242 Prisoner from Singapore
    1940-370 Prosecution of Subversive Associations Regulations

AA Department of the Army

Correspondence files, multiple number series 701 plus secondary number
1939-42
    Z55/714/31 Internment Camp Hay — Conditions
    255/714/37 OV Report on Hay camp
    255/714/64 Internees at Hay (inc. booklet on Kitchener Camp)
    255/716/221 OV Report 15 on Loveday
    255/717/18 OV Reports on Harvey camp
    255/717/65 Transfer Parkeston to Loveday (WA internees)

AA Department of Defence, Military Board

MP 95/3 Monthly Intelligence Summaries, 3rd Military District 1923-1936

AA Department of Labour and National Service

MP 574/1 General Correspondence 1940-1950
    210/2/4 Protests against release and employment internees
    220/2/6 Protests against employment of aliens

AA Drakeford Papers re Defence and Civil Aviation 1939-1957

MP 288/17 — item 1 War Book

Sydney
CA785 Collector of Customs, Sydney

SP 822/39 Relating to seizure of "Remo" 1940-1951

CA 912 Commonwealth Investigation Service, N.S.W.

SP 26/3 Correspondence relating to various investigations 1939-1946
    Military Police Intelligence Section reports
    Conference on Security, March 1942
    Weekly Review of Incoming Shortwave Broadcasts

SP 26/5 Report on European Emergency Committee

SP 26/6 Transcripts — Aliens Tribunal No. 2 N.S.W.

CA951 Commonwealth Police Force N.S.W.

ST 1604/1) Correspondence relating to various Investigations 1928-1951
SP 1714/1)
    item Policy 3 Other than Security Reasons
                  Released internees
                  Japanese internees' property
                  Unjustified or frivolous internments
    item 52 Loveday Internment group Intelligence reports
    N4673 British Fascist Society
    N18035 Naturalization File 1930-1948
    N26622 George F. Edelmann 1939-1946
    N27827 V.M. Kuringu
    N29007 Alfonso, Prince Del Drago
    N36990 Jewish-General, 1942-1945
    N38486 Intelligence Reports, Internee & POW camps 1944-1946
    N38529 Consular Archives and Furniture
    N39016 German Lutheran Church 1940-1947
    N39039 Walter Ladendorff 1939-1945
    N40344 Japanese Activities 1942-1946 (inc. Barnwell's Report)
    N40752 Count Von Luckner 1938-1946
    N41025 Repatriation of ex-Internees on Compassionate grounds 1946
    N41719 Dr J.H. Becker 1947-1953
    N42087 Capuchin Franciscan Fathers
    N33197 Dr Asmis
    N60318 Consul General Switzerland 1942-1945

ST 2476/10 Report of Fascist Activities in Australia 1940

ST 2476/20 Various Exhibits concerning the internment of Italians 1939-1941 (inc. Barnwell's report)

ST 2476/22 Investigations into the Activities of Aliens 1942 (inc. Italians in Vicinity Water canal and pipelines)

CA1878 Headquarters, Eastern Command [11] Australian Military Forces

SP 196/1 POW and Internees subject files 1939-1946
item 5 Files of deceased Japanese/Italians 1945-1947
(inc. Japanese repatriation)
item 17 Explanation of internee number prefixes

Adelaide
Attorney General's Department

Commonwealth Police. Investigation Service
AP 50/1 General Records of National Security
file SS 971 PWI camps — Nazi and Fascist Influences

AP 308/1 General Correspondence files
file 551004 Review of internments — other nationalities
551006 Aliens Advisory Classification Committee
55 1032 Temporary release — compassionate
551037 Notification of release
551057 Interned Justices of the Peace
SA 19912 Disposal of seized property
SA 21667 Loveday Group Intelligence report 1946

AP 501/1 General Records of National Security
file SS 974 Transfer of Tribunals and Advisory Committees to Security Service

AP 501/2 General Records of Fascio Activities
Unnumbered file Summary of "Club Italiano", "Italian Club" and "Venezia Club".
Report on Fascism (Barnwell's report)
German and Italian Consular Records
Correspondence dealing with Port Pirie Fascio
Fascio Port Pirie

AP 538/1 Inquiry Files, Alien Organisation Files
file SA 2048 Civil Alien Corps, Italia Libra protests
file SA 20499 Liaison between Nazis and Fascists
file SA 20502 Release of Lutheran Missionaries
file SA 21163 "True Italian" Movement

AP 589/1 General Correspondence files
file SS 1061 Documents to accompany internees
file SS 1064 Internees to Mental Homes
file SS 1067 Attempted Suicide — Internees
file SS 1091 Release of Internees Arrangements

Department of the Army. Southern Command

4th Military District. South Australia

AP 613/1 Security Classified General Correspondence

file 90/1/24 Aliens Control (Residential Prohibition)
file 90/1/70 Handling of OV's report on Loveday
file 90/1/117 Reply to OV's report
file 90/1/124 Correspondence courses — internees
file 90/1/139 Camp Leader No. 10 Loveday
file 90/1/205 Educational Facilities
file 90/1/238 Transfer No. 10 to 14 — Protest
92/1/4 History of Loveday Group
130/1/7 PWI — Employment
154/1/2 Security Measures — Loveday
162/1/64 Security against possible Japanese reaction to end of war
and invasion of Japan

AP 613/4 Miscellaneous Papers
Internees ex Dunera — Movement
Orders for Officer in Charge of Guard
Official Visitors Report No. 1
Official Visitors Report No. 3
Official Visitors Report No. 4

AP 613/10 General correspondence
file 123/1/313 Menu for Loveday Groups 1945

Brisbane
Attorney Generals Department

Commonwealth Investigation Service, Queensland
BP 242/1 Correspondence file, 1942-1950
    item Q31659 Secretary, German Club
    item Q33792 Overseas internees — Policy
    item Q33794 Release of Internees — Policy
    item Q39362 Japanese Internment — Action
    item Q40135 State Publicity Censor Reports (Part 1) 1943-1945
    item Q42665 Censorship — Miscellaneous
    item Q8375 Oswald Bonutto
    item Q8389 Augusto Orlandi

Department of Information

BP 361/1 Correspondence file
    item 1-11 Commonwealth Investigation Branch 1940-1945
    item 2-43 Security Service Reports 1942-1943

Perth

As most files held in Perth were personal and the Perth branch took the attitude that staff time would only be granted to clear a total of nine files on persons of five different countries. When these were sent one tenth of the pages were removed on the grounds of information given in confidence and distress or embarrassment to individuals. The pages were mutilated by screened material being physically cut out with a stanley knife and they were accompanied by a letter saying no work of this nature would be carried out again for this writer.

CA 908 Investiqation 3ranch, Western Australia

PP 205/1 Files relating to internees and POWs of various nationalities for the 1939/45 war
    [Name withheld] Dutch Indonesian Javanese, 1942-1944
    [Japanese internee, name withheld] 1941-1944
    [German internee, name withheld] 1944-1946
    [Italian internee, name withheld] 1940-1944

CA956 Commonwealth Police Force, Western Australia

PP 302/1 Correspondence files 1918-1959
    [Italian internee, name withheld] 1938-1946

PP 245/3 Internees and Prisoner of War Files 1939-1945
    item WA 39931]Albanian internee, name withheld] 1940-1943
    item WA 39997 [Japanese internee, name withheld] 1940-1943
    item WA 39999 [Italian internee, name withheld] 1940-1945
    item WA 40150 [German internee, name withheld] 1940-1950

War Memorial, Canberra

CRS A2663 Written Records Files, War of 1939-1945,
(AWM 54) Multiple Number System, c.1953-(1966)
    item 780 1-6 History of the Directorate of Prisoners of War and Internees 1939-1945

AWM 52 AIF and Militia Unit War Diaries, 1939-1945 War
    (Garrison Battalion Diaries were only made available on a very limited basis because internees' names were in the text so often, that screening and envelope covers would endanger the binding of the original.)
    17 Garrison Battalion — 8/7/21
    25 Garrison HQ — 8/7/29
    Loveday HQ — 8/7/42
    Tatura — 8/7/43

AWM 67 Gavin Long — Papers of Official Historian

AWM 140 Official Historian — Biographical Cards (1914-1919 War)

AWM 123 "Special Collection II", Records of Defence Committee, AHQ Intelligence Summary No. 170

    Blamey Papers 3 DRL 6643 item 54.7

QUEENSLAND STATE ARCHIVES

The following locations from the Police and Premier's Department records contain relevant material:

A/1191   Townsville District June-October 1940 — March 1942
(1942)   Lists of Internees (Master Warrants) February — June
         1942
         Metropolitan District April-August 1940 — April 1942
         Cairns District February — May 1942

A/11914 Townsville District February-April 1942
         Toowoomba District June 1940
         Longreach District July 1940
         Not Labelled February-November 1942
         Cairns District July-December 1940

A/11916 List of Internees Northern Command
         June-September 1940
         April-December 1942
         August-December 1943 Releases

A/11917 Miscellaneous and Index August-October 1939, May-June
         1940
         Cairns District April-June 1942

A/11918 June-November 1940
         April-May 1942

A/11919 Advisory Committees March 1941
         February-March 1942

A/11957 Various — May 1941-1944

A/6434   169/3 Council of Public Safety

A/6436   170/1 Statutory Rules 1939
         170/8 Guards and Manpower

A/6437   171/1 Statutory Rules 1939
         170/8 Guards and Manpower

A/6438   171/10 Regulation 35 revoked

A/6464   183/1 Queensland Agent-General May 1941

A/6465   183/3 Censorship Instructions 1942

A/6467   183/2 Clearance of areas, enemy landings
         184/3 Evacuees from Asia and Palestine

A/6472   186/1 Treatment of Internees at Stuart Gaol
         186/2 Administration Internees' Estates
         186/3 Member Cotton Board detained
         186/16 Lack of Defence Qld coast

A/6473   186/19 Aliens and land
         186/23 Closure of Italian-run hotels June 1940

A/6474   187/2 Carroll's report on Local Security Officers Sept.
         1940

187/4 State/Commonwealth Cooperation
187/9 Consulate of NEI
187/10 Air Raid Precautions Townsville Feb. 1942
187/13 Police Action in time of emergency

A/6475 187/14 Police War Instructions
187/15 Police Action in event of hostilities
187/17 Protest — employment of POWs

A/6477 188/20 Security Service arrangements in Qld
188/25 ARU protest — treatment of 'left" organisations

COMMONWEALTH PARLIAMENTARY DEBATES (war years and relevant sections to 1950)

VICTORIAN PARLIAMENTARY DEBATES (1916) Lutheran Schools Closure debate.

ACTS OF PARLIAMENT

National Security (General) Regulations
National Security (Aliens Control) Regulations
National Security (Internment Camp) Regulations
National Security (Aliens Service) Regulations

PERSONAL PAPERS, INTERVIEWEES AND CORRESPONDENTS, T.V. PROGRAMS

Personal Papers

Calwell Papers — (MS) MP 1444, National Library, Canberra (by kind permission of Elizabeth Calwell)

Eichbaum, Ludwig, Diary of Ludwig Eichbaum, Hut 28, Hay — MS 9538, La Trobe Library, Melbourne.

Evatt Papers — Flinders University, Adelaide (with consent of trustees)

Fitzpatrick Papers — MS 4765, National Library, Canberra

HMS Dunera — MS 9538, La Trobe Library, Melbourne

Jessie Street Papers — MS 2683, National Library, Canberra

Margaret Pierce Papers — MS 8782, La Trobe Library, Melbourne (by kind permission of A.C. Clarke)

Society of Friends Papers — MS 9250, La Trobe Library, Melbourne (by kind permission of A.C. Clarke)

Interviewees and Correspondents

Tom Aikens
E.A.Bevege

G.F. and Ben Chodziesner
A.C.Clarke

V.J.Kronenberg
Noel W.Lamidey
Hans Lindau
J.R.,T. and E.McDowell
Ian Moles
John Mordike
Illma O'Brien
Augusto Orlandi
Warren Perry

Tony Corbett
Ross Costanzo
Lyn Henderson
Olive Hirschfeld
Ethel Punshon
Paulo Scuderi
Andy Spaull
A.W. Skimin
Ruby Ward
Ben Warburton
John Whitelaw
Paul Wilson
Hugo Wolfson

and others who have asked not to be named.

Television Programs

"The Class of '39" on Channel 0/28, Melbourne, on 13, 20 and 27 February 1983.

ABC "Weekend Magazine", Channel 2, Melbourne, 14 October 1979.

NEWSPAPERS

The following newspapers have been used for inforrnation and for a guide for public opinion:

Age, Melbourne, 1941-2
Argus, Melbourne, 1938-47
Sydney Morning Herald, 1939-47
Townsville Daily Bulletin, 1942
Home Hill Observer, 1942

ARTICLES

Bailey, T.A., "The Sinking of the *Lusitania*" in *American Historical Review,* vol. 41 (October 1935).
Berger, George M., "Australia and the Refugees" in *The Australian Quarterly,* September and December 1941.
Bevege, Margaret, "Women's Experiences in North Queensland during World War II" in *Second Women and Labour Conference Papers, vol. 2, 1980.*
Carroll, Brian, "William Forgan-Smith: Dictator or Democrat?" in D.J. Murphy and R.B. Joyce (eds), *Queensland Political Portraits, 1859-1952,* University of Queensland Press, St Lucia,1978
Chodziesner, G.F., "How I came to Australia", roneoed sheets in possession of Ben Chodziesner, Melbourne.
Coulthard-Clark, Captain C.D.,"Australia's War-Time Security Service", in *Defence Force Journal,* no.16,May/June 1976.
Douman, M., "Townsville during World War I" in *Lectures in North Queensland History,* History Department, James Cook University, 1974.
Encel,S., "These Men are Dangerous" in *Nation,* September 1965.
Fischer, Gerhard, "Botany Bay revisited the transportation of

prisoners-of-war and civilian internees to Australia during the first world war", *Journal of the Australian War Memorial*, no. 5, October 1984.

Hasluck, Paul, "The Unfulfilled Patriot, Full of Steam" in *Age*, 28 July 19B4.

Hawley, Janet, "The Sugar Millionaires" in *Age*, 14 March 1981.

Kinne, G., "Nazi Stratagems and their Effects on Germans in Australia up to 1945;" in *Royal Australian Historical Society Journal*, vol. 66, pt l, (June 1980.)

Konig, Walter S.J., "Internment in Australia" in *Twentieth Century*, vol. 18, Spring 1963.

Kwiet, Konrad, "Be patient and reasonable!" :The internment of German-Jewish refugees in Australia, in *Australian Journal of Politics and History*, vol.31, no. 1 , 1985.

Loewald, K.G., "A Dunera Internee at Hay, 1940-41" in *Historical Studies*, vol. 17 , no.69, October 1977.

McCarthy, John, "Australia and the German Consul-Generals 1923-39" in *Australian Journal of Politics and History*, vol. 27, no. 3 , 1981.

Mayer, Henry, "Not yet the Dunera Story" in *24 Hours*, vol.4, no.12. Mayer, Henry, "The Dunera Affair: An Inside View", *The National Times*, 27 February-5 March 1983.

Menghetti, Diane, "Their Country, Not Mine", paper given at Second Australian Conference on Italian Culture and Italy Today, Frederick May Foundation for Italian Studies, University of Sydney, 6 August 1982.

Morris, E.Sydney, "Report on Visit to the Internment Camp, Hay, N.S.W.," roneoed sheets, provided by A . C . Clarke, Melbourne.

Nelson, H.N., "Loyalties at Sword-point: The Lutheran Missionaries in Wartime New Guinea , 1939-1945 " in *Australian Journal of Politics and History*, vol. 24, no. 2, August 1978.

Pierce, Margaret and Clarke, Alfred C., "Report on a Visit to Hay Internment Camps ", roneoed sheets.

Pyke, N.O.P., " An Outline History of Italian Immigration into Australia" in *The Australian Quarterly*, September 1948.

Selleck, R.J.W., ""The Trouble with my looking glass": a study of the attitude of Australians to Germans during the Great War", *Journal of Australian Studies*, no.6, (June 1980).

Vane, Captain Amoury, "The Surveillance of Northern Australia: The story of Stanner's Bush Commando 1942, *Defence Force Journal*, no.l4, Jan/Feb 1979.

Werder, Felix, "The *Dunera* Internees", *Age*, 8 September 1979.

Zainu'ddin, Ailsa G. Thomson, "Rose Inagaki: Is It a Crime To Marry a Foreigner?" in Farley Kelly and Marilyn Lake (eds), *Double Time: Women in Victoria's 150 Years*, Penguin Books, 1985.

BOOKS

Andrew, Christopher, *Secret Service: The Making of the British Intelligence Community*, Guild Publishing, London, 1985.

Andrews, E.M., *Isolationism and Appeasement in Australia: Reactions to the European Crises, 1935-1939*, Australian National University Press, Canberra, 1970.

Barcs, Emery, *Backyard of Mars: Memoirs of the 'Reffo' Period in Australia*, Wildcat Press, Sydney, 1980.

Bevege, Margaret, James, Margaret and Shute, Carmel (eds), *Worth Her Salt: Women at Work in Australia*, Hale and Iremonger, Sydney, 1982.

Blakeney, Michael, *Australia and the Jewish Refugees, 1939-1948*, Croom Helm, Sydney, 1985.

Bonutto, Oswald, *A Migrant's Story*, H.Pole, Brisbane, 1963.

Borrie, W.D., *Italians and Germans in Australia: A Study of Assimilation*, Cheshire, Melbourne, 1954.

Boyle, Andrew, *The Climate of Treason: Five Who Spied for Russia*, Hutchinson of London, 1979.

Cain, Frank, *The Origins of Political Surveillance in Australia*, Angus and Robertson, Australia, 1983.

Calwell, Arthur A., *Be just and fear not*, Rigby, Adelaide, 1978.

Carr-Gregg, Charlotte, *Japanese Prisoners of War in Revolt; The Outbreaks at Featherstone and Cowra during World War II*, University of Queensland Press, St Lucia, 1978.

Carruthers, Steven L., *Australia Under Siege: Japanese Submarine Raiders 1942*, Solus Books, Sydney, 1982.

Cohen-Portheim, Paul, *Time Stood Still: My Internment in England 1914-1918*, Duckworth, London, 1931.

Cresciani, Gianfranco, *Fascism, Anti-Fascism and Italians in Australia, 1922-1945*, ANU Press, Canberra, 1980.

Crowley, F.K. (ed.), *A New History of Australia*, Heinemann, Melbourne, 1974.

Crowley, F.K., *Modern Australia in Documents, 1939-1970*, Wren Publishing Company, Melbourne, 1973.

Dalziel, Allan, *Evatt the Enigma*, Lansdowne Press, Melbourne, 1967.

Daniels, Roger, *Concentration Camps, USA: Japanese Americans and World War II*, Holt, Rinehart and Winston, New York, 1971.

Edwards, P.G., *Prime Ministers and Diplomats: The Making of Australian Foreign Policy, 1901-1949*, Oxford University Press, Melbourne, 1983.

Evatt, H.V., *William Holman: Australian Labour Leader*, Angus and Robertson, Australia, 1940 (Famous Australian Lives Edition 1979).

Fitzgerald, Alan, *The Italian Farming Soldiers: Prisoners of War in Australia, 1941-1947*, Melbourne University Press, Melbourne, 1981.

Fitzpatrick, Brian, *The Australian Commonwealth: A picture of a community, 1901-1955*, Cheshire, Melbourne, 1956.

Frakes, George,E. and Solberg, Curtis B (eds), *Minorities in Californian History*, Random House,New York, 1971.

Gamba, Charles, *A Report on the Italian Fishermen of Fremantle*, Dept. of Economics, University of Western Australia, 1952.

Gillman, Peter and Leni, *Collar the Lot!: How Britain interned and expelled its wartime refugees*, Quartet, London, 1980.

Gordon, Harry, *Die like the carp!*, Cassell Australia, Stanmore, 1978.

Grodzins, Morton, *Americans Betrayed: politics and the Japanese evacuation*, University of Chicago Press, Chicago, 1949.

Gullett, H.S., *Sinai and Palestine*, 1923, (vol.VII of C.E.W. Bean[ed], *Official History of Australia in the war of 1914-1919*).

Hall, Richard, *The Secret State: Australia's Spy Industry*, Cassell Australia, Stanmore, 1978.

Hasluck, Paul, *The Government and the People, 1939-1941*, Australian War Memorial, Canberra, 1952.

Hasluck, Paul, *The Government and the People, 1942-1945*, Australian War Memorial, Canberra, 1970.

Hazlehurst, Cameron, *Menzies Observed*, George Allen & Unwin, Sydney, 1979.

Hetherington, John, *Blamey: Controversial Soldier*, Australian War Memorial, Canberra, 1973.

Horner, D.M., *Crisis of Command: Australian Generalship and the Japanese Threat 1941-1943*, ANU Press, Canberra, 1978.

Horner, D.M., *High Command: Australia and Allied Strategy, 1939-1945*, George Allen and Unwin, Sydney, 1982.

Horner, D.M.(ed.), *The Commanders: Australian military leadership in the twentieth century*, George Allen and Unwin, Sydney, 1984.

Huber, Rina, *From Pasta to Pavlova: A Comparative Study of Italian Settlers in Sydney and Griffith*, University of Queensland Press, St Lucia, 1977.

Index to Australian Military Forces: Appointments, Promotions, etc., LHQ Press, Melbourne, vol. 1, Oct.-Dec. 1943.

Internment in South Australia: History of Loveday, Loveday Internment Group Barmera, 1940-1946, Adelaide *Advertiser* Printing Office, Adelaide, 1946.

Johnston, George, *My Brother Jack*, Fontana, 1964.

Joske, Sir Percy, *Sir Robert Menzies, 1894-1978: a new informal memoir*, Angus and Robertson, Australia, 1978.

Kiernan, Colm, *Calwell: A Personal and Political Biography*, Nelson, West Melbourne, 1978.

Kristianson,G.L., *The Politics of Patriotism:The Pressure Group Activities of the Returned Servicemen's League*, ANU Press, Canberra, 1966.

Lamidey, Noel W., *Aliens Control in Australia, 1939-1945*, N. Lamidey, Sydney, 1974.

Lamidey, Noel W., *Partial Success: My years as a public servant*, N. Lamidey, Sydney, 1970.

Laughlin, Austin, *Boots and All: The Inside Story of the Secret War*, Colorgravure Publication, Melbourne, 1951.

La Violette, Forrest E., *The Canadian Japanese and World War ll*, University of Toronto Press, Canada, 1948.

Lockwood, Rupert, *Black Armada*, Australasian Book Society, Sydney South, 1975.

Loh, Morag (ed.), *With Courage in Their Cases: The experiences of thirty-five Italian immigrant workers and their families in Australia*, F.l.L.E.F., Melbourne, 1980.

Long, Gavin, *The Six Years War: A Concise History of Australia in the 1939-45 War*, The Australian War Memorial, Canberra, 1973.

Lowenstein, Wendy, *Weevils in the Flour: An oral record of the 1930s depression in Australia*, Hyland House, Melbourne, 1978.

Luck, Peter, *This Fabulous Century*, Lansdowne Press, Sydney, 1980.

McCarthy, John, *Australia and Imperial Defence 1918-39: A Study in Air and Sea Power*, University of Queensland Press, St Lucia, 1976.

MacKenzie, Kenneth Seaforth, *Dead Men Rising*, Jonathon Cape (1951), Angus and Robertson (1975).

McKernan, Michael, *All In!: Australia During the Second World War*, Nelson, Melbourne, 1983.

McKernan, Michael, *The Australian People and the Great War*, Nelson, West Melbourne, 1980.

McQueen, Humphrey, *Social Sketches of Australia, 1888-1975*, Penguin Books, Ringwood, 1978.

Menghetti, Diane, *The Red North — Studies in North Queensland History No. 3*, History Department, James Cook University of North Queensland, 1981.

Miyamoto, Kazuo, *Hawaii, End of the Rainbow*, Charles E. Tuttle Co., Vermont, 1964.

Moles, Ian, *A Majority of One*, University of Queensland Press, St Lucia, 1979.

Muirden, Bruce, *The Puzzled Patriots: The Story of the Australia First Movement*, Melbourne University Press, Melbourne, 1968.

Munro, Craig, *Wild Man of Letters: The Story of P.R. Stephensen*, Melbourne University Press, Melbourne, 1984.

On Guard with the Volunteer Defence Forces, Australian War Memorial, Canberra, 1944.

Patkin, Benzion, *The Dunera Internees*, Cassell Australia, Stanmore, 1979.

Pearl, Cyril, *The Dunera Scandal: Deported by Mistake*, Angus and Robertson, Australia, 1983.

Pelz, Werner, *Distant Strains of Triumph*, Victor Gollancz, London, 1964.

Price, Charles A., *German Settlers in South Australia*, Melbourne University Press, Melbourne, 1945.

Robertson, Eric, *The Japanese File: Pre-War Japanese Penetration in South-East Asia*, Heinemann Asia, Hong Kong, 1979.

Robertson, John and McCarthy, John, *Australian War Strategy, 1939-1945*, University of Queensland Press, St Lucia, 1985.

Robertson, John, *Australia at War, 1939-1945*, Heinemann, Melbourne, 1931.

Ross, Lloyd, *John Curtin: A Biography*, Macmillan, Melbourne, 1977.

Scott, Ernest, *Australia During the War*, Angus and Robertson, Sydney, 1936.

Sekuless Peter, *Jessie Street: A Rewarding but Unrewarded Life*, University of Queensland Press, St Lucia, 1978.

Sharpe, Alan, *Australian Crimes*, Ure Smith, Sydney, 1979.

Shirer, William L., *The Rise and Fall of the Third Reich: A History of Nazi Germany*, Book Club Associates, Great Britain, 1959.

Spender, Percy Claude, *Politics and a Man*, Collins, Sydney, 1972.

Stirling, Alfred, *Lord Bruce: The London Years*, Hawthorn Press, Melbourne, 1974.

Street, Jessie (Lady) M.G., *Truth or Repose*, Australasian Book Society, Sydney, 1966.

Tennant, Kylie, *Evatt: Politics and Justice*, Angus and Robertson, 1970.

The Army List of the Australian Military Forces, Government Printer, Melbourne, various volumes.

Thompson, Stephanie Lindsay, *Australia Through Italian Eyes: A study of settlers returning from Australia to Italy,* Oxford University Press, Melbourne, 1980.

Who's Who in Australia, The Herald and Weekly Times Limited, Melbourne, various years.

Watson, Don, *Brian Fitzpatrick: A Radical Life,* Hale & Iremonger, Sydney, 1979.

Wigmore, Lionel, *The Japanese Thrust,* Australian War Memorial, Canberra, 1957

Willyan, Charles, *Behind Barbed Wire in Australia: The Amazing Experiences of an Australian Citizen,* C.Willyan, Murchison,1948.

THESES

Davies, J.D., "Some Aspects of the Commonwealth Government's Response to the Presence of Germans and German Descendants in Australia, 1914-1918", PhD thesis, Melbourne University, 1982.

Henderson, Lyn, "Italians in the Hinchinbrook Shire, 1921-1939", BEd-BA Hons thesis, James Cook University of North Queensland, 1978.

Wiemann, Ursula, "German and Austrian Refugees in Melbourne, 1933-1947", MA thesis, Melbourne University, 1965-6.

INDEX

Official History of Internment, 37
Official Visitors, 36-38, 96-107, 178, 187-88, 190-93, 195-97, 236
onus of proof, 27, 40, 92, 116, 120
Oral History, xviii
Orange Showgrounds, 57, 68-69, 85, 91, 105
Orlandi, Augusto, 171-72, 182, 213-14, 235
Otabe, K., 137

pacifists, xv, 8, 70-71, 228
Parkeston camp, 179
Paterson, Fred, 173
Patkin, B., 235
Patti, Orazio, 216
Peace Movements, 11
Pearl, Cyril, 113
pearlers, 132-33
Pelz, Werner, 89
Personal Particulars form (Form A42), 2, 92
petitions, 153-55, 157
Philcox, Claude A., 214
Philp. Roslyn, 39, 125
Pierce, Margaret, 194
Pike, G.H., xvii, 135, 214
Pilcher, Venn, 113
Piscitelli, M., 187
Plas, Charles van der, 147
Platt, Linda (Pyjama Girl), 217-18
Police Special Branches, viii, 2, 19, 92
    as arresting officers, 131, 171
    in North Queensland, 156-57, 166, 167, 169
    in NSW, 12, 17, 30, 43
    as Reporting Officers, 80-83, 170-71, 174
instructions if invasion, 153
Police War Instructions, 17-18
policy, xv, xvii, xx
political balance of power, 109-10, 113, 129, 202, 230, 236
political prisoners (NEI), 147, 223-24
Posner, Leonard, 97
Price, Charles A., 14-15
Prime Minister's Department, xviii, 155
prisoners-of-war, 177
    Japanese, 133, 223
Prisoners of War and Internees, Directorate of. See Directorate of Prisoners of War and Internees
Proctor, P.G., 121

progress of war as factor, 158-59, 174-76, 199, 205, 227-28, 230
Protecting Power. See H. Hedinger, and E. Brack
public sentiment as factor, 112, 130, 139-40, 149, 199, 219, 227-28
Punshon, Ethel, 134, 189

Quakers. See Society of Friends
Qualia, Captain, 107
Queensland coastal areas, 156
Queensland Police Department, xviii
Queensland Premier's Department, xviii
Queensland Sugar Board, 205, 234
Quinland, F.J., 136

Racial League of Germans Abroad, 15
Raible, Bishop, 94
Ratcliff, Horace, 93, 201, 208
Ray, W.V., 190
reciprocity, 32-38, 85
Red Cross representative. See G. Morel.
Reed, G.S., xvii, 6, 62-63, 175-76, 210, 212-13
refugees, 1, 21, 25, 31, 54-55, 68, 77, 86-87, 89, 91-93, 111, 124, 211
    from Netherlands East Indies, 147, 158
Regulation 26, 94
Regulation 42A, 117-19
Reichelt, Nancy, 33
Reitano, Felix, 204
release from internment
    Albanians and Finns, 212
    Anglo-Persian oil employees, 222
    Australia First, 218-19
    Australians, 208-9
    Asians, 223-24
    in bulk, 213
    Germans, 219-23
    Italians, 211-18
    Straits Settlements, 222
    Templars, 221-22
    statistics, 241
Remo, 57, 59, 66
repatriation, 146, 220
reserved occupations, 159
residents
    long-term, 7, 130, 136, 138, 196, 198, 220
    short-term, 5, 130
    files on, 10
restrictions, 141, 215
returned soldiers, RSL, 78, 126, 156-57